Islamic Studies

Equipping the Christian Witness to Muslims

Revised and Expanded Second Edition

Kent Philpott

EVP

Earthen Vessel Publishing

ISLAMIC STUDIES: EQUIPPING THE CHRISTIAN WITNESS TO MUSLIMS
(2ND EDITION)

©2019 by Kent Philpott

All rights reserved.
Earthen Vessel Publishing, San Rafael, CA 94903
www.evpbooks.com

ISBN: 978-1-946794-13-0

Library of Congress Control Number: 2019943471

Cover and interior design by KLC Philpott

All Biblical Scripture quotations, unless otherwise indicated, are taken from the Holy Bible, English Standard Version. (ESV.), copyright © 2001 by Crossway Bibles, a publishing ministry of Good News Publishers. All rights reserved.

All Qur'an quotations, unless otherwise indicated, are taken from *The Holy Qur'an*. 10th ed. Translated by Abdullah Yusuf Ali. New Delhi: Kitab Bhavan, 2015.

Acknowledgments

So many to thank, so much work done by so many including my students who for two years worked with me through much of the content of this book.

Then there is Margaret Alvarez who summarized Ayaan Hirsi Ali's books.

Stephanie Adams who worked over the glossary and edited several of the major pieces of this puzzle.

Chuck Munson who edited blocks of material.

Patrick Dunleavy who made corrections and gave me insights.

Michelle Shelfer who brilliantly edited most of the second edition's new material.

My wife Katie who agonized with me over the past four years to complete the original book and then this second edition for publication and to whom is owed so much.

Then to the congregation of Miller Avenue Baptist Church in Mill Valley, California, who no doubt got tired of my speaking about Islam over and over, yet who never did say a bad word about it.

Contents

Preface	vi
Introduction	1
1 Islamic Studies Outline	3
2 A Summary of *Understanding Islamic Theology*	28
3 Sharia Law: An Introduction	68
4 Sharia Law: A Summary for Sunni Islam	70
5 Sharia Law: A Summary for Shia Islam	96
6 Ultimate Intentions of Islam	114
7 A Summary of *The Exorcist Tradition in Islam*	116
8 Commentary on the books by Ayaan Hirsi Ali	126
9 Commentary on *No god but God: The Origins, Evolution, and Future of Islam* by Reza Aslan	142
10 A Response to the Call for Reform by Ayaan Hirsi Ali and Reza Aslan	155
11 Basics of the Qur'anic Chapters	157
12 A Biographic Timeline of Muhammad's Life	161
13 The Crescent and Star Symbol	163
14 The Sira: The Biography of Muhammad	165
15 The Miracles of Muhammad and Jesus: A Comparison	169
16 Essays on Islam	175
A Follower of Muhammad? A Follower of Jesus	
Were the Crusaders and Inquisitors Christians?	
Looking at Muslims	
A Fundamental Error of Islam	
The Weakness of Islam	
Islam's Cultic Connection	
My First Essay on Islam	
Shame versus Guilt	
Abrogation or Progressive Revelation?	
Eid Al-Adha: Who Has it Right?	
The Making of an Extremist	
But . . . It *Is* Warfare!	
17 Who Is Gabriel?	224
18 Debating with Muslims	235

19	Was Jesus Crucified?	250
20	Answering A. Deedat's *Combat Kit Against Bible Thumpers*	260
21	Islamic Hygiene	287
22	Christian Hygiene?	292
23	Names Given to Muhammad in the Qur'an and Hadith	294
24	Twenty-Five Ways	296
25	Significant Muslim Populations	299
26	Three Religious Movements Associated with Islam	303
27	Ministries to Muslims	311
	Glossary: Terms Related to Islam	313
	Annotated Bibliography	335
	Index	344
	Other Books by Kent Philpott	353

Preface

Muslims are people loved of God and are not the Christian's enemies. As Paul stated,

> For we do not wrestle against flesh and blood, but against the rulers, against the authorities, against the cosmic powers over this present darkness, against the spiritual forces of evil in the heavenly places. (Ephesians 6:12)

That there exists an enemy is certain, but equally certain is that the enemy has been defeated through the work of Christ on the cross (see 1 John 3:8).

Jesus is the light of the world, and the work of the evangelical Christian is to let that light shine. Those who follow the Qur'an and the Prophet are walking in darkness, just as all of us who know Jesus as Savior once did.

The audience I am hoping will find this book to be of use is the evangelical Christian community, and by evangelical I do not refer to those traditionally understood to be evangelicals. I am thinking of all those, of whatever branch or denomination within the diverse Christian Family, who desire to present and proclaim the Good News of Jesus Christ to Muslim people.

After September 11 of 2001, it was some time before I ceased being fearful, angry, and hateful toward Muslims. I lumped all Muslims into the extremist category. Though I read about Muslims coming to faith, still I could not shake the antagonism I felt toward them. I did not distinguish between the radicals, moderates, liberals, and progressives in the diverse Muslim world.

Then, more than three years ago, I found I had a love for Muslim people. I can only credit that to the working of the Holy Spirit. From Amazon.com arrived book after book on Islamic-related subjects. In addition, I began teaching a course on Islam that continued for two years. I even began to attend the local Sunni mosque for their Friday prayer service. Now I have made many friends there, including the imams, and our little Miller Avenue Baptist Church, of which I have been pastor since 1984, cooperates in a food program with the mosque to help those in need.

For one and a half years I have been debating and discussing key issues with Muslims on television with my program "The Imam and the Pastor." I am the pastor in the series and the imam is Imam Abu Qadir Al-Amin, director of the San Francisco Muslim Community Center and a nationally know advocate for social justice. We completed eighteen one-hour programs. All eighteen can be viewed at our YouTube channel called The Imam and The Pastor.

We have not seen any conversions yet; we are still praying that the Holy Spirit will reveal Jesus to some.

Kent Philpott,
Mill Valley, California,
January 2019

Introduction

This volume is intended to be a handy reference for those who desire to understand the history, theology, and traditions of Islam, all in a single volume. It is also meant to equip those of the Christian faith in their witness to Muslim friends, neighbors, and acquaintances.

The first chapter is the study guide I developed for a class on Islam for The Saturday Seminary, a ministry of Miller Avenue Baptist Church in Mill Valley, California. It contains most of the important elements of Islam.

The second chapter is a summary of Patrick Sookhdeo's book, *Understanding Islamic Theology*. His is a most thorough presentation of Islam, and this summary pulls out most of his salient points.

Note: The first two chapters cover much of the same material by design; thus there is apparent and actual redundancy. Islam is complex, with many aspects to it and many different systems of thought, and the various sects and branches vary slightly or significantly from one another. Between Dr. Sookhdeo's outline and my own there is thus a greater chance of capturing a broader scope of how Islam is formulated.

Group discussion topics are interspersed throughout chapters two and three. The reader or class might imagine being in a debate with Muslims or that the goal is to be as knowledgeable as possible about Islam in order to more effectively witness to Muslims in a Western setting.

New to this edition is a fairly complete coverage of all the essentials of Shariah Law for both the Sunni and the Shia sects of Islam.

The sixth chapter condenses material presented by Dr. William Wagner from his book, *How Islam Plans to Change the World*.

The seventh chapter is a summary of *The Exorcist Tradition in Islam*, by Dr. Abu Ameenah Bilal Philips, and it is most enlightening about the extent to which the Muslim world is concerned with supernatural beings and their effects. Here is a subject that draws attention from Muslim leaders, an area that greatly concerns Muslim people.

The eighth chapter is a commentary on the four books written by Ayaan Hirsi Ali: *Infidel*, *The Caged Virgin*, *Nomad*, and *Heretic*. Ali is a former Muslim from Somalia who escaped a forced marriage and fled to Northern Europe where she became politically active and still acts as a voice against the abuse of women and for reform in Islam. She and her husband are both professors at Harvard University, and she is a frequent guest on Fox News.

The ninth chapter is a commentary on Reza Aslan's book, *No god but God*. Aslan is a Sufi, which is a religion stemming from Islam. He also calls for Islamic reform. Dr. Aslan is currently a professor at the University of California at Riverside. At the date of this book's publishing, Aslan has appeared on a television show series on CNN called "Believer," in which he explored unusual or fringe religious groups around the world.

Chapter ten presents possible responses to the calls for reform from within Islam.

Chapters eleven, twelve, thirteen, and fourteen present basic details of the Qur'anic chapters, a short outline of Muhammad's life, an explanation of Islam's Crescent and Star Symbol, and a brief summary of the *Sira*, the official biography of Muhammad (though now largely ignored), by Ibn Ishaq.

Chapter fifteen considers the differences in how Islam and Christianity claim miracles for Muhammed and Jesus.

Chapter sixteen contains a collection of essays I have written about Islam over the years.

Chapter seventeen is potentially the most explosive material in this book, since it questions the very basis of Muslim concepts of who actually spoke the Qur'an to Muhammed and therefore who Allah is.

Chapters eighteen, nineteen, and twenty deal with debating and use two works by Ahmed Deedat, material favored by Muslim debaters, as targets for response by Christians.

Chapters twenty-one and twenty-two deal with Islam's great concern for practical and ceremonial cleanliness in contrast with Christianity's less stringent approach.

The remaining chapters deal with various topics: the names of Muhammad; 25 Ways to Enter Paradise; an account of three religious movements that emanate from mainstream Islam—Bahai, Subud, and Sufism; significant Muslim populations of the world along with two maps; and a List of Christian Ministries to Muslims.

Next is an extensive glossary, which is a study in itself. Mastering the meanings of Islamic terms does not come quickly.

There is an annotated bibliography to make it easier for those who desire further study of Islam. The bibliography could be far longer, as more and more books on Islam are being published regularly.

Lastly, there is an index that should prove useful. The majority of the terms found in the glossary are not also found in the index.

Any of these materials may be quoted anywhere and for any purpose; permission is given to all who would find something of use.

There are any number of ways to spell key words, among which are: Qur'an (Koran, Quran); Shi'a (Shia, Shiite, Shi'ia); hadith (hadiths, Hadith, Hadiths); Sharia (Shariah, Sharia'); Muhammad (Mohammed); and there are many others. One of the problems with Arabic transliteration spellings is that many writers on Islam who are quoted here vary from one another. The spellings that seemed to be used by the majority of the scholars researched were chosen whenever the material is not a direct quotation.

1

ISLAMIC STUDIES OUTLINE

I. **Basic Beliefs**
   A. **Monotheism: Allah is the sole and almighty God.**
      1. This is called *Ta'whid*[1] in Arabic.
      2. Islam is monotheistic, in that it embraces one God only, as do Judaism and Christianity also.
      3. Islam is referred to as an Abrahamic religion, since the father of Islam is said to be Ishmael, the son of Abraham and Hagar, the Egyptian handmaiden to Abraham's wife Sarah.
      4. Those who embrace Islam are called Muslims, meaning "those who submit," and in the early period it meant, "those who submit to Allah and to Muhammad as Allah's prophet."
      5. Judaism is identified by Muslims as monotheistic, but Christianity is considered polytheistic due to the doctrine of the Trinity—the Father, Son, and Holy Spirit.
      6. Muslims especially repudiate the deity of Jesus and find the idea repugnant that God had a son, which infers that there is a sexual nature to God and that God had sexual relations with a woman—Mary.
      7. Islam emerged out of and was heavily influenced by both Judaism and Christianity as well as other religious belief systems such as Zoroastrianism, Gnosticism, and other pagan concepts, although Muhammad strongly rejected the paganism of his time.
   B. **Allah revealed ultimate truth to Muhammad, his final prophet.**
   C. **This truth was collected and written down in the Qur'an.**

---

[1] Throughout the remainder of this book, any Arabic term that is found in the Merriam-Webster Collegiate Dictionary, 2009 edition, will not be italicized; any Arabic term that is not found in that dictionary will be italicized the first time it is defined in a chapter but not always thereafter.

D. **There are Five Pillars of Islam that all Muslims must perform** (see VII):
   1. The *Shahada* or creed
   2. The *Salat* or daily prayers
   3. *Zakat* or almsgiving
   4. The *Sawm* of Ramadan
   5. The Hajj or pilgrimage to Mecca

E. **There are Six Articles of Belief** (see VIII).
   1. Belief in God and Tawhid
   2. Belief in angels
   3. Belief in the Islamic holy books
   4. Belief in the prophets and Messengers (mostly Sunnis)
   5. Belief in the Last Judgment and Resurrection
   6. Belief in predestination

DISCUSSION POINTS FOR EVANGELICAL WITNESS AND DEBATE

- Of critical importance is for Muslims to see that the God of the Bible is a Trinity, a three in one, an *echad* (Hebrew for "one" or "unity"), which does not violate monotheism. How might this be communicated to Muslims?
- Muslims are usually not willing to acknowledge external influences upon the Qur'an. Here the evangelical witness faces a dilemma. What are some ways the issue might be presented without terminating a dialogue?
- It is critical to distinguish between Islam's reliance on obedience and performance and Christianity's reliance on the grace of God in Christ Jesus. How might this distinction start to show up in your conversation with Muslims?

II. **The Qur'an, Hadith, and *Sira***

   A. The Qur'an, Islam's primary sacred Scripture, is believed to have been "recited" by Allah to Muhammad through the agency of the archangel Gabriel and stands therefore as the exact record of the true and final word of God. The word Qur'an can be translated as "reading" or "recitation." The regard is so high with which the Qur'an is held in the Muslim world, it touches on worship.
   1. The Qur'an is written in Arabic, and many Muslims consider that only the Arabic edition of the Qur'an is pristine and without distortion.
   2. Allah is the Arabic word used for God in the Qur'an and is used by most Arabs. In other languages, however, Allah is replaced with native words—for instance, *Tann* in Turkish and *Khoda* in Persian.
   3. The Qur'an is divided into 114 suras, or chapters. Some, the early softer recitations, were revealed in Mecca, and the later bulk were revealed in Medina. There is a decided difference in the nature of the revelations. The harsher ones were revealed later in Medina.

4. The Qur'an is considered the source book of Islamic principles and values. However, much of Islamic thought and practice comes from the hadith.

B. **The hadith is the written record of the life of Muhammad,** and it both supplements and interprets the Qur'an. Many Muslims contributed to the hadith, and its compilation is said to have begun during the 3rd caliphate, that of Othman (or Uthman), and mostly written during a period several generations after the death of Muhammad. Aisha, Muhammad's wife and the daughter of the first caliph, Abu Bakr, contributed heavily to the hadith, perhaps as many as 200,000 sayings.

1. The most valued of the hadith was collected by Al-Bukhari and Al-Muslim. There are several other collections which range from reliable to accepted forgeries.
2. It is usual for Muslims to divide the hadith into three categories: one, those that Muhammad directly spoke; two, those things that Muhammad did; three, what Muhammad declared to be permitted (Ar., *halal*) or declared to be forbidden (Ar., *haram*).

C. **The Sira is the biography of Muhammad**, and the most respected biography is written by Ibn Ishaq. In another section is a brief glance at the Sira (see the Table of Contents).

DISCUSSION POINTS FOR EVANGELICAL WITNESS AND DEBATE

- An evangelical witness to Muslims must be careful to avoid denigrating the Qur'an. At the same time, problems with the Qur'an are abundant. What are ways in which this dilemma can be overcome?
- "Allah" is the name of God for many people, including Arabic-speaking Christians, even today. Is it necessary to avoid the name Allah when speaking with Muslims?
- Must Muslims who have come to faith in Jesus begin using "God" in place of "Allah"?
- It is virtually impossible to become sufficiently knowledgeable of the hadith to effectively engage in debates or discussions about the hadith—for most Christians. But there are summaries, including in this present volume. Will this be enough preparation?
- Knowledge of the Sira is most quickly acquired. Muslims rarely know much of it. Would then a presentation of the many rather ridiculous sayings found therein prove of value?

III. The Meaning of the Word "Islam"

A. **Islam means wholeness, safeness, or peace** in the minds and hearts of Muslims, is often called the religion of peace. The word itself is means "voluntary submission to God." A devout Muslim is one who is submissive to Allah by serving him, following the tenants of Islam, and rejecting polytheism.

B. **Much of Islam is fear-based.** Among those fears are offending Allah, going to hell, being attacked by jinn (satans or demons), not being Islamic enough, being rejected by family and *ummah* (community), appearing to be weak, approving Western practices, and more. One's life in an Islamic community is observed and judged by many searching eyes, and thus there is little personal freedom in belief.

Those who are most extreme, the jihadist warriors and the honor brigade, have the most influence, so it is dangerous to oppose them.

DISCUSSION POINTS FOR EVANGELICAL WITNESS AND DEBATE

- Consider the word "voluntary." Is this an accurate description when the vast majority of Muslims are born into Islam? There is another sizable group who declare for Islam to avoid death. There are those who say they are Muslims to avoid the taxes imposed in Muslim-dominated countries on non-Muslims. And there are more who are required to state their submission to Islam who do not fit any of the above categories. Is it possible to use this topic in an evangelical witness?
- Fear of going to hell is used by Muslim leaders to excite conformity to Islamic ideals. Do Christians, who also believe in hell, do the same?

IV. Brief History

A. Muhammad

1. Muhammad was born, probably in AD 570, and died June 8, 632. In 610 Muhammad began receiving revelations from the archangel Gabriel and did so until his death. These revelations began to occur at the Cave of Hira, in a range of hills near Mecca. It was the custom of many Jews, Christians, Zoroastrians, and Gnostics to retire to secluded places in hopes of receiving spiritual visions and a direct connection with deity. These ascetics would fast, meditate, and stay awake for days in order to empty the mind and be open to dreams and visions. Muhammad, after a time, achieved trance-like states, during which the angel Gabriel, as he reported, spoke to him.

2. Muhammad reported his visits by Gabriel to his wife Khadija, who supported the idea that it was the angel speaking to her husband. Muhammad was not sure of the nature of the vision he had, but eventually adopted his wife's opinion. (There is an interesting hadith on this called "The Lap.")

3. Muhammad's home was Mecca of Arabia, in the area now called Saudi Arabia. He preached there of the revelations he received and was accepted by some as a legitimate prophet. Eventually, the civil authorities at Mecca rejected his claims and the content of the angelic revelations and persecuted Muhammad and his followers. Thus came the trek to Medina in 622, known as the *hijra* or immigration. In Medina, Muhammad established himself as a political and religious authority. The Islamic calendar is dated from the flight or immigration to Medina, making it year one.

4. In time, other tribes in Arabia rose up against Muhammad and his followers, and one by one these tribes were defeated in battle and brought under the rule of the early Muslims. In 629, Muhammad returned to Mecca and was received as a conqueror. By the time of his death, Muhammad had united all the tribes on the Arabian Peninsula into one religious and political unity. A tribe either converted to Islam, meaning that it swore allegiance to Muhammad as the true prophet of Allah, or the tribe had to

pay a tax to Islam. In time, Islamic warriors received a pension from this money source.

5. The Qurayzah, a Jewish tribal group, were banished for not embracing Islam. Then the dominant Jewish tribe, Banu Nadir, began opposing Muhammad and even attempted to assassinate him by dropping a large stone on him. They also were exiled from Medina. Eventually, all the non-Muslim forces opposing Muhammad were defeated. Then came what has been called "casting terror into their hearts"—murderous behavior intended to frighten others into submission. At the Battle of the Trench, after the forces of Islam were victorious, between 600 and 800 prisoners were beheaded, and according to more than one hadith, Muhammad participated in the slaughter.

DISCUSSION POINTS FOR EVANGELICAL WITNESS AND DEBATE

- Casting suspicion upon the veracity and credibility of the Qur'an in dialogue with Muslims may not achieve much. Is it yet a strategy worth employing?
- It is quite plain, based on the early history of Islam, that the bulk of Muhammad's followers in the seventh century were not persuaded but were rather coerced into aligning with Islam. Does the average Muslim care about this fact?
- Since it is not wise to denigrate Muhammad as a person in discussion with Muslims, how might one deal with his violent tendencies?

V. **Worldview**

A. **Creation:** Islam's basic worldview is that there was a creation somewhat like that found in the opening chapters of Genesis.

B. **The goal for Muslims is for Islam to dominate the entire globe and for sharia to be the world's rule of law.** This is to be accomplished by whatever means necessary. There will be "peace" only when this is fulfilled. (See chapter 6 for further discussion of this topic.)

C. **Resurrection:** There will be a final bodily resurrection, known in Islam as the "Day of Resurrection."

D. **Judgment:** After the resurrection there will be a judgment based on people's good and bad deeds. Good deeds—giving to the poor, prayer, and compassion toward animals—will earn a person who believes in Allah and in Allah's prophet Muhammad entrance into paradise. Out of this final judgment issues heaven for faithful Muslims and hell for all others.

E. **Predestination:** Predestination for Islam means that Allah has determined everything that will happen. Nothing happens except by the will of Allah. What Allah wills, and only what Allah wills, will come to pass. In fact, whatever happens must be Allah's will or it would not have happened, even if that which happens is contrary to the ethics of Islam as found in the Qur'an and the hadith. At the same time, however, humans have free will and must choose what is right or suffer for their disobedience.

DISCUSSION POINTS FOR EVANGELICAL WITNESS AND DEBATE

- Is the Muslim worldview sufficiently the same as that of the Bible that there is common ground with Muslims?
- Biblical Christianity's core goal is that the Gospel is to be proclaimed throughout the world. How is this different from the goal of Islam?
- Predestination and fatalism: does Islam distinguish between the two? How may a conversation on this point be introduced to Muslims?

VI. Allah

A. **Allah is almighty and incomparable**; he is transcendent, above and beyond nature, and communicates with humans by way of angels. Allah is all powerful and all knowing, merciful and compassionate. His ways are unknowable.

B. Muslims believe the basic purpose of humans is to **worship and serve Allah**.

VII. The Five Pillars of Islam

Performing the Five Pillars is obligatory for all Muslims. These are simultaneously considered a demonstration of faith, submission to Islam, and a desire to worship Allah. They are as follows:

A. The *Shahada* or creed

1. The primary creed of Islam, the shahada, must be recited in order to become a Muslim. The recitation is done under solemn oath and thereafter becomes part of the daily prayers.

2. The creed reads, "I testify there are no deities other than God alone, and I testify that Muhammad is the Messenger of God." Another version of the shahada is: "I believe Allah is God alone and that Muhammad is his messenger." (There are other variations.)

B. The *Salat* or daily prayers

1. The prayers, *salah* or *salat* (plural), are offered five times a day, beginning in the morning and extending in intervals until evening. Timings of the prayers vary, since they are set by a lunar calendar. The most important prayer is made Friday at the mosque, but if prevented from being at the mosque, praying can be done anywhere. This prayer time is usually sometime between 1 p.m. and 2 p.m. Certain washings of the feet and other ablutions are to be accomplished prior to entering the mosque.

2. The muezzin, either from a minaret or from inside the mosque itself, chants out the call to prayer, the *adhan*, and the first two words in Arabic are "*Allahu Akbar*." This prayer is thought to have the power to drive away jinn. The *iqamah*, the second call to prayer, is made just before the congregation begins the obligatory, or *fard*, prayer. The local imam will deliver a sermon in Arabic. The entire prayer service is usually about twenty-five minutes in length.

C. The *Zakat* or almsgiving

1. The zakat is an obligation and is not voluntary. It amounts to about 2.5% per year of a Muslim's income and is expected from those who can afford to give, thus not from the poor. The money raised by zakat also goes to cover the expenses of those who collect it. More can be given than the amount expected, and this additional offering is referred to as a *sadaqah*.

D. The *Sawm* of Ramadan

1. The sawm is a month long fast conducted during Ramadan. From dawn to dusk, food or drink is prohibited. At dusk a festive meal is celebrated. The fast is to express gratitude to Allah, acknowledge dependence on him, atone for sins, and serve as a reminder of the poor.

E. The Hajj or pilgrimage to Mecca

1. The hajj is expected to be made by every Muslim at least once in a lifetime, but only if one has the financial means and physical capacity to do so. While in Mecca the pilgrim walks seven times around the Kaaba (a large, black, cubic structure in a central square). This is termed circumambulating, with the left shoulder closest to the Kaaba, and recounts the journey Hagar took when she and Ishmael were sent away from Abraham by the urging of Sarah. The Kaaba is a holy building or shrine that houses the sacred black stone. On the final circling of the Kaaba, the pilgrim kisses the black stone.

The two main branches of Islam—Sunni and Shi'a—agree on the Five Pillars. Though not original to the foundations of Islam, some pious or radical Muslims consider the "lesser" or violent jihad to be a sixth pillar.

VIII. The Six Articles of Belief

In various places, along with the five pillars presented above, one will find the Six Articles of Belief, which are virtually identical to the five pillars but read somewhat differently. References for the Six Articles of belief are: Qur'an 2:98, 277, 285; and 4:136: *Iman* is the term used to describe those who believe in all six articles of belief.

- A. **Belief in God and Tawhid**
- B. **Belief in angels**
- C. **Belief in the Islamic holy books**
- D. **Belief in the prophets and Messengers** (for Sunni Muslims mostly)
- E. **Belief in the Last Judgment and Resurrection**
- F. **Belief in predestination** (Sunnis have a belief in Allah's unlimited power, while Shi'as see Allah's power as limited.)

DISCUSSION POINTS FOR EVANGELICAL WITNESS AND DEBATE

- In what ways are Islam's Allah and the God of the Bible alike? Is there common ground?

- Compare the Five Pillars of Islam and the Ten Commandments.
- Does Islam, in light of Allah's all determining will, have an actual ethic?
- Is Islam a religion of works or grace? May the difference between works and grace, as it impacts ordinary people, be a means of Gospel presentation? And if so, how?
- In the *Sira* by Ibn Ishaq, page 98-99, is the story of the "Four Men who Broke With Polytheism." That section opens with this sentence: "One day when the Quraysh had assembled on a feast day to venerate and circumambulate the idol to which they offered sacrifices, this being a feast which they held annually, four men drew apart secretly and agreed to keep their counsel in the bonds of friendship." The Arab tribe known as Quraysh, which was Muhammad's tribe, had the care and oversight of the Kaaba in Mecca. For some centuries, the Kaaba had been a pagan shrine which housed various idols. Muhammad preached there against polytheism and later instituted the hajj. In effect, Muhammad turned a pagan practice into an essential ritual for Muslims. May this be a point worth raising with Muslims today?

IX. Jihad

A. Though not an original pillar of Islam, it must be clearly identified that Islam does not distinguish between secular and religious authority; **there is no separation between church and state**. This has serious repercussions when it comes to matters of a military.

1. Jihad refers to a striving or a struggling, whether personal, as in the pursuit to serve Allah, or against what might be perceived as an attack on Islam itself. Muslims in non-Western countries may view through various forms of media Westerners engaged in what the pious consider sinful behavior and consider the entire culture represented to be offensive and an enemy to be fought. The Muslim is to fight against personal sin, the devil, or a visible enemy, and thus Jihad has a military component.

2. Many Muslims distinguish between the "greater" jihad, which is the advancement to spiritual and religious perfection, and the "lesser" jihad, which is the defense of Islam or the advancement of Islam.

3. Lesser jihad is to be exercised against non-Muslims, but often such jihad is carried on between differing sects of Islam, principally between Shi'a and Sunni. Jihad ideally is defensive in nature.

4. One of the principle tactics for Muslims is to assert that any violent action taken against Western countries is merely revenge for wrongs done to Muslims, either presently or in the past, even as far back as the Crusades a thousand years ago.

5. Some argue that the non-Muslim world is continually at war with Islam and Allah, and that it is the Muslim's duty to be engaged in violent jihad. (There is more on jihad in section XVI.)

DISCUSSION POINTS FOR EVANGELICAL WITNESS AND DEBATE

- Christians "strive" to be more like Jesus; is this the same as Islam's greater jihad? May

Christians speak to the hunger that many Muslims have to know God personally?
- "An attack on Islam," which may lead to a violent response, may be easily and broadly perceived by Muslims. How can this be avoided and still tell the truth in love?
- Is it any surprise that Muslims face a major conflict? On the one hand, Muslims want to be aware of what others are doing in the world, but they may then be fearful that the "honor brigade" is monitoring their internet account.
- Knowing the history of the Crusades (see the table of contents) and understanding what happened at that period of history may prove helpful in conversations with Muslims.

X. **Source of Authority**
   A. **Muhammad is considered the last prophet of God.**
      1. Adam, Noah, Abraham, Moses, and Jesus are also considered prophets of God, but Islam teaches that the revelation they received was not complete or final or that these Biblical revelations, both the Old and New Testaments, were misinterpreted and distorted over time. For Muslims, the final truth comes through Muhammad. Everything and anything else is considered heretical.
      2. The problem Muslims face here, however, is that in the Qur'an, especially in the early surahs, which were recitations received at Mecca before the flight to Medina, Jews and Christians and their Book are treated with respect and approval. But the messages from Allah through Gabriel to Muhammad changed in Medina. After that the Jews, the Christians, and others, along with their Scriptures, were denigrated.
   B. **Qur'an**
      1. The words that the archangel Gabriel spoke to Muhammad were said to first be memorized by his friends and associates, then passed on orally, then later written down in what we know as the Qur'an.
   C. **Sunnah and Hadith**
      1. In addition to the Qur'an, the record of the life and experiences of Muhammad, "the traditions," is called the sunnah and means "trodden path." The Sunnah is part of the hadith and together with the Qur'an comprises the core of the Muslim's authoritative teachings.
      2. The life examples of Muhammad, as found in the hadith, figure large in Islam. For instance, Muhammad had more than one wife, one wife was nine years old, he ate with his right hand only, he slept on his right side, and he wore a beard. He cast terror into the hearts of his enemies, often directed massacres, sold women and children into slavery in addition to other brutalities, and demanded demeaning gestures on the part of conquered people to demonstrate Islamic dominance. Muslims are expected to copy Muhammad's behavior and practices in our own times, at least according to the most faithful Muslims. Any deviation from the pattern of Muhammad is considered weakness if not apostasy.

3. There are a number of collections of hadith, but those collected by Al Bukhari and Al Muslim, two separate collections, are said to be the most trustworthy.

D. **The Sira, or biography of Muhammad**
1. The *Sira* is a third major source of authority for Islam. Originally compiled by Ibn Ishaq in Arabic, the most accessible English version is edited by A. Guillaume, published by Oxford Press. Supposedly, there are other biographies, but these accounts are not highly considered. In recent times, scant attention is paid to the *Sira* in either Arabic or translated, since it is easily apparent that its content is often of a mythological nature, and most Muslims probably wish they would escape critical attention.

DISCUSSION POINTS FOR EVANGELICAL WITNESS AND DEBATE

- Muhammad is considered the prime authority for all that is Islam. Thus, the Qur'an, hadith, and *Sira* have been sifted for centuries to determine exactly who Muhammad was and what he did. Christians do something of the same thing regarding Jesus. What are the differences between Muslims and Christians on this point?
- "To be like Jesus," Christians sing, and so we should. Do Muslims know what it is to be like Jesus? How may Christians communicate this to Muslim people?
- Should the *Sira*, the biography of Muhammad, be something Christians explore with Muslims? If so, the Christian witness will run into two problems. One, Muslims know little of what the *Sira* contains. Two, when material from the *Sira* is presented that is strange and contradictory to mainstream Muslim understanding, the Muslim will likely become defensive. Is it enough to present Jesus and leave Muhammad alone?

XI. Jesus

A. **Muslims believe Jesus is a true prophet of God**
1. Jesus is considered to be just like the prophets of the Old Testament: Adam, Noah, Moses, Abraham, and so on. This is made plain in Qur'an 6:83-86:

What was the reasoning About Us, which We gave to Abraham, (To Me) against his people : We raise whom We will, Degree after degree : For thy Lord is full Of wisdom and knowledge. We gave him Isaac And Jacob : all (three) We guided : And before him, We guided Noah, And among his progeny, David, Solomon, Job, Joseph, Moses, and Aaron : Thus do We reward Those who do good : And Zakariya and John, and Jesus and Elias : All in the ranks Of the Righteous : And Ismail and Elisha, And Jonas, and Lot : And to all WE gave Favor above the nations :

2. Note that this chapter in the Qur'an was "given" in Mecca and so has a much more conciliatory tone than the later parts of the Qur'an, the harsher recitations given in Medina. Note also that in Sura 6 verse 85 that the place of Jesus and "Zakariya and John" are out of sync historically.

B. The Arabic word for Jesus is *'Isa*,
   1. *'Isa* is a name often given to Muslim males.
   2. Arabic is a Semitic language, and it may be seen that *'Isa* comes close to the Hebrew spelling and pronunciation of Joshua and Hosea.
   3. Other passages in the Qur'an say of Jesus that:
      a) He was born of a virgin (19:16-21)
      b) He was the Messiah (4:171-172)
      c) He was without sin (19:19)
      d) He did miracles, even raising the dead (5:110)
      e) Jesus was not more than a messenger like the other prophets who died and are no more (5:75).
      f) He was not crucified and never died but went to heaven to be with God, and he has a major role to play on the Day of Judgment and actually descends to the earth (4:157-159).
   4. In contrast, Muhammad was not virgin born, was not the Messiah, was not without sin, and performed no miracles. In Qur'an 40:55 and 48:1-2, Allah commanded Muhammad to ask for forgiveness of his sins. Though not found in the Qur'an or hadith, it is said that Muhammad's miracle was the Qur'an itself.

DISCUSSION POINTS FOR EVANGELICAL WITNESS AND DEBATE

- Does it matter whether Jesus is referred to as Jesus or *'Isa*? As a follow up, does it matter whether the God of the Bible is referred to as Allah? We Christians differ among ourselves on these points, so just how important to evangelical witness is this difference?
- Considering what Islam says about Jesus, is it a question of "Yes, but" or "Yes, and"?
- The Islamic denial of the crucifixion of Jesus is perhaps the most critical of all points of difference between Muslims and Christians. This is the heart of the Gospel, and the Muslim heart and mind are braced to reject this fundamental truth. How can the evangelical Christian speak of Jesus' sacrifice on the cross?

XII. **Sin and Salvation**
   A. **Muslims do not believe in human inability**
      1. Every person has free will and is able to make right choices.
      2. But without Muhammad, the warner and sure guide to the straight path, and without the Qur'an, there is no chance of being in paradise.
   B. **Sin for Muslims**
      1. Sin is failing to live up to the obligations of the religion and is not seen as an offense against a holy God as it is in Christianity.
      2. Such failure may be overcome or set aside by the actions of the faithful Muslim. It is what is done not who you are that counts.

C. **Islamic salvation is by means of human effort.**
1. Through right action and right knowledge paradise may be attained, primarily by following the Five Pillars of Islam.

D. **Muslims have no assurance of salvation.**
1. Muhammad himself was not sure he would be in paradise.

E. **What about the jihadist who dies as a martyr?**
1. There is no absolute assurance of being in paradise, because Allah is a deceiver and will lead astray any and all he wills.

DISCUSSION POINTS FOR EVANGELICAL WITNESS AND DEBATE

- It is no wonder that Islam is capable of producing the most radical followers. Would even serious, Biblically-oriented and faithful Christians be seen by Muslims as weak and faithless? How can Christians demonstrate true faith and piety?
- Muslims speak much of sin, especially in the Friday prayers in the mosque. Sin is often understood as a lack of attending to the obligations imposed on Muslims. How may Christians speak of the holiness of God and their own personal unholiness?
- It is highly likely that Muslim people may have a sense of personal unworthiness, since the requirements of the religion are so very extensive, and a lifetime of being a truly observant Muslim can be shattered and erased in a single moment. Does this present an opportunity for the evangelical witness to present the assurance and peace there is in Christ?

XIII. **Supernatural Beings**
A. **Angels**
1. The belief in angels, whom Muslims believe are made of light, is central to Islam. The word angel translated into Arabic carries the meaning of messenger, just as the Greek word in the New Testament does. Gabriel, the angel who recited the Qur'an to Muhammad, had no free will but served and worshiped Allah in total obedience.
2. Angels record everything a person does and acquire the soul of the dead, thereupon delivering it to its proper destination.
3. Every Muslim is born with an angel on each shoulder. These angels are named *Munkar* and *Nakir*. The one on the right shoulder records good deeds, while the one on the left records bad deeds. These angels are very involved in the death of the person.
4. Islamic angelology is complex and confusing. It is also quite extensive, so that capturing it is not within the scope of this presentation.

B. **Satan and Demons**
1. Islam believes in a real Satan and demons. There are at least five categories of demons, which are called jinn, *garina*, *dews*, *als*, and *pari*. These fear-

some beings are involved in the affairs and lives of people and must be placated, warded off, or appealed to for assistance. They are a significant part of the religious and/or superstitious life of Muslims, in the Middle East especially. These "demons" are not the complete equivalent of the demons in the New Testament but are close. They are lower than angels in rank, can appear in human and animal form, and can exercise power over people. The genie in the bottle is a jinn, and jinn jinx people through spells.

2. The "evil eye" figures large in Muslim communities and is used to ward off the jinn in every Muslim home. On a practical everyday level, the religion has much to do with magical and superstitious practices in order to control and protect against jinn, especially in countries dominated by Islam. Traditional tribal cultures have also been mixed in to the point that many Muslims do not know which is which.

3. *Shaytan* is the word often used by Muslims for the Biblical Satan. It may also refer to a particularly evil jinn.

C. **Exorcism**

1. There are exorcists in Islam, those who specialize in warding off jinn and who also practice exorcising them.

2. Islamic dealings with evil spirits are most unlike those found in the New Testament or experienced by those who cast out demons today in the Christian community.

3. In chapter three is an extensive summary of Dr. Bilal Phillips' book entitled, *The Exorcist Tradition in Islam*. This work plainly demonstrates magic pitted against magic and is virtually the same as that practiced by the shamans.

4. The contrast between how Muslims and how Jesus and Christians today deal with the demonic could not be more pronounced.

DISCUSSION POINTS FOR EVANGELICAL WITNESS AND DEBATE

- The Christian and Islamic view of angels could not be greater. How might this difference serve as a point of witness?

- Muslims, especially mosque leaders, are well acquainted with jinn and the mischief they cause. Much of daily life for Muslims involves protection from the jinn. The concept of "hygiene" for Muslims often does not have as much to do with cleanliness as it does with completing protective rituals to ward off demons, much of it having to do with the toilet. Not all Christians are experienced with the casting out of demons, but for those who are, may this be an open door of ministry?

- Many Muslims live in fear of evil spirits. They know such are real and not a product of the imagination. Here is a definite point of connection with Muslims.

XIV. The Sharia Law

A. **"The path leading to the watering place"** is the Sharia Law, which makes sense for a religion that sprang from the desert in the seventh century.

1. The Law emerged out of the communities of Muslim scholars, and nearly all Muslims honor it. Indeed, to be a faithful Muslim is to live under Sharia—and just as it was administered in the seventh century.

2. Islam does not acknowledge the separation of religion and state but weds the two, with Islamic jurists being the dominant authorities. Anything less than this ideal state is not accepted except by Muslims who live in a non-Muslim majority culture.

3. Westerners generally consider Sharia Law to be harsh and austere; however, some have thought that Christians or even secular advocates could find accommodation with Muslims in certain areas such as family law, divorce, and financial matters.

4. Sharia Law is all encompassing; all aspects of life must submit to it. Though many Muslims chafe at the strictness of it, the powerful religious authorities will not tolerate deviance. Sharia is seen as the pattern of Muhammad's life and practices, and thus it must be followed in order to achieve paradise. An issue arises when authorities disagree with one another on how the Law should be interpreted.

5. The implementation of Sharia Law has much to do with the exercise of power, the wielding of real power over others, Muslim and non-Muslim alike.

6. Muslims hold that it is their mission to fight non-believers and specifically Christians until they willingly embrace Islam or until they submit to being ruled over by Muslims. This is seen in Qur'an 9:29:

Fight those who believe not In God nor the Last Day, nor hold that forbidden which hath been forbidden by God and His Apostle, not acknowledge the religion of Truth, (even if they are) of the People of the Book, until they pay the Jizya with willing submission, and feel themselves subdued.

B. **Muslims in Western countries make serious efforts to apply Sharia Law in the following circumstances:**

1. Areas having to do with marriage and divorce
2. A man's treatment of a wife and children
3. Allowing Muslims freedom to dress as is fitting to their traditions
4. Freedom to honor Allah in both public and private sectors
5. Often Sharia Law is secretly practiced in Muslim "ghettos." It can be expected that pressure to practice "cultural" tolerance—to allow Muslims to be Muslims and for the civil, legal, and police authorities to keep hands off—will increase as Muslim populations increase.

DISCUSSION POINTS FOR EVANGELICAL WITNESS AND DEBATE

- That Sharia Law must reign upon the earth is a central Muslim goal. All other forms of governance are viewed as inadequate and not honoring to Allah, for at least the pious Muslims. The contrast with the kingdom of God as Biblically understood is immense. How may the Biblical nature of the kingdom of God be presented to Muslim people?

- Pious Muslims are not concerned about updating their faith and view attempts to adopt modern liberal innovations to be antagonistic to real Islam. How may a different concept be presented to Muslims?

- The drive to institute Sharia Law is largely based on fear, fear of not being like Muhammad and thus risking being cast into hell. This very potent and all pervading fear stands as a barrier to the Gospel. How may such fear be countered?

XV. **Sects and Divisions in Islam**
  A. **Sunni vs. Shi'a History**
      1. After Muhammad's death in 632, there was a dispute over who would replace him. The Sunnis believed Muhammad's successor should be chosen on the basis of ability and character.
      2. Abu Bakr, a close friend of Muhammad, was named the first "caliph" or chief Muslim ruler. Abu Bakr's first undertaking was to put down a rebellion of some of the Arabian tribes known as the "Wars of Apostasy."
      3. It was during this time that they began to write down collections that became one volume called the Qur'an. Much controversy surrounds this and is a highly complex debate.
      4. Abu Bakr died of natural causes in 634 and there followed a succession of four of the early followers of Muhammad as caliph—Umar (Omar), Uthman (Othman), Ali, and Ali's son, Hasan.
      5. Umar was assassinated in 644, and Umar's replacement by Uthman caused considerable unrest. Uthman was assassinated in 656 and replaced by Ali. Ali was assassinated in 661.
      6. Turmoil continued for some time, the story of which is quite confusing and complicated, but eventually the battle over leadership resulted in a schism in the Muslim community.
      7. The fourth caliph, Ali ibn Ali Talib, was considered by one group to be the legitimate heir to lead Islam, and they were the Shi'a. Those who rejected Ali became known as the Sunni, those who follow the pattern or sunnah of the life of Muhammad. (There will be much more on the split between the Shi'a and the Sunni branches of Islam.) The Shi'a branch of Islam believes that the successors of Muhammad should be from the actual bloodline of Muhammad, and Ali was both Muhammad's adopted son and Muhammad's son-in-law, since Ali married Muhammad's youngest daughter, Fatima.
      8. Sunni versus Shi'a interpretations of the Qur'an and the hadith emerged

and diverged between the seventh and tenth centuries. During this period, Sharia Law developed, mostly within the Sunni branch and is more a way of life or a legal system within a belief system.

9. It is claimed that if attacked, Muslims of whatever branch will unit to fight a common enemy. This, however, is more of a slogan than a reality.

B. **Who are the Sunni?**

1. The Sunni branch is by far the largest, comprising between 80% to 90% of Muslims worldwide.

2. The Sunnis claim that Muhammad did not appoint a successor before he died and believe the Muslim community is to elect a successor. This is the Imam, and for Sunnis he is the leader of prayer, the one who "stands in front."

3. There are four schools of thought within Sunni Islam: Hanafi, Hanbali, Maliki, and Shafi'i. Followers of each accept followers of any of the other schools.

4. Sunni can also be designated *Ahl as-Sunnah* or followers of the way of Muhammad. Thus they give a high status to the hadith, the story of the habits and practices of Muhammad contained in six volumes.

5. Sunnis follow both the Qur'an and the hadith, but foremost is the Qur'an. They acknowledge the four first Caliphs as the legitimate successors to Muhammad.

6. Within the Sunni branch is an ultra-orthodox version of Islam known as Wahhabi, a puritanical Muslim sect founded in Arabia in the 18th century by Muhammad ibn-Abdul Wahhab and revived by ibn-Saud in the 20th century. Wahhabism esteems the first generation of Muhammad and his followers and strives to emulate their lives as examples to follow. These followers are often referred to as traditionalists.

C. **Who are the Shi'a?**

1. Shi'a is the second largest branch of Islam and comprises between 10% to 20% of Muslims worldwide.

2. Shi'as assert that on his final pilgrimage to Mecca, just before his death, Muhammad selected his son-in-law, Ali ibn Abi Talib, to be the leader of the new movement. "Shi" refers to follower and "a" refers to Ali, thus Shi'a. Shi'as reject the Sunni Muslim caliphs that began with Abu Bakr.

3. In Shi'a is the idea of the "hidden Imam." At one point in Shi'a history, in 872, one of their Imams, Muhammad al-Mahdi, is believed to have gone into hiding but did not die; this is called the Occultation. This hidden Imam, called the Mahdi, whose whereabouts are known only to a few, is expected to reappear at the end of time and restore the fortunes of Shi'a Islam and usher in the final period of grace. This concept of the Mahdi is also shared by some Sunni who believe the Mahdi will be a bloodline descendant of Muhammad. There have been a number of persons

who have claimed to be the Mahdi, the latest being Abdullah al-Qahtani (1935–1980), who led a few hundred followers to take over the Grand Mosque in Mecca in 1979, but the group was overcome by the Saudi Arabian military.

4. Shi'a has a number of offshoots, the largest of which is known as the Twelvers, those who are looking for the return of the Mahdi as the twelfth caliph. The Seveners are those who are looking for the return of the seventh caliph, who is now in occultation, the aforementioned Muhammad al-Mahdi.

D. **Liberalizing Influences**

1. The history of Islam with its power struggles, wars, and development of a multitude of sects is complex. In more recent times, from 1924 onward, Islam has seen a separation from traditional Islamic beliefs and practices and the corresponding growth of what might be termed liberal Islam. Liberal or progressive Islam attempts to adjust to the realities of the modern era. There is a reaction to this liberalization movement by extremists who fear the rise of an "accommodating" Islam. For instance, there has been a move to reinstitute and enforce women wearing the "Islamic veil" and a desire to return to Sharia Law.

E. **Sufism**

1. Many religions have a mystical version, and Sufism serves this purpose for Islam. Sufism combines an ascetic and mystical way of life and seeks to have direct experiences with deity.

2. Over time Sufism impacted Islam in direct ways, accounting for some of Islam's greatest achievements in terms of the arts and sciences. Indeed, the intellectual culture often claimed as a product of Islam was really due to Sufism.

3. Persecution of Sufism by Islam

   a) In recent times, both Sufi shrines and mosques have been vandalized, even destroyed by mainline Muslims.

   b) Sufis, unlike mainstream Islam, builds shrines for its saints, which is not pleasing to Muslim hardliners who consider the traditional mystical school of Islam heretical.

   c) Sufis have been killed, most notably in Pakistan, Kashmir, Somalia, Mali, Egypt, Libya, Tunisia, Russia, Dagestan, and Iran.

DISCUSSION POINTS FOR EVANGELICAL WITNESS AND DEBATE

- Christianity and Islam have in common competing branches. Sunni and Shi'a have murdered one another, and this kind of warfare is also part of Christian history. Our history of conflict cannot be denied, but it can be clarified, especially from a Biblical evangelical point of view, and it is here that the witness has an opportunity.

- Is it of value to know to which branch of Islam the evangelical witness is speaking? Perhaps, but maybe not, is the best answer. There are real differences, but Muslim is Muslim most of the time.

- Sufism is all together different. It is plain from Reza Aslan's book, *No god but God*, that a large difference exists. The Sufi claims to be Muslim and will often practice as one and appear almost indistinguishable from a Sunni or Shi'a Muslim, but it is in appearances only. The Sufi has more in common with the shaman who seeks to have a mystical experience with the divine. Might Sufis be more open to an evangelical witness? What approach would you take?

- Persecution of Shi'a by Sunni and the reverse, with both Sunni and Shi'a persecuting Sufis, is serious and deadly. Sufis merely think the Sunni and Shi'a are heading in the wrong direction, but the other two branches consider each of the others to be apostate and thus the worst of the worst, worthy of death. Here the evangelical witness may use John 3:16, the parable of the Good Samaritan, and other wonderful passages that speak of love for enemies.

XVI. The Crusades

    A. It is common for Muslims to point to the crusades as **a reason for Muslim violence today**. This seems disingenuous to most people, since the events occurred so long ago. Nevertheless, the themes of retaliation and revenge continue.

    B. As soon as Muhammad gained a foothold, he began to conquer tribes and territory in the Arabian Peninsula. After his death, his successors continued the **pattern of advancing Islam by the sword**, which continued for centuries.

        1. In 717, Muslim armies moved into Europe, conquered France, and began to invade further east into Germany and Poland. Islamic forces also traveled into the British Isles.

        2. In 732, an army lead by Charles Martel stopped Muslim expansion at the Battle of Tours-Poitiers. However, Islam continued to hold most of Spain for more than 700 years.

        3. Earlier, in the late seventh century, the Muslim army on the eastern front conquered the areas now known as Pakistan, Afghanistan, parts of India, and other areas of Central Asia.

        4. For centuries after that a kind of cold war existed.

    C. The run-up to the period of the actual Crusades

        1. The Seljuk Turks of Central Asia who converted to Sunni Islam moved aggressively west and began warring against Arabian Muslims and Byzantine Christians. They occupied modern day Turkey and began destroying churches and slaughtering Christians. They did the same to Jerusalem, destroying the Church of the Holy Sepulcher and building a mosque in its place.

        2. The Christian population was being decimated, and in 1093 the Byzantine Emperor, Alexius Comnenus, appealed to the Roman Pope and other

Western European kings and princes, asking for help against the Seljuk Turks. Thus began the Crusades.

    3. That there were Crusades, which began in 1095, is plain history.

  D. **The Purpose of the Crusades**

    1. The primary purpose of the crusades was to stop Muslim aggression and relieve Christians who had been overrun by Muslim armies. Of special interest was Jerusalem, yet it must be noted that the Christian armies, from the first to the last, did not attempt to conquer territory or peoples who had not been taken over previously by Muslims.

    2. The Crusades were defensive in nature, and Muslims claim the same for their warfare.

    3. Islam's beginnings were marked by war and aggression, and it continued despite periods of tolerance and peace. Again, it must be understood that the Crusades were a response to centuries of conquests by Muslims. Indeed, over two-thirds of the Christian world had fallen under the domination of Islam.

  E. **The Crusaders committed their share of atrocities.**

    1. A distinction should be made, however, between Christendom and genuine Christianity. The Crusaders were certainly part of Christendom, but given the state of the Church, the "visible" Church during those "dark ages" was something far differnt than the invisible Church of Jesus Christ.

  F. **The Crusade period accomplished very little:** there was no clear winner or loser.

    1. The First Crusade: 1095, Jerusalem was captured and held until 1187.

    2. The Second Crusade: 1147–1149, was largely a failure with nothing achieved.

    3. The Third Crusade: 1189–1192, under the leadership of Richard the Lionhearted, struggled over Jerusalem against the Muslim chieftain, Saladin, and failed in this attempt to recapture the city. However, he did take Cyprus and the City of Acre and was able to sign a treaty with Saladin to give Christians access to Jerusalem.

    4. The Fourth Crusade: 1201–1204, the Crusaders were sidetracked into the struggle for Constantinople, and little else was accomplished.

    5. The Fifth, 1218–1221; the Sixth, 1228–1229; and the Seventh, 1248–1250, were focused on Egypt with little accomplished.

DISCUSSION POINTS FOR EVANGELICAL WITNESS AND DEBATE

- To this day, radical Islam takes refuge in the concept of revenge, that Muslim violence is merely revenge for past violence against Muslims, and at the head of that list is the Crusades. Is the best approach for the evangelical witness to speak to the issue of the Crusades or not?

- Is it a worthwhile issue to pursue the distinction between the true or invisible Church and the visible Church or Christendom? It must be acknowledged that we have little to go on as to the nature and make-up of the church of the Crusade era.
- The reality of territory lost and gained may be a more plausible ground on which to make a statement, since the conquering of territory looms large for Muslims and is an indicator of their strength. It is here we are reminded that Jesus said His kingdom was not of this world.

XVII. *Taqiyya*

A. Origins of the permission to deceive

1. After the Battle of Badr against the Qaynuqa Jews, Muhammad became angry with a Jewish poet named Ka'b bin Al-Ashraf who poked fun at Muslim women. Muhammad asked for someone to step up and defend Islam and the honor of the prophet, that is, himself. A young man named Muhammad bin Maslama volunteered. But he requested that he be allowed to deceive the opposition. The Prophet of Islam again took the path of expediency over moral absolutes and replied, "You may say it."

2. Thus was born the principle of *taqiyya*, which may be defined as, To defend or promote Islam, Muslims are permitted to lie and deceive. Whatever one says for the sake of Allah and for Islam is forgiven.

3. "The Greatest Deceiver" is one of the 99 names of Allah.

B. Shi'a vs. Sunni use of Taqiyya

1. Though it is the Shi'a who are said to be more invested in taqiyya, it is practiced by most Muslims. Perhaps it has become so ingrained in the Muslim mindset that distortion of facts in defense of or promotion of Islam simply goes unnoticed. I have found both Shi'a and Sunni imams to repeatedly lie, even when they know they will be found out.

DISCUSSION POINTS FOR EVANGELICAL WITNESS AND DEBATE

- Permission to deceive was given by Muhammad in the seventh century, and so it continues. It is part of what being a Muslim is, and it seems not to come across to them as lying. The issue is, should the evangelical witness call attention to the untruth?
- Taqiyya is something we are all tempted to do, to protect and advance, and Christians do it as well, though it is not based on a timeless strategy. We do so out of a good motive or even ignorance, but there is still the untruth. Perhaps the Christian witness will be content to understand taqiyya and not get too excited about it. The audience often catches the deception regardless.

XVIII. Muslim Tolerance

A. How tolerant are Muslims when they are in a position of dominance?

1. The answer to this key question varies. In a country that is a self-proclaimed Muslim country, there is little tolerance; it is either convert,

submit, leave, or die. This is what most Westerners understand of life in Saudi Arabia and Iran.

B. Historically it must be noted that **Muslims have been tolerant of others**.

1. In some Muslim-majority countries over the centuries not even the *jizya* has been demanded of non-Muslims. The *jizya* is the obligatory tax placed upon People of the Book who refuse to convert to Islam.

2. Many in this modern era suspect that the days of tolerance are over or is only evident when Muslims are not in power and control.

C. **History is one thing, but the present day is another.**

1. Currently we see a worldwide rise in fundamentalist Islam, sometimes called the Salafi movement or Pious Ones movement. And it is shared by both Sunni and Shi'a Islam.

2. Perhaps the extreme forms of Islam arose out of desperation and flourished in Muslim countries that are largely poor and backward as compared to first and second world nations.

3. Perhaps it has been the result of increased ability to act in the world due to Middle Eastern oil money.

4. Perhaps it has been a fear brought on by a large proportion of Muslims becoming nominal in their faith.

5. Whatever the reason, Muslim tolerance is not what it used to be, and hard-line attitudes toward those within and without the Islamic faith have flourished.

DISCUSSION POINTS FOR EVANGELICAL WITNESS AND DEBATE

- In the face of potential violence, Christians are to be wise as serpents and harmless as doves. Easy enough to say, but not so easy to do. Certainly the evangelical witness does not engage in violence of any kind. And to be fearful is understandable, thus we do not judge one another as to our level of involvement. What may be some safe(r) avenues of witness?

- Are Christians who witness to Muslims protected by God from harm? Evidently not, in the broad outlook. But such has been noted.

XIX. Violent Jihad

A. **Sixth pillar of Islam?**

1. Some observers of Islam claim that violent jihad has become the sixth pillar of Islam. Those who follow daily news reports would likely agree. It occurs everyday wherever Muslims have some degree of presence.

B. **Does mainline Islam support it?**

1. The answer is that the Qur'an, the life of Muhammad, and the hadith do indeed support this.

2. It is historical fact that Muhammad did force conversion to Islam and either enslaved or murdered those who refused to convert. There is no way that Muslims today can or will deny this.

C. It will suffice here to quote from the Qur'an in regard to the necessity of Muslims practicing violent jihad.

1. Qur'an 2:190–193: "Fight in the cause of God Those who fight you, But do not transgress limits; For God loveth not transgressors. And slay them Wherever ye catch them, and drive them out of the holy places whence they drove you out, for persecution is worse than slaughter. And fight not with them at the Inviolable Place of Worship until they first attack you (there) then slay them. Such is the reward of disbelievers. But if they desist, then lo! Allah is Forgiving, Merciful. And fight them until persecution is no more, and religion is for Allah. But if they desist, then let there be no hostility except against wrong doers."

2. This sort of instruction continues in Sura 2 and verses 216, 217, 246; 4:74–78, 91, 104; 9:5, 36, 41, 84, 123; 47:4–6. One of the strongest messages is Qur'an 9:29: "Fight those who believe not In God nor the Last Day, Nor hold that forbidden Which hath been forbidden By God and His Apostle, Nor acknowledge the religion Of Truth, (even if they are) Of the People of the Book, Until they pay the Jizya With willing submission, And feel themselves subdued."

3. It should be noted that suras 2 and 9 of the Qur'an were received in Medina when Muhammad ran into conflict with tribes and peoples who would not submit to Islam. These suras abrogated or supplanted softer recitations received in Mecca earlier. One Imam, in my presence said the reverse, hoping to please or fool his Christian audience.

DISCUSSION POINTS FOR EVANGELICAL WITNESS AND DEBATE

- Political liberals tend to ignore or deny the idea that violent jihad is part and parcel of Islam. Generally, they believe this is a more loving attitude or that violence is more a matter of culture within the Muslim world and will fade away in time. They also resort to the claim that Islam has been "hijacked" by extremists. While these arguments may contain some truth, they may be disingenuous ways to excuse deadly violence.

- One fact will not go away, and that is that there are suras in the Qur'an that directly and clearly advocate for violent jihad. Moderate Muslims are mostly unaware of passages like Qur'an 9:29 or will claim ignorance if they can get away with it. Should the evangelical witness, even in American communities, protect those Muslims from hearing this truth?

- Abrogation, especially in the discussion of violent jihad, becomes a major issue. Here is where the Christian witness must be aware of the concept and know that the passages presenting violent jihad come later at Medina than the earlier soft passages that came in Mecca.

XX. Prospect for Missions to Islam in S.M. Zwemer, *Arabia: The Cradle of Islam*

Rev. Zwemer writes passionately about mission outreach to the Arab people. He was part of a wave of missionaries, mostly Calvinistic young men and women of British and Scottish heritage, many of whom died on the mission field. In chapter 35 of his most interesting and helpful book, published in 1900, he quotes from Dr. H. H. Jessup's book, *The Mohammedan Missionary Problem*, published in 1879, about "the missionary problem of the future" (page 374). Quoted now are the lists that the Rev. Dr. Jessup presented concerning the obstacles facing the mission to Muslims:

A. **Unfavorable features:**
   1. The union of the temporal and spiritual power
   2. The divorce between morality and religion
   3. Ishmaelitic intolerance
   4. Destruction of true family life
   5. The degradation of woman
   6. Gross immorality
   7. Untruthfulness
   8. Misrepresentation of Christian doctrine
   9. The aggressive spirit of Islam

B. **Favorable features:**
   1. Belief in the unity of God
   2. Reverence for the Old and New Testament
   3. Reverence for Christ
   4. Hatred of idolatry
   5. Abstinence from intoxicating drink
   6. The growing influence of Christian nations
   7. The universal belief of the Muslims that in the latter days there will be a universal apostasy from Islam.

Zwemer comments then that though there have been changes since Dr. Jessup wrote his book, the central truths remain true.

DISCUSSION POINTS FOR EVANGELICAL WITNESS AND DEBATE

- How does your experience and/or knowledge of outreach to Muslims tally with Dr. Jessup's views?
- Which of the items listed under "unfavorable features" seems to pose the greatest obstacle?
- Which of the items listed under "favorable features" seems to offer the most hope for reaching Muslims for Christ?

XXI. Trends

A. Islam will grow and spread around the world.

1. One factor influencing this is the high birth rate among Muslims.
2. Another factor is immigration.

   a) Immigration is often encouraged or planned and has been for centuries. The patient Islamic strategists are looking fifty or more years into the future.

   b) Turmoil in Muslim countries is a trigger to speed immigration to Western countries, deliberate or not.

B. Islam is highly evangelistic.

1. Millions of dollars, mostly flowing from Iran (Shi'ite) and Saudi Arabia (Sunni), are spent every day, and much of it goes toward the building of mosques and establishing Islamic learning centers in or near Western educational institutions.

C. There is a growing need for order and restraint.

1. This need comes even at the expense of liberties among Muslims. As the world's cultures head increasingly toward chaos of varying kinds in terms of economic, moral, and political disintegration, greater will be the desire for order.
2. The establishment of Sharia Law will increasingly become the agenda for many Muslims.

D. The early history of Islam is full of military style conversions.

1. Islam may well continue to be the same in the future.
2. Islam is a power religion in many respects, and the leaders of Islam are not afraid to use it, either to defend itself or to advance its authority, a kind of iron glove evangelism and a "casting of terror into the heart." This last phrase, casting terror into the heart, is a prominent strategy for Muslims. Bombings of markets and other venues where people gather is intended to bring fear into the hearts and minds of non-Muslims. It is however, a gross miscalculation of the strength of Western nations and their resolve.
3. The thinking is that Westerners will run for cover and either convert to Islam or accommodate them on many points that suit their agenda. Terror that inspires fear is a major feature of Islamic jihad.

E. However, much of the expansion of Islam for the near future will be by the ballot box.

1. Immigration shows Muslims spreading out worldwide.
2. Some of them will assimilate, but radicals do arise and lead others astray.
3. The average Muslim wields little power; power is in the hands of the leaders, and the leaders are often fearful of becoming weak or apostate.

F. **The treatment of women in Islam**
   1. This may be a factor that works against the religion despite publicity that tries to show Muslim women in a favorable light. Women cannot decide whom they will marry, are beaten by their husbands as a kind of duty, are often restricted in their movements, and are largely treated as property.
   2. Adultery is effectively sanctioned and often legalized through bizarre temporary marriages. Women's sexuality must be repressed, and female circumcision is considered necessary to curb sexual appetites (though this practice is largely cultural). It is not a stretch to consider that men and women in Islam are often fearful of one another. In some places, this dysfunctional life may produce change.

DISCUSSION POINTS FOR EVANGELICAL WITNESS AND DEBATE

- Whatever the future is moving toward, it is also nearing an end point where Jesus will return and the kingdom of God will have come. This is the solid ground of the evangelical witness, so death is merely the worst that can happen. Our witness is from strength, from the power of the Holy Spirit.
- The "hideous strength" that C. S. Lewis wrote about in his famous trilogy is merely hideous—strong but defeated. Heels may be bruised, but the head has been crushed (see Genesis 3:15). In that strength we go into the Muslim world and proclaim the Gospel of Peace.

2

A SUMMARY OF UNDERSTANDING ISLAMIC THEOLOGY

Note: Dr. Sookhdeo's book[1], in my opinion, is the most accessible, thorough, and well constructed summary of Islamic theology available to date. I have tried to put this summary in my own words, but in many cases I have quoted directly and without footnotes, as I did not want to clutter the manuscript for students and other readers.

INTRODUCTION TO PART I

Part I consists of three sections: The Sources of Islam, Introduction to Shari'ah, and a Detailed Study of the Structure of Shari'ah. The last two sections will be presented only briefly.

Chapter 1: THE SOURCES OF ISLAM

Dr. Sookhdeo focuses on the Qur'an and the hadith.[2] There is one other source of authority that he does not cover, and that is the *Sira* by Ibn Ishaq, which is the biography of Muhammad. Perhaps Sookhdeo does not cover it, because Muslims rarely appeal to it. In addition, a quick glance at Ibn Ishaq's work reveals why it is better for Muslims to ignore it.

The Qur'an[3]

Note: The word is spelled in a number of ways: Koran and Quran are two other spellings. Dr. Sookhdeo uses Qur'an in his *Understanding Islamic Theology* but Quran in *A Christian's pocket Guide to Islam*. Qur'an will be used throughout this section.

Qur'an is the title of the collection of the recitations (the term means "The Recita-

---

1 Patrick Sookhdeo, *Understanding Islamic Theology* (McLean, VA: Isaac Publishing, 2013).
2 "Hadith" is plural, thus, "the hadith" refers to the thousands of verses found in the major hadith collections, like Sahih Bukhari and Sahih Muslim, the two most respected collections. It will not be capitalized here, but others do so.
3 Much more on the Qur'an appears in Part II, and there will be considerable overlap between these two discussions.

tion") that Islam believes were given by the angel Gabriel to Muhammad over a period of twenty-three years. Many of the verses appear to come in answer to circumstances that troubled Muhammad.

Eighty-eight recitations were given at Mecca and twenty-six at Medina. The early ones given at Mecca are "softer" in tone regarding those who opposed Muhammad's message. The verses given in Mecca are, however, often superseded or abrogated by those given later at Medina where opposition increased in intensity.

The Qur'an contains 114 chapters, or suras, and 6,236 *ayas*, or verses. Each chapter has a title such as "The Cow," which is chapter two and is the longest in the Qur'an. Chapter 72 is "The Jinns." The Qur'an is similar in length to the New Testament.

It is said that Muhammad himself contributed nothing to the Qur'an. What he heard from the angel he passed along to others who memorized what he said. These men later either wrote down what they heard or repeated the recitations to others who either wrote them down or continued to repeat them until finally someone captured them in written form. Muslims deny that there were, early on, various versions of the Qur'an, but many scholars present evidence to the contrary.

Muslims esteem the Qur'an very highly—so highly that it is dangerous to speak ill of it in any way; it takes on almost magical or even divine properties.

Muslims believe the Qur'an supplants all other sacred writings, that it is in fact the final word of God to his final prophet, Muhammad. It is believed that the actual original Qur'an is written on a stone tablet in Paradise.

The Qur'an is considered to be the perfect guide from Allah for all of life and that it has been perfectly preserved over the centuries, quite unlike the Bible, which Muslims insist has been corrupted. The Qur'an occupies a place for Muslims similar to that of Jesus Christ for Christians, meaning that it has essentially been deified.

Muslims believe that only in the original Arabic is the Qur'an perfect and that all translations into other languages are tainted in some way. Parts of the Qur'an are spoken in Arabic every day by pious Muslims; however, most Muslims do not understand Arabic. The more of the Arabic Qur'an a Muslim has memorized, the higher he is held in esteem, and there are many who have memorized it in total. The hadith cover a far wider range of topics than the Qur'an, but the words of the sacred book have final and absolute authority.

Hard history often stands as a problem for some views of the Qur'an. It is clear that between AD 650 and 656 the third caliph, Othman, ordered that an official and standard text of the Qur'an be developed and that all other versions be destroyed (Muhammad died in AD 632). Indeed, Muslims have largely been able to deflect critical analysis of the Qur'an, usually by means of loud, sometimes violent, protestations, while at the same time applying liberal and often unreasonable and unscholarly critical analysis to the Bible.

Muslims consider that the Qur'an is Muhammad's one great miracle. It is said by Muslims that no one could ever write such truthful and beautiful words than those found in the Qur'an. Muhammad is not reported to have performed any miracles during his lifetime, at least as far as the Qur'an and hadith report. However, in the Sira, the biography of Muhammad, there are many interesting hero-type miracles attributed to Muhammad.

The earliest portion of the Qur'an is thought to be chapter 96, verses 1 to 5. Structurally, except for chapter one, the first chapters are the longest, with each succeeding chapter approximately shorter.

The Qur'an is written in a poetic manner like rhymed prose. It is said to have three primary subjects: Tawhid—the unity of God; *Risala*—prophet-hood; *Akhira*—last things.

DISCUSSION POINTS FOR EVANGELICAL WITNESS AND DEBATE

- Most Christians read and study the Bible. Many are well acquainted with it, and it is a large part of their lives. With Islam's attitude about translations of the Qur'an, can the same be said of the average Muslim?
- The original language of the Qur'an is Arabic. If I do not know Arabic, what benefit do I receive from it?
- Muslims are convinced the Bible has been corrupted. How might this issue be debated with a Muslim scholar?
- Would you say that Muslims worship the Qur'an or simply hold it in very high esteem?

The Hadith

The hadith reveal the pattern or way of life of Muhammad. They are collections of what Muhammad's wife Aisha and other companions of Muhammad reported about what he did and said, compiled mostly in the seventh century. The largest number of hadith come from Aisha.

Muhammad is considered the perfect man; thus, his manner of living and those things he taught are actually the most important source of truth for the lives of Muslims, past and present.

Personal Note: When a local imam came to our Saturday Seminary class and was asked what was the most important aspect of Muhammad's life to emulate, he reported it was his beard. "All good Muslims have a beard like Muhammad," he said, stroking his own.

The hadith are seen as the second most important authority for Muslims, the Qur'an holding first place. It is from the hadith that Shari'ah Law is derived. This is seen in the Qur'an itself. Surah 33:21 reads, "Ye have indeed in the Apostle of Allah a beautiful pattern (of conduct) for anyone whose hope is in Allah and the Final Day and who engages much in the praise of Allah." Also Surah 53:3 says, "Nor does he say (aught) of (his own) Desire. It is no less than inspiration sent down to him."

Note: a word or words in parentheses within verses of the Qur'an are added by editors of the particular translation of the Qur'an used, not this author, and are intended by them to clarify obscure readings.

In practice, hadith often take precedence over the literal Qur'anic statements, as various hadith explain, interpret, and expand the meaning of the Qur'an and are used to establish legal rulings. Without hadith much of the Qur'an is a closed book.

Traditional Islam considers hadith material to be true and reliable, except for questionable hadith (see criteria for determining this below), and is to be accepted as Muhammad's true words and deeds.

The main features of the hadith

Matn – the content of each hadith

Islamic scholars insist on the following: Each individual hadith has been examined as to its authenticity and reliability. All hadith thought to be erroneous have been deleted. The following are the criteria used in the examination of hadith:

- The hadith must not contradict the Qur'an or accepted doctrines of Islam.
- The hadith must not contradict other hadith accepted as reliable and authentic.
- The hadith must not contradict reason, laws of nature, or common experience.
- The hadith must not praise any tribe, place, or person.
- The hadith must not contain exact dates of future events.
- The hadith must not contradict accepted sayings of Muhammad or belittle his unique position.

The core considerations as to reliability depend on whether the transmitter, or author of the saying,

- Was an imam (respected hadith scholar)
- Was a hafiz (memorizer, preserver of the Qur'an)
- Is considered reliable and trustworthy
- Made mistakes
- Was weak
- Was abandoned by hadith specialists
- Was a liar who fabricated hadith

Collections of hadith

There are six Sunni collections that are considered most reliable:
1. Sahih Bukhari (d. 870)
2. Sahih Muslim (d. 874)
3. Sunan Ibn Majah (d. 886)
4. Sunan Abu Dawud (d. 889)
5. Jami' Tirmidhi (d. 892)
6. Sunan Nasa'I (d. 916)

Other important hadith writings are:
- The Muwatta' of Malik Ibn Anas (d. 795)
- The Musnad of Ibn Hanbal (d. 855)
- The Sunan of al-Darimi (d. 868)
- The Sunan of al-Daraqutni (d. 995)
- The Sunan of al-Bayhaqi (d. 1065)
- The Sunan of Ibn Mansure (d. 841)

- » The Sunan of al-Khashshi (d. 895)

Shi'a Muslims have their own set of hadith and consider many of the Sunni hadith to be corrupted or forged, especially those regarding the succession of the caliphate in which Ali was ignored or passed over in favor of Abu Bakr, Umar, and Uthman. The main Shi'a collections are:

- » Mohammad Ibn Yaqoob Abu Ja'far Kulaini (d. 939)
- » Usul al Kafi
- » Forroh al Kafi
- » Man la yahduruhu al-Faqih by Muhammad ibn Babuya (d. 991)
- » Tahdhib al-Akhkam and Al-Al-Istibsar, by Sheikh Muhammad at-Tusi, Shaykh al-Ta'ifa (d. 1067)

Classification of hadith

As to the original speaker:
Qudsi – divine: supposedly a revelation from Allah to Muhammad.
Marfu – elevated: a narration from Muhammad.
Mawquf – stopped: a narration from a Companion of Muhammad.
Maqtu' – severed: a narration from a successor.

As to the transmitter, or *isnad*, which is the history of the transmission chain of a particular hadith and is found at the introduction to a hadith, the classifications are:
Mutassil – continuous: an uninterrupted *isnad* which goes back to a Companion or a Successor.
Mursal – hurried: if the link between a successor and Muhammad is missing.
Munqati – broken: the link anywhere before the Successor is missing.
Mu'adal – perplexing: where the account omits two or more consecutive transmitters in the *isnad*.
Mu'allaq – hanging: where the reporter of the hadith omits the entire *isnad* and quotes Muhammad directly.

There are many other issues about the nature of the hadith, but the above covers most of the main categories.

DISCUSSION POINTS FOR EVANGELICAL WITNESS AND DEBATE

- Christians hope to be like Jesus. However, Christians do not necessarily want to look like, dress like, talk like, or live like Jesus did in first century Israel. Christians want to love Jesus, obey His commands, and follow Him throughout their lives. Muslims want to be like Muhammad in almost every way, including dress, manners, relations with women, treatment of those who oppose Islam, and much more. Is this difference significant?
- How much of contemporary life would have to be rejected and ignored in order for Muslims to be pious?
- Christians are clear that the Bible is the Word of God. Can the Muslim be confident that the Sunnah, or proper pattern for doctrine and practice, is the Word of Allah?
- Would entry into paradise depend upon the ability to be like Muhammad?

Chapter 2: INTRODUCTION TO SHARI'AH

Shari'ah is a transliteration into English of the Arabic word that means path or way. The compilation of all that is now considered the path or way is the Shari'ah Law system.

Shari'ah Law is all encompassing, defining in great detail the approved practices and doctrine for the faithful Muslim. It is not so much about right belief as it is about right practice. It concerns matters such as devotional life, worship, ritual purity, marriage and inheritance, criminal offences, commerce, and personal conduct, all down to the minutest details of behavior. It divides all of life into two categories, *haram* (that which is forbidden) and *halal* (that which is permitted).

Shari'ah is a legal system under which most or many Muslims desire to live. They believe it is God's will they follow Shari'ah and will work to bring the whole of the world's peoples under that legal system; it is actually seen as their religious duty to bring this about. Even in Western countries, Muslims hope to yet live under Shari'ah Law. Generally, this is a slow process, depending on how influential a Muslim community is. When the percentage of a population shows Islam to be a small minority, then there is little attempt to impose or lobby for Shari'ah Law. As the percentage increases so does the drive to more completely put Shari'ah in place.

Shari'ah Law is the constitution of Islam.

There are two other important distinctions to be noted. Shari'ah is what Allah has revealed in the Qur'an, the hadith, and the Sira. *Fiqh* is the body of interpretations of Shari'ah by Islamic scholars. Names or titles for these scholars include *'ulama*, *qadis*, and *muftis*. These scholars' work is to both interpret and apply Islamic law.

The *fuqaha'* are those who practice fiqh, which is a lifelong process.

Four Roots of the Law

The first root of Shari'ah is the Qur'an, but there are few legally-oriented regulations found in it. Second are the patterns of how Muhammad lived collected in the hadith and of which there are several hundred thousand. Third and fourth are what is called *ijma'*, meaning consensus, coupled with *qiyas*, which has to do with comparing that which is similar and making decisions on that basis.

The four roots of the Law loom large in Islam, since failure to live up to the legal expectations so derived from them will result in being condemned to hellfire.

The Five Schools of Law

There are four orthodox Sunni schools of the law called *madhab*:
7. The Hanafi School of law founded by Abu Hanifa (700-767) was developed in Iraq and governed the Ottoman Empire. About 30% of Islam looks to this law which is presently dominant in Turkey, Syria, the Balkans, and the Indian sub-continent.
8. The Maliki school was founded by Malik ibn Anas (715-795) in Medina. Malik developed a collection of hadith referred to as *Muwatta'*. Muslims in North and West Africa, Kuwait, and Bahrain follow this school.
9. The Shafi'i School founded by Muhammad ibn Idris al-Shafi'I (767-820) informs Muslims in Yemen, East Africa, Indonesia, Malaysia, and the Philippines.

10. The Hanbali School is predominant in Saudi Arabia, Oman, and Qatar. It was founded by Ahmad ibn Hanbal (780-855) who authored an extensive hadith collection known as *al-Musnad*. This was a rather small school until the founder of Wahhabism revived it in the 18th century.
11. Shi'a Islam has one school, the Twelver School, and the name of the school is derived from the twelve honored imams descended from Ali, the first imam of Shi'a Islam. The Twelver school is what governs Shi'a Islam wherever it is found, especially Iran, Iraq, Lebanon, the Arabian Peninsula, and the Indian sub-continent. This school has its own collection of hadith. It accepts the Qur'an as authoritative as well as the hadith and the ijma (the consensus of the community or ummah), but it rejects the qiyas (comparing of similar statements found in the Qur'an and hadith). The sunnah of Shi'a Islam includes the practice and sayings of the twelve Shi'a Imams, which are regarded as infallible and inspired.

Though there are differences in the schools, they all tend to accept each other's laws as orthodox.

Islamic laws focus on the categories of rituals (purity, prayer, alms, fasting, pilgrimage, and sometimes jihad) and social relations. Social laws involve criminal and family law, including marriage, divorce, and inheritance, and economic law, including trade, commerce, and contracts. Within criminal law is found the death penalty for apostates and adultery, including amputation of limbs for stealing.

Muslims often defend these harsh penalties by appealing to the even harsher practices found in the Arabian Peninsula where Islam took root during the seventh century. While this is certainly the case, the law has changed very little since then.

The focus of Islamic law is on right behavior and responsibility; how one feels in terms of the conscience is not at issue. Here we see the shame-based nature of Islam. Honor is most important. In Christianity, however, guilt and the freeing of a person's conscience is the issue—forgiveness and reconciliation is the goal.

Conclusion

Attempts at modernizing or liberalizing Shari'ah Law have not proven successful. Often those who try to reform Islam are intimidated, even assassinated, and are often viewed as being apostate.

Certainly the slide into corruption and immorality by Western nations alarms and horrifies Muslims, with the United States labeled as "The Great Satan." Muslims generally see the West and Christianity as one and the same, with both being idolatrous and wicked. Thus, faithful Muslims desire to see the world ruled by Shari'ah Law.

Saudi Arabia is probably the only nation to have fully implemented Shari'ah Law, but even there some Muslim critics accuse the nation of straying from the ideal course. Iran, Pakistan, and Sudan make efforts to comply with Shari'ah, as does northern Nigeria and parts of Malaysia.

Much of the tension, conflict, and division fomented in Muslim-dominated countries has to do with establishing a pure form of Islam where Shari'ah Law is operative. The world is well aware of how this effort is now spilling over into non-Muslim countries that have a significant Muslim presence.

Note: From my point of view, the extreme efforts to enforce Islamic ideals are based on a faulty notion. Law and its practice does not change the heart for long. Fear works in a twisted way in the human being. Compliance out of the threat of injury or death is not an expression of true faith.

DISCUSSION POINTS FOR EVANGELICAL WITNESS AND DEBATE

- Shari'ah Law is the constitution of Islam. In Islam, there is no distinction, ideally, between the religion and the state. Islam is all-governing; every part of life is to be included. Would it logically follow that Islam must rule all the people of the world or only where Muslims are the overwhelming majority?
- It would seem that all that is required is to be obedient to Islamic Law. With performance holding such priority, how would you present a higher role for faith and matters of the heart and mind?
- Should we assume that serious Muslims will engage in violence in countries where Islam predominates but Shari'ah Law is not in place? For instance, would they consider the political leaders of Turkey be to be tyrants that must be opposed? If so, what may be offered as another approach?

INTRODUCTION TO PART II

The Muslim Creed

Sookhdeo's introduction to The Muslim Creed—the core beliefs of Islam—properly begins with an examination of the fundamental difference between Islam and Christianity.

Iman is Arabic for faith, and in Islam faith has to do with intellectual assent to the factual truth of the Shahada and the Muslim Creed. The Shahada declares that Allah alone is God and that Muhammad is his messenger or apostle. Iman also must be accompanied by observing the central tenets of Islam, the Five Pillars of Islam.

Note: Faith as understood in Christianity is quite different. Biblical faith is a trust in Jesus Christ and His death on the cross wherein He atoned for or covered sin thus reconciling the forgiven sinner to God. This is all an expression of God's love, mercy, and grace.

Chapter 1: ALLAH

Allah loves those who do good, from Surah 3:31. Allah loves those who are patient in adversity (Surah 3:146), and Allah loves those who trust in him (Surah 3:159).

Allah does not love unbelievers (Surah 3:32), transgressors (Surah 5:87), or traitors (Surah 8:58).

Allah's love is primarily based upon what humans do or do not do.

Allah will not mislead, according to Surah 9:115, yet according to Surah 11:34 and 14:27, Allah will in fact lead astray or mislead those whom he wills.

Allah, The Arabic word, compares to the Hebrew *El*, or *Elohim*, but does not compare to Yahweh, the covenant name of God as revealed to Moses in Exodus 3.

Allah may be derived from El in Hebrew with "the" or "al" as a prefix, thus al-el. Allah likely means The Mighty God or The Mighty One.

Allah has ninety-nine names per Al-Tirmidhi, No. 724: "Allah Most High has ninety-nine names. He who retains them in his memory will enter Paradise." (See appendix D for a complete listing.)

That God cannot have partners or offspring is one of the defining doctrines of Islam. Muhammad did not actually attack Christianity while in Mecca at the beginning of his work. His preaching was aimed at the pagan polytheists in Arabia at that time. However, as time progressed, he viewed the Trinity as being comprised of three gods—the Creator, Jesus the Son of God, and Mary the mother of God.

Shirk is the unpardonable sin, which is having gods other than or associated with Allah. Shirk originally referred to pagan polytheistic religious concepts of deity but later to the idea that Mary and Jesus are both considered deity by Christians.

In Surah 5:116 is found "Allah will say, 'O Jesus the son of Mary! Didst thou say unto men, Worship me and my mother as gods in derogation of Allah?'" Jesus did not say this in the Gospels, so the source of the information is suspect, but we see in Surah 5, a later Medinan surah, the view of Islam at that time. Found In Surah 5:75 is the warning that those who believe in the Christian Trinity will be sent to hellfire.

Allah is completely transcendent, much as the Greek gods and goddesses were viewed. Allah only has contact with humans by means of angels. Thus Allah sends down his words to Muhammad through the angel Gabriel. This is closely identified with the Gnostics' view of deity that was current in seventh century Arabia. Allah may visit his creation but not indwell it, and thus he has no actual contact with humans. As the Gnostics denied that God could be in contact with created matter, thus Jesus could not be God in the flesh, so Islam's ultimate definition of God is similar to that of the Gnostics.

DISCUSSION POINTS FOR EVANGELICAL WITNESS AND DEBATE

- Allah did not come to be with humans, since he is utterly transcendent and above any contact with humans. Therefore, he communicated with Muhammad through an angel. God the Son, Jesus Christ, came to be with us to live among humans. Is this perhaps the greatest of all distinctions between Islam and Christianity?
- Allah loves those who do good and believe in him. The God of the Bible loves those who do not love Him and do not do good as well. Is this point significant in outreach to Muslims?
- What does it mean that Allah may lead astray? Might this make Muslim people insecure about whether they are on the right path?
- Is Gnostic thought intertwined with Islamic thought in regard to the essential nature of God?

Chapter 2: ANGELS AND JINN

Angels

Angels figure prominently in Islam. They act as mediators for the transcendent God. Anyone who denies them, according to Islamic authority, is an infidel. And why? Because of the role of Gabriel as the conduit through whom Allah sent down his message to humans.

In the Old Testament the Archangel Michael is a friend and protector of the Jewish people. In the Qur'an, Gabriel is an enemy of the Jewish people.

In Islamic thought Gabriel is the Holy Spirit. Many of the actions Christians associate with Christ or the Holy Spirit are performed by Gabriel in Islamic thought, and generally angels in the Islamic schema are credited with being divine agents in creation, revelation, and the Judgment.

Is there a kind of polytheism in Islam? The answer is evident when it is seen that there are three who are actually worshipped: Allah, the Qur'an, and angels. It could be argued that Muhammad is the fourth entity worshipped, based on exaggerated and heroic claims of purity and goodness attributed to him.

Allah is transcendent and only interacts with humans through angels. The idea that the Word of God became flesh and dwelt among people is impossible in Islam.

Angels are created beings, created in the light of God and have wings but may appear in human form. They both act as guardians of humans and record each human's actions. Every person is born with two angels who record all deeds done during his or her lifetime. One, the good angel, sits perennially on the right shoulder and records good deeds. On the left shoulder is an evil or demonic angel who records the bad deeds. These are the recording angels.

Jinn

The word "jinn" comes from the Arabic word for concealment, indicating that humans cannot see them. Muhammad emphasized that Islam served as a protection against jinn and other evil entities that populated the world of the pagans. There are both good and evil jinn, and the leader of the evil jinn is Satan, or Shaytan. Unlike in the Bible, there was no angelic fall or rebellion recorded in Islam, but Muhammad absorbed the dual concept of good and bad spiritual beings into Islam from previous pagan notions.

Muhammad was sent to the world of the jinn as well as to humans. In Christianity, there is only conflict with demons. In the Qur'an, Muhammad did meet with jinn, and they responded to his message. This is intended to show the superiority of Muhammad. There is even an indication that there were apostles among the converted jinn sent to humans, though this view is held by only a minority of Islamic scholars.

Jinn were created from smokeless fire or from the fire of a scorching wind, and angels were created from the light of God. These beings were created before humans, who were created from clay. Unlike sexless demons described in the Bible, the jinn can be male or female and thus can mate and have offspring despite being spirits. Another widespread belief is that jinn can disguise themselves as animals.

The night belongs to the evil jinn. Many Muslims live in great fear of the jinn, and this fear is intensified during the dark hours.

In the hadith are described various measures one can take to protect from the evil jinn. They can be warded off by reciting the Qur'an or by calling on the name of Allah. Many Muslims wear amulets and charms designed to ward off the jinn. The "Evil Eye" is one such amulet, and artistic renderings of a single "eye" are found painted or pasted on many ordinary household objects like cups and other utensils.

An important issue in folk Islam is the belief that jinn can enter a person through the nose, making personal hygiene and especially nose blowing an important activity. Evil jinn are thought to inhabit unclean places and things. Since some foods are unclean, jinn may thus be found in the markets. Before entering the toilet, Muslims will say a prayer for protection and perform other hygienic ablutions to ward off jinn.

The jinn are said to be restrained during Ramadan.

Since jinn can be converted to Islam, Muslims may attempt to accomplish this and make provision for them.

Muhammad had power over the jinn.

Satan

There is some confusion over the origin of Satan, who was originally called *Iblis*. Surah 2:34 implies Satan had been an angel who refused to worship Adam when ordered by Allah. However, Surah 7:12 and 18:50 indicate Satan was a jinn. (We recall that jinn were made from fire.) Islam has not reconciled the different accounts, though Satan is usually considered a jinn.

Islam does not share the doctrine of original sin with Christianity, but it does propose that Satan caused the original sin, that is, tempted or deceived Adam and Eve to rebel against God. Original sin for Islam therefore means the first sin and not a sin that spread to the entire human race.

Satan fulfills the role assigned to the "old self or man or nature" in Christian theology. The "works of the flesh" are the result of the activity of Satan, so humans are ultimately not responsible. It is Satan's whispering in humans' ears that leads them astray from the path of God. His aim is to get people to disbelieve Allah and apostatize from Islam thus joining Satan in hell. This is related to the evil angel acquired at birth that resides on the left shoulder. The Qur'an provides guidance against being led astray, which may be considered the central role of the Qur'an.

Satan's throne is upon the sea, from which he sends out his jinn to divide and weaken Muslims. Satan promotes infighting amongst Muslims. Division is evident where man-made boundaries that were created by Western powers separate Muslims from each other, thus proving to be the work of Satan.

Satan's power is said to reside in eastern Arabia. Some radical Muslims take this to mean Saudi Arabia, so rebellion against the House of Saud is actually loyalty to Allah for some Muslims. Islam hates America's diplomatic relations with Saudi Arabia.

Satan promotes atheism, agnosticism, and rationalist philosophical thought. Therefore Islam fights against the inroads of Western ways around the globe. Islam seems not to understand that the "West" is not Christian. Islam sees the decline in Western morality and the influence of the "church" as evidence the West is satanic. Church bells are particularly repulsive to Muslims, as they see them as instruments of the devil. The gong of the bell is seen as *noise* made by the evil one.

Islam must stand against Christian missionaries who come into Muslim countries, and doing so is considered to be fighting against Satan. Muslims also resent any attempts at Christian evangelism directed at them in Western countries and view such as satanic. However, Islam also attacks other world religions like Buddhism and Hinduism. By doing so, Muslims believe they are saving fellow Muslims from satanic systems of belief.

Islam holds that Satan encourages occult practices like magic, fortune telling, and witchcraft; however, in folk Islam, Muslims practice magical customs, turn to astrology for guidance, and use spells for not only healing but for the placing of curses on others.

Demon possession is a reality in Islam, and a bad dream is considered to be from Satan. On the other hand, dreams may be a supernatural means of communication from Allah via angels.

Other common notions associated with Satan are that he causes female menstruation and circulates in humans as blood does. Another reason for head coverings for women is that these work as protection against Satan and the jinn. The same holds for spitting or blowing the nose three times upon waking from a night's sleep (the jinn are thought to enter the human through the nose during the night).

Note: Chapter three contains an extended discussion of the jinn and Islam's exorcism traditions, of which there are an abundance.

DISCUSSION POINTS FOR EVANGELICAL WITNESS AND DEBATE

- The angel Gabriel, according to some in Islam, is the Holy Spirit. This marks a major difference between Islam and Christianity. How is it that Islam's view of Gabriel does not mean that the angel is worshipped?
- The notion of two angels on the shoulders, one evil the other good, each recording the good and the bad, are common to Islam. How does this idea impact the daily life of Muslims, and how might the fact that Jesus has defeated Satan comfort Muslim people?
- How do Muslims attempt to influence the two angels, placate the evil one and accommodate the good one? Again, what might you say to a Muslim who is preoccupied with these activities?
- Is this circumstance a bridge to communicate the finished work of Jesus to Muslims?

Chapter 3: THE BOOKS OF GOD

According to Islam there have been 104 books revealed by God: ten to Adam, fifty to Seth, thirty to Enoch, ten to Abraham, one to Moses, one to David, one to Jesus, and one to Muhammad.

One hundred of these books have been taken up to paradise. Concerning the remaining four, the Qur'an supersedes the books of Moses, David, and Jesus. The book ascribed to Moses is the whole Old Testament, excluding Psalms, which is ascribed to David. The book given to Jesus is the New Testament, especially the four gospels.

Surah 5:113 says: "Then will Allah say: 'O Jesus the son of Mary! ...Behold! I taught thee the Book and Wisdom the Law and the Gospel ...'"

The Qur'an as the Seal of Revelation

Muslims believe that inspiration is complete and no other revelations will be forthcoming. (However, there is an idea that some Islamic sects may yet bring forth revelation, but this is a minority opinion.)

Islam also believes that all the revelations have the same message. Muslims are required then to believe in all the revelations handed down from God, even from Moses, David, and Jesus. Of course, other exclusive claims found in the Qur'an supersede all of these. The concept of abrogation essentially denies any idea that "older" revelations such as the Bible are valid, if they differ from later ones in the Qur'an (see Surah 2:4-6).

The Nature and Mode of "Inspiration"

The Qur'an was "eternally preserved" in paradise and sent down from Allah through the angel Gabriel to Muhammad. We see this in Sahih Al-Bukhari, Vol. 6, Book 60, No. 378. Therefore, Muhammad was not involved in the composition of the Qur'an.

This method of revelation is perfectly contrary to the Christian doctrine that says the Bible was written by human beings who were inspired by the Holy Spirit. The writers of the Bible were active and not passive as was Muhammad. Thus, the Christian view of Scripture comes closer to how Muslims view the hadith.

Muhammad went into a state of trance whenever he received revelations from Allah through Gabriel. The trance or passive state of mind was a common goal during that period and during prior centuries of monks and contemplatives who sought inspiration and enlightenment while meditating long hours and days in the deserts of Arabia. We find a hint of this in Abu Dawud, Book 12, No. 2247a, which reads, "When the Apostle of Allah (peace be upon him) came to himself (after the revelation ended)..."

Note: In *The Way of the Shaman*, the cultural anthropologist turned shaman, Michael Harner, describes how shamans acquire their inspiration through contact with various spiritual entities: "The best [location at which] to acquire a guardian spirit is in a remote place or wilderness. The location may be a cave, the top of a mountain, or a tall waterfall or an isolated trail at night" (p. 51). One must wonder about Islam's origin. What was Muhammad doing in that cave? Another point of interest is Muhammad's Night Journey. I mention in *The Soul Journey: How Shamanism, Santeria, Wicca, and Charisma are Connected*, page 92, that "Once in the altered state of consciousness, one meets various entities that help during the soul journey..."

It is known that Muhammad experienced extreme sensations during the times he was receiving revelations. For instance, when it was cold he would sweat and when it was hot he would shiver.

Note: In Christianity, the Biblical writer is always fully conscious—"in the Spirit," as John in Revelation states, but aware and alert, not passive or in a trance.

Muhammad received revelations over the course of not less than twenty-two years.

In the Qur'an there appears to be hints of progressive revelation. This is seen in the differences in attitudes held about the Jews and Christians. Early on in Mecca these groups were treated with consideration and respect. This changed, and sharply so, when Muhammad and his companions made the pilgrimage to Medina. This in turn prompted the principle of abrogation in which later verses supersede earlier ones. In fact, it often appears that Muhammad is reacting to events as they occurred.

At the very beginning of Muhammad's encounter with Gabriel, he wondered if he was actually in contact with a jinn rather than an angel. This is stunningly apparent from a hadith reported by Aisha (the mother of the faithful believers and favorite wife of Muhammad) as found in the most trusted of all hadiths, Sahih Al-Bukhari, Vol. 1, Book 1, No. 3.

Muhammad was so harshly treated by what he thought was the angel Gabriel that he doubted it was an angel from Allah at all. He became depressed and considered throwing himself off the mountain of Hira. It was only through the intervention and convincing of Khadija, his wife, that Muhammad was prevented from doing so.

Just before his death, Muhammad received a large number of revelations (see Sahih Al-Bukhari, Vol. 6, Book 59, No. 650). The last revelation to Muhammad is thought by Muslims to be Surah 2:281. Others say 282 or 278; some include all three of these. And a minority view is that Surah 5:4 was the last recitation from Allah.

The Nature of the Qur'an

For Muslims, the Qur'an is a miracle, the great miracle that authenticates Muhammad, since he did not perform any other signs and wonders as Jesus did (although later writers of hadith attributed miracles in what may be viewed as typical hero stories).

The Arabic word for verses is "ayahs," which means "signs" in Arabic. And it must be read in Arabic. The Qur'an's miraculous nature is illustrated by the idea that only Muslims can understand it and that reading it in Arabic leads to automatic conversion to Islam.

Muslims are certain that neither the jinn nor any human could produce such a perfect book as the Qur'an. Muslims challenge unbelievers to produce anything so wonderful, even a sentence. We find this in Surah 10:38-41. The challenge is given, but nothing that is offered to meet that challenge by non-believers, however beautiful or well constructed, will do. Even the Psalms of David or the Proverbs of Solomon fail to measure up. To even consider the possibility of a worthy comparison would demonstrate weakness.

Shi'a Muslims claim that the Sunnis have tampered with the Qur'an, mainly in deleting passages that stated the succession to the caliphate after the death of Muhammad went to Ali.

There is evidence from the third caliph, Uthman, that the Qur'an has not always been as it now is. Apparently, there were several versions of the Qur'an, but all were destroyed by Uthman in the seventh century just before he established his own authorized version.

To be fair, the transmission of the Qur'an begs many questions, and there are differing opinions.

The Qur'an and Salvation

For Muslims, knowledge of the Qur'an's instructions is the key to salvation. This is seen in Surah 2:135–136:

> They say, 'Become Jews or Christians, and you will be rightly guided.' Say [Prophet], 'No, [ours is] the religion of Abraham, the upright, who did not worship any god besides God.' So [you believers], say, 'We believe in God and in what was sent down to us and what was sent down to Abraham, Ishmael, Isaac, Jacob, and the Tribes, and what was given to Moses, Jesus, and all the prophets by their Lord. We make no distinction between any of them, and we devote ourselves to Him.'

Islam does not view humans as being corrupted; therefore a saving event is not necessary. In Christianity, humans break God's laws, become sinners, and thus are alienated from God. God then acts in Christ on the cross to provide forgiveness of sin and salvation. It is all due to God's working and nothing on the part of the human.

Islam has no similar concept of grace; rather, humans must save themselves. Allah gives guidance as to how to achieve or earn salvation. Islam is truly a religion of works.

The doctrines for reaching paradise for Muslims are confusing and troubling even to Muslims. To die a martyr is the sure path and the only sure path. However, no one is ever sure of his or her status, as Allah is the "Greatest Deceiver" and may actually lead one astray.

Status of the Qur'an

The Qur'an has the same place in Islam as Jesus does in Christianity. A Muslim must revere the Qur'an as eternal and uncreated, the miraculous Word of God. In Christianity the Word became flesh; in Islam the Word became a book.

A problem arises for Muslims on this point: the Qur'an is elevated to a high status, one comparable to the position of Allah, approaching the status of deity. Islam comes close, if not actually crossing the line, of associating something with God that is not God, a kind of "Qur'anolatry."

Note: Muhammad is elevated to a very high status as well, and non-Muslim observers, Christian and non-Christian alike, have spoken of the Islamic "trinity" of Allah, Qur'an, and Muhammad.

The Muslim must practice what the Qur'an teaches—again, all is based on what a human can or cannot do. Muslims are not permitted to question the Qur'an. No critical examination of the Qur'an is possible; such would be anathema or blasphemy. To do so could result in death; thus few Muslims will take the risk. This is even truer in modern times. A critique of the Qur'an is viewed amongst Muslims as weakness at minimum, and leaders in the ummah would be especially careful not to suggest anything close to it.

Literary Dimensions, Compilation, and Collation of the Qur'an

There are 114 surahs or chapters in the Qur'an, of which 88 were written or revealed in Mecca and 26 in Medina. The surahs are arranged according to length, and the longest ones begin at surah 2 and gradually decrease in length. The surahs are not arranged according to subject matter nor are they chronological. Each surah has a title which is taken from the content of the surah. The first surah, titled "The Exordium," was revealed in Mecca and is to be recited by all Muslims everyday.

The Qur'an is not always simply read and understood. Perhaps as many as one fifth of the passages are nearly impossible to grasp (apart from the supposed miracle of understanding only available to Muslims). Some verses are referred to as *muhkam*, meaning they are clear and explicit. The *mutashabih* are not clear but are implicit or allegorical. The muhkam are said to be incapable of being misunderstood while the meaning of the mutashabih are known only to God—in the eyes of Sunni scholars. Shi'a scholars believe that the mutashabih verses are simply those with deeper meanings and are thus more difficult to comprehend.

There is a literary nature to the Qur'an evidenced by differing genres of writing. There are artistic, dramatic, pictorial, and imaginative styles of writing found in the Qur'an, but this can be a delicate topic among Muslim scholars.

The Qur'an was passed on in oral form at first, as some of Muhammad's early companions memorized them after he reported them. Written forms came later, some being written during Muhammad's lifetime but most after his death in 632. The complete compilation of the Qur'an took place under the leadership of Abu Bakr and 'Uthman. It is said that the first compilation came following the Battle of Yamama in 633, during which some *qurra*, or people who memorized the Qur'an, had been killed. We find reference to this in Sahih Al-Bukhari, Vol. 6, Book 61, No. 509.

In the aforementioned hadith, it is reported that Abu Bakr, the first caliph, objected to the necessity of collecting and recording the verses of the Qur'an, since Muhammad had not done so, illustrating the obsession with doing as Muhammad did during his lifetime.

Reliability of the Qur'an

As early as the eighth century Muslim scholars took notice of difficulties with the Qur'an and began the cataloguing of various problematic aspects of their sacred book. They listed shifts in style, voice, and subject matter, unfamiliar vocabulary, apparent omissions of text, grammatical incongruities, deviant readings, and more.

It is well known that many harsh-sounding passages in the Qur'an were smoothed out in translations from the Arabic original. In addition, there are hundreds of insertions of explanatory phrases and words by editors of varying translations of the Qur'an.

Note: Readers of translated Qur'ans may find that without the editorial help, many verses are simply unintelligible.

A discovery was made in 1972 of tens of thousands of fragments of Qur'anic parchments in the Great Mosque of Sana'a in Yemen. This has continued to cause Islamic scholars difficulty, as an examination of these reveals that the text of the Qur'an has evolved, a notion which is utterly contrary to Islamic understanding, because it demonstrates a human element in the authorship.

Note: In contrast, the Christian Bible, from Genesis to Revelation, clearly depicts the human hand, which is not denied but embraced. People moved by the Spirit of God wrote the Scripture, and over the years, errors, additions, and corrections crept in; this is why archaeologists and Biblical scholars examine some of the 5,000 texts of New Testament books in order to determine original texts, with the result that nearly 95% of the material has been declared certain to be original. Christians do not view the Bible as a document that magically descended from heaven. Christians believe the Bible is inspired or God-breathed but all through the agency of humans.

Abrogated Verses

The Arabic word *naksh* means that some verses have been abrogated or replaced by other verses. It is well known that in the Qur'an there are contradictory passages, and Muslim scholars do not deny this. The difficulties here are dealt with by claiming that later passages replace former passages, or that some passages were meant only for special situations, which changed over time.

In one of the later surahs, #2 and verse 106, an attempt to solve the problem of abrogation is plain:

> None of Our revelations do We abrogate or cause to be forgotten but We substitute something better or similar; knowest thou not that Allah hath power over all things?

Muslim apologists think that the above verse refers to Christian and Jewish Scripture. However, we find a similar message in Surah 13:39 and Surah 16:10. Sahih Al-Bukhari, Vol. 6, Book 60, No. 8 and No. 34 also speak to this issue.

Below are two instances where the Qur'an abrogates itself and another where a hadith abrogates a passage in the Qur'an:

» Early Muslims complained about how much time was required for prayer especially during the night as expounded in Surah 73:2–4. Then verse 20 abrogates this.

» Polytheists are not to be troubled in Surah 43:89, while Surah 2:190–2 says they must be slaughtered.

» Regarding temporal marriage, or *muta*, Surah 4:24 disallows it while Sahih Al-Bukhari, Vol. 7, Book 62, No. 52 allows it.

Three different types of abrogation are noted and can be found: (1) Sahih Muslim, Book 8, No. 3421—this is an example of abrogation of the recited verse together with the legal ruling; (2) Surah 33:50–52—this is an example of abrogation of the legal ruling with the recited verse; and (3) Sahih Al-Bukhari, Vol. 8, Book 82, No. 817—this is an example of abrogation of the recited verse with or without the legal ruling.

It should be noted that Surah 6:34 states, "There is none that can alter the Words (and decrees) of Allah."

Shi'ism and the Qur'an

Shi'a Muslims assert that Sunnis have tampered with the Qur'an, charging that verses upholding the succession of Islam to 'Ali have been deleted.

A Shi'a hadith is reported to have the following:

> Jabir says, "I heard Imam Baqar…saying: One who says that he has collected the whole Qur'an is a big liar." "Only 'Ali and the Imams collected it all and preserved it."

Another Shi'a hadith says that the real Qur'an will be presented at the return of the Twelfth Imam, and Shi'a Muslims believe this Qur'an to be 17,000 verses long as against the 6,236 verses of the present Qur'an.

Qur'anic Hermeneutics

The science of interpretation in Islam is called *tafsir*. There are three degrees of interpretation.

Tafsir bi'l-riwaya

This Arabic term means transmission and refers to comparing passages of the Qur'an with other Qur'anic passages, so that the Qur'an interprets itself. This is expanded to include Muhammad, the pious companions of the early days, and students of the companions, so that they also help understand the meaning of the Qur'an.

Tafsir bi'l-ra'y

This term means understanding the Qur'an based on human reasoning and applying other sound sources of information. This method is hotly debated, especially in the modern era.

Tafsir bi'I-ishara

This Arabic phrase describes a mystical method of interpreting the Qur'an. Mystics like the Sufis and others in Shi'a Islam interpret the Qur'an other than in a literal fashion. Allegory is one means of this, a process referred to as *ta'wil*.

This esoteric means of interpretation is not common with the ordinary Muslim but is practiced primarily by the "infallible" Imams of Shi'a.

DISCUSSION POINTS FOR EVANGELICAL WITNESS AND DEBATE

- Of the 104 books of God, Islam teaches that 100 have been taken up to paradise. How can anyone be certain of this? Where is the proof? If some books are still present, we know of only the final four: of Moses, David, Jesus, and Muhammad. What about the others?
- Dr. Sookhdeo gives evidence that Muhammad was in a trance state while receiving the recitations from Gabriel. Is there anything comparable in the New Testament?
- Abrogation, in which later recitations replace earlier recitations, is a necessary doctrine in Islam, or it would have to be admitted that contradictions are in the Qur'an. Does this impugn the integrity of either Muhammad or Allah?
- Might Shi'a Muslims be correct when they argue that Sunni Islam changed the Qur'an in order to deny the right of succession to Ali?
- Grace versus works for salvation is at the heart of the difference between Islam and Christianity. The challenge is for Christians to present the evangelical Gospel. How may Christians go about this?

Chapter 4: PROPHETS

According to Islam, God has sent prophets to every people group and tribe. Surah 10:47 is said to teach this: "Every community is sent a messenger, and when their messenger comes, they will be judged justly; they will not be wronged."

The ultimate and last prophet sent was Muhammad, who was both apostle and prophet. All apostles are prophets, but not all prophets are apostles (see Surah 6: 83–87). Muhammad was both sent by Allah and given the Qur'an, the prophetic message. However, the distinction between prophets and apostles is unclear.

Islam sees all the wise and holy men who lived from the foundation of the world to be Muslims. The fact that these pre-Islamic sages did not preach Islam as it is now is because their message was corrupted—only Muhammad got it right.

For Islam the greatest prophets are Adam, Noah, Abraham, Moses, Jesus, and Muhammad (see Surah 2:285, Surah 4:163–165, and Surah 6:84–87).

Adam

In Arabic, Adam is called *Safi Allah,* meaning "Chosen One of God." In Surah 23:12–14 we find that Adam was made from clay, dust, and a clot—the clot being made of sperm. It comes close to the Biblical account of Adam's creation. Adam was also created in the image of God, but the "image" seems to be more physical than spiritual.

Adam, Islam claims, was created on Friday, and that is the reason Islam's primary day of worship is Friday. Adam is considered the first caliph on earth.

Surah 7:19–27 describes events in the garden, and the parallels between that and the Biblical account are evident.

Adam's disobedience of eating the forbidden fruit does not impact the rest of humankind as it does in the Bible. Adam simply was not able to withstand Satan's temptation. However, humans are vulnerable to being disobedient due to weakness or infirmity, which is passed down generationally (see Sahih Muslim, Book 32, No. 6319).

Noah

Islam has a difficulty concerning Noah and his relation to Adam. Two hadith indicate that Noah, not Adam, was the first apostle and prophet of Islam. This is found in Sahih Al-Bukhari, Vol. 9, Book 93, No. 507 and 532.

Noah is called *Nabi Allah*, meaning "The Prophet of God." Like Adam, he is a prophet but does not bring down a book. Noah is not an apostle; he earns the title prophet due to his strong preaching and submission to the will of God.

According to hadith, Noah commanded the jinn in that he had control over snakes (see Abu Dawud, Book 41, No. 5240). Also Noah, per Sahih Al-Bukhari, Vol. 8, Book 73, No. 194, talked about the antichrist, the Ad-Dajjal. Noah reported that the antichrist "is blind in one eye, whereas Allah is not so."

Abraham

The Arabic title for Abraham, which is often spelled Ibrahim, is *Khalil Allah*, which means Friend of God (see Sahih Muslim Book 1, No. 380). Abraham was awarded the title Friend of God for his strong preaching against idolatry and his submission to God. He was neither Jew nor Christian but was a true Muslim. This is seen in Surah 3:67–68. Abraham is referred to as the "Protector of those who have faith." Abraham was a model for Muslims to follow, because he withstood pagan worship in his day (see Surah 16: 120–123).

Details regarding the sacrifice of Isaac in the Bible are altered in the Qur'an (see Surah 37:100–109). For Islam the issue was a test of obedience and not faith. Though it is not stated in the Qur'an, Muslims believe it was Ishmael and not Isaac who was about to be sacrificed. The fiqh, or jurisprudence, in the Hanafi Manual, states that the sacrificial son was Ishmael.

Note: see Essay Ten in Appendix A, "*Eid al-Adha*: Who has it right?" for more on this topic.

It is interesting to note that hadith present Abraham as lying on three occasions, which is not counted against him, as he was a prophet (see Sahih Al-Bukhari, Vol. 4, Book 55, No. 578).

Hadith also record that Abraham was thrown into a fire by pagans, but he survived (see Surah 21:68–69). It is thought this story was borrowed from accounts of the fiery furnace in the book of Daniel, with Abraham substituted for the three friends of Daniel.

Abraham, on the Day of Resurrection, is to be the first person "to be dressed," that is, resurrected (see Sahih Al-Bukhari, Vol. 8, Book 76, No. 533). Even considering all these accolades, Abraham is still inferior to Muhammad (see Sahih Muslim, Book 1, No. 380).

Moses

Moses' title is *Kalim Allah*, meaning Speaker with (or Confidant of) God, and he is the prophet most often mentioned in the Qur'an. Moses was chosen by God to be both a prophet and apostle according to Surah 19:51–52. Accounts of Moses in the Qur'an are similar to those found in the Bible but with differences.

One of the significant events involving Moses is his being in the presence of God during the forty days on Mt. Sinai while receiving the Law. The "Beatific Vision," or beholding the face of God, is considered the chief reward for the faithful Muslim.

Moses in Islamic tradition, unlike the Biblical account of his receiving two tablets, was given six tablets, two of which were "withdrawn," yielding four tablets finally. Muhammad, however, was given more; he received "seven long surahs" (see Abu Dawud, Book 8. No. 1454).

Surah 7:143 is problematic for Muslims, since it records Moses saying, "I am the first to believe," or "I am the first of (true) believers," whereas Adam is usually said to be the first to believe in Islam, and Noah is often called the first prophet.

It will not surprise Christians to learn that Islamic scholars have interpreted Deuteronomy 18:15, "The LORD your God will raise up for you a prophet like me from among your own brothers. You must listen to him," as referring to Muhammad. The debate on this prediction goes on and on and around one point primarily: Muhammad was an Arab, unlike the Levite Jew Moses, thus not "among your own brothers."

Another abiding issue Muslims face is found in Sahih Al-Bukhari, Vol. 6 Book 60, No. 249, where Moses described himself as greater than anyone else on earth, and was thereupon admonished by Allah for such a fraudulent claim.

Jesus

In Arabic Jesus is *'Isa*. The exact meaning of the name is uncertain.

Jesus is held to be the last prophet before Muhammad. Surah 19:30 has Jesus saying, "He said, 'I am indeed a servant of Allah: He hath given me revelation and made me a prophet....'" However, Jesus is merely one in a long line of prophets, equal to but not greater than other prophets of Islam.

Islam believes that Jesus is the Messiah but does not define or clarify the meaning of the title, so it is essentially a meaningless designation.

Jesus is also the Word of God, but not the final word; Jesus is merely "a" and not "the" word of God (see Surah 4:171 and 3:45 and Sahih Al-Bukhari, Vol. 6, Book 60, No. 236).

Ruḥ Allah or Spirit of God is a title given to Jesus in Islam, but it is one not applied to Jesus in the New Testament. This Spirit of God, however, is not the same as the Holy Spirit (*Ruh-al-Quddus*) in Islam. Jesus, in Islam, is the Spirit of God, and the angel Gabriel is the Holy Spirit. Hadith Sahih Al-Bukhari, Vol. 4, Book 55, No. 644 and Sahih Muslim, Book 1, No. 380 both testify to this.

Islam judges that Christianity believes in a family of gods: God the Father, Mary the mother, and Jesus who is the offspring of a sexual union between God and Mary. Surah 6:101 speaks to this distorted view: "To him (Allah) is due the primal origin of the heavens and the earth: how can He have a son when He hath no consort? He created all things and He hath full knowledge of all things."

So Christians are considered to have elevated a mere man to the status of deity. Thus, Christians are accused of committing shirk, meaning to associate others with Allah. Surah 5:17; 3:45ff; and 19:88ff speak to the issue.

Note: Due to the confused understanding of Biblical Christianity during the seventh century in the Arabian Peninsula held by both Jews and Christians, it is no wonder that Muhammad rejected the errant views of the Trinity that were extant during that period. As a preacher against paganism, he was bound to level the charge of polytheism against the Christians.

An interesting confusion found in the Qur'an, especially Surah 3:35–37 and 19:28, has to do with Mary (Miriam in the Qur'an), the mother of Jesus. She is named as the sister of Aaron and Moses, and her parents are said to be Zechariah, the father of John the Baptist, who was only six months older than Jesus. It must be noted that Moses, Aaron, and their sister named Miriam lived anywhere from 1,300 to 1,500 years before the days of Jesus, Mary his mother, and Zechariah, father of John the Baptist. Thus, Islam proposes a chronological and genealogical impossibility.

There is more: the Qur'an has Jesus being born in a desolate place under a date palm tree (see Surah 19:22–23). However, the prophet Micah says the Messiah would be born in Bethlehem, and the Gospels record that this is indeed where Jesus was born, nearly a millennium and a half after the days of Moses and Aaron.

The Qur'an seems to have been influenced by the *Gospel of Thomas*, a second century Gnostic document, that assigns miraculous signs to Jesus, e.g., giving life to clay birds he made so that they fly away (see Surah 3:46 and 5:110).

Islam claims that Jesus came to proclaim Islam and establish Shari'ah Law. In order to do this, Allah sent down the *Injil* or Gospel (see Surah 5:49). However, in Muslim eyes the Gospel has been corrupted, which they must believe in order to authenticate Islamic doctrine.

Surah 61:6 speaks of Isa predicting the coming of Muhammad:

> And remember Isa the son of Mary said: 'O Children of Israel! I am the apostle of Allah (sent) to you confirming the Law (which came) before me and giving glad Tidings of an Apostle to come after me whose name shall be Ahmad' (from The Holy Qur'an, A.Y. Ali translator).

Note: Several versions of the Qur'an have been consulted, and they do not always agree with each other. This is so when it comes to Surah 61:6. Here *The Glorious Qur'an* reads differently from *The Holy Qur'an*, as translated by Abdullah Yusuf Ali. Several editions of the Qur'an are usually necessary to consult in many cases.

Note: Islam considers Jesus' original disciples to be Muslims and not Jews or Christians.

Islam absolutely denies the death of Jesus on the cross (which is understandable, considering it would go against all that Islam says about works salvation). Surah 4:157 states it clearly:

> and said, 'We have killed the Messiah, Jesus, son of Mary, the Messenger of God.' (They did not kill him, nor did they crucify him, though it was made to appear like that to them; those that disagreed about him are full of doubt, with no knowledge to follow, only supposition: they certainly did not kill him—

Note: The word in the verse, "appear" is reminiscent of the Gnostic belief that it only appeared that the one dying on the cross was Jesus, a concept that is commonly referred to as Docetism from the Greek word "to appear or seem." One famous Gnostic, Basilides, held that it was actually Simon of Cyrene who was crucified and not Jesus. Simon, according to the Bible, was compelled by Roman soldiers to carry the cross to the execution site when Jesus stumbled and fell under its weight. Some Gnostics, and in turn Islam, believe it was Simon who was crucified while Jesus stood at a distance and laughed at the mistake. Other Gnostics believed it was Judas who was crucified and not Jesus.

Muslim salvation is based on obedience to Islam, whereas Christian salvation is anchored on blood atonement—Jesus' sacrifice on the cross where our sin was placed upon Him.

Let it be noted that some Muslim commentators, Al-Baydawi and Ibn Kathir, accept that Jesus did die but not on a cross. However, primary in Muslim thought is hate for the cross and a desire to "break the cross," which means "destroy Christianity."

Islam blames the Jews for *attempting* to kill Jesus and likewise blames the Jews for harboring the same plan—to kill Muhammad.

Jesus, according to Islamic teaching, now resides in paradise enjoying a sensual life (a notion that would horrify Christians), while he awaits the Day of Judgment.

However, Jesus does play an important role when the Day of Judgment comes. Jesus, according to Islam, descends from paradise, thus displaying one of the main signs of the last days. When Jesus returns he will destroy the false Messiah or antichrist and his forces. We see this in Sahih Muslim, 1348. Isa—Jesus—will point all to Muhammad as the true prophet and on the Day of Judgment will destroy the Jewish and Christian religions and make Islam the only religion of the entire world. Jews and Christians are considered pigs and thus unclean. Islam will thereby become incredibly wealthy by capturing all the booty left behind by the dead Jews and Christians.

Muhammad

In the Qur'an Muhammad is spoken of as the Apostle of God and the Seal of the Prophets, the one chosen to be the greatest and last prophet. This is seen in many surahs, including Surah 5:4 and 33:40. Muhammad brings the final word from God concerning salvation history. He will also be the first to be resurrected (see Al-Tirmidhi, No. 1519).

A problem is presented in a hadith by Abu Dawud, in Book 8, No. 1535: "The Prophet (peace be upon him) used to seek refuge in Allah from five things; cowardliness, niggardliness, the evils of old age, evil thoughts, and punishment in the grave."

Muhammad is not completely glamorized in Islam. He is the "warner" only, and he worries about his going to paradise, which is one reason for the term, "Peace be upon him," being either spoken or written whenever his name is spoken or written. The phrase is a prayer and a hope and is more than simply honoring to Muhammad; it asks that Allah should have peace upon the Prophet and allow him into Paradise. In this regard, it may be asked, why would Muhammad require supplication and prayers for forgiveness, if he were perfect and without sin? It should be noted that the Sunni and Shi'a branches of Islam disagree on this point. Sunnis contend he was without error from the time his prophetic ministry began, while Shi'a opt for his pureness from birth.

Islamic tradition says that Muhammad was known as *al-Amin*, which means "Trusted One." His trustworthiness and truthfulness is attested to in Surah 69:44–51":

> If [the Prophet] had attributed some fabrication to Us, We would certainly have seized his right hand and cut off his lifeblood, and none of you could have defended him. This [Qur'an] is a reminder for those who are aware of God. We know that some of you consider it to be lies–this will be a source of bitter regret for the disbelievers–but it is in fact the certain Truth.

Despite the above appeal to complete truthfulness and sinlessness, Sahih Al-Bukhari, Vol. 1, Book 12, No. 711 contradicts this:

> O Allah! Set me apart from my sins (faults) as the East and the West are set apart from each other and clean me from sins as a white garment is cleaned of dirt (after thorough washing). O Allah! Wash off my sins with water, snow and hail."

DISCUSSION POINTS FOR EVANGELICAL WITNESS AND DEBATE

- Muhammad is said to be both apostle (one sent from Allah) and prophet (sent with a message). Islam claims all apostles and prophets sent by Allah are Muslims, including Adam, Noah, Abraham, Moses, and so on, including Jesus. First, is the definition of "Muslim" here too broad? Second, how might one counter this concept?

- Muslims assert that Adam was born on a Friday, and thus Friday is the Muslim holy day, according to Sahih Muslim, Book 39, No. 6707. Is this a point to be debated or disputed with Muslims?

- Muslims claim that it was Ishmael rather than Isaac whom Abraham was to sacrifice. The Qur'an does not teach this, but a lesser hadith mentions this. How might this position be discussed? And, is it an important issue?
- Muslims present Moses as being the first one to believe (see Qur'an 7:142–143). However, Adam is held to be the first believer, and Noah is often called the first prophet (see Qur'an 7:143). Moses is said to have received more than two tablets from God (see Abu Dawud, Book 8, No. 1454). How would these issues be debated, if indeed they were thought worthy of contention?
- Muhammad is the final messenger of Allah, thus superseding all others (see Qur'an 33:40). Religious leaders, founders, and prophets, such as Joseph Smith of the Latter Day Saints and groups like Bahai, were also each founded by a "prophet" and considered heretical by Muslims. How is this different from mainstream Christian assertions?

Chapter 5: JUDGMENT

Death (*Maut*) and the Intermediate State

That all will die is a central doctrine of Islam—there is no transmigration of a soul, no reincarnation, no absorption into anything divine. Surah 3:185 says,

> Every soul shall have a taste of death: and only on the Day of Judgment shall you be paid your full recompense. Only he who is saved far from the fire and admitted to the garden will have attained the object (of life): for the life of this world is but goods and chattels of deception.

Death comes at "God's leave." Allah is the Lord of Death, and death does not occur apart from his will. Islam clearly teaches that God has predetermined the time for each person to die. Death becomes the servant of God. Surah 2:28 says,

> How can ye reject the faith in Allah? Seeing that ye were without life and He gave you life; then will He cause you to die and will again bring you to life; and again to Him will ye return.

God therefore determines a person's death in every detail, and the above Surah makes it sound as though everyone will "return" to God, although Islam does not actually teach this.

Angels and death

Angels are very much involved in death; an angel extracts the soul from the dead body (see Surah 32:11), which can be painful (see Surah 50:17–19). The soul extraction of unbelievers is much worse, however (see Surah 8:50–51).

A pair of angels are assigned to each person, one on the right shoulder and one on the left. These angels are involved in bringing about death, as seen in Surah 6:61–62:

> He is the Supreme Master over His subjects. He sends out recorders to watch over you until, when death overtakes any of you, those sent by Us take his soul—they never fail in their duty. Then they will all be returned to God, their true Lord. The Judgment truly belongs to Him, and He is the swiftest of reckoners.

The names of these angels are Munkar and Nakir. When death occurs, two angels (these or others) come to the body in the grave and examine it to see if there has been true faith in Muhammad and a patterning of the person's life after his (see Surahs 16:28; 8:50; and 6:93). It is assumed that if one has the right attitude about Muhammad there will likewise be a right attitude about Allah (see Sahih Al-Bukhari, Book 4, No. 184).

For the faithful, death is like a gate that opens to a glorious future. Those who do not have faith will experience punishment prior to entry into hellfire; angels punish infidels and evil people in their graves (see Abu Dawud, Book 40, No. 4735). The punishment is so terrible that the cries of the wicked in the grave can be heard by the living (see Sahih Al-Bukhari, Vol. 1, Book 4, No. 215). In fact, all non-Muslims, pagans, Jews, Christians, Hindus, Buddhists, atheists, and so on, will be punished in their graves. The hadith, Al-Tirmidhi, No. 510, goes into detail about the role that angels play in death.

Torment of the Grave

Muhammad spoke often of the torment of the grave. And even he had to take refuge from the punishments of the grave, which is interesting, if Muhammad was the perfect and sinless believer (see Sahih Al-Bukhari, Vol. 2, Book 23, No. 459). Muhammad instructed his followers to seek refuge from punishment, saying the only way to escape it was to die as a martyr (see Al-Tirmidhi, No. 1967).

Death: The Hereafter: Intermediate States, Punishment in the Grave, and the Abode of Souls

Islamic authoritative literature agrees that each person will be questioned after his death, whether he is buried or not. Even if a person were eaten by carnivorous animals or burnt to ashes and thrown in the air or emptied into the sea, he or she will be questioned about his or her deeds and rewarded with good or evil, depending on his or her deeds in life. Both the body and the soul together experience punishment or reward.

Islam has a doctrine of an intermediate state as do some Christian churches and denominations (see Surah 23:100).

Note: The Bible does not directly teach an intermediate state.

The Islamic intermediate state is called *barzakh*. It means an interval, a separation, or a partition. Some souls morph into the form of green birds that roam around in paradise, and these would likely be souls of the martyrs. The souls of some martyrs, however, are unable to enter paradise if they have outstanding debts, especially having failed to pay the zakat tax.

There are four abodes of the soul, and each abode is bigger and greater than the previous one.

» 1st abode: This is the womb of the mother, where there is confinement, compression, seclusion, and three layers of darkness.

» 2nd abode: This is the earthly existence of the person, where good and evil are done and which determine success or failure after death.

» 3rd abode: This is the abode of barzakh, which is large and spacious.

- » 4th abode: This is the abode of eternity, either paradise or hell. Beyond these four there are no others.

Allah allows the movement of the soul from one abode to the other, and the movement ceases when it reaches the place to which it was predestined.

Regarding the children of Muslims and non-Muslims: Islam believes in infant salvation of Muslim children; indeed, those who die prior to the age of puberty go to paradise. All non-Muslims, however, go to hellfire, whatever their age.

The Last Day

Belief in the Last Day is central to Islam and is as important as belief in Allah.

Surah 2:62 says it clearly:

> Those who believe (in the Qur'an) and those who follow the Jewish (Scriptures) and the Christians and the Sabians and those who believe in Allah and the last day and work righteousness shall have their reward with their Lord; on them shall be no fear nor shall they grieve.

In the first line, notice that "in the Qur'an" is in brackets, thus not original but added by an editor somewhere along the line and does reveal how central belief in the Last Day is to Islam. Muhammad was a "warner" in that he warned of the necessity of believing in the Last Day, the Day of Judgment. It is apparent that Muhammad borrowed from other religions' concepts as well as vocabulary about the end of the world, and no more so than from the Bible, both Old and New Testaments.

There are several different terms used in the Qur'an to describe the Last Day:
- » Day of Assembly (see Surah 42:7).
- » Day of Noise and clamor (see Surah 101:1–11).
- » Day of Judgment (see Surah 83:10–11 and 16–20).
- » Day of Meeting (see Surah 40:15–18).
- » Day of Reckoning or Account (see Surah 38:26).
- » Day of Resurrection (see Surah 50:41–45).
- » Hour of Doom (see Surah 7:187).

Only Allah knows the hour of judgment, but it will occur on a Friday. This is said to be the day that Adam was created, the day he entered paradise, and also the day he was expelled from paradise.

The last hour will come suddenly. Surah 43:61 reads, "And (Jesus) shall be a Sign (for the coming of) the Hour (of Judgment): therefore have no doubt about the (Hour) but follow ye Me; this is a Straight way."

In the hadith, Sahih Al-Bukhari, Vol. 9, Book 88, No. 237, the signs of the Last Day are stated: (1) Two big groups fight each other whereupon there will be a great number of casualties on both sides and they will be following one and the same religious doctrine; (2) About thirty *dajjals* (liars) appear, and each one of them will claim that he is Allah's Messenger; (3) Religious knowledge is taken away (by the death of religious scholars); (4) Earthquakes will increase in number; (5) Time will pass quickly; (6) Afflictions will appear; (7) *al-harj*, (i.e. killing) will increase; (8) Wealth will be in abundance; (9) People will compete with one another in constructing high buildings; (10) A man passing by a grave of someone will say, "Would that I were in his place;" and (11) Not until the sun rises from the West.

This hadith is from Al-Bukhari and therefore is considered authentic and reliable.

Analysis of the Signs

The ad-Dajjal is the Antichrist and is central to Islam. According to Sahih Al-Bukhari, Vol. 4, Book 55, No. 553, the Antichrist is one-eyed. Also, the word kafir or infidel is written on his forehead (Vol. 9, Book 88, No. 245). In Vol. 4, Book 55, No. 649, Al-Bukhari relates that Ad-Dajjal "is blind in the right eye and his eye looks like a bulging out grape."

Interestingly, it is the second coming of Christ that destroys the Antichrist. Here we see so many obvious parallels with the New Testament. According to Surah 43:61, the second coming of Christ is a sign of the coming of the Last Hour. Jesus will come announcing that he has embraced Islam and will be killed and buried next to Muhammad in Medina.

Some hadith, but not the best attested, state that Antichrist would come in Muhammad's lifetime and that the Antichrist would emerge from the East, since Satan's seat of power is in eastern Arabia.

The Antichrist will not wreak havoc upon either Mecca or Medina, and he will have a goodly following among the Iranian Jews. This proves difficult for Islam, given the few Jews still living in Iran.

One of the signs is that toward the end there will be a radical decline of both faith and morals on the earth, which is attributed to the failure of religious leaders.

Another sign or marker of the Last Hour is that there will be a rule of twelve caliphs and all from the Qurayshi tribe. This is from Sahih Muslim, Book 20, No. 4483:

> …the Messenger of Allah (peace be upon him) says…'The Islamic religion will continue until the Hour has been established, or you have been ruled by twelve Caliphs, all of them being from the Quraysh…'"

Another sign is that there will be deep divisions in Islam before the Last Hour, principally seen in a race to build mosques (see abu Dawud, Book 2, No. 449).

Gog and Magog (see Surah 21:96–98), a beast (see Surah 27:82), and heavenly portents (see Surah 70:8; 75:8–11; and 81:1–2) will be signs of the Last Hour.

And there will be wars, of course, and this creates some problems for Islam, as the wars predicted were to be fought against the eastern Roman Empire, the Byzantines, the Persians, the Turks, and against other Arab tribes. However, these are now all Islamic countries, and the Byzantines have not existed for many centuries. Many thought the Last Hour would come close to the death of Muhammad in 632 (see Sahih Al-Bukhari, Vol. 4, Book 53, No. 40).

An event having to do with the Last Hour, occurring just at the end, is the killing of Jews. Oddly, even trees and other flora will reveal to Muslims the plans of the Jews. From Sahih Al-Bukhari, Vol. 4, Book 52, No. 176:

> Allah's Messenger (peace be upon him) said, "You (i.e. Muslims) will fight

with the Jews till some of them will hide behind stones. The stones will (betray them) saying, 'O 'Abdullah (i.e. slave of Allah)! There is a Jew hiding behind me, so kill him.'"

Another sign of the end is that smoke will cover the earth (see Surah 44:10–11 and Sahih Al-Bukhari, Vol. 6, Book 60, No. 297). In that same hadith, No. 245, we find,

> Five things have passed, i.e. the smoke, the defeat of the Romans, the splitting of the moon, Al-Batsha (the defeat of the infidels in the battle of Badr) and Al-Lizam (the punishment).

There will be worldwide fire, wind, and rain. And as already mentioned, time will speed up. Sahih Bukhari, Vol. 2, Book 17, No. 146:

> The Prophet (peace be upon him) said, 'The Hour (Last Day) will not be established until (religious) knowledge will be taken away (by the death of religious learned men), earthquakes will be very frequent, time will pass quickly, afflictions will appear, murders will increase and money will overflow amongst you."

The Coming of the Mahdi

As time nears for the Last Day, there will be major moral and religious decline worldwide. The Antichrist and Beast will appear and cause great trouble. The Mahdi, who appears before the return of Jesus, will restore the world to righteousness and justice. The Sunni branch of Islam maintains this, while the Shi'a branch equates the Mahdi with the Twelfth Imam.

The Mahdi, according to hadith, will be of the family of Muhammad and is a direct descendant of Fatima, the youngest daughter of Muhammad and who became the wife of Ali, the father of Hasan and Hussein. This is especially important for Shi'a Islam which split away from the Sunni over the succession after Muhammad's death. Of special significance is the collection of hadith by Abu Dawud: Book 36, No. 4271:

> The Prophet (peace be upon him) said: The Mahdi will be of my family, of the descendants of Fatimah. 'Abdullah ibn Ja'far said: I heard AbulMalih praising 'Ali ibn Nufyi and describing his good qualities.

Book 36, No. 4172:

> The Prophet (peace be upon him) said: The Mahdi will be of my stock, and will have a broad forehead and a prominent nose. He will fill the earth with equity and justice as it was filled with oppression and tyranny, and he will rule for seven years.

The only way to be prepared for the Last Day is to believe in Muhammad (see Sahih Al-Bukhari, Vol. 9, Book 89, No 267).

Miscellaneous extraordinary events associated with the Last Day

Animals and non-living objects will speak to people; in fact some errant Muslims and non-believers will be changed into apes and pigs. Surah 2:65 reads, "As ye know of those of you who broke the Sabbath, bow We said unto them: Be ye apes, despised and hated!" (see Surah 4:47 and Sahih Al-Bukhari, Vol. 2, Book 24, No. 539 and No. 485).

Humans will be judged on the way they treat animals. Even animals will be judged and sacrificial animals will be resurrected (see Sahih Muslim, Book 5, No. 2166, Book 32, No. 6252, and Al-Tirmidhi, No. 446).

The Last Day Sequence of Events

The Sounding of the Trumpet

> And the Day that the Trumpet will be sounded then will be smitten with terror those who are in the heavens and those who are on earth except such as Allah will please (to exempt): and all shall come to His (Presence) as beings conscious of their lowliness (Surah 27:87). (See also Surah 23:101; 36:51; 39:67–68; and 50:20.)

The Descent of the Records

Two angels sit on the shoulders of all people. The one on the left records evil deeds and the one on the right records good deeds. Surah 82:10–12 reads, "But verily over you (are appointed angels) to protect you. Kind and honorable writing down (your deeds): They know (and understand) all that ye do."

According to Surah 69:18ff and 84:7ff, while humans are waiting for the Judgment to begin, the righteous ones will be given a record book or scroll in their right hands, but the unrighteous will receive the book or scroll in their left hands or behind their backs (see Surah 17:13–140).

The Weighing of the Deeds

Great scales are used at the Judgment to weigh everyone's deeds. Some believe this will take place in Jerusalem. The angels Michael and Gabriel will oversee this event. The deeds will either be heavy or light.

> Then those whose balance (of good deeds) is heavy they will attain salvation: But those whose balance is light will be those who have lost their souls, in hell will they abide (Surah 23:1–2). (See also Surah 42:17; 57:25; and 55:7.)

In addition to angels, people's limbs, arms, and legs will speak against them. This is referred to as "The Testimony of the Limbs" and is not to be taken lightly:

> On the Day when their tongues their hands and their feet will bear witness against them as to their actions. On that Day Allah will pay them back (all) their just dues and they will realize that Allah is the (very) Truth that makes all things manifest" (Surah 24:24–25). (See also Sahih Muslim, Book 42, No. 7079.)

Islamic jurisprudence or fiqh indicates that humans will be judged in regard to unpaid zakat or taxes.

The Bridge over Hell

This bridge or *sirat* is a path over which all must walk and, according to fiqh, is finer than a hair and sharper than a sword. There is nothing in the Qur'an about a bridge, but Muslims take it very seriously, because hadith literature is clear on the subject (see Sahih

Al-Bukhari, Vol. 9, Book 93, No. 532).

The righteous—those who believe in Muhammad—will cross easily, but others will fall into hellfire. We see this in Surah 19:68–72. The bridge crossing is supposed to help Muslims work out their differences with each other so there will be harmony in paradise.

The Prophet's Cistern

At the end of the bridge is a lake, reservoir, or cistern filled with delicious liquid from which the righteous are allowed to drink before they enter paradise. This wonderful liquid is to be a foretaste of the pleasures that are to come (see Surah 2:25; 3:15; and 108:1–3).

Note: One cannot help but be reminded of the Arabian Peninsula and the harsh life of the desert that Muhammad and his companions knew. Paradise is the reverse of desert life where one was always living on the edge.

Like the bridge, Muslims must believe in the Prophet's cistern. Hadith literature speaks of the cistern as well as the bridge. It is said that Muhammad will be the first to taste the wonderful water of the cistern.

The Prophet's Intercession

There are two sides to the intercessory work of Muhammad—affirmative and non-affirmative. For negative deeds and unbelief, Muhammad does not intercede (see Surah 2:48; 2:254; 74:48; and 82:19). For positive deeds and belief, Muhammad does intercede (see Surah 39:44). Surah 6:51 says, however, that only Allah may intercede.

Intercession is said to be Muhammad's chief work (see Sahih Al-Bukhari, Vol. 2, Book 24, No. 553; Vol. 9, Book 93, No. 507; and Vol. 1, Book 7, No. 331). The last part of Bukhari's Vol. 1, Book 7, No. 331 reads, "Every prophet used to be sent to his nation only but I have been sent to all mankind."

Abu Dawud, Book 14, No. 2516 takes the intercessory work of Muhammad a much larger step forward: "The Prophet (peace be upon him) said: The intercession of a martyr will be accepted for seventy members of his family (see also Al-Tirmidhi, No. 1471).

Note: This last point, that the martyr's death results in the martyr bringing seventy family members to paradise with him or her, serves as an inducement to engage in violent jihad.

Also it must be noted how large the "warner's" role is. It is akin to the role of Jesus as redeemer and Savior. Muhammad is absolutely central and pivotal for the salvation of any and all Muslims. It is very much a god-like role. Not only that, but Muhammad is actually able to remove people from hellfire and bring them to paradise.

This is testified to by Sahih Al-Bukhari, Vol. 8, Book 76, No. 571:

> The Prophet said, "Some people will be taken out of the Fire through the intercession of Muhammad, they will enter Paradise and will be called Al-Jahannamiyin (the Hell Fire people)."

(Also see Sahih Muslim, Book 1, No. 396, No. 357 and Sahih Al-Bukhari, Vol. 8, Book 76, No. 563.)

Only Muslims will enter paradise; all the rest will enter hell.

Eschatological Cosmology

The old universe will be rolled up like a scroll and all will be made new. This description bears clear resemblance to accounts in the Book of Revelation and in 2 Peter (see Sahih Al-Bukhari, Vol. 6, Book 60, No. 335 and 336). This will take place while people are crossing the bridge, or sirat, over hell on the way to paradise (see Sahih Muslim, Book 39, No. 6709).

DISCUSSION POINTS FOR EVANGELICAL WITNESS AND DEBATE

- Christians and Muslims agree there will be a Day of Judgment, and for Muslims the Last Day takes on a much more prominent place than in Christianity. How might this serve as a bridge for discussion between Christians and Muslims?
- Islam holds to an intermediate state similar to the purgatory of Roman Catholicism. Is this a point to which to call attention?
- All die according to the dictates of Allah who predestines their death. How might this concept impact the lives of Muslim people?
- Final destinations or degrees of punishments depend upon deeds far more than anything else in Islam. This differs markedly from the doctrine of grace in Christianity. How might this difference be injected into a conversation?"
- The sirat bridge over hell, narrow and razor sharp, must be crossed by all who would enter paradise. How might this Islamic doctrine be an opening for a Christian witness?

Chapter 6: ESCHATOLOGICAL ABODES

Al-A'raf

Similar to the idea of purgatory, al-A'raf is a holding place between paradise and hell. In Islam those in paradise can speak with those in hell and vice versa (see Surah 7:44–51). In the hadith by Sahih Al-Bukhari, Vol. 1, Book 2, No. 22 is the concept that Muslims may be purged of evil before entering paradise.

Al-Jahannam, Al-Nar, and Dozakh (synonyms for hell)

Islamic jurisprudence, or fiqh, generally teaches that hell is the permanent abode of those who are not Muslims and for Muslims who turned away from Islam. Hell is temporary for Muslims who did evil deeds, and Muhammad will intercede for them.

The great penalty for those in hell is that they will never have the Beatific Vision, which is to behold the presence of Allah.

Qur'anic Depiction of Hell

Summarizing Surah 38:56–65 we find the following description of what hell is like:

> An evil journey's end; an evil resting place where the inhabitants will burn and roast in the fire; people will drink boiling fetid water; other torments in extremes; the inhabitants do not welcome new arrivals; the inhabitants of hell

constantly fight with one another.

Note: One cannot help but think that drinking "boiling fetid water" is certainly a torment desert dwellers would take notice of.

Though it is difficult to provide source material here, hell is usually divided, with some differences between sects of Islam, into seven tiers:

1. Jahannam or a purgatorial hell for Muslims – Surah 19:68-72
2. Laza is a blazing fire for Christians – Surah 70:15-18
3. Al-Hutama is an intense fire for the Jews – Surah 105:4-9
4. Sa'ir is a flaming fire for the Sabeans – Surah 4:10
5. Saqar is a scorching fire for the Magicians or Zoroastrians – Surah 54:55
6. Al-Jahim is a huge hot fire for idolaters – Surah 2:119
7. Hawiya is a bottomless pit for hypocrites – Surah 101:8

Description of Hell in the Hadith

Islamic hell seems to be the reverse and evil mirror image of paradise. For non-Muslims, hell is a place of utter and endless torment beyond imagination. Hadith that speak to this are Sahih Muslim, Book 1, No. 357; Sahih Al-Bukhari, Vol. 9, Book 87, No. 155 and No. 177. The fire of hell is more intense than fire on earth and grows progressively hotter. Hell has human characteristics, in that hell speaks to the inhabitants; it also eats (see Al-Muwatta, Book 1, No. 1.7.27). The only relief from hell fire is on Islamic holy days when the fires are not kindled.

There are trees in hell, but they give no shade and smell awful (see Sahih Al-Bukhari, Vol. 6, Book 60, No. 240). The fruit of the trees is disgusting, unlike the fruit in paradise.

Sahih Muslim, Book 40, No. 6853, details the nature of the citizens of hell. The very worst of hell is for Muslims who war against other Muslims, and those who drink alcohol on earth will only be able to drink the discharge from the wounds of those tortured in hell (see Abu Dawud, Book 26, No. 3672).

Inhabitants of hell are subjected to tedious, repetitious striving, since hell is eternal. There is no escaping hell, as it has walls like a prison (see Al-Tirmidhi, No. 1507). Like a prison, it is guarded, said in the Qur'an by nineteen angels and in the hadith by seventy angels (see Sahih Muslim, Book 40, No. 6810). The angel Malik is the Custodian of hell (see Sahih Al-Bukhari, Vol. 6, Book 60, No. 344).

The majority of the inhabitants of hell are women, which is because of their ungratefulness. From Al-Muwatta, Book 12, No. 12.1.2 is found:

> Then I saw the Fire—and I have never seen anything more hideous than what I saw today— and I saw that most of its people were women. They said, Why, Messenger of Allah? He said, Because of their ungratefulness (kufr). Someone said, Are they ungrateful to Allah? He said, They are ungrateful to their husbands and they are ungrateful for good behavior (towards them). Even if you were to behave well towards one of them for a whole lifetime and then she went to see you do something (that she did not like) she would say that she had never seen anything good from you.

(Also see Sahih Al-Bukhari, Vol. 2, Book 24, No. 541.)

Jews, Christians, pagans, and false professors of Islam can only look forward to hell—Christians because they commit shirk, associating others with Allah. This is the unpardonable sin (see Sahih Al-Bukhari, Vol. 2, Book 23, No. 330).

There is a huge emphasis placed on reading the Qur'an and being able to recite it as well as doing the Five Pillars of Islam. Muslims are not to engage in private or personal interpretations of the Qur'an, which is anathema and would lead to hellfire. In Al-Tirmidhi, No. 83 we read, "He who speaks about the Qur'an on the basis of his personal opinion (only) will find his abode in Hell-Fire."

Some people are predestined to hell. Some hadith suggest that all but one sect of Islam will go into eternal hell (see Al-Tirmidhi, No. 56). Part of that passage reads, "Then (the Companions) said: Allah's Messenger, which (sect) is that? Whereupon he said: It is the one in which I and my companions belong."

Note: This would be the Sunni branch or perhaps more narrowly defined as the particular tribe Muhammad belonged to.

The failure to perform ablutions correctly also leads to hell. From Sahih Al-Bukhari, Vol. 1, Book 4, No. 166 we find,

> I heard Abu Huraira saying as he passed by us while the people were performing ablution from a utensil containing water, "Perform ablution perfectly and thoroughly for Abud Qasim (the Prophet) said, Save your heels from the Hell-fire."

It might be said that not many Muslims will remain in hell or that they have a chance to escape it after a time of suffering. Only the martyrs have any real assurance of not going to hell at all. However, Allah forgives those whom he will and sends to hell those whom he will.

Islamic salvation also depends on two other major issues: consensus and the caliphate. In regard to consensus, one must be in conformity with the ummah, holding to and practicing only what the ummah approves. Thus, Muslims will be reluctant to innovate. Then one must be obedient to the caliphate, the only true leader of the Islamic community (see Sahih Al-Bukhari, Vol. 8, Book 76, No. 587; Vol. 9, Book 84. No. 57; and Al-Tirmidhi, No. 57).

Making the hajj pilgrimage is as close as Islam comes to a concept of salvation apart from suicide missions.

Note: The description of those who enter hell is extensive, complex, even confusing, but the above summarizes the majority of the concepts.

Paradise

In Arabic, paradise is *al-janna,* meanimg garden, and Islam states there are four different gardens. Surah 55:46 says: "But for such as fear the time when they will stand before (the Judgment Seat of) their Lord there will be two Gardens," followed later by verse 62: "And besides these two there are two other Gardens."

There are four stages then of paradise: *Janna* (garden), *Adu* (Eden), *Firdaws* (Paradise), and *Sama* (Firmament).

In Islam, paradise is very different from the Christian view of heaven. Muslim paradise is the utmost in physical comfort and pleasure. There are beautiful women who never lose their virginity no matter how many sexual encounters they experience; there is the finest wine that does not intoxicate and which is drunk out of expensive cups; and the men have thrones to sit upon. There is the Beatific Vision, which is seeing Allah, but the main focus is on sexual pleasure and luxury (see Surah 76:5–9; 78:31–33; 83:22–28). Muslim men will enjoy sexual relations with women, or female spirits might be a better designation, and these are referred to as *hooris* or *kawaa'ib*. *Kawaa'ib* means "voluptuous maidens" (see Surah 44:51-55).

Note: It is apparent that the Islamic paradise is everything that life in Arabia was not.

There is clear indication that the men in paradise will also enjoy the sexual pleasures of young boys who are never worn out. Surah 52:24 reads, "Round about them will serve (devoted) to them youths (handsome) as Pearls well-guarded." Also, Surah 56:17 says, "Round about them will (serve) youths of perpetual (freshness)." It must be understood that the Arabic for "youths" is *ghalman*, which refers to little boys who are passive partners in the homosexual act.

Note: This is one area where the contrast between Islam and Christianity could not possibly be greater.

Whatever is forbidden now will be permitted in paradise, which serves as a powerful motivation for Muslim people, but mostly for men. Fornication, adultery, and homosexuality are prohibited—haram—now, but in Paradise all will be halal—permitted.

There is little for women to enjoy in paradise. In this world, this side of the Last Day, women are not to be sexual in nature, which is one reason for their veiling. In paradise, the women, real or spirit, are seductive in their nudity or scanty dress. Their primary function is to serve men with an emphasis on sexual satisfaction.

Surah 13:23 shows that married women, at least, will enter paradise; however, little will change there as they continue to serve their husbands. They do not enjoy the pleasures that the men do; there are no handsome men for them.

Bassamat Alfarah

This term refers to the "smile of joy" that is to be on the face of the martyr at the time of his or her death. The martyr is the one who will assuredly achieve salvation (see Surah 9:20). In battle with enemies of Islam, any one who displays cowardice or is a pacifist or conscientious objector will not go to paradise. In fact, any Muslim who is not ready to die as a mujahad is considered an apostate and therefore headed for hellfire.

Paradise in the Hadith

The description of paradise in the hadith is very similar to that found in the Qur'an. Paradise has all that desert tribal people would value and long for, and much of the descriptions of paradise seem to come straight out of the Bible. A distinct contrast must be acknowledged, however. In the Bible, heaven is described using metaphors that are not meant to be taken literally. In the Qur'an, they are to be taken literally.

The hadith describe tree trunks made of gold in paradise, and faithful Muslims are promised to have a date tree planted for them. (In Muhammad's day such a tree was a status symbol.) There is a problem here, however, as Al-Tirmidhi, No. 736 states,

> Allah's Messenger (peace be upon him) said that he met Abraham on the night he was taken up to Heaven, and he said, "Convey my greeting to your people, Muhammad, and tell them that Paradise has good soil and sweet water, that it consists of level, treeless plain, and that its plants are 'Glory be to Allah', 'Praise be to Allah', 'There is no god but Allah', and 'Allah is most great'.

Khadijah, Muhammad's first wife, was promised a palace in paradise (see Sahih Al-Bukhari, Vol. 5, Book 58, No. 164). Muhammad's companions, the *Sahabah*, are also promised palaces in paradise (see Sahih Al-Bukhari, Vol. 5, Book 57, No. 28). Muhammad is also promised a palace (see Sahih Al-Bukhari, Vol. 9, Book 87, No. 171).

Paradise dwellers are not immune to carnal temptations. There is also a bustling market in paradise, but no trade occurs there. Lavish wealth is displayed, and beautiful people are everywhere (see Sahih Muslim, Book 40, No. 6792 and Al-Tirmidhi, No. 1492).

Throughout paradise Muslims remain in their prime of life (see Al-Tirmidhi, No. 1484), but a kind of metamorphosis can also take place, e.g., some people are changed into green birds (see al-Tirmidhi, No. 512). Also, Muslims are changed into shining lights, and bodily functions that are distasteful disappear (see Sahih Al-Bukhari, Vol. 4, Book 55, No. 544).

Paradise is unimaginably wonderful with a brightness that would outshine the stars (see Sahih Al-Bukhari, Vol. 6, Book 60, No. 573 and Al-Tirmidhi, No. 1483).

Paradise is, of course, promised to martyrs, but those considered martyrs is a broader category than those killed while engaging in violent jihad. It can include Muslims who die due to illnesses, pregnancy, or accidents (see Al-Tirmidhi, No. 497). These individuals enter paradise without experiencing any sort of purging as do other Muslims. The martyrs are especially favored with sexual satisfaction, far more so than ordinary Muslims. Seventy of a martyr's relatives also gain entry to paradise (see Al-Tirmidhi, No. 1967). Martyrs go to the best of all the four Paradises, firdaws.

Paradise is also a place of brotherhood and luxury. We see something of this in Sahih Al-Bukhari, Vol. 4, Book 54, No. 468:

> Allah's Apostle said, "The first group (of people) who will enter Paradise will be (glittering) like the moon when it is full. They will not spit or blow their noses or relieve nature. Their utensils will be of gold and their combs of gold and silver: in their censers the aloes-wood will be used, and their sweat will smell like musk. Every one of them will have two wives; the marrow of the bones of the wives' legs will be seen through the flesh out of excessive beauty. They (i.e. the people of Paradise) will neither have differences nor hatred amongst themselves; their hearts will be as if one heart, and they will be glorifying Allah in the morning and in the evening."

Every man will have two hooris as well, while the martyrs have seventy-two. This is in addition to the two wives. In paradise then, every man's sexual vigor is increased one hundred fold so as not to disappoint wives and hooris (see Al-Tirmidhi, No. 1482). Muhammad is said to have possessed great sexual prowess during his lifetime. "Anas bin Malik said, 'The Prophet used to visit all his wives in a round, during the day and night and they were eleven in number'"(Sahih Al-Bukhari, Vol. 7, book 62, No. 169).

Note: One wonders if the promises to faithful Muslims, especially martyrs, is not intended to instill patience with a sub-level existence many Muslims experience.

Of interest is the hadith by Sahih Al-Bukhari, Vol. 4, Book 53, No. 391, that says, "Whoever killed a person having a treaty with the Muslims shall not smell the smell of Paradise though its smell is perceived from a distance of forty years." This seems to be ignored when one considers the killing of non-Muslims who live in Muslim-dominated countries.

Muslim children automatically go to paradise and are provided with wet-nurses (see Sahih Al-Bukhari, Vol. 2, Book 23, No. 464), and aborted or still-born fetuses go directly to paradise (see Sahih Al-Bukhari, Vol. 2, Book 23, No. 441).

There is an interesting hadith, Al-Tirmidhi, No. 36, that is worth quoting:

> Khadijah asked Allah's Messenger (peace be upon him) about her children who had died in the days of ignorance. Thereupon Allah's Messenger (peace be upon him) said: They are in Hell Fire, and when he saw the sign of disgust on her face, he said: If you were to see their station you would hate them. She said: Allah's Messenger, what about my child that was born of your loins? He said: It is in Paradise. Then Allah's Messenger (peace be upon him) said: verily the believers and their children will be in Paradise and the polytheists and their children in the Hell Fire.

Note: "Days of ignorance" refer to the time prior to the revelations to Muhammad. Also, it is plain that Muhammad changes his opinion to comfort Khadijah.

Piety or *Takwah*

Martyrs enter paradise at once, but the primary preferred way to Paradise is Islamic piety, that is, doing what the religion demands from the faithful Muslim. As mentioned earlier, doing the Five Pillars of Islam is highly important. And the performing of these acts of devotion are to be just that, performance for the glory of Allah. We find in Sahih Al-Bukhari, Vol. 1, Book 10, No. 548 "My father said, 'Allah's Apostle (peace be upon him) said, "Whoever prays the two cool prayers (Aur and Fajr) will go to Paradise."'

Reciting the Qur'an in Arabic is a key achievement. Understanding Arabic and thus the meaning and intent of the Qur'an is secondary. This thus injects a magical element into Islam.

A big part of Islamic piety is knowledge—knowledge of Islam first, but all forms of knowledge count.

Obeying and being in consensus with the ummah is of great importance. Attendance at the mosque, especially for the congregational prayers on Friday, is a must. Anyone who builds a mosque gains entry to paradise (see Sahih Al-Bukhari, Vol. 1, Book 8, No. 441).

Charitable giving is also required, but according to Abu Dawud, Book 9, No. 1678, it is a giving in order to receive in like kind in paradise.

A pious Muslim may pray for dead Muslims, somewhat like in the Roman Catholic Church where prayers are said for those in purgatory.

Those making the hajj pilgrimage from Jerusalem to Mecca are promised forgiveness of sins and entry into paradise (see Abu Dawud, Book, 10, No. 1737).

Anyone who supplies military arms to Muslim fighters, the mujahidin, will go to paradise (see Sahih Al-Bukhari, Vol. 4, Book 55).

The greeting, "Peace be upon you" when spoken from the heart also guarantees paradise (see Sahih Muslim, Book 1, No. 96). Muslims are only to greet other Muslims this way. Jews and Christians, on the other hand, may be insulted:

> Reported Allah's Messenger (may peace be upon him) as saying: "Do not greet the Jews and the Christians before they greet you and when you meet any one of them on the roads force him to go to the narrowest part of it."

The intention above is to humiliate (see Al-Risala (Maliki Manual) Chapter 43).

Jews and Christians who are subject to Muslims in Muslim-dominated countries must be made to submit to Muslims, and Muslims are free, even obligated, to humiliate them. Infidels, as in polytheists or pagans, must be forced to convert or be killed; apostates, that is, those who leave Islam, are to either reconvert or be killed; and those of other sects, like Sufis (but really for the Sunni the Shi'a and the Shi'a the Sunni), must be fought and annihilated.

Allah has ninety-nine names, and part of piety is to act out or live out the meanings of those names. In Sahih Al-Bukhari, Vol. 8, Book 75, No 419 is found,

> Allah has ninety-nine Names, one hundred minus one, and whoever believes in their meanings and acts accordingly will enter Paradise; and Allah is Witr (one) and loves the Witr (i.e. odd numbers).

Obeying Muhammad is a key to piety, and doing those things will earn a Muslim paradise. Surah 4:80 says, "He who obeys the Apostle obeys Allah."

This figures more prominently in Islam than one might think. Among so many other things, it is necessary to repeat and pray, "Peace be upon him," in order to enter paradise. The pious Muslim is to pray that Muhammad will be given the role of Wasilah, or intercessor. Muhammad's role in the position of intercessor means that Muhammad will plead to Allah that individual Muslims be allowed into paradise.

The pious Muslim, having done all that is required, may then receive the ultimate, the Beatific Vision. This is promised in Qur'an 9:72–73; 10:26; and 75:22–23.

Note: The Beatific Visions is a viewing of or seeing Allah. Biblically speaking, direct and personal fellowship with the God of all creation, the maker of heaven and earth, is the ultimate intention of the Triune God.

DISCUSSION POINTS FOR EVANGELICAL WITNESS AND DEBATE

- Both Islam and Christianity hold to a belief in an actual heaven and hell. How do these two ultimate destinations differ one from another?
- Islam's paradise demands a world like the earth we live on. The Christian heaven is beyond description and decidedly otherworldly. The Bible describes a dissolving of the

entire universe. Is there a point here worth debating with Muslims?

- The descriptions of paradise in hadith are rather fantastic. They are decidedly misogynous as well. Women do not fare nearly as well as men in the Islamic hereafter. Is there an opportunity here for discussion?
- The way to paradise for Muslims is all up to personal piety. Paradise is achieved or earned, all based on "works righteousness." It is the age-old works versus grace controversy. Is there a window open here to explain grace?
- A question may be posed as to whether Muhammad is in paradise, and if so, why the continued repeating of, "Peace be upon him"?

Chapter 7: PREDESTINATION

That Allah knows all and nothing happens outside the will of Allah suggests predestination, even fatalism.

So much of Islam has to do with the necessity of belief in Muhammad and Allah accompanied with the performance of religious ritual, that Islamic predestination is a stark internal contradiction with human responsibility.

Note: In Biblical Christianity there is an emphasis on the foreknowledge of God and His predestination, while the person foreknown and predestined and elected still has the freedom to obey and trust and follow his or her Lord. Biblical predestination has to do with a person's salvation and not with individual acts, good or evil.

Faith in Allah's predestination is mandatory for all Muslims. From Al-Risala (Maliki Manual), under the title "Determination" we find the following:

> Another precept is the belief in divine foreordainment, whether it be for good or for evil, and whether it be pleasant or distasteful. All of that has been ordained by Allah our Lord. The beginnings of affairs are in His hand and they take place by His decree. He knows all things before they happen, and they happen in accordance with His knowledge. Neither words nor deeds can proceed from His servants except by His decree. He would also have a prior knowledge of that.

Note: Regardless of what takes place, whether good or bad, i.e., a killing, a rape, an atrocity of any kind—all are foreordained. Such extreme predestination begs the question of whether of not there is an actual ethic or code of conduct in Islam.

The issue of predestination in Islam is clouded by references to Allah's veiling of the minds of unbelievers and that Allah "schemes" against them as well. The veiling idea is found in Surah 2:2–7, and the scheming notion is found in Surah 3:54: "And they (the disbelievers) schemed, and Allah schemed (against them): and Allah is the best of schemers."

The Arabic word for schemer is *makara* and usually means deceiver. The concept is that Allah will bring to destruction those whom he wishes. Indeed, Allah is known to lead astray those whom he chooses; thus one is not really sure where he or she stands, with the possible exception of martyrs.

The destination of all persons was determined at the creation of Adam, from the very beginning (see Al-Tirmidhi, No. 38).

Note: This is not too dissimilar from what is called hyper-Calvinism, except there the Biblical predestinating is based upon the love of God for His creation.

In the hadith, therefore, and also the Qur'an, is the idea of comprehensive predetermination. "For Allah will surely accomplish His purpose: verily for all things has Allah appointed a due proportion" (Surah 65:3). (Also see Surah 35:11-13).

No one is a Muslim, and a faithful Muslim at that, except by the will of Allah (see Surah 81:28-29).

Clashing with the stern and strict predestination recorded above is Surah 4:79: "Whatever good (O man!) happens to thee is from God; But whatever evil happens To thee, is from thy (own) soul."

This conflict is not resolved, and thus it cannot be said that Islam is completely fatalistic, except when it comes to death. If one is to live, or if one is to die—all is in the hands of Allah and determined a long time ago. This, it is said, will result in bravery on the battlefield.

Several different schools of thought have arisen in Islam to cope with the real or apparent contradictions:

» The Jabrians deny all human free will or responsibility.

» The Qadarians deny predestination by Allah, since Allah cannot be charged with evil.

» The Ash'arians combine both the above, with God causing the act but the act is the responsibility of humans. This is the position of the Sunni.

Expressions that echo fatalism are: *Maktub*-it is written; *Maqdur*-it is decided; *Kismat*-it is my lot; and Inshallah-God Willing.

Surah 45:24-27 and Surah 11:3 seem to indicate that Muhammad rejected fatalism in favor of the mercy of Allah, which confuses to some degree the emphasis of absolute predestination. This is a debate with many sides to it.

DISCUSSION POINTS FOR EVANGELICAL WITNESS AND DEBATE

- Is there assurance of salvation in Islam? Is this issue an open door for a clear presentation of the Gospel of grace?

- How might a discussion between a contrast between Surah 81:28-29 and Surah 4:79 be structured?

- The issue of fatalism is a potential quagmire. Yet Muslims take solace in the idea that whatever they do is the will of Allah. How might a discussion on this issue be raised?

Appendix 1: THE GOSPEL OF BARNABAS

The *Gospel of Barnabas* is Appendix I in Dr. Patrick Sookhdeo's book *Understanding Islamic Theology*. Following is a brief outline of it, based on its importance to Islamic apologetics.

There is a Biblical character named Barnabas, who accompanied Paul on his first missionary journey, as reported in the Book of Acts. The author of the *Gospel of Barnabas* is not Paul's companion. The *Gospel of Barnabas* is also not to be confused with either the *Epistle of Barnabas* nor with the *Acts of Barnabas*, both of which belong to apocryphal literature and were written long after the Barnabas of the Bible was dead.

The only version of the *Gospel of Barnabas* extant are in Italian and housed in Vienna; there are also fragments of it from a Spanish version.

There are internal clues in the Barnabas writing that indicate parts of it were composed in the fifth century at the earliest. However, it may well be a medieval forgery. Not only that, the author of Barnabas plagiarizes the fourteenth-century works of Dante. Dr. Sookhdeo is complete in his explanation and proof that the *Gospel of Barnabas* is a false writing.

The reason this small segment comes at this point is that Islamic scholars may cite this document as evidence that first century Christians, even persons noted in the Christian Bible such as Barnabas, denied the Messiahship of Jesus and other core Christian doctrines. Essentially it is a grasping at straws and actually detracts from any debate about the issue.

A Special note about Dr. Patrick Sookhdeo

Patrick Sookhdeo's book, *Understanding Islamic Theology*, published by Isaac Publishing in 2013, proved to be very valuable in attempting to understand Islam. Our church used his book as the primary text for our Saturday Seminary Islamic Studies class. It is simply written, clear, comprehensive, and was perfect for our purposes. Only later did it come to light that the author was being accused of several serious moral breeches.

Contact with the publisher and conversation with the staff at The Barnabas Fund, of which Dr. Sookhdeo is head, gave valuable insight, as did internet articles, both pro and con. In the end, this author reasoned that what happened to Dr. Sookhdeo has happened to many who take up the task of exposing and critiquing Islam. It is always the same—attack the messenger rather than the message. In 2016, The Barnabas Fund released a position paper in regard to the charges against Dr. Sookhdeo. For further investigation, please search the internet for "Dr. Patrick Sookhdeo and The Barnabas Fund" and decide for yourself.

The best site might be:

http://www.episcopalcafe.com/the-barnabas-aid-international-board-of-trustees-make-a-statement-regarding-the-return-of-dr-patrick-sookhdeo/

Of chief concern for this book was whether Dr. Sookhdeo's book was accurate in regard to his presentation of Islam. My fifteen years of researching Islam yields the conclusion that the material in his book is trustworthy and reliable. If a reader would judge my work based on whether or not I was sinless enough to be acceptable, then no one would read what I write. And the same is likely true for any of us.

Both the publisher and Dr. Sookhdeo have given permission to quote, even extensively, from *Understanding Islamic Theology*.

3

SHARIA LAW: AN INTRODUCTION

What Muslims and Non-Muslims Need to Know about Sharia Law

Introduction

Many Muslims know little of Sharia law, though some aspects of it are taught to them as children. The clerics, imams, and muftis are conversant with Sharia, but even these will hold varying opinions on even core elements of this very complex code of law.

Sharia law is highly important to Muslims because they view it as the perfect and complete, eternal, and universal will of Allah and as that form of governance practiced by Muhammad and his faithful companions. This is the first and most important fact non-Muslims need to understand about Islam. The Islamic agenda is for the entire globe to be under Sharia law.

Non-Muslims have little idea of Sharia law, and even those things we think we know are often incorrect. This essay is an attempt to present the essentials of Sharia law in as simple a manner as possible by presenting actual legal descriptions on major subjects.

The complete codes of law are lengthy. For Shia Islam, I use as my reference *The Laws of Islam* by the Grand Ayatullah Sayyid M. Taqi al-Husayni al-Modarresi (480 pages). For Sunni Islam, I use *Shari'ah: Islamic Law* by 'Abd ar-Rahman I. Doi, revised and expanded by 'Abdassamad Clarke (704 pages). It is of course not possible to present all the myriad of laws and opinions of Islamic law for either Shia or Sunni Islam. I have chosen to focus on central themes only.

In Sunni Islam there are four schools of interpretation, and in Shia there is one, and they will often differ from each other, sometimes to an extreme degree.

At certain points I will express my own opinions, which will be indicated by a shaded box reading: **Note:** followed by my thoughts.

Comparing Sharia and the Gospel

According to Islam, the way to Paradise is to conform and submit to Sharia law. Sharia is literally translated "the way" or "the way to water," the latter making sense in that Islam developed in a desert region.

In Islam the way to life is a code of laws; in Christianity the way to life is a person, Jesus Christ. For Muslims the central authority behind Sharia law is the Prophet Muhammad himself—primarily his exemplary life and practice as recorded in the Qur'an, the hadith, and the *Sira*.[1]

In order to attain Paradise, Muslims must live a life as close as possible to that of Muhammad and the faithful companions, i.e., Abu Bakr, Umar, Uthman, Ali, and many other seventh-century followers of Muhammad. This way of life is defined in Sharia law by means of thousands of laws that help rightly guide Muslims. The imam is a prophet or preacher, one who is a divinely appointed leader into right guidance and not one who gives prophesy. Following the imam is essential to have proper guidance. Islam teaches that the real problem humans face is ignorance, and so they must be guided to live the right life. Once people learn what to believe, *aqeeda*,[2] and how to live, Sharia, they will earn the pleasure of Allah. Islam sees the world living in darkness and is thus is compelled to dispel error by teaching Sharia and enforcing its laws.

Muslims reject Christianity's core doctrine that forgiveness of sin and all wrongdoing is a gift of grace. In addition, Islam rejects the Biblical truth that no Christian goes to hell. Muslims ask then, why should any Christian do good? The answer to that question is that forgiveness produces a desire to please God and be a faithful follower of Jesus and do what He commanded. This concept is not understood by Muslims. They cannot accept the core Biblical and Christian truth that no one can earn salvation through their works.

Summary

To restate, the sources of Sharia law are the Qur'an, the hadith, and the *Sira*, but most importantly it developed from the interpretations of Islamic scholars and jurists over long centuries.

The mission of Islam is that all the people of the world should live under Sharia law, which alone can turn people from living in ignorance.

---

1   Ishaq's *Sirat Rasul Allah, The Life of Muhammad*, Introduction by A. Guillaume (Oxford: Oxford University Press, 1967). The *Sira* is much less appealed to in recent decades due to the often strange and fanciful stories about Muhammad found therein.

2   *Aqeeda*, or what must be believed, is: (1) Allah is not a father, nor a son; Allah is a monad—an absolute unity (2) the prophets (3) the divinely inspired books (4) angels and the unseen (5) the day of judgment and (6) Allah's predestining sovereignty. These are the six articles of faith.

4

SHARIA LAW: A SUMMARY FOR SUNNI ISLAM

Based on *Shari'ah Islamic Law* by Professor 'Abd ar Rahman I. Doi

Note: As with Shariah law for Shia Islam, the material is complex, and instead of just shy of five hundred pages, our reference source for Sunni Islam by Professor Doi is seven hundred pages. Again, support for the laws begins with the Qur'an, then material from the hadith is presented, followed by the rulings of the jurists, the legal authorities. And again, it is not possible to present all the rulings. I have chosen areas of Sunni jurisprudence that might be of greatest assistance in discussions with Muslim people. I have retained British spellings and punctuation.

Chapter 1: Din and Society

Din means the practice of religion, living the faith of Islam in real life. The focus is on doing what is permitted (what one is obligated to do: halal) and not doing that which is not permitted (that which is forbidden: haram).

Shariah law, then, has to do with that which is obligatory and that which is forbidden. Usually that which is forbidden is in contrast with that which is permitted, but the author uses the word *obligatory* as close to or the same as *demanded* or *expected*. Imam Doi says, "The Islamic Shariah is a broad and generous way whose obligations and prohibitions are minimal and easily understandable" (p. 11).

Part I: Principles of the Shariah and the Madhabs

Chapter 2: What is Shariah?[1]

"Shariah is an Arabic word meaning the road to be followed. Literally it means 'the way to a watering place.'...Thus it is only Shariah that liberates man from servitude to

---

1 There are various ways "Shariah" is spelled. Imam Doi uses "Shari'ah," but here I use "Shariah."

other than Allah. This is the only reason why Muslims are obliged to strive for the implementation of this path, and no other path" (p. 23).

"Three things are mentioned as gifts of Allah. They are the Book, the Balance, and iron, which stand as emblems of three things which hold society together, *viz.* revelation, which commands good and forbids evil; justice, which gives to each person his due; and the strong force of the law, which maintains sanctions against evildoers" (p. 24).

Note: By "Book" is meant the Qur'an, the "Balance" refers to the Day of Judgment, and "iron" is to enforce right and punish wrong. This is how Shariah works in a Muslim-dominated country, but it has less impact elsewhere. However, what goes on inside tight-knit Muslim enclaves in Western countries is anyone's guess.

Allah is the lawgiver and can protect better than any person. The *ummah,* which is the whole nation of Islam, is Allah's trustee. And the ummah also plays a significant interpretative role. The "Ummah enjoys a derivative rule-making power and not an absolute law-creating prerogative." Imam Doi sees the whole of Islam as united, "one vast homogeneous commonwealth of people who have a common goal and a common destiny and who are guided by a common ideology in all matters both spiritual and temporal. The entire Muslim Ummah lives under the Shariah to which every member has to submit, with sovereignty belonging to Allah alone" (p. 27).

Professor Doi sees Islam as a democracy where interpretations of law can be presented, except in cases where Allah has clearly presented his own law, which cannot ever be altered.

The jurists, and only the appointed experts, which are appointed by Allah, then act under Allah. These jurists, in examining the Qur'an and Sunnah, are responsible to make proper interpretations, which are necessary due to the changing of times and circumstances. So then, Imam Doi states: "The reason why there is a greater degree of stability in the Shariah compared to any other man-made legislation in the world is due to its Divine origin" (p. 28).

There are four primary sources for Shariah law. First, the Qur'an; the second is the Sunnah, which is the practice of the Prophet Muhammad; the third source is the *ijma,* or consensus of the ʿulama; and the fourth is *qiyas,* or analogical deduction.

In the Qur'an it is said there are five hundred verses that contain legal rulings. These deal with marriage, polygyny, dower, maintenance, rights and obligations of the spouses, divorce and various modes of dissolution of marriage, the period or retreat after divorce, fosterage, contracts, loans, deposits, weights and measures, removal of injury, oaths and vows, punishments for crimes, wills, inheritance, equity, fraternity, liberty, justice to all, principles of governance, fundamental human rights, laws of war and peace, judicial administration, and much more (p. 28).

Due to the complete and unerring nature of Shariah law, no authority in any Muslim land can change or nullify this rule of law for Muslims.

Note: The above list, in my view, is rather overreaching. It makes the Qur'an out to be a detailed law book, but it is not that at all. One has to search diligently and employ an energetic imagination to arrive at such a conclusion as to the viability of the Qur'an in terms of legal pronouncements. It is my impression that Imam Doi does his best to paint Islam's code of law as the most complete and comprehensive law code ever devised.

It is plain to see, then, why Muslims desire to live under Shariah law and will do so even if such practice violates the laws of whatever nation they may live in. It is also evident that living under Shariah law would be similar to living under a very strict and powerful dictatorship.

Though Shariah originated with direct commands from Allah, still there is the provision or power to interpret the divine law "by means of analogical deduction and through other processes" (p. 28). Yet, it is insisted, "The Qur'an, therefore, is the best commentary on the Qur'an and the main source of the Sharia."

Besides the four sources of Shariah law—the Qur'an, Sunnah, consensus, and analogical deduction—there is a fifth source: juristic preference or equity. This helps provide elasticity and adaptability to the entire Islamic legal system. Imam Malik ibn Anas (795 CE), founder of one of the Sunni schools of law, developed this concept. This fifth source is meant to examine those issues having to do with the public interest and those that are not specifically defined in Shariah law.

In Shariah law there is no separate judiciary for civil, criminal, and military matters. The core principles of Shariah are:

1. 1. The larger interests of society take precedence over the interests of the individual.
2. 2. Although "relieving hardship" and "promoting benefit" are both among the prime objectives of Shariah, the former takes precedence over the latter.
3. 3. A bigger loss cannot be inflicted to relieve a smaller loss, or a bigger benefit cannot be sacrificed for a smaller one. Conversely, a smaller harm can be inflicted to avoid a bigger harm, or a smaller benefit can be sacrificed for a larger benefit.

As for the *qadi*, or judge, these are of three types: one will go to the Garden, and the other two will end up in the Fire. The two who go to the Fire judge unjustly and judge out of ignorance.

From the Sunnah of the Prophet it is found that every judge must observe the following in his task of administering justice:

1. The equality of all litigants
2. The defendant and the litigant must appear before the qadi.
3. The defendant should be given the right to take an oath.
4. The judge must be careful in awarding *hadd* punishments. (Hadd punishments are meant to be a deterrent.)

Note: There are no juries of one's peers or others in Shariah law.

Chapter 3: The Noble Qur'an: The First Textual Source of Shariah

"The Qur'an is divided into 114 chapters and contains 86,430 words and 323,760 letters of the alphabet. The total number of verses is 6,666. There are fourteen, some say fifteen, and others eleven, places in the Qur'an where the words used are so commanding that the reciter must prostrate in awe to glorify Allah."

The Qur'an was revealed a little at a time to Muhammad over the course of twenty-two years, two months, and twenty-two days. The first revelation began the fifteenth night of the month of Ramadan when Muhammad was forty-one years old. The first revelation was given at the Cave of Hira, and was as follows: "Recite: In the Name of your Lord who created, created man from clots of blood. Recite: And your Lord is the Most Generous" (Qur'an 96:1–3).

The last verse of the Qur'an to be recited to Muhammad is: "Today I have perfected your din for you and completed My blessing upon you and I am pleased with Islam as a din for you" (Qur'an 5:3). Muhammad was sixty-three at the time (p. 48).

The issue, then, is interpretation, and the word for this in Arabic is *tafsir*. There are three conditions for interpreting the Qur'an:

1. Every word should be explained with its real meaning so that it shows the reality of its objective. In order to achieve this, the scholar has to employ linguistic knowledge and grammar.
2. Everything should be explained with reference to the context of the main theme of the revelation.
3. The interpretation should not be contrary to the sayings of the Companions, who witnessed the coming of the revelations to the Messenger of Allah.

There were three main schools on interpreting the Qur'an: One, developed toward the end of the seventh century, is that of *Makkah* (Mecca). The second school was that of Iraq. Ibn Masud was the master of the school in the early years of the eighth century. Then there was the school of *Madina* (Medina), the first capital of Islam, and the lead scholar was Ubayy ibn Ka'b. This was also in the early decades of the eighth century.

Then came the four great imams: Imam Malik, Imam Abu Hanifah, Imam ash-Shafi'I, and Imam Ahmad ibn Hanbal. These Imams established the principles of the science of Islamic jurisprudence (p. 55).

Rules were developed to determine the value and validity of the hadith that are ascribed to Muhammad, whether they are weak or strong. This is called developing the *isnad*. Two of these credited with this work are Muhammad al-Tabari and al-Bukhari. It is al-Bukhari who is credited with collecting the most respected and authoritative hadith. His thirty-volume book presents interpretation of the Qur'an by noting what was said by the Companions.

Professor Doi cautions, "It is very risky to undertake the interpretation of the Noble Qur'an on the basis of personal opinion. A case in point is given in regard to the *tafsir* or interpretation of Qur'an 4:15: 'If any of your women commit fornication, four of you must be witnesses against them. If they bear witness, detain them in their homes until death releases them or Allah ordains another procedure for their case.'"

Some commentators say the fornication was among the women only, with no men involved. Other commentators say the verse refers to fornication with men or women. Others say this verse has been abrogated, or superseded, by another verse of the Qur'an: "A woman and a man who commit fornication: flog both of them with one hundred lashes and do not let compassion for either of them possess you where Allah's din is concerned, if you have iman in Allah and the Last Day. A number of mu'minun should witness their punishment" (*Iman* means faith; *mu'minun* refers to the faithful Muslims [p. 62]).

In light of the differences, it is said that the Qur'an has two systems of interpretations. One is "clear judgments" and the other is "open to interpretation." So then, the

Qur'an can be divided into two portions, not arranged separately but intermingled. The first is "clear judgments" and is the nucleus or foundation of the Book. The second, "open to interpretation," is figurative, metaphorical, and allegorical.

Note: Following Professor Doi's presentation of the many problems involved in interpreting the Qur'an, he states:

> The Prophet has, for his own part, transmitted every word and letter of the Noble Qur'an to humanity and explained all of them with clear details to preclude every possibility of confusion or change in their form, content and meaning. He did it with such vigour and assiduity that Allah even had to say: "Perhaps you may destroy yourself with grief, chasing after them, if they do not have iman in these words." Qur'an 18:6

This seems to cloud the issue all the more. What the quote from the Qur'an has to do with tafsir [interpretation] is anyone's guess.

A summary of the qualities necessary for a judge to interpret the Qur'an is:

1. He should never entertain any doubts as to the principles and injunctions contained in the verses of the Qur'an, for Allah says: "That is the Book, without any doubt" (Qur'an 2:1).
2. He must be a right-acting man, a person of *taqwa*, as the Qur'an gives guidance to those who are God fearing. "It contains guidance for those who have *taqwa*" (Qur'an 2:1).
3. He should believe in Allah and the unseen and must not be an atheist or a deviant in his faith. "In it is guidance for those who have *taqwa*" (Qur'an 2:1).
4. He must be regular in his five daily prayers, for the Qur'an says, "And who establish *salah* [prayer]" (Qur'an 2:2).
5. He must be charitable: "And (in it is guidance for those who) give of what We have provided for them" (Qur'an 2:2).

Note: *taqwa* [or *takwa*] refers to purity; thus a judge must be perfect in his obedience to Islam.

Chapter 4: The Sunnah: Second Textual Source of the Shariah

Essentially, the Sunnah explains and interprets the Qur'an. The pattern of life of Muhammad as reported by his faithful companions after his death makes up the hadith. It is said that Muhammad only reported what had been recited to him by the angel Gabriel, who only recited what Allah had given. This is backed up by Qur'an 53:2–4: "Your companion is not misguided or misled, nor does he speak from whim. It is nothing but Revelation revealed."

It is said that the above verses were revealed to counter three false charges that the Jewish tribe Quraysh made against Muhammad:

1. That he was going astray either through a defect in intelligence or through carelessness

2. That he was being misled or deceived by evil spirits (jinn) and so was majnun (possessed by a jinn)
3. That he was speaking whimsically or impulsively, or from a selfish desire to impress with his own personality (p. 74)

After the death of Muhammad in 632, the judgments regarding Shariah law needed to be based on a variety of issues—the Qur'an and the hadith—thus the hadith, which revealed the pattern of life of Muhammad, acquired increasing importance.

In Shariah law, actions are divided into five classes (pp. 80–81):

1. Fard: This is an obligatory duty for which there is a reward, and the neglect of which brings a punishment, of both a legal and divine nature.
2. *Mandub* or *mustahabb*: This is a recommended action for which there is a divine reward, but if the action is not taken, there is no punishment.
3. *Ja'iz* or *Mubah*: This is an action that is permissible with no legal consequences. But it may be considered an act of worship if obedience to Allah is the reason for the action.
4. *Makruh*: This is a disapproved act. If undertaken, it does not bring divine punishment, but if abandoned there is a divine reward.
5. *Haram*: This is an act punishable both in this world and by Allah, and if abandoned there is a divine reward.

Professor Doi wants to be clear that the Qur'an is not a book of law, history, or sociology. It is a book of guidance so that "His creatures" will lead better and more descent lives (p. 82).

"The Noble Qur'an, even with its wealth of detail, needs the additional element of *fatwa* (legal judgment) and tradition, and the hadith were collected to fulfill this need" (p. 82).

Note: Guidance, not salvation, is the chief concern. Right guidance results in favor with Allah and thus may possibly lead to the Garden, or Paradise. This is in sharp distinction from the message of the Christian Scripture that salvation is on the basis of God's grace and mercy.

About the hadith, there are six collections, the latest dating from the sixth century of Islam. There are other collections of the sayings and practices of Muhammad considered valuable by some scholars. The six accepted collections are:

1. The Sahih of al-Bukhari (d. 870 CE)
2. The Sahih of Muslim (d. 875 CE)
3. The Sunan of Ibn Majah (d. 887 CE)
4. The Sunan of Abu Dawud (d. 888 CE)
5. The Jami of at-Tirmidhi (d. 892 CE)
6. The Sunan of an-Nasa'I (d. 915 CE)

It is said that each compiler carefully selected only the most trusted of the sayings and doings of Muhammad. The author Doi writes: "Al-Bukhari, for example, examined and memorized 600,000 traditions of which he chose to include in this Sahih only 7,397."

Note: Other sources declare that Al-Bukhari collected 300,000 traditions, memorized

200,000, and included in his hadith approximately 7,275 with repetition and about 2,230 without repetition.[2] The reason for the discrepancy may be due to the constant concern of Islamic writers to puff up Islam and make it sound more well grounded in history than it really is.

In the process of evaluating the various hadith accounts, scholars found it necessary to evaluate the veracity of the hundreds of thousands of items. So a system referred to as *isnad* developed, which ranks the material as:

- Excellent
- Good
- Fair
- Weak
- Fabricated
- Untrue

"Therefore, the isnad is almost as important an element in a hadith as the *matn* (saying) itself" (p. 86).

In terms of the content of the hadith, the following principles were established:

1. The text should not be contrary to the text or the teachings of the Qur'an or the agreed-upon basic principles of Islam.
2. Hadith should not be against the dictates of reason or the laws of nature or common sense.
3. Hadith should not be contrary to other hadith already accepted by the authorities of this science as reliable and authentic according to the proper criteria.
4. Hadith which sing lavish praise of the excellence of any tribe, place, or persons should generally be regarded as suspect.
5. Hadith that contain dates and minute details of future events should be regarded as suspect.
6. Hadith that contain some remarks attributed to the Prophet that are not in keeping with the Islamic belief about the nature of prophethood and the position of the Prophet or which contain expressions that are not suitable or appropriate for him should also be regarded as suspect (pp. 87–88).

Note: It is quite clear that the scholars of Islam, both in ancient and more contemporary times, are able to apply Shariah law according to not much more than expediency.

Of those hadith designated "*Sahih*," there are only two, that of al-Bukhari and Muslim, considered the authentic hadith and are stated to be so after applying all the tests (p. 89).

Chapter 5: Ijma-The Third Textual Source of Shariah

Ijma is the Arabic word for "consensus" and refers to the consensus or mutual agreement of "juristic opinions of the learned *'ulama* of the *Ummah* after the death of the Messenger of Allah and can be defined as the consensus of the Companions of the Prophet and the unanimous agreement reached on the decisions taken by subsequent learned *muftis* and jurists on

---

2 Dr. Muhammad Muhsin, *Sahih Al-Bukhari* (Houston: Dar-us-Salam, 1997), 19.

various matters" (p. 98). ('*Ulama* is the ruling jurists and *ummah* is the Muslim community.)

The Qur'an, the Sunnah, and consensus, then, are the textual sources for Shariah law. Further "intellectual sources" are the qiyas and *ijtihad*. (*Qiyas* has to do with analogical deduction, and *ijtihad* has to do with deductive logic.)

These processes are vital to Islam, as is made clear from Qur'an 4:115: "But if anyone opposes the Messenger after the guidance has become clear to him, and follows other than the path of the *mu'minun*, We will hand him over to whatever he has turned to, and We will roast him in Hell. What an evil destination!"

Essentially, *ijma* aims at arriving at practical solutions. For example, "In the field of family law it is agreed that since the Qur'an proscribes marriages with mothers and daughters then, by the same token, grandmothers and granddaughters, however far removed, fall within the prohibited degrees" (p. 100).

Ijma is divided into three broad categories:

1. Consensus verbally articulated
2. Consensus expressed by deed
3. Consensus expressed by silence over an issue, by not expressing disagreement with or opposition to it

Ijma can also be subdivided into either regular consensus or irregular consensus.

Chapter 6: The Intellectual Principles of Shariah

The first principle is *qiyas*: analogical deduction. This is the "legal principle introduced in order to arrive at logical legal conclusions" (p. 108).

Not all Islamic scholars agree to the principle of *qiyas*, and these are termed anti-*qiyas*. They argue that Allah revealed the Qur'an for guidance and no more, no less. Every Muslim must then look alone to the Qur'an. A supporting verse is: "We have not omitted anything from the Book—then they will be gathered to their Lord" (Qur'an 6:38).

The pro-*qiyas* people also look to the Qur'an, chapter 59 and verse 3 for support: "People of insight, take note!" The passage, for the pro-*qiyas* followers, means that people must use their common sense to deduce Islamic law. The author, Professor Doi, is pro-*qiyas*, especially when the outcome does not go against the Qur'an.

Then secondly, *ijtihad* is the use of one's intellect to arrive at a solution or judgment. It is said that "*qiyas* or analogical reasoning, then, is a particular form of *ijtihad*" (p. 118). "*Ijtihad*, therefore, is exercise of reasoning by a jurist to arrive at a logical conclusion to a legal issue, and to deduce the conclusion as to the effectiveness of a legal precept in Islam" (p. 118).

In order to use *qiyas* and *ijtihad* a Muslim jurist must have the following qualities: he must be a genuine Muslim, not a nominal Muslim—a practicing one, not omitting any of the obligations of Islam. This last point is a matter of a difference of opinions. To omit obligations to some leads to *kufr* (to be treated as an apostate), while others consider it to be a major wrong action, and sometimes a capital offense (p. 121).

An example of the application of *ijma* and or *ijtihad* has to do with wine, because it causes intoxication. "Therefore, other intoxicants like spirits and beer, and drugs like heroin, cocaine and marijuana are prohibited by analogical reasoning, because they also lead to intoxication and loss of one's senses" (p. 122).

Chapter 7: The Four Schools of *Fiqh* and Their Imams

Imams Abu Hanifah, Malik, ash-Shafi'i, and Ahmad ibn Hanbal are the founders of the four Sunni schools of law. (*Fiqh* refers to Islamic law.)

It is said: "If one closely examines the *fiqh* of the four schools, one will never come across substantial difference in the basic matters" (p. 131).

Note: The quote above is typical of Islamic "sacred deception" (*taqiyya*). There are substantial differences among the four schools, but this must not be openly admitted. However, in more recent times, with the aid of the Internet and access to Muslim sources, the facts reveal the differences and contradictions.

Imam Abu **Hanifah** comes from Iraq and was the first school of fiqh to be founded. It is said he was born in 699 CE and died in 767 CE. He died, then, some 135 years after Muhammad's death in 632 CE, and also after the deaths of all the first four successors, Abu Bakr, Umar, Uthman, and Ali.

Imam **Malik** ibn Anas was born in Madinah in 712 CE, while others say in 713 CE. His family came from Yemen.

The next imam, **ash-Shafi'i**, is reported to have said: "There has not been placed on the earth a book which is closer to the Qur'an than the book of Malik." In addition, it is reported that he said, "There is nothing more useful after the Book of Allah than the Muwatta' of Malik" (pp. 154–155).

"Imam Muhammad ibn Idris **ash-Shafi'i** died in 938 CE and he belonged to the tribe of Quraysh and was thus a relative of the Prophet Muhammad" (p. 157). It is said that he studied the schools of both Hanafi and Malik.

Imam Ahmad ibn Muhammad **ibn Hanbal** was born in 780 CE. His father, Muhammad, is reported to have been a warrior and lived in Basra in Iraq. He began studying Islamic law at age sixteen and is reported to have memorized almost a million hadith. He based his opinions entirely on the Qur'an and the hadith. He died in 856 CE.

By the end of the ninth century CE, the four major Sunni schools had come to agree on a common ground, namely that the primary sources of Islamic law are:

1. The Qur'an
2. The Sunnah
3. *Ijma* (juristic consensus)
4. *Qiyas* (reasoning by analogy)

Part II: The Categories of Fiqh

Chapter 8: The Categories of Fiqh in the Shariah

The five categories of fiqh based on the Qur'an and the Sunnah are:

1. The obligatory
2. The recommended
3. The permissible

4. The disliked
5. The forbidden

The obligatory "is that which the Shariah demands with binding force that it be done."

The recommended "is that which the Shariah demands that it be done but not with binding force."

The forbidden "is that which the Shariah demands with binding force that it be abandoned."

The disliked "is that which the Shariah demands be abandoned but not with binding force."

The permissible "is that which the Shariah neither demands that it be done nor abandoned" (pp. 173–174).

There is not to be a double standard in Islam; what applies to the average Muslim also applies to the imam—Arabs and non-Arabs alike.

That which is forbidden, or haram, is also haram in Islam. "Anything that facilitates or leads to an act of adultery, theft, brigandage or murder, is also haram. One who brews, sells and distributes wine is committing haram just as much as a the person who drinks the alcohol, and in fact he is more wrongdoing since his act leads more than one person to do something haram, whereas the solitary drinker only destroys himself" (p. 179).

It is understood that Muslims must abstain from eating the following (pp. 186–187):

1. Pork. The pig is an animal whose habits—such as eating excrement and on occasion, its own young—are well known.
2. Carrion that has died a natural death or was killed in some manner
3. Blood poured from an animal by force—eating or drinking blood is forbidden
4. The flesh of a strangled animal
5. The flesh of an animal beaten to death
6. The flesh of an animal that dies in a fall
7. The flesh of an animal that is gored to death
8. The flesh of an animal a part of which is eaten by a wild beast
9. The flesh of an animal that dies a natural death
10. The flesh of an animal slaughtered for worship of an idol
11. Beasts of prey with canine teeth

"Hunting for the purpose of sport alone is detestable in the eyes of Shariah, but hunting for a purpose other than sport is lawful" (p. 189).

Part III: Family Relations

Chapter 9: *Az-Zawaj*, Marriage

"Allah created men and women for them to provide company for one another, love one another, procreate and live in peace and tranquility obeying the command of Allah and the direction of his Messenger" (p. 195).

Qur'an 16:72: "Allah has given you wives from among yourselves, and given you children and grandchildren from your wives, and provided good things for you."

Celibacy is not approved in Islam; rather marriage is considered an article of faith. Even in the Garden or Paradise men and women will have mates: "They will have there spouses of perfect purity" (Qur'an 2:24).

Muhammad wanted men to marry as soon as they were able. "Extra-marital relations are categorically prohibited except for a man's relations with his slave women" (p. 197).

A Muslim couple's lovemaking is a part of true worship of the Creator if one intends it thus (p. 198). The second purpose of marriage is to respond to the basic biological instinct of procreation, and parents are legally responsible for the education and maintenance of their children.

Imams Hanifah, Hanbal, and Malik considered marriage to be recommended, and for some to be obligatory, while Imam ash-Shafi'i said it was permissible.

It is reported in a hadith that the Messenger of Allah said: "Marriage is my Sunnah, so whoever does not practise my Sunnah is not of me" (p. 205).

Before marriage, a groom and a bride are not allowed to be together alone, because the Prophet said that when they are alone, another is present: *Shaytan* (Satan). Therefore, there is no idea of courtship in Islam. Both parties must consent to the marriage per Qur'an 2:232.

Marriage is a covenant, meaning a solemn agreement between them and which must be recorded in writing. No one can be coerced into marriage.

A man must not have more than four wives at a time (p. 210).

Note: Wealthy men in Muslim-dominated countries may have as many as four wives. The younger men often then are deprived and resort to other forms of sexuality. In Western countries where the law allows one wife, some Muslim men who are determined to live like Muhammad and be obedient to the Sunnah will have more than one wife. This is done in two ways: firstly, by keeping a wife in the Western country and another in another country; secondly, by keeping one legal wife and others to whom the husband is not legally married.

Chapter 10: The Marital Relationship in Islam

From Qur'an 4:34 we find that men have charge of women because Allah has preferred men above women and because men spend their wealth on women. Right-acting women are obedient, safeguarding their husband's interests in his absence as Allah has guarded them. If there are women whose disobedience is feared, they may be admonished, refused intimate relations, and then beaten. But if they obey, it is forbidden to look for a way to punish them.

Note: The idea of Allah giving guidance to beat women in certain circumstances has created numerous defenses of this practice in Western countries in particular. This we see in the following.

"Wife-beating is discouraged by the Messenger of Allah and by Muslim jurists. However, if the wife's behaviour is against the injunctions of Allah and the Sunnah of the Prophet, beating her in a light manner may become necessary. However, the Prophet has enjoined that she must not be beaten on the face or in such a way as may leave a mark on her body" (p. 217).

Note: It is not permissible for a Muslim to marry someone who associates others with Allah, and this would mean Christians. However, it is permitted for Muslim men to marry "People of the Book," meaning Jews and not Christians, though Christians are also People of the Book.

Imam Malik said marriage with a Jewish or Christian woman is permitted but generally discouraged and can be considered abhorrent (p. 223).

Chapter 11: Polygyny

Polygyny is the marrying of more than one wife. It is stated by Professor Doi that such a practice was common long before the era of Islam. When Islam emerged, polygyny was embraced but limited to four wives. The only Qur'anic verse that refers to polygyny is 4:3: "If you are afraid of not behaving justly towards orphans, then marry other permissible women, two, three or four. But if you are afraid of not treating them equally, then only one, or those you own as slaves."

Muslim jurists developed conditions for having more than one wife:

1. The husband should have enough financial capacity to look after the needs of the additional wives he has undertaken.
2. The husband must do equal justice to them all. Each wife should be treated equally in fulfilling their conjugal and other rights.

Polygyny is then permitted on the basis of both the Qur'an and the Sunnah.

Note: There is no attempt to clear up the circumstances of Muhammad's more than four wives. This fact is largely ignored and/or explained away, but it is part of the pattern, or Sunnah, of the Prophet.

Chapter 12: Unlawful Forms of Marriage

Mut'ah is the term for a temporary marriage. "Mut'ah is a forbidden form of marriage which is contracted for a short period in exchange for a fixed remuneration. It was a pre-Islamic contract which was allowed in the early formative period of Islam before the Shariah of Islam reached its completion" (p. 249).

Doi states that mut'ah marriage is harmful to society and is nothing more than prostitution. "There is consensus of the 'ulama that it is unlawful" (p. 250). The Shia branch of Islam, however, does permit it even today. Professor Doi decries the impact of this practice as it becomes known to those outside of Islam.

Chapter 13: *Mahr* (Dowry)

Mahr is a marriage gift made by the bridegroom to the bride. This is based upon Qur'an 4:4: "Give women their dowry [*saduqat*] as an outright gift." Generally, in European history, a dowry is paid by the bride to the bridegroom. In Islam, however, it is the opposite.

There are several circumstances that determine the amount of a dowry. These are:

educational qualifications, professional standing, and the wealth and social status of the bridegroom. Then there are the negotiations between the families. But the dowry belongs to the bride exclusively. Even in the event of a divorce, the dowry remains with the wife.

Chapter 14: *Talaq*: Divorce in Shariah

Talaq literally means to set an animal free.

"In Islam marriage is a contract and the contract should be made to work but not forced to work when it becomes impossible" (p. 266). The goal of Shariah law here is to establish a healthy family unit through marriage. Qur'an 4:35 and 4:130 speak of procedures to be undertaken in case of divorce.

Note: The seemingly lofty goal of Islam is stated [above], but the words are crafted so that just about anything could happen. Doi also states that other religions do not even allow divorce [p. 267], so that Islam's practice appears more equitable. My suspicion is that he has in mind the strong prohibitions the Roman Catholic Church and many very conservative Protestant groups enjoin. Yet it is well known that divorce is common among all Christian groups.

Divorce may be given orally or in writing, and it does not need to take place in the presence of witnesses. Yet the Qur'an says: "Then when they have reached the end of their 'iddah either retain them with correctness and courtesy or part from them with correctness and courtesy. Call two upright men from among yourselves as witnesses" (Qur'an 65:2).

If, in extreme circumstances, divorce must be announced, it is necessary to ascertain three things: the man should be sane, not be a minor, and should be of independent discretion. This announcing is rather complex, but if the man should say, "I divorce you" three times, and not necessarily on the same occasion, meeting other requirements, the divorce is complete.

Now if the statements of divorce are separated over a period of time, a time when the husband might change his mind, "the marriage between the parties subsists and the husband retains his marital authority over his wife. He may therefore, have access to his wife even without her permission and can treat her as his wife" (p. 276).

The process of divorce can be ended by saying words like "I take you back," or the return can be effected through an action like resuming sexual relations, or kissing each other" (p. 278). There is a limit, though, on how many times a divorce can begin and end—three times is that limit. It must be noted that among the four schools of fiqh in Islam, there are differences of opinion.

Note: The husband can force his wife to have sex with him.

The laws regarding divorce and separation are highly complex and, to me, confusing. Then, given the variations among the four schools of jurisprudence in Islam, detailing these does not seem profitable.

Chapter 15: *Khul'*: Divorce at the Request of the Wife

Khul' means the removing of clothing from the body and is derived from Qur'an 2:187, where a wife is the subject: "They are clothing for you and you for them."

In Shariah law, a wife can divorce her husband if sufficient grounds exist (p. 297). A ground for divorce would be if the husband were cruel. We find warrant for this is Qur'an 4:128: "If a woman fears cruelty or aversion on her husband's part, there is nothing wrong in the couple becoming reconciled. Reconciliation is better. But people are prone to selfish greed. If you do good and have *taqwa*, Allah is aware of what you do."

Khul' must only be sought in extreme circumstances. The Messenger of Allah said: "If any woman asks her husband for divorce without any specific harm [done her], the fragrance of the Garden will be unlawful to her" (Qur'an 8:174) (p. 300).

A jurist (*qadi*) can grant divorce for:

1. Habitual ill-treatment of the wife
2. Non-fulfillment of the terms of the marriage contract
3. Insanity
4. Incurable incompetency
5. Quitting the conjugal domicile without making provision for the wife
6. Any other similar cause which in the opinion of the *qadi* justifies a divorce

Chapter 16: *'Iddah*: The Period of Waiting; Guidance from Qur'an and Sunnah

'Iddah means number and refers to the woman's required waiting period before remarriage after the death of a husband or separation or divorce from him (p. 307). The Qur'an speaks to this: "Divorced women should wait by themselves for three menstrual cycles" (Qur'an 2:228).

If a woman is past menstruation or has not yet menstruated, she is to wait three months. But the time for pregnant women is when they give birth.

Here is a summation of *'iddah*:

1. Three menstruations for women who still menstruate
2. Three months for women who have not reached or have passed the age of menstruation
3. Four months and ten days for widows
4. For pregnant women, whether divorced or widowed, until they deliver
5. No time period for women whose marriage is not yet consummated

Chapter 17: Maintenance, Custody, and Guardianship

There are directions for the maintenance of a divorced wife when the husband is poor. Also, a mother should nurse their children for two full years, according to Qur'an 2:233. After two years, the child should be weaned, according to Qur'an 31:14.

There are laws regarding the maintenance of parents, poor relatives, orphans, and the destitute in general. Regarding parents, Qur'an 17:23–24 speaks to this:

> Your Lord has decreed that you should worship no one but Him, and that you should show kindness to your parents. Whether one or both of them reach old age with you, do not say "Ugh!" to them out of irritation and do not be harsh with them but speak to them with gentleness and generosity. Take them under

your wing, out of mercy, with due humility and say: "Lord, show mercy to them as they did in looking after me when I was small."

Part IV: Crime and Punishment

Chapter 18: Criminal Law and Punishment

"When a group within the society denies the rights of another group, it must be taken to task" (p. 338).

Criminal law is referred to as *'Uqubat*, which means "consequences." Shariah law emphasizes fulfilling the rights of all individuals as well as the public at large. "A Muslim will be punished for a crime committed even if it was carried out far away from the Islamic community" (p. 340).

"The qadi or jurist or Shariah judge must abide by the fixed laws of both the Qur'an and the Sunnah. If not, this qadi becomes a wrongdoer."

Hadd (hudud is its plural) is Arabic for prevention, restraint, or prohibition. It contains the restrictive and preventive ordinances, or statutes, of Allah concerning things that are either *halal*, or permitted, or things *haram*, unlawful or forbidden.

Here is a list of thirteen crimes that require punishment:

1. Killing
2. Injury
3. Adultery
4. Unsubstantiated accusations of fornication or adultery
5. Drinking wine
6. Theft
7. Rebellion
8. Brigandage
9. Reneging on Islam
10. Heresy
11. Cursing Allah and cursing the prophets and angels
12. Working magic
13. Giving up prayer and fasting

There are special *hudud* for abandonment of the obligations of Islam (p. 341). The list is:

1. Someone who refuses to pray
2. Someone has not reneged but affirms the prayer and yet says, "I will not pray." He is given a respite until the time of the next prayer. If he does not pray, he is killed.
3. Someone refusing to pay *zakah*. It is taken from him by force, and if he dies, his blood is of no consequence.
4. Someone refusing to go on hajj. He is left to Allah.

The *zakah* is a tax and is paid into the *bayt al-mal*, or public treasury. Abu Bakr, the second caliph following Muhammad, was sent out against a tribe that refused to pay the Muslim tax since such action was "tantamount to denial of one of the fundamental pillars of Islam, rebellion against the caliph and a violation of the rights of the poor" (p. 342).

Note: Muhammad maintained his armies, to some extent, by means of the collection of this tax.

There are four classifications of punishments.

1. Physical punishments that include amputation of a hand, flogging, and stoning to death
2. Restrictions of freedom, which includes imprisonment or exile
3. Imposition of compensatory payments, as in the case of manslaughter and causing injury to others
4. Warnings given by a *qadi*

Hadd punishments are awarded in the following seven cases:

1. Penalties exacted for committing murder, manslaughter, or bodily harm
2. Punishment for theft: the amputation of a hand
3. Punishment for fornication or adultery: stoning for a married person and one hundred lashes for an unmarried person
4. Punishment for unsubstantiated allegations of sexual impropriety: eighty lashes
5. Punishment for renouncing Islam: death
6. Punishment for inebriation: eighty lashes
7. Punishment for highway robbery: crucifixion, death, amputation of an alternate leg and arm, or exile, according to the seriousness of the crime and at the discretion of the qadi or *amir*

Punishment for acts that are not listed above, called ta'zir, are intended to disgrace the criminal for a shameful act. Such punishments may include lashes, imprisonment, fine, or a warning.

Punishments are intended for the criminal alone and not for any family member. A child will not be given hadd punishment for a crime, nor will an insane person. If a crime is committed while one is asleep he will not be punished (p. 350). The same is true for one who commits crime while under duress. However, they are not forgiven.

Chapter 19: Criminal Law and Punishment Continued

Qur'an 5:32 reads: "So We decreed for the tribe of Israel that if someone kills another person—unless it is in retaliation for someone else or for causing corruption in the earth—it is as if he had murdered all mankind. And if anyone gives life to another person, it is as if he had given life to all mankind."

Note: This passage from the Qur'an can be used in many ways. The current application is that if anyone acts against Islam, genuine or perceived as it is today, terrorism is justified even when the perceived injury occurred many centuries earlier. Islam views all that is not Islam as enemy and any action taken against any Muslim at any place or time as a punishable act. Terrorists will justify their actions because of the Crusades a millenium ago.

In jihad against the enemies of Islam, it is natural that some of the combatants will be killed. However, one forfeits one's right to life in the following situations:

1. In the law of retaliation applied against someone who killed someone else intentionally
2. Capital punishment for traitors who plot to overthrow or rebel against Islamic governance
3. A married man or woman who is given the hadd punishment for adultery
4. For highway robbery, which we will examine in more depth later, but which according to some includes crimes like breaking and entering

Any form of abortion is haram with the exception of the necessity of saving the life of the mother.

Killing a Muslim is haram. "As for anyone who kills a mu'min deliberately, his repayment is Hell, remaining in it timelessly, for ever. Allah is angry with him and has cursed him, and has prepared for him a terrible punishment" (Qur'an 4:93).

One does not have the right to commit suicide. Islamic belief is that there is a great punishment awaiting the suicide in the next world. In the Qur'an, Allah commands: "And kill not one another" (Qur'an 4:29). The author Doi states, "This also applies to so-called suicide bombers" (p. 356).

Note: This last law providing "great punishment" for a suicide bomber is at variance with the widely known belief that one sure way—and perhaps the only sure way—to Paradise is to die in violent jihad. Here is a typical example of sacred deception. A Muslim reading the words on page 356 would understand the statement to be fabricated.

"You who have imam! Retaliation is prescribed for you in the case of people killed: free man for free man, slave for slave, female for female (Qur'an 2:178).

"When a homicide is pardoned, he is to be given one hundred strokes of the cane and imprisoned for a year" (p. 363).

Concerning adultery and fornication: "It is immaterial whether one or both parties have their own spouses or are unmarried. It is also immaterial whether it is with the consent of both parties" (p. 363). According to Ibn Abi'd Dunya, such action is akin to associating partners with Allah. "The Prophet is reported to have said that if a person commits adultery, Allah will open for him in his grave eight doors of Hell from which will emerge scorpions and snakes to trouble him until the Day of Rising" (p. 364).

There are other forbidden acts that can lead to adultery. There is "adultery of the legs," meaning to walk toward a woman with bad intentions, "adultery of the hands," which has to do with touching, patting, or caressing, and "adultery of the eyes," or casting lustful glances.

One hadith, from 'Ubadah ibn as-Samit, reported the Prophet said that if an offender is not married and commits adultery, he should be given one hundred lashes and exiled for one year. But if married, give one hundred lashes and stone to death (p. 366).

Professor Doi suggests that the harsh punishments are intended to act as a deterrent. Islam commands purity of the sex life both for men and women, thus punishments are carried out publically for all to see.

Sodomy, whether perpetrated on men or women, "is an act intended to satisfy a sexual perversion, for which there is a hadd punishment when it is practiced by men on men" (p. 369). Allah, in Qur'an 7:80–81, called sodomy or homosexual behavior for men depraved.

There is a hadith, that of Al-Bayhaqi, Shu'ab al-imam, that reports: "Whoever has anal intercourse with his wife, Allah will not look at him on the Day of Rising." And in addition, the Prophet said: "If a man commits an act of sex with a man, they are both adulterers and if a woman commits such an act with a woman, then both of them are adulteresses" (p. 371). Yet other hadith say that both partners in sodomy must be stoned to death.

Among the four schools of fiqh there are differing interpretations concerning sodomy; some recommend light punishment and others not light.

Bestiality—sex with animals—is addressed. From At-Tirmidhi come these words: "Whoever you find who has had sexual relations with an animal then kill him and kill the animal." Other jurists say that only the human is to be killed.

Acts of adultery must be witnessed by four other people in order to be punished, and so it is said: "During the whole life of the Prophet, not a single case of adultery was established by evidence of four eye-witnesses" (p. 374).

If a Muslim man were to find his wife committing adultery, he would still have to produce four upstanding male witnesses who had seen the act, which is generally impossible. In that case, the husband would have to swear an oath in the Shariah court four times to the fact of the adultery, and also invoke a curse upon himself if he was not telling the truth. But more, if the wife four times swears an oath that she is innocent and invokes a curse upon herself to prove that she is innocent, she will be acquitted.

Note: The requirement to have four witnesses to an act of adultery for a conviction is ludicrous at best. And the eyewitnesses have to have the best credentials. This silly concept is intended to show how perfect were the early days of Islam and how pure were Muhammad and his companions. In reality, this charade succinctly illustrates the Muslim practice of sacred deception, or, telling of lies to promote, defend, or advance Islam. One of the interesting statements found in this chapter of Doi is: "Every Muslim is supposed to guard the honour and respect of a fellow man and not expose the hidden failings of any other Muslim" [p. 376].

In Qur'an 5:33 we find: "The reprisal against those who wage war on Allah and His Messenger, and go about the earth corrupting it, is that they should be killed or crucified, or have their alternate hands and feet cut off, or be banished from the land."

Then, anyone who commits robbery, disrupting another's way of life, deserves capital punishment. So, for robbery or brigandage the punishment includes execution, cutting off the head, crucifixion, cutting off the right hand and left foot, or exile from the land (imprisonment outside the person's hometown).

From the hadith by Ibn Hisham, *Sira*, the Life of Muhammad, Vol. 2, pp. 271–272:

> When the Prophet Muhammad and his Companions had just returned to Madinah after the battle of the Ditch, the archangel Jibril appeared and commanded the Prophet to punish the Jews of Bani Qurayzah for their violation of their agreement and for conspiring with the enemy while the battle of the Ditch was in progress. The Jews asked that their judgment be left to Sa'd ibn Mu'adh of the tribe of Aws who were their allies. The Prophet accepted their request and made Sa' ibn Mu'adh the judge. Sa'd gave judgment according

to the Tawrah that all the fighting men should be put to death, and that the women and children should become slaves of the Muslims, and the verdict was carried out. Nevertheless, each man was offered Islam, and thus life, before execution but they refused.

In cases of theft, we have Qur'an 5:38: "As for thieves, both male and female, cut off their hands in reprisal for what they have done: an object lesson from Allah. Allah is Almighty, All-Wise." The jurists Hanifah and Malik have differing opinions as to the extent of the punishment.

In the section about intoxicants, "Drinking wine or alcohol and taking intoxicating drugs are forbidden in Islam." Qur'an 2:219 says: "They will ask you about alcoholic drinks and gambling. Say, 'There is great wrong in both of them and also certain benefits for mankind. But the wrong in them is greater than the benefit.'"

Professor Doi's comment here is: "The above verse as well as indicating its benefits pointed out the evils of wine-drinking but did not prohibit it." He appeals to Qur'an 4:42, "You who have iman! Do not approach the prayer when you are drunk, so that you will know what you are saying." However, Qur'an 5:90–91 is quoted where Allah abrogates 4:42, in that he says drinking intoxicants and gambling are the work of Shaytan. It is concluded then that all hemp, hashish, marijuana, opium, heroin, methadone, cocaine, ecstasy, and other drugs are equally haram. And the jurists of the four schools agree that a drunkard must be punished by flogging (p. 399).

Reneging on Islam (*riddah*) is turning to another religion or to no religion at all, i.e., atheism, and this through either actions or words. "Rejection of the Obligatory practices, like salah, zahah, siyam (Fasting in the month of Ramadan), and Hajj Pilgrimage also amount to acts of Riddah. Likewise, if one imitates the practices of non-Muslims in their religion or their prayers etc., and dresses in their clothing and attends their places of worship it is considered an act of reneging on Islam" (p. 400).

The hadd punishment for reneging is clear in the hadith: "Whosoever changes his din [from Islam to something else] then kill him" (Al-Bukhari, citation not given). Professor Doi states: "The punishment by death in the case of reneging on Islam has been unanimously agreed upon by all four schools of Islam jurisprudence" (p. 401).

Note: The crime here is apostasy. Only a Muslim can commit it. Shia Muslims tend to see Sunni Muslims as apostates and the reverse is true, and that is why each will send suicide bombers into the other's mosques.

In battle against non-Muslims, or against apostates, it is forbidden "to flee from the enemy unless they are more than twice the Muslims either in numbers or in force and power, in which case it is permissible to flee" (p. 403).

Chapter 20: Mirath: Laws of Inheritance

The laws of inheritance are lengthy and complex and differ among the four schools. An overall look at Islamic inheritance is: "The rules regulating inheritance in the Shariah are based on the principle that property which belonged to the deceased should devolve on those who by reason of consanguinity or marital relations can expect to be beneficiaries of it in proportion to the strength of their claim" (p. 413).

In Qur'an 4:7: "Men receive a share of what their parents and relatives leave, and women receive a share of what their parents and relatives leave, a fixed share, no matter whether it is a little or a lot."

From pages 424 to 431 are diagrams that depict how inheritance works depending upon varying circumstances.

The impediments to succession of anything that might be inherited are:

1. Homicide
2. Difference of religion
3. Slavery

One who commits homicide does not inherit. Someone of a different religion does not inherit. Slavery is also a bar—that is, a slave will not inherit anything from an owner or master. The slave is treated as property and can be inherited.

Funeral costs are to be kept at a minimum, and to cut these, every corpse has a seamless shroud. "According to the Hanafi School, the husband is responsible for a wife's funeral expenses even though he himself is dead and even if the wife is rich" (p. 438).

Chapter 21: Shares of Each Heir

Islamic law concerning inheritance is complex to the point that it must be looked at case by case. In general, though, it can be said that male heirs receive the bulk of any estate.

Note: Essentially, Islamic law determines the distribution of any wealth following a death. It is not possible to make personal decisions. There seems to be distrust on Islam's part of an individual making a decision as to how much and to whom inheritance might go.

Chapter 22: Disposal of Property

This chapter is largely an expansion into areas discussed in the previous chapters.

The lead paragraph for chapter 22 reads: "In the jahiliyyah (times of ignorance) period before Islam, Arabs disposed of their property as they liked because no law concerning bequests or inheritance existed to guide them. They could make a bequest in favour of anyone, depriving their own parents, children and wives. At times the bequest was made in favour of rich and influential members of the clan."

Note: It may appear that Islamic laws of inheritance are an improvement over the times of ignorance, referring to that era prior to Muhammad's ascension. In reality, it is an intrusion of the Muslim clerics into the lives of the ummah, the Muslim community.

Chapter 23: *Tijarah*: Trade and Commerce

Islam calls for honesty in business dealings. "You who have iman! Do not consume one another's property by false means, but only by means of mutually agreed trade. And do not kill yourselves. Allah is Most Merciful to you" (Qur'an 4:29).

Professor Doi states: "The Qur'an thus enjoins the cardinal values of equity, justice, mutual co-operation and self-sacrifice for organizing the socio-economic fabric of Islamic society" (p. 546).

Men and women can equally engage in business, buying and selling one to the other.

A major section in this chapter has to do with the laws of contract, detailing the ins and outs of offer and acceptance.

Note: This material applies to business between Muslims, for the most part. Certainly this would be expected during the times when the Qur'an and the hadith were coming into being. I question whether or not the laws dealing with business apply to the non-Muslim world. Could it be that sacred deception is permitted in such situations?

Chapter 24: Distribution of Wealth

Under the heading "Ill-gotten Wealth" is: "Money or property which is acquired through unjust means is definitely unclean and unlawful, and anyone who makes use of it or spends it on his or his family's needs does himself and them great harm. As the Prophet has warned, such a person's prayers will not find acceptance with Allah, his supplications will not be answered, his petitions will not be granted, and if he does good deeds they will avail him nothing. In the Next world, there will be no share for him in the special favours of Allah, exalted is He, unless Allah forgives him" (p. 580).

Usury, or interest charged on money or goods loaned, is considered wrong for Muslims. It is said that Allah permitted trade but not riba, meaning usury.

Qur'an 2:278: "If you do not [forgo riba], know that it means war from Allah and His Messenger. But if you make tawbah you may have your capital, without wronging and without being wronged." The idea is that charging usury does not increase wealth, but rather the opposite.

Note: Qur'an 30:39 looks like something a modern health-wealth preacher might say: "What you give with usurious intent, aiming to get back a greater amount from people's wealth, does not become greater with Allah. But anything you give as *Zakah* seeking the Face of Allah—all who do that will get back twice as much."

If one receives a gift after giving a loan, he commits usury. Even a small amount of money received for giving a loan is a "far greater crime than adultery" (p. 587). This is supported by a hadith from At-Tabarani. Muslims are warned that usury leads to poverty, and this, again, is supported by a hadith from At-Tabarani.

Professor Doi provides this history of usury in Arabia: "The thoroughness of the Prophetic condemnation of usury which was made after the dawn of Islam, leaves no room for any part for it, however indirect, in our transactions. The Messenger of Allah cursed the receiver [literally, the eater] of interest, and the clerk who writes the bond, and the two witnesses thereof, and declared them all equally culpable" (p. 589).

Aspects of usury and gambling that the Prophet forbade are:

1. Selling commodities or land not possessed by the seller
2. Selling animals still unborn
3. Selling birds and fish not yet caught
4. Selling a ewe which had not been milked for a long time to impress on the buyer

falsely that it is mild and always abundant
5. Selling commodities the defects of which have been disguised
6. Selling commodities while allowing the buyer to touch them only, without seeing or examining them
7. Selling a piece of cloth without exposing it adequately to the buyer
8. Selling commodities haphazardly without weighing or measuring
9. Selling agricultural produce that is not yet ripe
10. Prearranging with a man to bid a high price for a commodity, so as to induce others to buy it at a higher price

The *bayt al-mal* is the public treasury, and the wealth therein is to be treated as the Muslims' wealth. It is considered Allah's trust, and the leader of Islam is a trustee whose duty it is to spend it on the common good for all Muslims. This leader is to receive only a fixed stipend.

The sources for the funds that go into the bayt al-mal are:

1. *Zakah*, which is one of the five pillars of Islam. It demands that 2.5 percent of "held monetary wealth" is to be used for the welfare of the ummah. This tax is payable on wealth in terms of cash, gold and silver, trade merchandise, certain crops, and herds of cattle and flocks of sheep and goats. Non-Muslims are exempted from the payment of zakah.
2. *Sadaqah* is voluntary generosity to the poor, over and above the zakah. It is to be used "for the sake of Allah to relieve the problems and sufferings of fellow human beings" (p. 603).
3. *Jizah* is the annual poll tax levied on non-Muslims living under Islamic governance. Payment of this tax exempts them from military service. Qur'an 9:29 establishes this tax: "Fight those of the people who were given the Book who do not have iman in Allah and the Last Day and do not make haram what Allah and His Messenger have made haram and do not take as their din the din of Truth, until they pay the jizah with their own hands in a state of complete abasement."
4. *Kharaj* is a tax levied on the produce of landed property owned by non-Muslims living under Islamic governance. This can amount to 10 or 20 percent.
5. *Fay'* is property captured from the enemy without fighting any battles with them.
6. *'Ushr (Zakah)* is a tax of 10 percent to be paid on the produce grown with natural rainfall, watering by springs and rivers, of the landed property of Muslims.
7. *'Ushr* is a 10 percent tax on wealth made on trade of the People of the Book when they carry out business outside the land in which they reside.
8. *Khums* is a 20 percent tax of whatever a Muslim army obtains as booty when fighting with enemies and gains a victory and is paid on what wealth is left after paying the fighting men. This is based on Qur'an 8:41: "Know that when you take any booty a fifth of it belongs to Allah, and to the Messenger, and to close relatives, orphans, the very poor and travellers."
9. *Dara'ib* is a levy made by an Islamic ruler in the event of an emergency.
10. If an estate is left by someone who has no heirs, the estate goes to the *bayt al-mal*.

There are also rulings as to the right of the poor and handicapped. Miserliness is roundly condemned in Shariah law. "Give your relatives their due, and the very poor and travellers but do not squander what you have" (Qur'an 17:26). Muslims are instructed to earn a lawful living and not merely depend on charity.

Note: Professor Doi decries Western economics and banking systems, claiming that Islamic forms are far superior. I view it as a desperate and untruthful presentation. Muslim-dominated countries are amongst the poorest in the world, and the unemployment rates are very high. To be a full-fledged and faithful Muslim requires most of every day and would preclude most employment opportunities. My experience shows me that in non-Muslim-dominated countries, few Muslims pay the taxes they are called to pay. Again, in this chapter, we find evidence of sacred deception.

Part VII: External and Other Relations

Chapter 25: Siyar: Military Campaigns and International Relations

Note: Sadly, this chapter is mostly sacred deception intended to make the Islamic community appear harmless and peace loving.

Chapter 26: Non-Muslims and the Shariah

"Non-Muslims who live under Islamic governance and enjoy the rights enshrined in the contract they make under the Shariah are called *ahl adh-dhimman* or *dhimmis*, covenanted people" (p. 648). These people are guaranteed the protection of their life, property, and honor, just as Muslims are. Dhimmis are "people of the abode of Islam."

Jurists have created three classifications of non-Muslim citizens:

1. Those who have not fought but have negotiated a treaty in which is mention of their jizyah and the kharaj payment on their lands. The Muslim ruler is duty bound to observe all the conditions of their treaty.
2. Those who have been fought and conquered, and are compelled to pay the jizah
3. Those who are passing through, for example as traders

"Since the dhimmis are under dhimmat-Allah, the protection of Allah, they enjoy religious, administrative and political autonomy—a right guaranteed to them in return for their loyalty and the payment of the tax, called jizyah, which is utilized in the defense and administration of the commonweal" (p. 651).

The fundamental rights of non-Muslims are:

1. Their protection from all external threats
2. Their protection from all internal tyranny and persecution

Professor Doi clearly states that neither the religion of Islam nor the Shariah law can be forced on anyone against their will "according to the teachings of the Qur'an and the Sunnah of the Prophet" (p. 660). Qur'an 2:255 is cited in this regard: "There is no coercion into the din. Right guidance has become clearly distinct from error."

"According to the Shariah, all mankind is one entity, all are the people of Muhammad, but divided into those who accept him and those who reject him, and yet Muslims should think of the well-being of all human beings. All the provisions granted by the Shariah are meant for the welfare of the world. These provisions of the Shariah were revealed 1,400 years ago" (pp. 661–662).

Note: Qur'an 2 was revealed in Medina and early on [the first year] when Muhammad had little opposition. But later he ran into trouble with Jewish and Christian tribes. And in Medina other revelations were received that abrogated Qur'an 2:255 and all the nice things said about the People of the Book. So what we have in this chapter is intended to deceive the modern reader, since the falseness of Professor Doi's comments in this particular chapter is clear to anyone who is acquainted with daily news reports.

Chapter 27: Jihad

It is reported in hadith that the Messenger of Allah, Muhammad, defined the "way of Allah" in this way: "'So who is in the way of Allah?' He said, 'Whoever fights so that the Word of Allah may be uppermost then he is in the way of Allah'" (from Abu Musa al-Ash'ari).

The earliest permission to conduct jihad is found in Qur'an 22:39–40:

> Permission to fight is given to those who are fought against because they have been wronged—truly Allah has the power to come to their support—those who were expelled from their homes without any right, merely for saying "Our Lord is Allah" (if Allah had not driven some people back by means of others, monasteries, churches, synagogues and mosques, where Allah's name is mentioned much, would have been pulled down and destroyed. Allah will certainly help those who help Him—Allah is All-Strong, Almighty).

In the Qur'an 2:190 we find: "Fight in the Way of Allah against those who fight you, but do not go beyond the limits. Allah does not love those who go beyond the limits." This is followed by 2:193: "Fight them until there is no more fitnah and the din belongs to Allah alone. If they cease, there should be no enmity towards any but wrongdoers."

Permission was given to wage jihad in order to protect the Muslims and to preserve their fledgling community. "Permission for jihad was granted at that time so that the order of Allah could be established firmly on earth" (p. 668). Therefore, it was in the second year after the flight, or Hijrah, to Medina that jihad was made obligatory, as seen in Qur'an 2:216: "Fighting is prescribed for you even if it is hateful to you. It may be that you hate something when it is good for you and it may be that you love something when it is bad for you. Allah knows and you do not know."

Jihad is fard, or obligatory, just as are iman (faith), taharah (purification), salah (prayers), zakah (tax), siyam (fasting), and hajj (pilgrimage). Qur'an 4:171 reads: "You who have iman! Take all necessary precautions, then go out to fight in separate groups or go out as one body."

Jihad is obligatory for the following:

1. Those who are Muslim
2. Those who are male
3. Those who are sane

4. Those who have reached the age of puberty
5. Those who have sufficient means to maintain their families until they return from jihad

Qur'an 48:18: "There is not constraint on the blind, nor on the lame, nor on the sick. We will admit all who obey Allah and His Messenger into Gardens with rivers flowing under them. But We will punish with a painful punishment anyone who turns his back."

"Women can also render service in jihad by giving water to the warriors and bandaging and nursing the wounded" (p. 674).

Jihad is not only fighting, using force. It can also be practiced through the use of speech and writing, particularly when the wrongdoer is the established authority (p. 675). And jihad can be conducted with money and property, meaning to materially support warriors.

Before waging jihad, Muslim forces should summon their enemies to accept Islam. If they refuse to become dhimmis and pay the tax, they can be fought. "Fight those of the people who were given the Book who do not have iman in Allah and the Last Day and do not make haram what Allah and His Messenger have made haram and do not take as their din the din of truth, until they pay the jizyah with their own hands in a state of complete abasement" (Qur'an 9:29).

Other instructions about waging jihad include: no civilians are to be harmed; no cases of high handedness; no devastation of houses and crops; old people, invalids, women, and children must not be killed unless they engage in fighting; no places of worship can be destroyed, nor their priests and monks killed (p. 679).

As concerning prisoners of war, Muslims have five choices:

1. They may be killed
2. Ransom them
3. Enslave them
4. Set them free
5. Take jizyah from them

All the choices are made on the basis of how an enemy fought and other personal concerns. Prisoners must not be tortured or punished and they must be cared for. But captives are not to be taken until many have been killed. "It is not fitting for a prophet to take captives until he has let much blood in the land. You desire the goods of the dunya, whereas Allah desires the akhirah. Allah is Almighty, All-Wise" (Qur'an 8:68).

Note: Despite the words of Professor Doi, the Muslim fighters we read about nearly every day in the newspapers are definitely not following through on the "high ideals" for jihad. Not even close! So, is this merely more sacred deception?

In the above verse from the Qur'an, the dunya are the captives and akhirah is the blood of the enemies. Two of my Qur'ans obscure this verse altogether in order, one would suppose, to hide the vicious intent of the verse.

In terms of spoils of war, the amir, or Islamic ruler, takes one fifth of it and the fighters divide the rest.

"Casting terror into enemies' hearts" that is mentioned in the hadith by Sahih Muslim is fundamentally different from terrorism, Professor Doi claims. The professor claims that Muhammad conducted himself "miraculously"—unlike, for instance, the terrorism practiced in the French Revolution.

The terrorism, including suicide bombing, that we see in the present battles fought by the Islamic State, and other Islamic militants, is unacceptable in Shariah law, and completely haram or forbidden—so the professor states (pp. 683–684).

Note: It is expected that Professor Doi would want to distance himself and mainline Islam from what the Islamic State and other Muslim groups are doing presently. Yet these terrorists claim they are following the Sunnah of Muhammad while declaring that to *not* do so is not Islamic. Who has it right?

One final word: Is it possible that Professor Doi thinks he can fool those of us who keep up with world news? Or is it simply that he must present Islam in the best possible light and as such, is perpetrating another form of jihad—that of the pen?

5

SHARIA LAW: A SUMMARY FOR SHIA ISLAM

Based on *The Laws of Islam*[1] by Ayatullah Modarresi

The rulings found in this source are complex and lengthy, and there is much redundancy. The format for *The Laws of Islam* is this: the subject of the law is presented, then support for the law in the Qur'an and hadith are presented, then extensive rulings are given from the chief jurists of Shia Islam having to do with the interpretation and implementation of the laws. It is not possible to present more than a smattering of the more important aspects of Shia Shariah law. Grand Ayatullah Sayyid M. Taqi al-Husayni al-Modarresi's book is available through Amazon.

Part One: Islamic Doctrines from the Qur'an and Sunna

Here the central doctrines of Islam are stated and attested to by both the Qur'an and the Sunna.

First: About divine unity, or Tawhid, which means the unity of Allah, who is a monad and has no partners.

Second: Concerning divine justice, or 'Adi, which means that Allah wrongs no one. The scales of justice determine outcomes in terms of Paradise or hellfire, the weight of good deeds versus bad deeds.

Third: Concerning divine messages and messengers, which refer to the revelation of the Qur'an from Allah through Gabriel, then through Muhammad, with Muhammad being the final messenger or prophet. Islam is to prevail over all religions, as attested to in Quran 9:33: "It is He who has sent His Messenger with the guidance and the religion of truth, that He may make it prevail over all religions, though the polytheists should be averse." Then Qur'an 3:132: "And obey Allah and the Messenger so that you may be granted (His) mercy." The Sunna and the hadith show that Muhammad is the seal and

---

[1] Grand Ayatullah Sayyid M. Taqi al-Husayni al-Modarresi, *The Laws of Islam* (Enlight Press, 2016).

the peak of the prophets. To obey Allah is to obey Muhammad and copy Muhammad's pattern of life.

Note: Though there is much said about the mercy of Allah, it is obvious that Islam is a works-based religion. Faith in Allah and Muhammad is one thing, but this does not result in assurance of Paradise. What matters is tipping the scales by good deeds outweighing bad deeds.

Fourth: Concerning *imamate* (the imamate is the council of imams, the ruling body of Shia Islam) and imams—just as the message is not complete without a messenger, the religion is not complete without a leader, or imam. This imam is appointed by Allah alone and not by people, since the imam is assisted by Allah and knows Allah, his religion, and its disciplines, and is far removed from worldly concerns and ambitions. "When Allah chooses one of His servants to hold authority over others, He opens his chest, deposits springs of wisdom in his heart, and inspires him with knowledge" (p. 32). This concept finds support in Qur'an 32:24: "And amongst them We appointed imams to guide (the people) by Our command, when they had been patient and had conviction in Our signs."

The imam is "like the luminous full moon, is a fire upon the hill, is a rain cloud, bringing a downpour of relief, is a trusted friend, is Allah's trustee upon His earth, purifies mankind of sins and cleanses them of imperfections, is peerless in his era, no one else comes close" (p. 35).

The concept of a grand ruling imam is so central in Shia Islam that it is said by Imam al-Sadiq, "Whoever spends a night, not knowing the Imam of his time, shall die the death of ignorance" (p. 37).

In Shia Islam there are Twelve Imams. From a leading imam, Safi, come these words: "The Imams after me are twelve, so whoever loves and follows them has attained success and salvation, and whoever refrains from them has strayed and erred."

These words are said to be a quote from Muhammad, who goes on to say to 'Ali, who is the first imam after whom there will be eleven others and the last being the Mahdi "who shall fill the earth with justice and fairness. So woe to those who hate them! O 'Ali! Were a man to love you and your offspring, so Allah would resurrect him with you and your progeny, and you are all with me in the highest levels. You are the divider between Paradise and Hellfire. Those who love you will enter Paradise and those who hate you will enter Hell" (pp. 37–38).

Following this is a lengthy section on the Shia Muslim's responsibility to the imam.

Note: This fourth point sharply separates Shia Islam from Sunni Islam. The imams of Shia Islam are the ones to be obeyed, both in their past rulings and in their current rulings. Not being under the authority of a Shia imam means one is on the wrong path and will end up in hell. Thus arises the animosity between Sunni and Shia Muslims, with each seeing the other as apostate. It is famously boasted that Sunni and Shia Muslims will unite, if necessary, against a common foe such as the polytheists, i.e., Christians.

Fifth: Concerning the resurrection and the afterlife, these two doctrinal items are part of what a Muslim must believe, and are attested to in Qur'an 45:26: "Say, 'It is Allah who gives you life, then he makes you die. Then He will gather you on the Day of Resurrection, in which there is no doubt. But most people do not know.'"

Note: As a result of this quote from the Qur'an, Islam believes that Allah sets the very moment of death, which cannot be changed by even a second.

Part Two: Rulings for Acts of Worship ('*Ibadat*)

Islam, as the seal of divine messages, details every aspect of life including "doctrines, ethics, worship, individual and social conduct, and mankind's connection to everything in the universe" (p. 50). Indeed, "Whoever takes Islam as a religion must follow the way of Islam completely in all aspects of one's life, adopting its behaviours and practices according to the divine laws" (p. 50).

These rulings are based on the Qur'an, the Sunna, reason, and consensus of the leading jurists—this last is known as *fiqh*. Following the verdicts is necessary, since it is acknowledged that few if any have the time to "spare" to determine properly the right courses of action and belief. Therefore, the imamate is necessary. This is referred to as *taqlid*, which is acting in accordance with the opinion of a jurist, or *mujtahid*, who possesses the necessary qualifications. One of these qualifications is *bulugh* and refers to one who has reached the legal age of maturity.

It is held by most Shia authorities that "a person does not have to follow the most-learned jurist. Instead it is more appropriate that they choose the one who is best in piety, learning, and practical competence" (p. 51). The conditions for being a mujtahid are:

1. At the age of legal maturity
2. Of sound mind
3. Of correct belief
4. Of just conduct
5. Male
6. Living
7. Of pure birth, that he was not born from fornication or adultery

Note: In reality this allows a Muslim to find a jurist they think will favor them.

In regard to maturity, bulugh, or age, is this: "A male child reaches maturity, normally, at fifteen years of age, while a female child reaches maturity at twelve, though a female child can reach maturity as young as nine in some conditions" (p. 54).

Note: Here is a clear case of defending Muhammad's marriage to nine-year-old Aisha, a historical fact that Muslims traditionally are embarrassed about. Also, since a female cannot be a jurist, there is no reason other than to present a twelve-year- or even nine-year-old female as being mature.

Ritual Purity

Those who are jurists must be ritually clean. In a hadith by Mizan al-Hikma, the Prophet said, "Clean yourselves as much as you are able, for verily Allah built Islam upon cleanliness and none shall enter Paradise save he who is clean."

Note: Though the topic of ritual cleansing is a major aspect of Shariah law, let it be noted here that this cleanliness has nothing to do with the heart or the mind—the inner core of who a person is. Rather, it has literally to do with bodily cleanliness, mostly focusing on sweat, dirt, urine, feces, and bodily fluids emanating from sexual activity. The reason ritual cleanliness is so important is because jinn are believed to be attracted to dirt, sweat, urine, feces, and bodily emissions.

The purifying agents are: water, of which there are two kinds: unmixed (water in its natural state), and mixed (any other form of water).

For illustration purposes, a hadith from Wasa'il al-Shi'a, v. 1, p. 113, h. 2 is given: "'Ali b. Ja'far asked his brother, Imam Musa b. J'far about chickens, pigeons and the like, which have stepped in dung, and then enter the water: can one perform ablutions for prayer from that water: So he said: 'No, unless the volume of water was so much that it amounted to (at least) one kurr'" (p. 63).

Water purifies when properly applied—this is *wudu*. But absent water, earth, sand, or dust may be used. This is tayammum. The most complete method for ritual purity is ghusl, which is a full bath and which is necessary after sexual intercourse. Without it, a daily prayer would not count in earning Allah's favor.

The sun, that is sunshine, also works to achieve ritual purity. Whatever the sun shines upon has become purified.

And there are other purifiers as illustrated by Wasa'il al-Shi'a in regard to a question: "What if I meet a dhimmi (a non-Muslim living under the protection of Muslims) and he shakes my hand? He (Imam al-Sadiq) said, 'Wipe it with dust or against a wall.' I said, 'And what about the one who bears enmity towards the holy household or their followers?' He said: 'Wash your hand'" (p. 73).

In answer to the question, "What is ritual impurity?" ten things are to be avoided: urine, feces, semen, carrion, blood, dogs, pigs, disbelievers, intoxicants and beer, the sweat of an excrement-eating animal, and the sweat of someone in a state of major ritual impurity due to illicit sexual intercourse (pp. 75–76).

Wudu, which is purification by means of water, is the most common form used to attain ritual purity. Imam al-Sadiq said: "Whoever performs wudu', then uses a towel, will receive one goodness; but whoever performs wudu' and does not use a towel until after his wudu' dries, he will receive thirty goodnesses" (p. 92).

Flatulence, or breaking wind, is also a major concern. A jurist's ruling is: "Flatulence invalidates *wudu'* if it comes from the anus, whether it is accompanied by sound or not" (p. 95). Again, Imam al-Sadiq, "Whoever intentionally leaves a single hair in a state of major ritual impurity will be in the fire."

Another interesting ruling is: "A person enters a state of post-coital ritual impurity by penetrative sexual intercourse. This is when the private parts meet; so if a man's penis or part of it enters the vagina or rectum, then he has become ritually impure, as has his partner. As for someone who penetrates an animal there is uncertainty, but obligatory precautions requires that they perform *ghusl*" (pp. 98–99).

Ghusl, the washing of the entire body, is the most thorough method to achieve ritual purity, as evidenced by this: "It is best for a man who is in a state of post-coital impurity to urinate before making ghusl. That way, if he emits some moisture after ghusl but is uncertain that it is semen, he need not pay it any heed. And then, if there are multiple reasons for performing ghusl (for instance, if one is in a state of major ritual impurity and it is Friday), one can perform a single ghusl with the intention of fulfilling them all, and they will be rewarded for all of them, God-willing" (p. 103).

Note: The rules regarding ritual purity are many and complex. Exacting procedures are outlined by the jurists regarding proper washings with water, dirt, dust, and so on. These ritual washings are to precede the five daily prayers. It is not necessary here to outline the lengthy rulings to achieve ritual purity except to say that it would be a full time job to be in an ongoing state of favor with Allah. It seems that most people would be in a constant state of denial or condemnation in an attempt to be an exemplary Muslim.

As to leaving "a single hair in a state of major ritual impurity," this nearly always has to do with sexual intercourse, even between a husband and wife, and seems to be rather strange at minimum. It may be that the jurist's goal is to create an atmosphere of fear among ordinary Muslims and thereby subjugate them to compliance on all points.

Sexual relations with animals is mentioned from time to time. Also, the issue of the status of homosexual intercourse may be what is referred to. It seems that there are few, if any, limits, just so long as ritual purity is maintained.

It must be noted that little, if any, attention is given to women's ritual purity. It is present, but just barely.

With *tayammum*, the use of dirt, sand, or dust instead of water to achieve wudu', there is a ruling that consists of two wipings. It reads: "After striking both your palms on the ground, or placing them upon it, you wipe your face from your hairline to the bridge of your nose and the top of your eyebrows. It is more appropriate to wipe you eyebrows as well" (p. 108).

There are special rulings about menstruating women. First of all, "all acts of worship which require ritual purity, such as prayer, fasting, circumambulation, and seclusion in a mosque, are forbidden to her. If a woman begins menstruating in the middle of prayer, her prayer is invalidated (and should be abandoned) even if she began bleeding just before *taslim*." (*Taslim* is the greeting of peace said just prior to the ending of the prayer.)

It is forbidden for a menstruating woman to touch the text of the Qur'an, to touch the names of Allah, the Prophet, or an imam. Also, she is forbidden to recite verses of the Qur'an. She is not allowed to loiter or remain in the mosque. The rulings go on into rather bizarre topics.

Adornment, particularly of men, is addressed in many rulings of the jurists. For instance, a Muslim "is a pleasant and attractive person who loves adornment by looking after his hair, beard, and clothes. He trims his hair, perfumes and anoints his body, and uses hair dye if needed. This is how cleanliness and adornment enter the life of the believer from every angle" (p. 131).

Pubic hair and under-arm hair is to be plucked, at least every forty days. If not plucked, then other measures are to be used, and this for men and women.

There are extensive rulings regarding the use of the lavatory. The following lengthy quote gives the reader insight into the rigorous precautions that must be taken by the faithful:

A man's private parts are his penis, testicles, and rectum, though it appears that his buttocks conceal his rectum. A woman's private parts are her vagina and rectum with regards to other women like herself, she must cover them with any covering possible from every onlooker, even the insane, or minors capable of discerning the difference between right and wrong. Covering, here, means to conceal the skin, though precaution requires that it cover the shape as well. In addition to this, a woman must cover her entire body—from non-mahram men. It is forbidden for a Muslim to look at the private parts of another Muslim, aside from women who are permitted to him either as wives or concubines, and obligatory precaution requires him not to look at the private parts of a disbeliever as well. (p. 135)

Regarding the *Qibla*, the direction of the Ka'ba in Mecca, Muslims are not permitted to face the Qibla while urinating or defecating. And it makes no difference if one is in a building or in a desert. However, "if one does not know the location of the Qibla, then it is neither obligatory to observe this, nor is it obligatory to force a child or insane person to do so, even if it would be better" (p. 136).

Cleansing following defecation is important. "One must wash the (entrance of the) urethra twice, though three times is better, and it is not enough to remove the physical ritual impurity without water if one is able to use water. It suffices to wash the rectum until all fecal matter has disappeared; there is no need to check its odour or colour if no matter visibly remains" (p. 137).

In regard to bathing the body of the deceased, women should bath other women and men other men. Deceased children under five are exempt from this rule.

Anointing the deceased with camphor must be on seven places: the forehead, palms of the hands, the knees, and the two toes. It is best to include the nose as well (p. 149).

Rulings Regarding Prayer

Prayer is a central part of the life of a Muslim. Generally, the prayers are learned early in life and, when memorized, are repeated daily. There are times of spontaneous prayer as well, but these are not covered by rulings. Indeed, for a Muslim, prayer is a principal sign of faith.

"Let us heed the words of Allah's Messenger when he said: 'Whoever completes his wudu', beautifies his prayers, pays his zakat, suppresses his anger, restrains his tongue, seeks forgiveness for his sins, and cares deeply for the Household of his Prophet, has surely completed the realities of faith, and the gates of Paradise are flung open for him'" (p. 160).

Here are the "Preliminary rules for prayer." Prayers should always be made while facing the Sacred Mosque.

- A.   Allah has made five sorts of prayer obligatory for the Muslim:
    1. The five daily prayers
    2. The prayer of signs
    3. The prayer for obligatory circumambulation
    4. The prayer for the deceased

5. Compensatory prayers for those prayers missed by parents, which fall to the eldest child when they are deceased.

B. The daily prayers are five obligatory prayers:
1. *Zuhr*, four units called the "middle prayer"
2. *'Asr*, four units
3. *Maghrib*, three units
4. *Isha'*, four units
5. *Fajr*, two units

Note: The "units" are memorized prayers and are not given in the book. They are short statements repeated rapidly. Before, during, and after the units are a number of prescribed bodily movements.

Muslims are warned that the prayers are not to be taken lightly, and, in fact, the faithfulness in prayer will be the first thing questioned upon arrival in Paradise (p. 166).

Praying also has to do with Satan. "And since there are narrations affirming that Satan is always terrified of a believer so long as the believer keeps praying his five daily prayers on time, why would any of us squander these prayers? Why wouldn't we pray them on time? Why wouldn't we slam shut the door through which Satan creeps, and allow major sins to enter by treating our prayers with disdain?" (p. 166).

Women, when they begin menstruating, must wear a headscarf while praying. Men, when praying, must cover their private parts, everything between their navel and knees. Women must cover their entire body, including hair and head, except for their face, hands to the wrist, and the tops and bottoms of their feet (p. 176).

Prayers are invalidated by any form of ritual impurity. And "there are ten places where one should not pray: upon mud, water, in a lavatory, upon graves, in the middle of the road, upon an anthill, the resting place of camels, where water flows, upon wetlands, and upon ice or snow (pp. 181–182).

Bowing in prayer is obligatory, as is a bending of one's back, and all or some of the fingers must touch one's knees.

There are twelve things that invalidate prayer:

1. Being deprived of one of the act's conditional requirements during prayer
2. Experiencing a loss of ritual purity during prayer
3. Joining one's hands together
4. Turning away from the Qibla
5. Speaking
6. Guffawing
7. Crying for worldly matters
8. Doing something which effaces the outward form of prayer
9. Eating or drinking
10. Saying "amin" after reciting Surat al-Fatih
11. Adding or omitting something
12. Experiencing doubts which invalidate the prayer

Other actions that invalidate prayer:
1. Per # 5, intentionally uttering a word made up of two or more
2. syllables
3. Per # 6, guffawing means to laugh loudly, at length, and to tremble from laughter.

There is no problem with smiling.

The eldest son in a family must make up for the missed prayers and fasts of his parents after their death when such prayers were missed for valid reasons (p. 226). It is also permitted to hire a person to make up for missed prayers and fasts of the deceased. Or, a non-family member may volunteer to do this for free (p. 227).

The Imam of the Congregation

To be an imam of a congregation, one must have the following qualities:

1. Legal maturity according to precaution, although some traditions state that a boy who has not yet matured can still lead prayers
2. Sanity
3. Faith (that is, he must be a Twelver Shia)
4. Justness
5. Legitimate birth
6. Male. A woman can only lead women.

Friday is the chief day of prayer for Muslims; it is a holy day. And the Friday prayers are obligatory for all except those who are elderly, disabled, or for other reasons that make it difficult to attend.

There are prayers for signs—natural events like a solar eclipse, a lunar eclipse, an earthquake, and other extraordinary natural events (p. 243).

Note: Being faithful at praying is essentially for all Muslims. It is something one must do, not something that may be done. It is not a communication with God so much as it is ritualistic performance. Praying commends oneself to God and is rewarded as such.

Christian prayer is utterly different from Islamic prayer. Jesus said, "When you pray" and did not give times or methods. Nor did He promise rewards for praying or consequences for not praying. For the Christian, praying is a coming into the presence of God and making requests, confessing, offering praises, and giving thanks. Christians are invited to pray, not commanded to pray.

Fasting

"Fasting is an act of worship made obligatory on the faithful in this age, just as it was made obligatory for those who lived in previous ages. It is one of the pillars of the religion and marks of faith" (p. 246).

The reason for fasting is "to nurture the spirit of piety, not just to practice restraining the self from its lawful desires, but to enable it to better resist unlawful ones" (p. 246).

Fasting takes place during the month of Ramadan because that is the month of the Qur'an, and the Qur'an is Allah's book and gives guidance for all the faithful on every point of living. Fasting prepares the Muslim to receive the guidance of the Qur'an.

Fasting during Ramadan is so important that Imam al-Sadiq said: "Whoever (intentionally and prematurely) breaks his fast (even) one day during the month of Ramadan, the spirit of faith leaves him" (p. 247).

"In the rulings it is said that fasting means avoiding sexual intercourse, food, and drink, and each of these categories contains a number of sub-categories such as masturbation, foreplay for one who suffers premature ejaculation, and intentionally remaining in a sate of major ritual impurity until daybreak" (p. 252).

Additional rulings are:

1. Rectal intercourse is forbidden and invalidates the fast of both parties.
2. Intercourse with eunuchs or animals is forbidden (both of them are major sins, whether one is fasting or not).
3. Masturbation is also forbidden, and whoever seeks to climax whether by touching, kissing, or even looking at the other gender, images of them, or pornographic films—or even someone who attempts to ejaculate by imagining things—has invalidated his fast.
4. If anyone does the above without intending to ejaculate, but then does so accidentally, there is nothing upon him.
5. In terms of etiquettes of fasting, one jurist has said: "The one who fasts is engaged in worship even when he sleeps on his bed, so long as he does not backbite another Muslim" (p. 259).

Paying *Khums*

Khums is the one-fifth tax given to the Muslim community on all income. From Qur'an 8:41 we find: "Know that whatever thing you may come by, a fifth (khums) of it is for Allah and the Messenger, for the relatives and the orphans, for the needy and the traveller, if you have faith in Allah and what We sent down to Our servant on the Day of Separation, the day when the two hosts met; and Allah has power over all things" (p. 266).

To give khums is also referred to as jihad. Qur'an 9:41 is quoted to support this: "Go forth, whether (armed) lightly or heavily, and wage jihad with your possessions and persons in the way of Allah. This is better for you, should you know" (p. 267).

Giving khums is jihad because of the warfare Islam is engaged in around the world. The world's values pour into the Muslim religion and corrupt it, and thus it is necessary to fight against this onslaught. "That is because today we are facing a deliberate cultural assault to destroy the symbols of our religion, corrupt the values of our society and alienate our youth from them. Do you not see how our enemies began to enter our society through satellite channels, the internet, and movies?" (p. 268).

The general ruling on "war booty" is: "War booty is that which is captured by the victor in warfare, such as weapons and supplies, military encampments and perhaps even fortresses, such as the fort at Khaybar. *Khums* is due on all of these. As for lands which fall into the possession of the Muslims after the conquest, which are called 'conquered by force' the most likely ruling is that there is no need to pay *Khums* on them as they are not customarily treated as booty" (p. 269).

Paying Zakat

Zakat is the alms tax that is to be given for those who are in need. It is called a charity tax.

The importance of paying zakat is likened to that of prayer. Wasa'il al-Shi'a said: "There is no worshipper who withholds anything from the zakat on his wealth but that Allah makes that, on Judgment Day, a serpent of fire encircling his neck, biting his flesh, until the accounting is complete. And it is as Allah Almighty says: 'They will be collared with what they were miserly with on Judgment Day,' meaning what they were stingy with of zakat."

Zakat must be paid on nine things:

1. Camels
2. Cows
3. Sheep
4. Gold
5. Silver
6. Wheat
7. Barley
8. Dates
9. Raisins

Zakat can be spent on the following:

1. The poor
2. The needy
3. Those who collect the zakat
4. Those whose hearts are to be reconciled
5. For the freeing of slaves
6. For debtors
7. In Allah's way
8. The wayfarer

The definition of "whose hearts are to be reconciled" is interesting. It refers to non-Muslims, disbelievers, who are given *zakat* to secure their allegiance, cement their friendship with the Muslims, attract them to Islam, repel their evil, or to make use of them in specific areas such as jihad.

The *zakat* can also be used for "those Muslims whose faith is weak, who are given zakat with the goal of cementing their connection to Islamic society" (p. 286).

Those receiving *zakat* must meet four conditions:

1. Not disbelievers
2. Not to support immorality
3. Not given to one already receiving aid
4. Cannot be a Hashemite (this refers to the ruling royal family of Jordan).

The Pilgrimage (Hajj)

The hajj, one of the pillars of Islam, is a visit to Allah's House, the Holy Sanctuary, the Ka'ba in Mecca, along with other sacred sites. Muslims are expected, at least once in a lifetime, to make the pilgrimage.

From a hadith of Wasa'il al-Shi'a we have: "The reason for making the pilgrimage obligatory at least one time is that Allah Almighty set the obligations according to the strength of the least of the people. So from these obligations, the obligatory pilgrimage (hajj) is once, then He wished the stronger people (perform it more) according to their level of endurance" (p. 293).

The criteria to be fulfilled to make the hajj are: legal maturity, soundness of mind, freedom, and ability.

One must be in a state of consecration on hajj. Among those things that violate consecration are:

1. Hunting
2. Sexual activities and anything related to them
3. Smelling pleasant odours or scenting oneself
4. A man wearing clothes other than those required
5. Looking at oneself in a mirror
6. Wearing shoes and socks
7. Sinning
8. Disputation
9. Killing insects that feed on the body (mosquitos)
10. Wearing a ring for decoration
11. A woman wearing a bracelet for decoration
12. Using makeup
13. Removing hair
14. A man covering his head or a woman covering her face
15. A man travelling under shade
16. Causing oneself to bleed
17. Trimming one's fingernails
18. Cutting down trees or plants
19. Bearing arms

Jihad

An introductory footnote to this section reads: "The concept of jihad has been the subject of severe distortion and manipulation at the hands of imposters and extremists. In this section, His Eminence briefly outlines the true Islamic definition of the term, and provides some of the broad rulings that govern its application" (p. 298).

As to the jihad of the self, we have this: "The best of worship is abstinence of the stomach and privates." The point is to wholly dedicate oneself to Allah. Also, it is "volunteering to fight in an effort to raise the banner of truth, enjoin good, forbid evil and resist tyranny" (p. 299).

Note: Two kinds of jihad are usually presented in Muslim literature. The first, and always stated to be the most important, is "combat against the self." This refers to personal growth, becoming all that a Muslim should be. The second is jihad for Islam, meaning to protect, defend, and expand Islam in whatever means necessary.

From the last paragraph on page 299 above, we see that this form of jihad can be variously interpreted. To "forbid evil" covers a multitude of circumstances, including warring against the West because of its permitting of evil—at least in the eyes of a Muslim.

Jihad is an individual obligation, meaning each and every Muslim is obligated to engage in this means of forbidding evil. It includes "defending Muslims and the religion of Islam against danger. It could also be a strongly emphasized recommendation, such as struggling to convey the message of Islam and (peacefully) spread the true religion" (p. 299).

In answer to the question, Against whom should we struggle? the answer is: "Jihad has four aspects: commanding virtue, forbidding vice, to be honest among the citizenry, and to fight against *al-fasiqin* (those who openly commit acts of disobedience to Allah)" (p. 300). It is also obligatory to struggle against "the disbelievers in your vicinity" (p. 300).

Abu 'Abd Allah said, "All the goodness is in the sword and under the shadow of the sword. No people rise but by the sword, and the sword is the key of Paradise and the Fire." This is from Wasa'il al-Shi'a, one of the most respected of those who convey the pattern of life of Muhammad (p. 300).

An interesting example from the Sunna authority of Shia is: "Two boys were leaping on a rooster and plucked out its feathers, not leaving a single on it. Nearby, an old man was standing in prayer, and did nothing to order or forbid them, so Allah commanded the earth to swallow him up" (p. 307).

Then, two telling rulings are: "Good is whatever Allah has commanded, and evil is whatever he has forbidden, whether the doer of the deed knows this or not" (p. 307). "When there is a danger posed to Islam and Muslims, such as the appearance of innovations and the spread of corruption, which threatens the very existence of the faith or the lives of Muslims, or anything as serious as this, then forbidding this kind of evil becomes jihad in Allah's way. In the case, the aforementioned conditions for enjoining good and forbidding evil no longer apply; the rules for jihad apply instead" (pp. 311–312).

Note: "Allah's way" means violent jihad. "Innovations" may be interpreted by Muslims as almost anything coming from a Western culture.

Part Three: Selected Rulings for Transactions and Contracts

Qur'an 24:55 is quoted at the outset of this third part: "Allah has promised those of you who have faith and do righteous deeds that He will surely make them successors in the earth, just as He made those who were before them successors, and he will surely establish for them their religion which He has approved for them, and that He will surely change their state to security after their fear, while they worship Me, not ascribing any partners to Me. And whoever is ungrateful after that—it is they who are the transgressors."

In a section about justice in Islamic society is a list of the means of implementing justice:
1. Sending messengers
2. Sending down and setting up the scale (of justice), the most important manifestation of which is an imam who judges between people with fairness
3. Revealing scriptures with laws

4. Sending down iron (weapons), containing great might to confront those who wrong others
5. Encouraging those who (legitimately) fight to assist Allah and His messengers with iron (weapons) (p. 323).

Note: The warlike and violent nature of implementing justice, which would be perfectly fitting to seventh century Arabia, is obvious. Islam, except where compelled otherwise, prefers the old ways of Allah.

Much attention is given to the "righteous jurists." These alone, the imams, shall make decisions. Qur'an 4:105 and 5:42 are quoted to substantiate this (p. 335).

Concerning abortion, which was common in seventh century Arabia, is the ruling: "It appears that the (primary) form of child killing today is abortion, when the child is in its earliest stage of life in the womb. The crime of abortion is widespread in many lands; it has even become legal in some. We must confront this crime by any means available to us" (p. 338).

Speaking of the early years, those of Muhammad and his companions, it is said that "Allah would never destroy a town until He had exhausted every means to guide them; 'This is because your Lord would never destroy the towns unjustly while their people were unaware'" (Qur'an 6:131) (p. 338).

For many pages, various aspects of social commerce and engagement is discussed, most of which is common for many of the world's societies. Much of it centers on the family. "The family is the social unit responsible for preserving the values of Muslim society, the most important of which are the spirits of mutual cooperation and kindness. The ideal home furnishes these values—in the form of a family—with ease" (p. 353).

Reconciliation and Family Matters

And then, "The Messenger of Allah said: 'The love of a believer for a believer, for the sake of Allah, is among the greatest branches of the faith'" (from the ruling by Al-Mahdsin).

On brotherhood and reconciliation is a saying attributed to Ali', head of Shia Islam, made at the time of his death to his sons al-Hasan and al-Husayn: "I advise the two of you, and all of my sons, and my family and whomever my message reaches, to fear Allah, settle your affair, and reconciliation between each other. For surely I heard your grandfather, the Messenger of Allah, saying: 'Reconciling discord (between people) is better than all of prayer and fasting'" (p. 360).

Note: It must be remembered that Shariah law found here is for Shia Muslims and may or may not apply to Sunni Muslims. Sunni Muslims may be counted among the disbelievers, and vice versa.

Rulings regarding family, the roles of husband and wife, the caring and upbringing of children, and their education are outlined in great detail.

Laws Regarding Business Transactions

Imam al-Sadiq is quoted as saying, "There is no good in anyone who does not enjoy gathering wealth from a lawful source to meet his needs, support his religion, and maintain ties with his relatives" (p. 367).

In regard to business contracts: "The basis of all contracts is the obligation to fulfill them according to what both parties agreed upon. It is impermissible to default on them because Allah has commanded us to fulfill them, just as he has commanded us to fulfill all pledges. There is no difference between contracts that were common in the time of Allah's Messenger and the Imams, and those which have come into being since then (such as contracts for insurance, imports, exports, and international economic and business agreements), or will come into being in the future" (p. 370).

One of the limits of a contract has to do with usury, or the charging of interest on a loan. Qur'an 2:275 is quoted to show that Allah had so communicated this principle to Muhammad through Gabriel.

A chief ruling in this area is: "As a general rule, Islam has forbidden any kind of contract for something inherently unlawful and forbidden, because when Allah forbids a thing or its consumption, it is unlawful to assign it a monetary value" (p. 375).

Regarding alcohol, "It is impermissible to work in the field of intoxicants in any way, shape or form, and the same applies to illicit drugs: one may not produce, transport, sell, purchase, store, or advertise them. Anything (even peripherally) connected to the activities of producing, trading, and otherwise servicing them is forbidden" (p. 376).

It is also "impermissible to conduct transactions involving pigs, whether living or dead, or for their flesh, hide, or any other part of them" (p. 376).

Part of the Sunna, or pattern of life of Muhammad and his companions, is, "Whoever defrauds a Muslim in buying or selling is not from us, and he will be raised on the Day of resurrection with the Jews, for they are the ones who defraud the Muslims most!" (p. 377).

In regard to gambling: "Games using tools of gambling with bets, which are forbidden, games using tools of gambling, but without betting; it is obligatory precaution to avoid these, especially in the cases of backgammon and chess, about which we have many traditions.... An exception to the prohibition on betting is placing bets on horse racing and archery; these are permissible" (p. 377).

There is a ruling on music and singing: "Singing and things connected to music, and using any kind of forbidden instruments or entertainment, is prohibited, even if the singing is done with words from the Qur'an, supplications, or poetry about things that would be lawful in and of itself" (p. 378).

It is forbidden to earn a living by singing in any way, shape, or form, whether being paid to perform, or crafting and selling its instruments, or renting them out, and any other contract that involves music and singing.

"Also forbidden are audio and videocassettes, CDs, etc., which contain singing. It is forbidden to share, produce, buy, sell, or rent them, or form any sort of contract concerning them."

Note: Many of the rulings regarding singing and music have to do with the fact these were not practiced during the days of Muhammad and his companions. The goal of all Islam is to be like Muhammad and his faithful companions.

At this point, I will merely list the some of the major headings and sub-categories dealing with contracts and agreements.

1. Rules for selling
2. Rules for settlement
3. Rules for sharecropping
4. Rules for bail
5. Rules pertaining to loans and debts
6. Rules for collateral
7. Rules for borrowing
8. Rules for deposits
9. Rules pertaining to legal impediments
10. Rules pertaining to the usurpation and destruction of property
11. Rules for vows and covenants
12. Kinds of vows
13. Rules for competitions
14. Rules for the final will and testament
15. Rules pertaining to the gaze

Rules for Marriage and Family Life

Qur'an 24:2: "As for the fornicatress and the fornicator, strike each of them a hundred lashes, and let not pity for them overcome you in Allah's law, if you believe in Allah and the Last Day, and let their punishment be witnessed by a group of the faithful."

And then, Qur'an 24:4: "As for those who accuse honourable women and do not bring four witnesses, strike them eighty lashes, and never accept any testimony from them after that, and they are transgressors" (p. 426).

These penalties are meant to enshrine the sanctity of the family and protect it from rumourmongers (p. 426).

Note: At issue is whether either punishments or requirements are ever enforced in non-Muslim-dominated countries. Some sources say yes, others no. Some sources wonder if this form of practice occurs at all. Based on testimonies found in the website The Clarion Project,[2] one would have to think such punishments are meted out.

One cannot help but wonder how four witnesses, per Qur'an 24:4, could possibly be witness to a woman violating the marriage contract.

It is noted that "Allah purified social life from sexualisation by forbidding women from making a display of themselves, and by prohibiting them from displaying their charms (save that which is apparent of them)" (p. 427).

Note: The full covering of women, except for the face and parts of the hands, is practiced in many Muslim-dominated countries. Men do not have to cover up and seem to be very weak when it comes to controlling their sexual drives. I have not found one word addressing the controlling of the sexual appetites of men. It is almost as though men are uncontrollable, and the burden of preventing men from losing control falls to women.

As to the "gaze," Imam al-Sadiq said: "The first glance is for you, the second is against you and not for you, and in the third is your ruin" (Wasa'il al-shi'a).

---

2 clarionproject.org/

Also, the imam said: "A Muslim woman should not uncover herself among Jewish or Christian women, for they may describe her (hair or physique) to their husbands" (p. 430).

Muslim men should not initiate a greeting with a woman, exchange the peace, nor invite them to eat with them or shake hands.

"It is permissible for every man and woman to look at other members of the same gender so long as it is not furtive, lustful, or intended to be seductive, excluding the private parts, as only a spouse may see these and they must be covered from all others" (p. 430).

"A man is allowed to hear the voice of a non-mahram woman so long as he does not listen with lust or furtively, though it is recommended precaution that he does not do so anyway save in situations of need or necessity as dictated by custom" (p. 431).

"It is forbidden for a woman to cause a man (apart from her husband) to hear her voice when she makes it alluring by making it sound pleasant and soft" (p. 431).

"It is impermissible to shake hands with a woman except from behind clothing, without applying pressure to her hand" (p. 431).

"A man may look at a woman's face, hands, hair, and pleasant features, as long as he is likely to take her as a wife. It is obligatory precaution that he restricts himself to looking at only those women he already intends to marry" (p. 431).

It is forbidden to marry a Jewess or Christian woman. But if a Muslim man did so he would have to forbid her from drinking wine or eating pork, yet the marriage to such a woman would bring shame upon him (p. 432).

A ruling however is: "A Muslim man cannot marry a polytheist woman, as for marrying such women, such as Jews and Christians, the strongest opinion is its permissibility, though it is severely discouraged, and they must be educated in the Islamic practices or ritual purity, cleanliness, and abstain from wine, pork, etc. As for Zoroastrian women, it is obligatory precaution to avoid contracting permanent marriage with them" (p. 432).

Note: Zoroastrian women could be temporarily [*muta*] married, maybe for an hour, a day, or longer.

Another ruling is: "Fornication which occurs after a marriage has been solemnized and consummated has no effect on the marriage's validity. If a man marries a woman and then fornicates with her mother or daughter, his wife is not forbidden to him. But if this occurs before consummation, then it is precaution for him to leave her" (p. 434).

A ruling on the grounds of sodomy: "If one man sodomizes another, even if entry was only partial, he is forbidden from marrying the latter's mother or any of her ancestors, his daughter and any of her descendants, or his sister. It makes no difference whether the passive party is an adult or child, and the same applies—as a matter of precaution—even if the active party is a child, even though the strongest opinion is that he is not forbidden" (p. 437).

Note: The issue of homosexual behavior is complex in Muslim literature. That it is widely practiced, but denied, is evident and is the reason for the strange wording of the rulings, as above.

In regard to legal guardians for a marriage contract, it has been narrated from Abu ja'far al-Baqir, "The woman who is financially independent and not foolish, who has no master over her, can be married without the permission of a guardian" (p. 438).

A ruling as to guardianship: "The legal guardians for a marriage contract are the father and paternal grandfather, and so on up the patrilineal line, meaning that the father's maternal grandfather is never included." It is customary that a woman cannot marry without the permission of a male relative, even if that relative is a child (p. 438).

Rulings as to a defect in a man: "Any defect in the man which renders marital life impossible or causes unbearable hardship, confers upon his wife the right to separate from him and annul their marriage." Examples are: madness, castration, impotence, being sentenced to death, imprisonment, drug addiction and refusing to quit, their genetics do not match, addicted to indecencies, or has infectious diseases" (p. 442).

Rulings as to a defect in a woman: "A woman may be returned for four things: vitiligo, leprosy, insanity, or with an outgrowth or swelling in the vagina which prevents intercourse. Also due to madness, bowel ailment, blindness, and lameness. Also if it had been stated that the woman was a virgin but was not, she may be returned" (p. 442).

Rules on Temporary Marriage—*Muta*

Bakr b. Muhammad narrated, "I hate for a Muslim man to depart this world while there remains some characteristic from among those of the Messenger of Allah that he did not practice" (from Wasa'il al-Shi'a) (p. 445).

Imam al-Baqir said, "The pleasure of the believer is in three things: temporary marriage with women, spreading joy to his brothers, and praying at night" (p. 446).

Imam al-Sadiq said: "Temporary marriage is a recommended act for men, and I dislike it for a man to depart from this world until he performs temporary marriage even if only once" (p. 446).

Muta, or temporary marriage, is supported by Qur'an 4:24, and with the introductory words, "This is Allah's ordinance for you."

The author, Grand Ayatullah al-Modarresi, writes: "Allah's religion is a religion of human nature. Sexual desire is a human instinct like any other, and the religion of Islam has provided the proper means of satisfying it—including permanent and temporary marriage—while, at the same time, forbidding indecency, taking paramours, homosexuality, and any other illegitimate means of satisfying this desire" (p. 446).

Note: The above paragraph quoted from the author al-Modarresi is an example of Islamic sacred deception, or not being truthful in order to protect, defend, or advance Islam. Any form of sexuality for Muslim men [not Muslim women] is permitted on some flimsy basis or another, including sex with infants.

Again from Imam al-Sadiq: "It is not a problem for a man to enter into a temporary marriage with a Jewish or Christian woman so long as he is a freeman." This same imam also said it was permissible to enter into muta with a Zoroastrian woman (p. 448).

Rulings on Divorce

The two imams, al-Baqir and al-Sadiq, agree: "There is nothing (no divorce) until the man says to the woman clearly and before two (male) just witnesses: 'You are divorced;' or he says to her 'Begin your waiting period,' wishing (to indicate) divorce by that" (p. 456).

The wife being divorced must be a permanent wife, as there is no divorce in temporary marriage; she must not be menstruating or experiencing puerperal bleeding, and she must be free from menses, and her husband should not have had intercourse with her since her last period (p. 457).

"If a man divorces his wife three times, between which he has returned to her twice (meaning he returned to her after the first and second divorces), his wife is forbidden to him after the third divorce. But if she then marries another husband and he either divorces her or dies, the first husband is able to marry her once again, according to the conditions laid down in the detailed manual of Islamic law (p. 462).

In Conclusion—A Contemporary News Item

From the January 9, 2018, edition of the *San Francisco Chronicle*, page A4, is an article by Thomas Erdbrink, a *New York Times* writer, titled "Iran: Leader Scolds Critics of Protesters." There is a photo with the explanatory note: "President Hassan Rouhani says protesters object to both the poor economy and widespread corruption."

The telling paragraph in the article reads: "Rouhani, a moderate, has been seeking a relaxation in social controls, but he faces resistance from hard-liners in neglected power centers like the judiciary, vetting councils and the state news media. They want to keep in place the framework of Islamic laws that effectively dictate how people should live, despite enormous changes in Iranian society in the past decade alone."

Iran is under Islamic Shia Shariah law, the focus of this essay. Iran's religious leadership, the judiciary, and Ayatollah Ali Khamenei blame the West for the protests, along with Israel and Saudi Arabia. The Islamic power structure wants all social media banned. One interesting move the Islamic leaders have made is to shut down all English classes in elementary schools—all to halt the spread of Western influence.

Note: When visiting Turkey some years ago, my brother Bruce and I saw that many of the youth of the nation were abandoning Islam. We arrived in the midst of protests against the government and talked to many of these youth. Every person we spoke with had issues with the corrupt government and Islamic religion. To reject one was to reject the other; and the government cracked down ruthlessly on the protesters. This is exactly what is going on in Iran. And it shows the power struggle up close. Due to many factors, especially the Internet, Muslims around the world see what others enjoy, while they live a seventh-century way of life.

The question is, will slavery to an outmoded and severe set of laws or freedom prevail?

6

Ultimate Intentions of Islam

Although briefly mentioned in other sections of this book, I want to call more attention to the ways in which Muslims, both Sunni and Shia, spread their message and work toward their ultimate goals. For an extensive presentation of this, go to Dr. William Wagner's book, *How Islam Plans to Change the World*.[1] Dr. Wagner is president of Olivet University, located in Mill Valley, California.

Dawa

Dawa (it is variously spelled) refers to Muslim evangelism, and Muslims are very evangelistic. They are as engaged in spreading their faith as evangelical Christians are, and it is possible that more Muslim money is put to their cause than Christian money to ours.

Muslims are very patient in their outreach efforts. The year 2080 is a date forecasted to mark the time when Islam will have brought the entire world under Shariah law. They are working with ten-year, thirty-year, and fifty-year plans to bring this about. And Sunni and Shia Islam compete with each other in these efforts.

Strategy for the Spread of Islam

The first tool of Muslim growth is **missions**—that is, establishing outreaches as part of dawa. Missions might consist of chaplaincy work in prisons, which is a major area of dawa, especially in America. Increasingly, Muslim missions take the form of funding a chair of Islamic Studies in a college or university. Or the missionary strategy might consist in the creation of an Islamic study center, or the establishing of a relief center primarily for Muslims. This form of evangelism is costly and is growing across America.

The second strategy for the spreading of Islam is **jihad**—the use of force to subjugate people and force conversion. There are two forms of jihad in Islam. The first is the bettering of the person—the inner struggle to become more like Muhammad. The second is the use of force, if necessary. Muslims will rarely acknowledge this, as it does not have a good

---

1 Dr. William Wagner, *How Islam Plans to Change the World* (Grand Rapids, MI: Kregel Publications, 2012).

sound to it—violence, warfare. But it goes on and in many places in the world. Some of the wars Muslims are engaged in are aimed at conquering people groups for the purpose of bringing them into Islam.

It is a solid principle of Islam that dying in violent jihad not only sends the jihadist directly to Paradise, but also enables seventy-two family members to go to Paradise as well. For some, sadly, this would be a strong motivator.

The third tool for spreading Islam is the building of **mosques**. Most Muslims understand that building a mosque means automatic inclusion in Paradise.

The mosque where I have attended Jummah prayers on Fridays for the past four-years was so built: as a commitment to Islam using the congregants' worldly possessions. And this location was formerly a Baptist church. More and more, as Christianity declines, Muslims love to buy up old churches and conduct a remodeling project.

Fourth, Islamic growth is furthered by **immigration**. With nation against nation and wars and rumors of war, to use biblical phraseology, peoples of the world are displaced, and this works as a strategy in the spreading of Islam. Where Muslims go, mosques will be built and dawa will be practiced.

Fifth, in countries that allow plural marriages, Islam will increase dramatically with men having from two to four wives and **many children** born to each.

Patience

Muslims are patient; they have history behind them. Islam spreads almost unseen by observers. As a population of Muslims grows in an area, little by little, they will make their presence felt. At first, when they are a tiny percentage of the population, they lie low. As this percentage increases, so will their social and political presence.

Islam hates Western democracy, though when Muslim presence is small, no one would see this. The goal is to end democratic governing and establish Shariah law in its place.

At present, in a growing number of pockets within Western nations, Muslims have achieved the goal of self-government, especially in such fields as family law. Even police will not enter some of these insular communities. For Muslims, this inroad is just the first step toward the larger goal of worldwide Islamic rule. Whether this will ever come to fruition is anyone's guess, yet this is the objective for every believing and faithful Muslim.

7

A Summary of *The Exorcist Tradition in Islam*

Personal Introduction:

While attending the Mill Valley Islamic Center's Mosque in January of 2016, I noticed a book on a shelf in the foyer, and during the prayer time I skimmed through this book by Dr. Abu Ameenah Bilal Philips.[1] I was stunned and had to read it. The Imam Abdullah allowed me to take it home on the promise to return it the next Friday. I bought a copy online, read every word, and began to prepare this section of Islamic Studies.

The Exorcist Tradition in Islam (hereafter, *Exorcist Tradition*) confirmed so much I already knew about "folk" Islam. Here, however, information I thought relevant to only rural Muslim folk was actually mainstream for Muslims everywhere. It also confirmed what I already knew and had written about over the years, including my first published book by Zondervan Publishing House in 1973, entitled *A Manual of Demonology and the Occult*. During the late 1960s and throughout the 1970s, I actively and extensively engaged in what Dr. Philips refers to as exorcism but which I call deliverance ministry, as in the Lord's Prayer, "deliver us from evil" (see Matthew 6:13). Then, in more recent times, I wrote *Deliver us from Evil: How Jesus Casts out Demons Today*, published by Earthen Vessel Publishing in 2015.

When I returned Dr. Philips book, I also gave the Imam a copy of the new book mentioned above, which he gladly received and in which he eagerly expressed interest. It seemed necessary to me then to prepare this present chapter to assist those who might deal with this subject in their witness to Muslims.

Notes on the introduction to *The Exorcist Tradition in Islam*

Dr. Philips gives the following reason for the writing of his book:

> In the last ten years, an upsurge of interest among Muslims about possession and the spirit-world has led to the republication of most of the classical texts on this subject (p. 7).

---

1 Dr. Abu Ameenah Bilal Philips, *The Exorcist Tradition in Islam* (Birmingham, England, UK: Al-Hidaayah Publishing & Distribution Ltd., 2007).

He also says there has been a growing number of exorcists among Muslims. This interest then is the prime reason for Dr. Philips' book, and his work is based upon sources that are accepted by Muslim scholars as being authentic and reliable.

Chapter One is "The Spirit World," where the focus is on three areas: the human spirit, jinn, and angels. Chapter Two is: "Spirit Possession," in which he discusses the reasons for possession, partial possession, magic, the Evil Eye, exorcism, the validity of the need for exorcism, the exorcist, and methods of exorcism. Chapter Three is "Modern Muslim Exorcists." A questionnaire developed by Dr. Philips was presented to Muslim exorcists, the results of which are presented along with a profile of the 20th century Muslim exorcist and a survey of Christian exorcists. Chapter Four is the author's opinions about exorcism. There is an appendix that consists of interviews with seventeen exorcists, followed by an index of Qur'anic verses and hadith dealing with the subject, and concluding with a bibliography. Following now is commentary on these chapters.

Chapter One: "The Spirit World"

In Islam there are three different categories or species of created entities: human souls, angels, and jinn, all of which are considered rational yet invisible beings. Humans have bodies that are inhabited by human spirits or souls. Both the terms *ruh* and *nafs* are used in reference to the human spirit or soul. In this section I will use the word "soul" for the human spirit.

Souls

At death Sunni Muslims believe the soul dies, based on Qur'an 3:185; 28:88; and 40:11.

When a person dies, there is some disagreement among Islamic scholars about what happens to the human spirit or soul between death and the Day of Resurrection. A dominant idea is that they return to the *barzakh*, the place from which they originally came. It is from the *barzakh* that souls are "blown by angels into the human embryos" (p. 21).[2]

Upon death the souls of the prophets await the Day of Resurrection in the highest level of paradise, the seventh heaven. This is a lesser place than that of the martyrs, whose souls change into green birds in paradise (Abu Dawud, page 455, no. 3). In this hadith, it is also said that if the martyr leaves behind unpaid debt, he or she will not enter paradise.

The souls of the ordinary believer will not enter the bodies of green birds in paradise; they will, however, exist in the form of birds but are not allowed to roam around in paradise, unlike those of the martyrs.

The souls of disobedient believers are held in their graves and punished for their sins. Two kinds of disobedient believers are mentioned by Muhammad as recorded in Sahih al-Bukhari, vol. 1, p. 141, no. 215 and by Sahih Muslim, vol. 1, pp. 171–172, no. 575: "Surely, they are being punished right now, and not for major offences. One of them was not careful to protect himself from the splash of his urine, and the other used to spread rumors."

The souls of disbelievers sorrow greatly. These souls remain in the grave and are punished until the Day of Resurrection.

---

2   *Barzakh* is a Persian word that means separation, that is, a spiritual state in which souls wait before being blown into humans while in the womb.

Souls of believers have contact with each other just before they die, and the souls already having died inquire as to the lot and fare of acquaintances yet living.

Some Muslim esoterics, called *Batini*, believe that perfect souls leave their human bodies and educate living Muslims in order to improve their souls.

Angels

Although angels take the form of males, as in Gabriel who appeared to Muhammad, they are considered to be neuter with no actual sexual gender.

Names are given to some angels in Islam: *Jibril* or Gabriel is the angel of revelation (Qur'an 26:192–193);[3] *Mikail* or Michael is responsible for rain; *Israfil* is the angel who will blow the horn at the time of the end of the world; *Malik* is the name of the guardian angel of hell (Qur'an 43:77) who lights hellfire and makes sure no one escapes; *Munkar* and *Nakir* are the two angels who will determine, after a person is dead, whether he or she was a faithful Muslim; *Harut* and *Marut* were angels who were sent to the people of Babylon to determine if they had real faith or not (Qur'an 2:102); and *Raqib* and *'Atid* are the two angels who sit on the shoulder of each Muslim recording their good and bad deeds (Qur'an 50:17–18). The following passages in the Qur'an speak of recording angels who are not named: 82:10–11 and 50:17–18.

Angels have authority over the heavens and the earth. Angels determine or set in motion all that happens (Qur'an 79:5 and 51:4), yet they are merely servants of Allah. Angels are able to travel at incredible speeds.

Some angels are able to read the minds of humans, and some know the acts that were planned by people but never carried out. Angels are in constant contact with humans, from birth to death and after death. Angels are assigned to each person at the moment of conception. They inspire people to do good and guard them from doing evil (Qur'an 13:11). There are also angels who pray to Allah for people about certain matters.

One thing angels do not do is possess humans as jinn do, nor do they incite people to do evil.

Jinn

Jinn are hidden from human sight. The Arabic word for jinn is *janna* and means that which is concealed or hidden. Jinn is the plural form and jinni is the singular form.

The belief in jinn is shared with Jews and Christians, but most modern day Jews, as well as some Christians, disavow the existence of jinn or demons.

Jinn originate from fire (Qur'an 15:27; 55:15) and were created before humans existed (Qur'an 15:26–27). Since jinn are created beings, they also experience death (Qur'an 28:88; 55:26; 46:18).

Satan, or *Shaytan*, is close to the concept of devil or demon. There are those who say Satan was not an angel but only a jinn; however there are those who disagree and believe *Iblis*, which is the personal name of Satan, was among the angels, but he refused to bow down to Adam and thus became a demon or even the devil (Qur'an 7:11 and also Qur'an 26:75–78).

Though jinn are invisible to humans, some animals can see them. Some believe that certain jinn, like the angels, can assume human shapes and forms. Some jinn take animal

---

3 Where no citation is given, the authority comes from multiple hadith.

shapes on a constant basis.

Note: Here is a connection with "spirit animals" common to Shamanism and neo-pagan groups like Wicca.

There are three different kinds of jinn. One type flies in the air all of the time; others take the form of dogs and snakes; and others wander the earth. These latter jinn are referred to as *qarin*, which means companion, and they will accompany a person from their birth to their death.

There are jinn who listen in on the conversations of angels, who inhabit a lower level of heaven, and then report their findings to fortunetellers (Qur'an 72:8–9; 15:17–18).

Jinn can be Muslims or non-Muslims. One treats a Muslim jinn differently, almost reverently, but not so a non-Muslim jinn. Satan is a non-Muslim devil.

Some Muslim scholars contend, and are supported by some hadith, that camels are jinn or are created from jinn.

Some hadith say that jinn eat and drink, and do so with the left hand.

Some, mostly Sunni scholars, teach that jinn can have sexual relations with humans and may have offspring, based on Qur'an 72:6. There are hadith that report that Muhammad habitually said when entering the toilet, "O Allah, surely I seek refuge in You from evil male and female jinn." This particular saying was collected from all six of the major hadith, i.e., Sahih al-Bukhari, vol. 1, pp. 105–106, no. 144 and Sahih Muslim, vol. p. 205, no. 729. In addition, Qur'an 55:74 and 18:50 indicate that jinn deflower females.

Hinn are the lowest category of jinn and appear as black dogs.

Jinn, like angels, are able to travel large distances very rapidly. They are also able to affect the human mind by implanting evil thoughts. Some jinn sleep and eat with humans without the humans being aware of it. Jinn may cause humans to be ill.

At a person's death, even a Muslim, jinn will attempt to cause him or her to go astray and leave the straight path of Allah.

Jinn are the only possible source of possession of a human being; human spirits or souls or angels do not possess humans. Jinn can cause both physical and mental problems.

Chapter Two: "Spirit Possession"

Sar is the most commonly used term for possession by jinn, and only jinn can possess a human being. This word is also used to denote epilepsy and literally means, "to throw down." *Mass* is also a term used to refer to spirit possession but is also used to describe mental illness or madness. A possessed person is called a *mansus*. An insane person is called a *majnun*.

Not all Muslim scholars hold to the idea that jinn possess people; some are more likely to see marks of possession as mental or physical illness; major Islamic scholars, however, do attest to spirit possession. In fact, it is said that if one denies spirit possession of human beings it is akin to apostasy and a denial of the Qur'an.

Qur'anic evidence for spirit possession is found in Qur'an 2:275: "Those who devour interest rise up like one stumbling from Satan's touch." The hadith are used to substantiate this as well, several of which have wording like, "Verily, Satan flows in the bloodstream of Adam's descendants" (Sahih Muslim, vol. 3, pp. 1187–1188). In addition, Qur'an 14:22

suggests the possibility of spirit possession, but such is not absolutely clear from the passage itself.

The Sunnah, the pattern of truth found in hadith, support spirit possession by jinn, and not only the possibility of such but also its reality.

Spirit possession occurs from lack of faith in Allah, not performing prayers, lustful inclinations of jinn, or horseplay. Major trouble may occur if jinn become angry. The example given by Dr. Philips is interesting: a person accidentally splattering urine on or pouring hot water on the unseen jinn will make the jinn angry, who in retaliation may possess the offender. In general, jinn tend to be harsh, ignorant, and volatile.

Jinn fool mediums into thinking that they, the medium, can call up spirits of the dead, who even impersonate deceased ancestors, often using unknown languages that no one can understand.

Objects, animate or inanimate, may also be possessed, as Jinn can dwell in both. One example is that rats, which are possessed by jinn, force the necessity of putting out a candle's flame at night less the rat use it to burn a person (see Qur'an 7:148 and 20:86–89).

Jinn may also appear in visions, while a person is awake or asleep, in order to lead the faithful Muslim astray.

Sihr is Arabic for magic and refers to whatever is caused by hidden forces. It can also refer to speech that is subtle and strange, and Muhammad is reported to have said, "Some forms of speech are magic" (Sahih al-Bukhari, vo. 7, p. 445, no. 662).

In Sharia Law, magic is defined as "a contract or incantation, spoken or written, or something done which will affect the body, heart or mind of the one bewitched without actually coming in contact with him." It is said that Allah may allow such magical deception to occur.

Islamic scholars generally disavow the use of amulets and charms meant to ward off evil jinn, curses, and in order to achieve good fortune. There is a division amongst Muslim scholars as to the reality of magic, yet it is widely practiced, since in the Qur'an and the Sunnah magical practices are mentioned. Evidence of this is found in Qur'an 2:102; 113:4; and 7:116. Qur'an 113:4 reads, "And (I seek refuge) from the evil of the witches who blow on knots." The blowing on knots, rope, or animal hair was a mechanism by which spells were cast.

The Qur'anic verses 7:117 and 20:66 also refer to the reality of magical practices. Magic works through the power of jinn and Satan directly. It is evident then that spirit possession and magic are linked together, the second being dependent upon the first.

The Evil Eye is known to all Muslims and is a major issue for them. It essentially refers to an evil glance or look, which is thought to have a powerful impact upon the person looked upon. Sahih Muslim, vol. 3, p. 1192, no. 5427 says, "The effect of the evil eye (al-'ayn) is real, for if there were anything which could overtake destiny, it would have been (the effect of) the evil eye." This effect is caused by jinn.

Exorcism is the term used for the expulsion of evil spirits. The name of Allah may be invoked along with a number of other rituals such as the recitation of formulas, prayers, and the use of various artifacts, charms and amulets, thought to have spiritual power. A popular practice is for the exorcist to recite the Qur'an over a cup of water, which is then drunk by the patient. Beatings are frequently used to drive evil jinn out.

Exorcism treatments, according to Islamic Law, are divided into prohibited and permitted categories. Prohibited and permitted treatments are those stated to be so by

Islamic Law, but whatever measures prove to be of value belong to Allah.

In Islam there is no official position known as the exorcist, but different tribes and language groups employ various titles, such as *'amil* in India and Pakistan.

The methodology of exorcism generally involves the following steps:

1. The undoing of charms, where the spirit possession was the result of magic. Such charms are weakened or cancelled. Once a charm has been removed the spell is neutralized.
2. The possessing spirit is commanded to leave. The exorcist may engage the spirit in conversation. The jinn may be evil or good, Muslim or non-Muslim. Non-Muslim spirits may be converted to Islam. The possessing spirits can be corrected and admonished.
3. If a jinn refuses to leave, curses may be spoken by the exorcist. Offending jinn can be scolded, threatened, and "Allah's curse" may be used against it.
4. Recitations from the Qur'an may be used for physical healing as well as driving out jinn. Such authority is found in Qur'an 17:82 and 10:57.
5. *Ayah al-Kursi* means "Verse of the Footstool" (Qur'an 2:255), which the Prophet said was the greatest verse in the Qur'an as it relates to humans. This verse is said to have power when it is read over a spirit-possessed person.
6. Surah al-Baqarah is the second chapter in the Qur'an, also known as "The Cow." In Sahih Muslim, vol. 2, p. 337, no. 1707, Muhammad is reported to have said, "The devil flees from a house in which Surah al-Baqarah is read." There are 286 verses in that chapter, the longest in the Qur'an.
7. The *Basmalah* is a term that means, "In the name of Allah" or "God the Merciful, the Compassionate." This is spoken often by Muslims and is a kind of prayer or incantation. When spoken it is said to weaken or disarm Satan and the jinn.
8. *Ta'awwudh* is a word that means taking refuge or protection from Satan in Allah (Qur'an 41:36 and 23:97–98). It is powerful to ward off evil jinn and Satan. If a person remembers Allah when entering a house and while eating, then devils will not be welcome.
9. *Adhan* and *iqamah* are both calls to prayer and are said to have the ability to drive away demons.
10. Prophetic Prayers, found in various hadith, can cure illnesses and ward off jinn.
11. Natural medicines such as dates may be used to ward off physical trouble caused by jinn. A bath can protect against the evil eye (Sahih Muslim, vol. 3, p. 1192, no. 5427).
12. Beating can be used when all else fails. It is thought that only the jinn experience the pain inflicted on the possessed person. The pain causes the jinn to depart.

Chapter Three: "Modern Muslim Exorcist"

Methods of Exorcism

A number of exorcists from the following seven countries were interviewed to determine the methods they used in exorcisms.

Egypt: Recitation of the Qur'an; Crushed lotus leaves in water and Qur'an read over it then drunk; drinking and bathing; communication with jinn; command to leave; Adhan called in right ear and Uqamah in the left ear; Qur'an read over water and olive oil, water then drunk and oil rubbed on body.

Saudi Arabia: Qur'an recited; grasping the neck; beating; Qur'an read over olive oil and water, oil rubbed and water drunk; string tied around finger and toes followed by beating; communication with jinn; command to leave; jinn bound with an oath to leave; blowing; slapping.

Pakistan: Scented oil poured on cotton and Qur'an read over it and given to smell; Qur'an verses recited in the patient's ear; patient shaken; a lock of hair of the patient's wrapped around the finger of the exorcist; beating; Amulets with Qur'anic verses tied around patient's arm; Qur'an read over water and drunk; Nails with Qur'anic verses read over them hammered in the four corners of the patient's house; communication with jinn; jinn scolded and commanded to leave; incantation before lighting lamps and blowing over lamps causes jinn to leave patient, enter lamp and be burned; Qur'an recited over oil and poured in patient's ear; knot tied in patient's hair to imprison the jinn; bound with oath to leave; Patient tied; Qur'an recited; amulet put around patient's neck or right arm; charm burnt and smoke inhaled.

India: Patient recites over Qur'an; Qur'an recited over water then drunk and bathed with; Qur'an recited over patient; blowing; patient tied down, talismans made of lines, numerology and knowledge of names; charms written in saffron ink on plate, washed with milk and drunk; amulets with Qur'anic verses given to patient; communication with jinn; a lock of hair grabbed to arrest the jinn; knot tied in patient's hair; prayers; amulet worn around neck for seven days.

Trinidad: Qur'an recited over water and drunk; Qur'an recited and blown in patient's face; supplications; prayers; command to leave; mustard oil put in patient's right palm and Qur'an recited over patient with blowing; mustard oil placed in patient's ear and sealed; nostrils pinched closed and palm with mustard oil held in front of mouth; patient's limbs massaged and pressed to determine location of jinn; communication with jinn; jinn driven upward to head and hair; tied lock of hair cut off; beating.

Bahrain: Patient faces Mecca, and line is drawn in front of him and another drawn around him, along with supplications; Qur'anic verses are recited; light beating; communication with jinn; command to leave.

Sudan: Exorcist touches aching body part with hand; Qur'anic verses recited; point of pain blown upon; administered only at sunrise or sunset; Qur'anic verses written on plate or bowl, then washed with water, patient drinks water and water rubbed over body; Qur'an verses or their numerical equivalent written on paper and burned while patient inhales the fumes; amulets with Qur'anic verses written on are tied to patient's ankle, waist, or neck; beating; fasting from meat and dairy products.

General notes:

Other means of treatment are the following: the patient made unconscious by depressing the jugular veins, supposing the jinn will expose itself thereby; the jinn may be arrested by tying knots in a patient's hair, the patient's fingers and toes may be tied to arrest the jinn;

amulets with Qur'anic verses written on them may be used; other occult sciences may also be employed.

Most of those requesting exorcism are women. The jinn may be Muslim or non-Muslim. Exorcists attempt to convert non-Muslim jinn. In India and Pakistan there are few real cases of exorcism. Most are possessed by a single jinn. These jinn may be male or female.

Signs of possession are the following: change of personality; physical changes; mental changes; spiritual changes. In this last category is included strong reactions to the Qur'an and/or to the adhan (the call to prayer), reaction to anything to do with the Qur'an as water drunk which the Qur'an has been recited over; abandonment of religious practices.

Reasons for possession are the following: retaliation for harming the jinn and the patient is then possessed out of revenge; jinn love or lust in that the jinn want to have carnal love relations with the patient; mischief in which evil, non-Muslim jinn possess due to their love of sin; magic where a spell or curse is placed on the patient by other humans.

Chapter Four: Discussion

The author states, "Muslims today erroneously attribute the power to expel jinn to the exorcist himself, rather than the mercy of Allah, which is available to any believer" (p. 195).

The chief and most effective element in Islamic exorcism is the use of the Qur'an. Dr. Philips writes, "Since the time of the Prophet Mohammad (peace be upon him) exorcism by Qur'anic recitation became an indisputable part of canonical prophetic tradition (the Sunnah)" (p. 196). He continues, "The practice of blowing over the demonically possessed patients or on the location where the patient complains of pain is unanimously applied by modern exorcists throughout the Muslim world at different points during their exorcising" (p. 196).

The Qur'an is seen as a magical book, especially in regard to exorcism. This much is made plain in the description of the methods used by Muslim exorcists. An example is the reading over cups of water and/or olive oil, which apparently magically infuses the Qur'an into the liquids, then when drunk expels jinn. Dr. Philips admits that neither Muhammad nor his companions used such a means for exorcism, but such treatment did arise in the Muslim community at a later time. And this practice was based upon Qur'an 17:82 and 10:57, in addition to passages in the Sunnah. He is clear that the use of amulets and talismans is a deviation from standard Islamic practices. The use of occult sciences and numerology is an even greater deviation. As to beating, the opinion is mixed, and Dr. Philips mentions that some patients died as a result of a beating.

The author states that the methodology of exorcism has changed little over the past fourteen centuries, and that Islam does not have persons cast in the role of exorcists (p. 205).

Dr. Philips says "much of the theory and practice of exorcism in Islam agrees with that of Christianity" (p. 204). It is clear that Muslim exorcists are not to employ any techniques that would involve *shirk*, which would be the association of any other deity with

Allah. In regard to Christian exorcism, preferably called deliverance ministry, he is aware that such ministry fashioned after what is seen in the New Testament is effectual, but only because of shirk. He means that those who cast out demons "in the name of Jesus" see results because the jinn, hearing something evil spoken—*shirk*—will leave a possessed person.

On this point, however, I must disagree, as I have shown in two books on the subject and after decades of active engagement with the actual and literal casting out of demons that only Jesus and those who act in his name actually cast out demons.[4]

Muslims and Christians both authenticate demon possession and the expelling of demons. The Muslims do so essentially in the name of Allah. Casting out demons in the name of Jesus, however, while proving demon possession, is far different from exorcism in the name of Allah. It is evident that the exorcists from the various countries whose methodologies are presented in chapter three rarely, if ever, commanded jinn to leave "in the name of Allah." Other magical means were used.

The issue of the effectiveness of Christian deliverance ministry, which employs no magical elements, is problematic. Dr. Philips readily admits the following:

> The question which remains to be answered regarding the Islamic view of exorcism is, "How does Islam explain successful exorcisms performed by Christians over the centuries, when it considers Christianity to be a false religion" (p. 210).

Dr. Philips' reasoning, and that of other Muslims who consider the issue, is that casting out of demons by Christians "in the name of Jesus" works because jinn react upon the employment of shirk, which the jinn regard as evil and so are motivated to leave the possessed person, but he also confusingly asserts that Christians cast out demons "in the name of God" and not in the name of Jesus, which would be effective.

Dr. Philips asserts that those who attempt to exorcize demons in the name of Jesus or in the name of Muhammad are in the same category of error as any of the pagan religionists, which he contends is mere sorcery. And when demons do leave, or appear to leave, it reinforces the notion that there is power in such incantations.

> Consequently, the jinn leave the diabolically possessed during Christian and pagan exorcisms by their own free will, having accomplished their malevolent goal of misguiding mankind as promised by Satan in the Qur'an.[5]

Then Qur'an 7:16–17; 15:39; and 38:82 are quoted as proof.

A final remark:

Generally Christians do not consider saying "in the name of Jesus" to be a magical phrase or spell or incantation, or anything magical at all. I have been part of dozens of situations where demons were cast out without the words, "in the name of Jesus" even being spoken. The phrase simply means that Jesus has defeated Satan and the demonic kingdom by means of His death, burial, resurrection, ascension, and being seated at the right hand of

---

4 Kent Philpott, *Deliver Us from Evil: How Jesus Casts Out Demons Today* (San Rafael, CA: Earthen Vessel Publishing, 2015).

5 Quoted from page 211.

the Father in heaven. It is that Jesus has defeated all that belongs to Satan and the jinn. "The reason the son of God appeared was to destroy the works of the devil" (1 John 3:8). And this Muslims simply cannot accept.

There are many points where Islam and Christianity connect, and exorcism (deliverance) is one of them. Perhaps it is one of the most significant connectors. Dr. Philips' book makes abundantly and sadly clear that Islam has no real way of dealing with the demonic kingdom except by various incantations, prayers, and rituals, which seem not to be effective. Indeed, the average Muslim is at the mercy of a most vicious foe. Combating magic with magic is deceptive, ineffectual, and dangerous.

It is in the realm of spiritual warfare where Bible-based Christians will be able to connect with Muslims and share the love of God with them. Certainly Jesus Christ is the only One who casts out demons, and this is one ministry Christians will be able to bring to Muslim friends.

8

COMMENTARY ON THE BOOKS BY AYAAN HIRSI ALI

Ayaan Hirsi Ali needs no introduction to the many who have followed her efforts to relieve the plight of women and girls in Islamic nations and ghettos wherever they may be found. *Infidel*, a New York Times bestseller, especially impacted me a great deal. In it Ali recounts how she became an immigrant fleeing from an arranged marriage to an older Muslim man and found her way to The Netherlands. She tells the story of how she moved from being a devout Muslim believing in Allah to a position of atheism.

In nearly two decades of studying Islam, my attraction has generally been to non-Christians who write about Islam, since they give more confidence that the purpose is not Islam-bashing or fear mongering. Hirsi Ali does in fact leave Islam, thus becoming an infidel, but her heart reveals someone who hopes to encourage Muslims to think carefully about their religion and fearlessly examine it.

Following are highlights or summaries of Ayaan Hirsi Ali's four books, beginning with the first published.

The Caged Virgin, An Emancipation Proclamation for Women and Islam [1]

Ayaan's parents raised her to be a good Muslim. Islam dominated the lives of her family down to the smallest details. Islam was the family's ideology, political conviction, moral standard, law, and identity. She considered herself as one submitted to Islam, which was Allah's will for her. She was taught that Islam set her apart from the rest of the world, the world of non-Muslims, and that Muslims alone are chosen by God. Others are *kaffir*, unbelievers, and thus are antisocial, impure, barbaric, not circumcised, immoral, unscrupulous, and above all, obscene. The kaffir have no respect for women; their girls and women are whores; many of the men are homosexual; and men and women have sex without being married. The unfaithful are cursed, and God will punish them most atrociously in the hereafter. This was her unquestioned understanding.

---

1 Ayaan Hirsi Ali, *The Caged Virgin: An Emancipation Proclamation for Women and Islam* (New York: Atria Paperback, a Division of Simon & Shuster, Inc., 2002).

As time went on, and as she discovered a larger world, she began to take a more critical look at her faith and discovered three important elements of Islam that had not struck her before.

The first of these is that Allah demands total submission, with the result that a Muslim's relationship with God is based on fear.

The second is that Islam knows only one source for its morality—the Prophet Muhammad and what he did and did not do.

The third is that Islam is strongly dominated by a sexual morality derived from tribal Arab values that date from the time the Prophet received his instructions from Allah.

She then realized that any Muslim who asks critical questions about Islam is branded a "deserter."

She understands that there are three kinds of Muslims in the West. The first is a silent minority that does not live according to the doctrines of Islam. They may say they are Muslim for varying reasons, but in their hearts and minds they are not actually Muslim.

The second grouping strongly identifies with Islam and is offended by any form of criticism of the faith. For generations these Muslims have come to think that their distress has nothing to do with the religion itself but is generated by outsiders' oppression, particularly by Western nations. These Muslims feel an emotional bond with their oppressed brothers and sisters elsewhere in the world.

Thirdly, there are the progressive Muslims who see themselves trapped in a cage and are willing to risk a public examination of their religion.

Ayaan believes, and this is a continual theme throughout her books, that the way out of the cage is to cease blaming others for the backwardness of Muslim cultures worldwide.

The constant trouble is that the fundamentalists, hardliners, or pious ones blame "questioning" Muslims and accuse them of not living their lives according to Islamic doctrine. The Islamic pious ones tend to believe that their religion suffers because of the failure of moderate Muslims to follow strict Islamic practices and laws.

Ayaan calls attention to how many Muslims live their lives wherein "rows of saints, ghosts, angels, and little demons play significant supporting parts." Islamic daily life is spiritual but unhealthily so—a world filled with spiritual entities that must be placated, avoided, or appeased. The Muslim world is one, she contends, of continual communication with spirits of the dead.

Ayaan points out that ordinary Muslims, not just the fundamentalists, are caught up in a word of spiritual beings in their daily lives. But it is this last grouping that most easily become radicalized and will more willingly engage in acts of terror.

The zealous pious ones teach that all of a Muslim's life must be focused on obeying the myriad of Islamic rules and laws in order to go to paradise. The result is that most Muslims see their lives as governed by a strong fatalism and thus may give up on life altogether.

Ayaan sees that the Western liberal response to Islam, whereby Islam is seen as having been hijacked by radicals, obscures the fact that Islam itself is wrong and dangerous. Political leaders, for whatever reasons, are fearful or reluctant to say that the religion itself is flawed and twisted.

She also points out that the decreasing number of young Muslims who attend Mosque is deceptive, because they nevertheless retain a strong Muslim identity.

One of the problems Ayaan perceives is that few have analyzed the origins of Islam from a sociological point of view. Among Muslims, the tribe and/or clan is central, and each Muslim is to be obedient to the tribal leaders. The ummah, or Muslim community, always comes first, and the general culture is shame-based, in that great emphasis is placed on avoiding bringing shame on the family, the clan, or the tribe. Much of this shame has to do with women and sexuality.

In terms of Muslim integration into non-Muslim cultures, much has to do with how women are regarded and treated in Islam. For instance, the best that women can look forward to in paradise are dates and grapes, if they make it to paradise at all. But most staggering is what Ayaan refers to as "stitching" and has to do with female genital mutilation. Stitching is especially popular in African Islamic countries, such as Somalia, Eritrea, Sudan, Nigeria, and Egypt, and also in Indonesia.

Ayaan points out that Muslim advancement in education, science, the arts, and so on, is very small, because Muslims are so very often discouraged from engaging with the Western world in such matters. Instead, poverty, violence, and decline are widespread. Ayaan is certain that in order to change this situation, the moral fabric of Islam must undergo a revolution. Indeed, a large proportion of current political conflicts involve Muslims, most of whom live in dire circumstances. Starvation, disease, overpopulation, and unemployment are widespread. Much of this has to do with political leaders who are really little more than dictators who base their system of governance on some form of Sharia Law.

She believes that the Jewish and Christian faiths are also flawed and that their members or adherents also need to free themselves from oppressive rules and regulations.

Terrorists and other Muslims who are fundamentalists believe that people are born to serve Allah through a series of obligations that are prescribed in an ancient body of writings. These laws govern and control all aspects of life, from birth to the grave. Many such laws are petty and absurd, such as the necessity of properly blowing one's nose in the morning and with which foot to step into a bathroom.

Muslims are taught they must kill those among them who leave their faith, the apostates, and be hostile to people of other religions. The murder of non-Muslim innocent people is sanctioned, with no consideration made for male or female, young or old, civilian or military. All who oppose Islam, all who are unbelievers, are subject to death. Though this is a fact, it is often concealed by stating that Islam is the religion of peace.

Note: Peace for Muslims generally has little to do with peace between nations. Rather, peace will reign when the globe is dominated by Islam.

In a culture based on Sharia Law, women are subordinate to men. They must be confined to their homes, beaten if found disobedient, forced into marriage, and hidden behind the veil. The hands of thieves are cut off, and capital punishment is performed on crowded public squares in front of cheering crowds. Terrorists seek to impose this way of life not only in Islamic countries, but in Western societies within the safety of Muslim ghettoes, of which there are a growing number.

Muhammad looms very large amongst Muslims, which forces them to deny or reject concrete and historical facts, including the following: Muhammad used military tactics that included mass killing, torture, targeted assassination, and lying, among other embarrassing events, and which are difficult for Muslims to admit or even consider. On the other hand, the highly questionable deeds done by Muhammad and his armies form a justification for modern acts of terror.

The fear or threat of being cast into hellfire is the single most effective hold fundamentalists have over young men and women. This is a principal tactic used to indoctrinate and intimidate young and impressionable youth.

European Muslims may be generally grouped into three categories. First are the jihadists who are ready to shed innocent blood, supported by the fundamentalists, who do not kill or maim, but provide the terrorists with various forms of assistance. Second are the very opposite of these (although small in number but growing in numbers and influence) who question the relevance and moral soundness of Muhammad's example. This last group may be referred to as "reformers." The third are undecided Muslims. They generally agree with Islam's doctrines but that they should apply only to Muslims and not to others, i.e., Westerners.

Ayaan brings up the issue of spreading the faith—proselytizing. It is mostly the case that non-Islamic religions are prohibited from building houses of worship, schools, graveyards, and more in places where Islam is dominant. She asks, if Muslims can proselytize in Vatican City, why can't Christians proselytize in Mecca? Why are Jews and Christians and atheists in the West the ones fighting genocide in Darfur? Why does it pass unnoticed in Muslim lands when Shi'as kill Sunnis and Sunnis kill Shi'as by the thousands?

One of Ayaan's most potent presentations has to do with women. She notes that obsessive subjugation of women is one of the things that makes Islam so reprehensible. From Riyadh to Tehran, from Islamabad to Cairo, Muslims are taught to believe that if the lives of women are improved, it will lead to a deterioration of Islam itself. If women were not held in careful check, then Islam simply could not cope with it. And, so very importantly, the decline of Islam then would mean the loss of power for the religious authorities—women are a threat to the power structure. This is a major and controlling reason why Muslim authorities are so desperate to cage in women. This is also why the West is so hated, since the West tends to value and uplift women.

Of course, there are the female apologists who continue to trumpet the good lives women have in Islam.

Note: Until recently, it was usual to see spots on television and on the internet where Muslim women, wearing the hijab, would appear in a cameo proclaiming how wonderful Islam is. "It is the religion of peace" they would say. These ads are few and far between now.

Ayaan strongly proclaims that she is not a Muslim, and this is because she "lost her fear of the Holy Book, the terror of being burned alive after [she] die[s], and being forced to drink the bitter Dari." She goes on: "I am not a Muslim, because I lost respect for the book and its author and his messenger. I lost respect for them because of their bloodthirsty demands to kill and hate. I now feel the common humanity with those whom I once shunned: the Jews, Christians, atheists, gays, and sinners of all stripes and colors" (p. 175).

EIGHT

Infidel [2]

Note: For the next three of Ayaan's books, beginning here with *Infidel*, repetition of earlier material will be avoided in favor of focusing on new insights and discussions. When there are redundancies, it is to emphasize a critical and important point.

Looking back at her life, Ali admits that Islam gave her a sense of peace and an assurance of life after death.

Islam, specifically its book and its leaders, are not to be argued with or questioned. Islam means "submission," and this is complete and total. A Muslim submits here and now in order to enter paradise later. That is the whole thing, and it all depends on being a good Muslim. She confesses that she was failing as a Muslim.

Note: One of the more interesting doctrines of Islam is that there are angels on a person's right and left shoulders. One records the good deeds done (right shoulder angel) and the other the bad deeds (left shoulder angel).

She states, "When I prayed, I felt that the angel on my left shoulder was growing weary of writing down all my sins" (p. 132). She supposed that once she got to paradise, the good deeds book would be very thin, and the other as thick as the unabridged Oxford Dictionary. She wanted to feel like a worthy Muslim, but it was not going to be. She assumed that Allah did not want her.

To make a long story short, Ayaan, to avoid an arranged marriage, escaped from her family and clan and managed to get to The Netherlands. There she began a whole new life, even becoming a member of that nation's parliament. Now free to do and think as she pleased, she moved further and further away from Islam.

The Netherlands (Holland) had mechanisms in place whereby immigrants could integrate into that society. Ayaan did so, and over the course of time made the necessary adjustments. The social welfare system made this possible. Ayaan notes that, taken as a whole, Muslims in Holland make disproportionately heavy claims on social welfare and disability benefits and yet are disproportionately involved in crime.

Ayaan states that it was while in Holland that she left Islam behind and became an atheist. At first she was reluctant to go public with her new faith position, because for a Muslim, to be an apostate is the worst thing possible. She knew that Christians could cease to believe in God, as it is a personal matter. But for a Muslim to cease believing in Allah can be lethal.

Now she began to analyze what was important to her. For one, she wanted her new country to wake up and stop tolerating the oppression of Muslim women in its midst. Indeed, she felt that the government must take action to protect Muslim women and at the same time punish their oppressors. Then she wanted to generate a debate among Muslims about reforming Islam; she hoped Muslims would take a hard look at the tenets of their religion. She recognized that such a critique could only take place in the West, since this would never be possible in any Muslim-majority country.

Ali hoped Muslim women would come to see and admit just how awful, how unac-

---

2 Ayaan Hirsi Ali, *Infidel* (New York; Atria Paperback, a Division of Simon & Shuster, Inc., 2007).

ceptable, their plight was. One obstacle was that most Muslim women living in Western countries had no means of comparison. She wanted Muslim women to develop a "vocabulary of resistance."

Ayaan, having also lived in Saudi Arabia and Kenya, as well as Somalia, understood that the mode of thinking in these countries prevented any inner dialogue within Islam in terms of being able to engage in critical thinking. Rather, the entire culture reinforces a fundamentalist way of thinking and acting. The whole system depends upon and preserves a feudal mind-set and which is largely based on upholding honor and avoiding shame.

She had become aware that although Islam denigrates the West for their technology and other scientific advances, which the purists view as sinful, they nevertheless take advantage of these and in a most hypocritical manner.

If Islam is seen by the West as just another culture that must be preserved, and no fault or error is associated with it, and if Islam is counted as merely one of the world's great religions, then no real progress will be made.

Avenues for transition must be opened up for Muslim people to be free of the tyranny imposed by the hard liners. She points out, especially in regard to women, that hundreds of millions of Muslim women live in arranged, forced marriages and that some six thousand young girls underdo female genital mutilation every single day. She asks how it is that the West, let alone educated Muslims, turn a blind eye to these atrocities and thereby perpetuate such incredible abuse, all in the name of diversity, tolerance, and political correctness. The apologists for Islam continue with the idea that Islam is the religion of peace, that Islam stands for compassion and tolerance, yet even a cursory examination of all that is Islam belies this presumption, at minimum.

Toward the end of *Infidel*, on page 348, Ayaan writes,

> The message of this book, if it must have a message, is that we in the West would be wrong to prolong the pain of that transition unnecessarily, by elevating cultures full of bigotry and hatred toward women to the stature of respectable alternative ways of life.

Nomad: From Islam to America [3]

In the preface Ayaan states that a radical minority of Muslims strongly holds to the notion that Islam is under siege and blames the West for all of it. They hope to establish a caliphate, which at some point in the future will rule the entire rest of the world.

Note: Ali wrote this prior to the rise of Al-Baghdadi's caliphate, the Islamic State or ISIS in Iraq and Syria.

Some Muslims fear that the rise of extremism will trigger a backlash against Muslims living in the West. At the time of the writing of *Nomad* this rise had not come into full flower. The radicals, however, were aware of the potential and began to raise the defense that Muslims were only protecting themselves from Western persecution. And it is in the ghettos where smallish groups of radicals fan the flames of fear and hatred.

Ali sees the agents for change and for integration residing in three institutions:

---

3   Ayaan Hirsi Ali, (New York: Atria Paperback, a Division of Simon & Shuster, Inc., 2010).

The first is public education, the second is the feminist movement, and the third is the community of Christian churches.

Though she is an atheist, Ali understands that many Muslims need a spiritual anchor in their lives. She is aware of Muslims being attracted to Jesus Christ and who find Christ a more humane person than Muhammad.

At the heart of the clash of values between the tribal cultures of Islam and Western modernity are three universal human passions: sex, money, and violence. Her argument here is complex and somewhat difficult to grasp. Sex in Muslim societies is tinged, to put it mildly, with shame. Sex is viewed as necessary for procreation and the pleasure of men, with women's sexual needs largely ignored. Money is the necessary means to power, and therefore the ability to engage in violent acts to spread Islam. Taken together, the right understanding of sex, money, and violence, with violence the ubiquitous method of settling affairs—these are roadblocks to integration.

Ali's mother and grandmother figure large in her growing up. She recalls her grandmother talking to dead ancestors and forefathers. Ali was warned not to upset dead family members and that women are responsible to ensure the carrying out of virtuous deeds and continual attendance to practices meant to secure the spiritual well being of the family.

Note: Here Ayaan opens a window, however slightly, into a world of fear, superstition, magical practices, and the never ending ordeal of placating the evil as well as the benign jinn.

Ali brings up *taqqiyah*, which amounts to pretending to be someone you are not. She says that making up stories that were untrue was taught to her as a young child. Taqquiyah is a practice so common among Muslims that they lose a sense of reality.

Note: Taqqiyah is the distorting of truth or lying in order to defend or promote Islam. Muhammad, as recorded in the Qur'an, sanctioned and practiced this. As I have found over and over, it is second nature to many Muslims, seeming to be so natural a process they are largely unaware of their deceptive behavior.

Ayaan found that American liberals are not fond of her communicating the awful plight of women in Muslim-majority countries, that they shy away from speaking out against the blatant abuse of women there. She observed that American conservatives deal more realistically with this issue.

She is reminded that as a young person she was attracted to dynamic young radical teachers of Islam who gave her a sense of significance and gave her a vision of having an important role to fulfill in life. These preachers of radical Islam reject the weird superstitions about the jinn and strange folk traditions and focus on the doctrines of the Qur'an and the mistreatment of Muslims today that must be avenged. These preachers held up the saintly and pure life of Muhammad and the pious companions of the seventh century and challenged their students to believe and act as they did. She points out that this very thing has been going on in Europe for a long while now, to the point that many young Muslims, both men and women, radicalized and poised for action, have become like a "fifth column."

So Ayaan raises the question: Can a person be a Muslim and an American patriot at the same time? Her answer is: Only if you don't care about being a Muslim.

She cites a poll taken among Muslims between the ages of eighteen and twenty-nine, living in America, which asked if suicide bombing is permitted for a Muslim to advance the cause of Islam. Yes, said 26% of the respondents.

Speaking of her Islamic studies at age sixteen in Nairobi, Kenya, at what she calls a revivalist mosque, she describes how a teacher taught her and her classmates to reject the old time superstition of the grandmothers. Ayaan observed that peculiar to the revivalist mosque in contradistinction to the old style mosques, women flocked to them. She suggests, "If you see women flocking to the mosque to pray, perhaps you should be suspicious."

Little by little is the idea. Muslim religious leaders are very patient. At first the instruction has to do with how to live a good life, one that is pleasing to Muhammad and Allah. Part of that is not making friends with anyone who is not Muslim. Some steps down that path, and it may be miles later, violent jihad's legitimacy and necessity asserts itself. Muslims are taught from birth not to question but to submit. This is the education process that underlies the violent defense of Islam.

Continuing Ayaan's coverage about women in Islam, she reveals the fact that limiting men's access to sex with women is a central focus of the code of honor and shame. After marriage, the woman must be faithful to her husband and is responsible for much of the veiling, making sure women never appear in public without a male escort and keeping women and girls quartered in the home. The wife can never refer to her husband by his first name but must refer to him as *rajel*, meaning "my lord."

Virginity of the female is of major importance. It is better for a Muslim girl to die than lose her virginity to anyone but her husband. And the woman (girl) and her family will lose respect and be shamed, even if the virginity is lost via rape. Women can be stoned to death for being raped. After all, a man is not responsible for his lustful ways—it is always the female's fault.

Women in Islam are the sexual property of their husbands.

Indeed, once the hymen is broken, the female is then considered dirty, filthy, and diseased. Even the natural female menstruation tarnishes the female, as she is seen as engaged in something evil, even contaminated by jinn.

Ali notes that one of the reasons contemporary Islamic teachers avoid the reality of the jinn is that it seems to present other deities than Allah.

Many Muslims see Western schooling to be an agent of corruption for their children. And, Ayaan admits, it does in fact do so. It gives students a look at the world that is not dominated by Islamic teaching; therefore, the hard liners consider it to be dangerous.

Islamic apologists tend to insist that Muslim women's subjection and ill treatment, which must now be admitted due to media coverage, is due to cultural factors rather than being inherent in Islam itself. Of course, the two influences are connected, even though such tribal shame was present prior to the advent of Islam. Islam nevertheless incorporated and sanctified the tribal culture of the Arabian Peninsula into the Qur'an and hadith.

Qur'anic passages that present women as property are straightforward. For instance, the permission, even command, that husbands "beat the disobedient wife" are well known, just as well known as is "Kill the infidel." Muslim teachers and apologists do their best to make these passages obscure with editorial fences built around them. Their tactics result in phrases that do not seem as harsh, as in "Don't beat her on the face," "Don't beat her to break her bones," and "Use only a small stick."

Note: I have several editions of the Qur'an. When I discuss certain passages with Muslims I will hear, "Well, you are using the wrong version of the Qur'an." Yet, all the editions I have are virtually the same. And it is interesting that in the actual text are many added words and phrases in parenthesis, which are inserted by editors intending to assist the reader. In my view, they serve to soften the harsh and obvious meaning. Then at the bottom of the page, often far longer than the text, are found scholar's notes of explanation of the text, most of which intend again to soften the harsh tone of the passages.

The Qur'an is very troublesome for those who wish to reform Islam, for to suggest there is even a hint of a problem challenges the whole basis of the religion. The whole ediface falls with a small crack.

Ali then writes about how the Jewish and Christian tribes in particular, who heard Muhammad preach and recite what he said came from Gabriel, called attention to long passages that were obviously lifted right out of the Old and New Testaments.

The Muslim fundamentalists are therefore stuck. They cannot modernize; they can only obscure. Ayaan uses the word "cognitive dissonance" in this regard. On the one hand are the difficult passages, and on the other the need to do and be like Muhammad and the early Muslims. The result is a Qur'an that is claimed to be perfect but misunderstood. This cognitive dissonance may lead to the idea that the West is engaged in a severe attempt to destroy the one true religion. And the chief enemy is the Jews.

Note: The traditionalists of Islam believe the Qur'an to be as eternal as Allah and that the original Qur'an is on a special table in heaven. It seems to me that Islam has a trinity of Allah, Muhammad, and the Qur'an. All three are worshipped in a very real sense. Islamic apologists deny this, of course.

In regard to the Jewish people, Ayaan sees three different propaganda tracks that result in anti-Semitism: One, increase the number of people who see the Jews as enemies. Two, use Islam to promote anti-Semitism. Three, picture Islam to be the underdog.

She points out that modern wars are not fought in the classic style, where enemies square off on a battlefield. Islam knows that the West is stronger militarily but that Muslims have numbers on their side. The targets of Muslim hate speech—women, gay people, infidels, Christians, atheists, and Jews—are divided among themselves, and the more so the better. Surely factions within Islam may kill one another, as with the Shi'a and Sunni Muslims viewing each other as heretics, and Muslims in Arabia may despise African Muslims, and the Muslims in Turkey and Iran may look down on Arab Muslims, but they still believe, hope may be a better word, that in the face of an Islam versus the West conflict, Muslims will unite and fight as one.

Note: My view is that such uniting is a fiction. In country after country, Yemen, Syria, Turkey, Iraq, Afghanistan, Egypt, Libya, and much more, such is clearly not the case.

For Muslims to be united there must be a common foe. At the top of the list of enemies are the Jews, who are pictured as the elite, wealthy power brokers who control the world. America is right up there—the Great Satan—as are apostates, and it is the apostates, those Muslims who leave Islam, who are hated the most.

Islam is all consuming—it is religion and state all rolled into one, and Islam is violent, and Muslims clearly understand that violent jihad will be the means by which Islam will dominate the world. And from day one, every Muslim is taught to be violent and accept violence as a way of advancing Islam.

Ayaan speaks directly about honor killing, which primarily has to do with a girl or woman who shames the family and clan. The only way to expunge the shame is for the female "offender" to be killed. Oddly, no dishonor comes to the person, usually a family member, father, mother, or brother, who does the actual deed.

The female's offense almost always involves sex. Even being alone with a man who is not a family member is enough to provoke an honor killing. To resist a forced marriage, like Ayaan did, is sufficient cause. A young teen dating a boy of her own choice can also be a trigger. Ayaan adds that there are even more trivial matters such as mere suspicion, which can serve as a catalyst.

Ayaan became an atheist, yet she recognized that the Christian Church had a possible role to play in reforming Islam. In conversation with a Father Bodar, she explained that Christians ought to engage in *dawa* or evangelism with Muslims. Muslims engage in dawa, which is attempting to bring non-Muslims into Islam, and Christians should do the reverse. She told him Christians need to compete, since it would be a powerful tool in reversing Islamization. She spoke of Muslim ghettos in the West that are being neglected.

Note: Ayaan's urging for Christians to evangelize Muslims is one major reason I began to reach out to Muslims in my community.

Ali suspects that most Muslims are sincerely searching for God, a God who is forgiving, a God one does not have to fear. Muslims already believe in a higher power that will lead and guide them. Ayaan thinks the Christian concept of God meets the description of the God Muslims are looking for.

She notes that most Muslims are horrified at the violence perpetrated in the name of Islam. She is also aware that most Muslims know little of their own religion and know little or nothing about the Qur'an or the hadith.

She does comment on her understanding of the Apostle Paul, thinking that he had contempt for women.

Note: On this point, Christians take differing positions, and my view is that Paul's view of women is not what many contemporary Westerners would applaud, but certainly women are treated by Paul, and especially by Jesus, as being the equal of men in God's eyes.

Ayaan goes so far as to urge atheists and classical liberals like herself to support and encourage Christian outreach to Muslims.

She is critical of Christian leaders who waste time and resources in interfaith dialogue with Muslims. She urges Christians to proclaim the God "who has sent his son to die for all sinners out of love for mankind" (p. 247).

Muslim evangelists work not to save from poverty, drug addiction, and homelessness, but to raise up a cadre of young soldiers to fight violent jihad.

Ayaan would prefer Muslims to believe in a religious leader like Jesus who said,

"Render to Caesar the things that are Caesar's, and to God the things that are God's," rather than a warrior like Muhammad, who demanded that the pious seek to gain power by the sword.

But she wonders if America has strong enough Christian networks to do the evangelistic work that is needed.

Ali then assures us, "I am not a Christian and have no plans to convert."

Heretic: Why Islam Needs a Reformation Now

In *Heretic*,[4] Ayaan recognizes that the radicals, extremists, and fundamentalists are motivated by a political ideology that is embedded in Islam itself. In reality, this group, though a minority, understands the goal of Islam, which is plain in the Qur'an and in the hadith—yes, in the very life and teachings of the Prophet Muhammad himself—nothing less than world domination.

With this understanding, she hopes to engage in dialogue with those whom she says are closer to Mecca than Medina. She is speaking of the "softer" Muhammad living in Mecca at the outset of the appearances of the angel Gabriel, when the Jews and Christians, the people of the Book, were not seen as enemies. When, due to opposition, Muhammad had to immigrate to Medina, the nature of the recitations changed dramatically. She hopes this group, the larger segment of Islam, will hear her call for reformation.

In her present state, as an apostate, there is little chance her voice will be heard by "moderate" Muslims. Therefore she casts herself into the position of a heretic. A heretic is one who deviates from the norm and may yet have an audience.

Ali's goal is critical thinking on the part of Muslims, that they truly think about their religion. This "third group"—those who are willing to ask the hard questions—is whom she addresses in this fourth volume. She knows, however, that a vast majority of Muslims, especially those from Pakistan, Bangladesh, and Iraq believe people like her should be put to death.

Note: the killings of those who are in disagreement with a religion serve only to demonstrate the weakness of that religion. It is my impression, developed over fifteen years of reading, writing, and researching Islam, that Muslim leaders are concerned that their religion cannot stand up to scrutiny.

Ali presents five areas in which reform is needed (p. 24):

» Muhammad's semi-divine and infallible status along with the literalist reading of the Qur'an, particularly those parts that were revealed in Medina;

» The investment in life after death instead of life before death;

» Re-evaluation of and application of Sharia Law, that body of legislation derived from the Qur'an, the hadith, and understandings developed out of Islamic jurisprudence;

» The practice of self-empowered individuals to enforce Islamic law by commanding right and forbidding wrong;

---

4 Ayaan Hersi Ali, *Heretic* (New York: Harper, 2015).

» The imperative to wage jihad, or holy war.

Ayaan reminds her readers of her credentials, or why she is able to speak as she does. Her history is known: raised a practicing Muslim for almost half her life; attended madrassas and memorized large parts of the Qur'an; as a child, lived in Mecca for a time and frequently visited the Grand Mosque; as a teenager, joined the Muslim Brotherhood.

She stopped praying, fasting, and wearing a hijab. More seriously, she violated at least two of the six major Qur'anic *hudood* restrictions. The hudood prescribe fixed punishments for (1) consumption of alcohol, (2) fornication or adultery, (3) apostasy, (4) theft, (5) robbery, and (6) falsely accusing someone of illicit sexual relations. She confesses, or rather, announces that she broke #1 and #2.

Ayaan wonders whether all who question Islam must either leave the faith or embrace violent jihad. She proposes a third option, but it demands the recognition that the trouble with Islam is embedded in Islam itself. To do what she did, leaving Islam all together, is the best. But few will do so. To preserve a healthy conscience, feel comfortable with toleration of differences in faith, embrace equality between men and women, and experience the good things of life, a Muslim will likely have to abandon Islam.

Standing in the way of that third option, to simply leave Islam, is "the honor brigade." This loosely-organized, worldwide coalition is designed to thwart even a questioning of Islam. Muslim leadership understands that questioning Islam or allowing people to take a hard look at it would mean the departure of large numbers. Allowing innovations, even small reforms, might trigger a strong reaction from the honor brigade. It is this tactic that is preventing Islam from taking its place as one of the world's best or most credible religions. In Buddhism, Hinduism, Christianity, and other religions, critique is common. In Islam such may be punishable by death.

Islam is decentralized, making it highly inflexible and slow to change. The new radical Islam resists change and rejects much of what the rest of the world embraces.

Ayaan does not advocate the overthrow of Islam. *Reforming* Islam is her hope, and her five theses for reform are based on the list of areas in need of reform presented above:

» Ensure that Muhammad and the Qur'an are open to interpretation and criticism.

» Give priority to this life, not the afterlife.

» Shackle Sharia Law and end its supremacy over secular law.

» End the practice of individuals "commanding right, forbidding wrong."

» Abandon the call to jihad.

In chapter 3, "Muhammad and the Qur'an," Ayaan describes the violent turn Muhammad took in his struggle to establish his fledgling movement.

From Sahih Muslim, a major collection of hadith, it is reported that Muhammad took the lead in nineteen military battles and fought in many of them himself. He also sold women and children into slavery after slaughtering the men. Muhammad became a man of war.

From Sahih Bukhari, the most revered collection of hadith, there are at least four hundred stories describing attacks on enemies led by Muhammad. These were intended to squash opposition, not by persuasion but by force, and to acquire booty to pay his troops.

As is well known, honor and shame play a major role in Islamic culture.

Honoring the family, the clan, and the tribe is instilled in children from day one. It can be dangerous, tragic even, if a person brings dishonor to the family or clan. Dishonor usually involves sex, and women are at the center of it. If an event occurs that shames a family, death may be the result. The killing of a family member who causes shame, as in a father killing a daughter or a son, strangely does not bring dishonor but honor.

Central to Muslim practice is having a large family, which is behind many of the marriage customs like arranged marriages, early age of marriage for both boys and girls, and polygamy. The clan or tribe is an extended kinship group whose numbers are increased by means of the above customs. The result is that "the space between generations shrinks, and the number of descendants grows" (p. 86).

Ultimate dishonor is to question the authority of Muhammad, the Qur'an, and the dictates of Sharia Law. In fact, to question the Qur'an at all is considered an act of heresy and can be punishable by death. To have a family member do so is unacceptable.

The Qur'an, especially the surahs recited in Medina, provides justification for the most violent of actions against any apostates or unbelievers besides many other activities that most other cultures would abhor.

Ali does not hesitate to question the authority of the Qur'an. She points out that there are many problems with the origin of the Qur'an and its transmission. Yes, the Qur'an states there is no coercion or compulsion in religion—from Surah 2:256—but then there are also verses that command believers to fight all non-Muslims till they either convert or submit to Islam—Surah 8:39; 9:5; and 9:29.

Jihad is a word that is found many times in the Qur'an. See Surah 2:218; 3:143; 8:72-75; 9:16, 20, 41, 86; and 61:11. She quotes al-Ghazali, a medieval Muslim scholar who wrote, "Blind obedience to God is the best evidence of our Islam." And many Muslims consider al-Ghazali to be second in authority behind Muhammad.

Ali states that a first critical step in moving toward reform is to admit the humanness of Muhammad as well as the human element in the Qur'an and the hadith. A second critical step, especially in regard to violent jihad, is to focus on this life and not the next. And then, the necessity of defending and advancing Islam as a means to a Islamic Paradise must be abandoned.

Islam gives little value to this present life. Islam is a religion that loves death more than life. To die a martyr is the highest status one could attain. And to die killing apostates and heretics and infidels is the great desire. Her conviction is that Islam "must be challenged and changed. Islam teaches that there is nothing so glorious as taking an infidel's life—and so much the better if the act of murder costs you your own life" (p. 117).

On page 120, Ayaan quotes Ismail Radwan, an Islamic university professor and spokesman for Hamas in Gaza, as he explains what the reward will be for those who die for Islam:

> When the *shahid* (Martyr for Allah) meets the Lord, all his sins are forgiven from the first gush of blood, and he is exempted from the torments of the grave. He sees his place in Paradise. He is shielded from the Great Shock and marries 72 Dark-Eyed [Virgins]. He is a heavenly advocate for 70 members of his family. On his head is placed a crown of honor, one stone of which is worth more than all there is in this world.

Hamas in Gaza is not the only place in Islam-dominated cultures where little children are outfitted as suicide bombers.

Note: Of course, not all Muslims, in fact a smallish minority, whole-heartedly embrace the extreme notions advocated by Ismail Radwan, but these voices are generally silent. If such voices were to be heard, they would invite accusations of weakness, which is just one step from apostasy.

Islam embraces the doctrine of fatalism. Whatever happens has been determined and actualized by Allah, therefore rendering human responsibility to almost insignificance, and this regards everything in life such as caring for children and the environment. It is this fatalism that prevents innovation and thwarts social and economic advances, thus ensuring that Islamic cultures remain backward.

Muslims strive to live under Sharia Law, but it prevents them from moving forward. Here are some of these laws: beheadings–47:4; crucifixion–5:33; amputations–5:38; stoning–in the hadith, Abu Dawud, book 38, no. 4413. Allah even warns, in regards to those caught in adultery, "Let not compassion move you" (24:2).

Sharia Law has a short list of those things that can be done, known as *halal* and thus permitted, and a long list of those things that are forbidden, known as *haram*.

Apostasy is the number one offense, which is when a Muslim stops submitting to Islam. Apostates are to be killed.

Homosexuality: according to the hadith Abu Dawud, book 38, no. 4447, "If you find anyone doing as Lot's people did, kill the one who does it, and the one to whom it is done."

One of Ayaan's laments is the blindness of much of the Western countries who "bend over backward to accommodate Muslim 'sensitivities' and often excuse or look the other way when Muslims violate universal human rights—even when they do so in our own countries" (p. 150).

She admits there are countries, such as Pakistan, that never will turn away from strict Islamic Sharia Law. But that does not mean authorities in Western countries should let Muslim communities operate under that Islamic law system. She writes, "Under no circumstances should Western countries allow Muslims to form self-governing enclaves in which women and other supposedly second-class citizens can be treated in ways that belong in the seventh century" (p. 152).

In chapter six, "Social Control Begins At Home," Ali illustrates what Muslims consider to be immodest behavior. The list of immodest behavior mostly has females in mind. Singing, looking out a window, talking to a man who is not a relative, marrying for love, and resisting an arranged marriage are but a few.

In a discussion about homosexuality she notes, "there are significant gay and lesbian populations in all Islamic nations. Because affairs with women are so logistically difficult, for example, Arab men have long turned to other men to satisfy their sexual needs. In Afghanistan, wealthy tribesmen are known to purchase young boys for their personal pleasure" (p. 166).

She makes the plea to Western countries not to ignore murder, rape, forced marriages, and other clear and plain crime. Right and wrong—halal and haram—cannot be defined by Sharia Law but by the laws of the nation state. Where right is commanded and the wrong forbidden, there is no real freedom.

Ali points out that Western observers of Islam often blame colonialism, cultural differences, and other sociological and environmental factors as the root causes for the dysfunctional ways of many Muslims. The difficulty Muslims have with integration into and acceptance of Western values is also blamed on causes peculiar to Muslim culture rather than the reality that the religion itself is the foundational problem.

One of the chief failures of the West is not understanding that the goal of Islam is to dominate the entire globe. According to fundamental Islamic doctrine, all people are to convert to Islam, submit to Islam, or be killed—and that this can only come through violent jihad. It is as simple as that, but even in the face of clear admissions by Islamic authorities, many in the West disregard such declarations.

Of course, jihad is usually presented to Muslim youth as a struggle to become more like Muhammad. This is the "greater" jihad, but the title is deceiving. Verses in the Qur'an that speak of jihad are 9.5; 8.60; 8.39; and 8.65.

A statement Ayaan applies to herself and her situation is one that would apply across the board: "It is not just an apostate like me who must now live in fear; even moderate Muslims face threats" (p. 184).

She points out that in surah 5:51, Muslims are warned, "Take not the Jews and the Christians for your friends and protectors."

This is Christophobia, which is little mentioned in the West. That there is Islamophobia in the West and that it is growing due to events is a reality. Yet this pales into insignificance alongside Christophobia and hatred for the Jews in Muslim countries and communities.

Attacks on Christians and all that is the West, which is generally considered Christian, is not necessarily planned by a central authoritative Islamic group but is the result of widespread anti-Christian sentiments among Muslims.

Ayaan clearly notes that Saudi Arabia funds much anti-West and anti-Christian violence. She concludes that if Muslims don't disown the call for violent jihad, Westerners should at least deny that Islam is a religion of peace.

Apartheid is something Ali says exists among Muslims, especially with the extremists, where people are singled out due to the color of their skin, their gender, sexual orientation, and religion, and for Muslims it extends to whether they are religious enough. She especially challenges so-called feminists and liberals to stop overlooking and excusing the behavior of Islamists.

Ayaan says there is a battle going on within Islam today, between what she refers to as the Medina and the Mecca Muslims. Muhammad, while yet in Mecca, was far more conciliatory and benevolent than the Muhammad of Medina. And so the Qur'an amply shows. This gives her hope that a Muslim Reformation may be coming.

Ali quotes from Malala Yousafzai, the Nobel Prize winning teen:

> The extremists are afraid of books and pens. The power of education frightens them. They are afraid of women. The power of the voice of women frightens them. That is why they are blasting schools every day—because they were and they are afraid of change, afraid of the equality that we will bring to our society. They think that God is a tiny, little conservative being who would send girls to the hell just because of going to school (p. 229).

Cabu Musab al-Suri, a leader with Al-Qaeda, wrote a book entitled *The Call to Global Islamic Resistance*. In it he lists the enemies of Islam: Jews, America, Israel, Free Masons, Christians, Hindus, apostates (including established Muslim leaders and officials), hypocritical scholars, educational systems, satellite TV channels, sports, and all arts and entertainment venues. By presenting the foregoing, Ayaan wants her readers to understand the scope of the issue.

For there to be a reformation of Islam there are some clear stepping stones that must be taken. Muslim leaders must change their view of the Qur'an, and to accept that it is not the sole source of truth. Next, that this life counts as much or more than life after death. Also, that Sharia Law is secondary to the laws of any given nation state. Abandon conformity to that which is forbidden and that which is permitted and allow for genuine freedom of expression. And, of chief and immediate concern, renounce violent jihad against non-Muslims and those who choose to leave Islam.

Ayaan quotes Voltaire to express what she hopes will be a guiding and mature stance for all people: "I disapprove of what you say," he is said to have written to Claude Helvetius, "but I will defend to the death your right to say it."

Some concluding thoughts

Ayaan Hirsi Ali's fourth and most recent book urges reform in Islam. Certainly reform is needed, but I question whether this will occur in the foreseeable future. As long as a liberal agenda predominates in Western countries, which is unable to identify the danger lurking in Islam, then the Islamic religion will simply continue to grow in numbers, strength, and power, and it may indeed one day dominate the entire globe.

Ali has many enemies. All of the Mosque leaders and informed Muslims to whom I have mentioned her name knew of her and articulated very close to the same attacks on her as though they were memorized. Never once did an imam or mufti deal with the content of Ali's arguments about Islam. No, only attacks upon her person, primarily that she is an apostate. To me it means that she has struck a deep cord, which authenticates her work all the more.

9

COMMENTARY ON
NO GOD BUT GOD: THE ORIGINS, EVOLUTION, AND FUTURE OF ISLAM

Reza Aslan is an Iranian-American author, public intellectual, religious studies scholar, producer and TV host, born May 3, 1972. He has written three books on religion: *No god but God: The Origins, Evolution, and Future of Islam*; *Beyond Fundamentalism: Confronting Religious Extremism in the Age of Globalization*; and *Zealot: The Life and Times of Jesus of Nazareth*. Aslan is a member of the American Academy of Religion, the Society of Biblical Literature, and the International Qur'anic Studies Association. He is also a professor of creative writing at the University of California, Riverside.

Note: This present commentary is but a brief summary of the major topics found in *No god but God*.[1] No attempt is made to present a summary of the entire contents of the book, but rather the focus is on unique material not found in Ali's work. Many whole blocks of Aslan's material are worthy of quoting and reporting. There were parts where Aslan distorted, or perhaps accidently misrepresented Christianity, but all things considered, his work deserves attention and respect.

Between the publisher page and the table of contents one finds the familiar Islamic recitation, "In the name of God, the Compassionate, the Merciful." Further, at the conclusion of the preface to the updated version (the book was first copyrighted in 2005) is found "Inshallah," meaning "God willing." These distinctly Muslim phrases let us know that Aslan identifies himself as a Muslim. It is one of the reasons the book is important for Christians and other non-Muslims to read.

Although the author was raised Shi'a Muslim, he describes himself according to the Sufi tradition. In contrast, in Ayaan Hirsi Ali's four books, we hear from a non-Christian who knows Islam intimately and has the courage to say what most Muslims, including ex-Muslims, would not reveal publically.

In his prologue, Aslan distinguishes between a clash of civilizations and a clash of monotheisms; the conflict is described as being between religions that, by their very monotheistic nature, cannot tolerate multiple stories of faith leading to a single Divine Presence. Aslan, like Ali, is concerned that Islam should experience reform.

---

1 Reza Aslan, *No god but God: The Origins, Evolution, and Future of Islam* (New York: Random House Trade Paperbacks, 2011).

Chapter One: "The Sanctuary in the Desert: Pre-Islamic Arabia"

The author looks at Arabia as it was in the sixth century, in the period before the adult years of Muhammad, who was probably born in AD 570.

In Mecca, pagan Arabs guarded the *Ka'ba*, meaning the cube, and within this squat, roofless, box-shaped edifice made of stones were representations of many gods, including Hubal, the Syrian god of the moon; al-Uzza, the Egyptian goddess Isis, which the Greeks called Aphrodite; al-Kutba, the Nabataean god of writing and divination; and even Jesus, the incarnate god of the Christians, along with his holy mother, Mary. Polytheistic tribalism united in a single worship in a single location—this was religion in Arabia.

Polytheism was widespread in the Arabian Peninsula, and Judaism, Christianity, and Zoroastrianism were also present. In many ways these blended and co-existed. But there was also Hanifism.

Hanifism was a pagan religion that was prominent in western Arabia, known as the Hijaz in the sixth century, and was a religion with which Muhammad would have been familiar. It was monotheistic, not polytheistic. A Hanifi leader, Zayd, preached against polytheism prior to Muhammad's time. Hanifism then pre-dated Muhammad's preaching against the pagan polytheism celebrated at the Ka'ba.

Was Zayd, the Hanifi prophet of monotheism, the John the Baptist preparing the way for Muhammad?

Chapter Two: "The Keeper of the Keys: Muhammad in Mecca"

Here Aslan recounts the story of Muhammad and how he became the Prophet. Sitting alone in a cave on Mt. Hira, the angel Gabriel commanded him, "Recite," and it began. The experiences of Muhammad on Mt. Hira were peculiar in that strange phenomena accompanied it—talking trees and more—and they greatly disturbed him. Aslan writes, "These aural and visual hallucinations continued right up to the moment in which he was called by God at Mt. Hira" (p. 37).

Visions and dreams were traditional in the sense that others from differing religious positions experienced the same things. Muhammad wondered and complained to his wife Khadija that he was going mad with all he was enduring. He had become a seer, a prophet, like others in that region and era.

Muhammad was not the first in that place and time to preach the oneness of God. There was Luqman and Suwayd who preached that there was no god but God (see Surah 31). Muhammad then was not the first with this message. His, however, was more than mere rhetoric; Muhammad's preaching was demanding, uncompromising, and intolerant of other views. This was the difference. Such was the zeal of Muhammad and abu Bakr, the first Muslim, that it made immigration to Medina (*Yathrib*) necessary.

Chapter Three: "The City of the Prophet: The First Muslims"

The Emigrants, or Companions of Muhammad, those who made the *hijra* or trek from Mecca to Medina, had to build a base for their mission. As the Muslim community grew, conflict with others emerged. Muhammad at first compromised with the polytheism of the tribes in and around Medina, which was essentially a community of tribes gathered around a bountiful oasis rather than a city.

In this chapter Aslan tells of the death of Muhammad and the rise of the early ummah or community of Muslims. He also tells the story of the development of the hadith, the account of the writing down of the things that Muhammad said and did that form the holy pattern of life for Muslims. Several hundred thousand hadith were known, and it became apparent that not all were trustworthy. In time, they were ranked from strong to weak and further to fraudulent. Aslan references a Hungarian scholar, Ignaz Goldziher, who found some of the hadith to have been taken from the Torah and the New Testament gospels; even the Lord's Prayer, almost in its entirety was found in a hadith. By the ninth century, Muslim legal scholars were putting these into two categories—those that were meant for financial gain and those used to support a doctrine or theology.

Aslan continues with other details about the hadith that are rather stunning, most of which I had never read about before. One such is that one sixth of all the reliable hadith apparently came from Aisha, Muhammad's wife whom he married when she was nine years old.

Of particular importance is the way women have been denigrated in the hadith, which is a real barrier to any kind of reform. Some Muslim women advocate returning to the Islam of Mecca, a time before the immigration to Medina, when women were seen in a better light.

Chapter Four: "Fight in the Way of God: The Meaning of Jihad"

At first in Medina, Muhammad's community and the Jewish tribes were not belligerent toward each other. Indeed, early on Muhammad taught the Muslims to pray toward Jerusalem not Mecca. However, in Medina Muhammad underwent significant change, to put it mildly. Clashes with other tribes, on the one hand, placed the fledgling community in danger. But of greater import was how he saw himself: the messenger and apostle of Allah, certainly, but now that role was enlarged to a global religious figure called to bring the true religion to the entire world.

Muhammad and the early Muslim community did engage in war, and brutally so. The need to survive was real enough; the fledgling Muslim community had to defend itself. Then, after Islam had taken root, conquest and expansion certainly resulted in conflict, with violence toward Christians, Jews, and others accompanying the early expansion of Islam into Europe. Neither the Qur'an nor Muhammad, however, endorsed the blanket killing of nonbelievers. This is evident in passages such as 2:256; 18:29; 10:100; and 109:6. Muslim leaders were very much aware of this.

During much of Islam's middle history, Jews and Christians, after being restricted from church building and evangelism, and after agreeing to pay the tax placed upon them as *dhimmi*, were not bothered.

Moving forward many centuries, to the modern era, Aslan notes that in Iran, thus Shi'a Islam, the Ayatollah Khomeini advocated the killing of nonbelievers who would not embrace Islam. From 1979 on, there was an increasing call for violent jihad.

With Sunni Islam, the same process developed, and this centered in Saudi Arabia under the leadership of the Islamic philosopher, Abdullah Yusuf, who greatly influenced

Osama bin Laden. Now violent jihad became far more than a defensive tactic.

Aslan has a most interesting presentation of how Muhammad viewed the relationship between what he received from Allah and what had been revealed to the Jews and Christians, the "People of the Book." This relationship was quite generous, as evidenced in Qur'an 3:84 where it is said, "We make no distinction between any of them." Certainly Islam sees itself as the final, last, and full revelation and Muhammad as the final or seal of the prophets. Indeed, it is possible that Muhammad considered that his Muslims and the Jews and Christians formed a "single divine ummah" or community. Naturally, Islamic scholars eventually rejected such an idea.

The issue of the Christian Trinity, perhaps not fully understood in the early days of Islam, became a major factor in how Muslims looked at Christians. For them, the Trinity was seen as three gods, thus violating the principle of *tawhid*, that Allah has no partner. Islam did, and does, understand the Trinity to be a father God who had sexual relations with a goddess, Mary, which produced a human god, Jesus. Seen in that light, Muslims would then be correct in their view—Christianity would be polytheistic.

The greatest sin for Muslims is *shirk,* meaning associating anything or anyone in "partnership" with God. Thus Christians commit this gravest of sins, and the penalty is death (see Qur'an 2:116).

Note: The triune God is one, as Deuteronomy 6:4 declares and which Christians also endorse. God is a unity, an echad, one yet three. The three all have the same nature, will, and ultimate essence. Christians do not and have never held to polytheism.

Aslan expresses sincere regret that the three Abrahamic faiths are so divided.

Chapter Five: "The Rightly Guided Ones: The Successors to Muhammad"

Abu Bakr, Umar, Uthman, and Ali, the rightly guided ones—the first four caliphs—set the pattern for Islam during the time the hadith were compiled and the Qur'an was collected in its final form. But there is debate surrounding this particular issue.

Abu Bakr and especially Umar were warriors, defending and expanding Islam. It was Uthman who presided over the collection of the oral recitations into a single fixed text in AD 650, after it was noted that the *Qurra*, those who had memorized the Qur'an, were dying off. Uthman ordered that all other copies and versions of the Qur'an be burnt, thus alienating many important members of the ummah.

Abu Bakr was an old man when Muhammad died and was the only one of the first four pious ones not to be assassinated by fellow Muslims.

Uthman did not earn the reputation of being very pious, however. A group who objected to variations in religious doctrine and practice, known as the Kharijites, were the first fundamentalists of Islam. Aslan states, "What makes the Kharijites so important to Islamic history, however, is that they represent the first self-conscious attempts at defining a distinctive Muslim identity" (p. 135). And it was a severe test, requiring stringent observance, practice, and belief. It became all too easy to be labeled *kafir* or nonbeliever, and the penalty for failure was excommunication from the ummah. These then were the first Muslim extremists.

Chapter Six: "This Religion Is a Science: The Development of Islamic Theology and Law"

Concerning the Qur'an, there are two positions a Muslim might hold. The **rationalists** are those who believe the Qur'an was created by God, that it had a beginning. The result is that the Qur'an can be discussed and thought about in a reasonable manner. The **traditionalists** are those who believe the Qur'an is uncreated and coeternal with God; therefore, its statements must not be open to reason and questioning. One can never ask, "Why?" This second view is held by fundamentalists and extremists and by unknown numbers of others. The Qur'an must be understood today and tomorrow just as it was in the seventh century according to the traditionalists.

Note: Based on other material, traditionalists believe the original, uncreated Qur'an sits upon a grand table in paradise. It comes very close to being worshipped as a god and whose verses, when read in Arabic, have almost magical properties. Muslim exorcists so value the Qur'an that its use is essential in any attempt to drive out unclean jinn. To even hear the Qur'an spoken in Arabic has great power, whether one understands Arabic or not. I have often asked Muslims after the Friday prayers if they understood the sermon that was in Arabic, and the reply is almost always no. Translations of the Qur'an will not do either. In debates with Muslims, not being able to read the Qur'an in Arabic is usually fatal in terms of winning the debate.

Aslan also distinguishes between religions as being based on either orthopraxy or orthodoxy. Orthopraxic religions, meaning those based on right practice, include Judaism and Islam. Christianity is orthodoxic in that the focus is on doctrine and faith. In Islam the emphasis is on right and proper performance of rites and rituals. This is why Muslim scholars, jurists, and other leaders are so intent on doing right and not doing wrong. Therefore, questions of theology, or *kalam*, are impossible to separate from questions of law, or *fiqh*. It is what Ayaan Hirsi Ali means when she speaks of permitting right and forbidding wrong.

Note: It has been my repeated experience that the average Muslim knows little of the doctrines of their faith. At first it was surprising to find Muslims who actually did not believe in anything at all, some even being atheists despite the fact they regularly visit a mosque for Friday prayers.

Here is where Aslan describes the Five Pillars of Islam, and in a most interesting and detailed manner. The first is the Shahadah, the statement of belief that Allah alone is God and Muhammad is his prophet. This is the only one of the pillars that has to do with belief. The prayers, Ramadan fast, almsgiving, and the Hajj, which is the pilgrimage to Mecca, are the four major rituals that maintain a Muslim's status as Muslim.

In further discussion of the place of the Qur'an, Aslan mentions that the Qur'an is Mohammad's miracle, thus he is able to stand beside Moses and Jesus who performed miracles. Muhammad's role was that of a conduit, receiving the very words of God without error.

Aslan writes of two ways the Qur'an may be interpreted. One, *tafsir*, is to interpret it literally. *Ta'wil* is concerned with the hidden or esoteric meanings, supposing there is concealed knowledge that is open to only a few.

Shariah Law is the "core and kernel of Islam." Aslan now looks at the five categories of behavior which are covered in that law. They are (1) actions that are obligatory, in that their performance is rewarded but their omission is punished; (2) actions that are meritorious, in that their performance may be rewarded, but their neglect is not punished; (3) actions that are neutral and indifferent; (4) actions that are considered reprehensible, though not necessarily punished; and (5) actions that are forbidden and punished.

In this section, Aslan mentions Sufism. Sufis tend "to regard the Shariah as merely the starting point of righteousness; true faith, they say, requires moving beyond the law" (p. 164).

Continuing his discussion of the hadith, Aslan talks of the *isnad*, which has to do with the trail of transmission of various statements found in the hadith. Some are strong, others are weak, and, interestingly, those that receive the strong rating tend to be those that support the position of the traditionalists.

Then there is the place of the jurists, the legal experts of Islam. Aslan notes that there is almost a "blind acceptance of juridical precedent" (p. 167), and when it appears that the Qur'an and hadith are not clear on an issue, the legal experts may issue a fatwa, which may or may not be accepted by the community.

In this context, the major judicial schools are mentioned. There is the Shafi School found in Southeast Asia; the Maliki School, found mostly in West Africa; the Hanafi School, found mostly in Central Asia and the Indian subcontinent; and the Hanbali School, found mostly in the Middle East. These four schools are Sunni, and for Shi'a, there is the Shi'ite School.

The *ulama* are the power brokers in Islam, the legal experts and scholars who determine most things that might impact the entire community. They may operate on the basis of consensus when issues cannot be resolved with an appeal to the Qur'an and/or the hadith. In some Muslim countries, such as Iran, Saudi Arabia, and the Sudan, the ulama command the religion and the state.

One of the reasons, perhaps the primary reason, why Islam has not been able to innovate or move into the modern era is that the ulama is comprised of traditionalists. Power is nearly absolute when the state enforces the will of the religious leaders.

Here is the problem, according to Aslan. The legal experts, the religious powerful, are not cohesive in their understandings. With four schools of legal opinions for the Sunni and one for the Shi'a, each one seeing Sharia Law as fixed, infallible, sacred, and divine, yet coupled with their respective differences—there is little hope for a unified future, let alone one that meets minimum standards of democracy and human rights.

Aslan concludes this chapter by presenting three possibilities for incorporating Sharia into the legal systems of a modern Islamic state. One, simply apply Sharia Law and exclude other factors of modernization (such as Saudi Arabia and Afghanistan under the Taliban); two, traditionalists' view of Sharia can be declared legitimate but ignored except in family, divorce, and inheritance law (as with Egypt and Pakistan); three, attempt to fuse traditionalist thinking about Sharia into a democratic, constitutional framework (only Iran has attempted this with little or uneven success).

Chapter Seven: "In the Footsteps of Martyrs: From Shi'ism to Khomeinism"

Aslan presents the origin of Shi'a Islam, which is the Shiite branch of Islam that was developed by those who thought Ali should be the head of the Muslim community.

It was not to be; thus Shi'a Islam emerged in the later part of the seventh century. Husayn ibn Ali, Muhammad's adopted grandson and husband to his youngest daughter, Fatima, was probably intended by Muhammad himself to succeed him. A brave and mighty warrior, Ali and his forces were defeated in battle, and he was beheaded by the Sunni Shimr. This was AD 661.

Ali's oldest son, Hasan, then led his father's followers. After Hasan was likely poisoned in 669, the second son of Ali and Fatima, Husayn, became head of the struggling Muslim community. The history is convoluted and complex, but Husayn was martyred at Karbala, and his followers created a new religion around this event, though anchored in Islamic thought.

The legend is that Husayn's coming to certain death at Karbala was a sacrifice and was told beforehand to Adam, Noah, Abraham, Moses, Jesus, Muhammad, Ali, and Fatima. Thus it was the will of Allah to complete the faith that Muhammad had initiated. Sunni Islam would be one thing, a step in the right direction, but Shi'a is the completion of the process.

Shi'a Islam then is established on the martyrdom of Ali. It developed on the concept of sacrifice and atonement, which is in opposition to Sunni Islam. And it all has to do with the death and beheading of Husayn. Rituals portraying the sacrifice grew up until these became the heart and soul of Shi'a. It is said, "A tear shed for Husayn washes away a hundred sins" (p. 183). In the eyes of the Sunni branch Shi'a became a false religion.

Corresponding to the pilgrimage to Mecca and the Ka'ba, are the rites and rituals occurring during the first ten days of the month of *Musharram*. These conclude with the *Ashura*, which are essentially dramatic lamentation gatherings. During this time the *Ta'zieh*, or passion play that acts out the martyrdom of Husyan, is presented.

Note: The events that take place in our own time with the ecstatic crowds and whippings and blood often make it into the news.

The Shi'a believe that to achieve salvation, the intercession of Muhammad, Ali, and the grandsons, Hasan and Husyan, is required. This mediation work is in addition to the intercession of the Imams who administer the divine revelation.

The head of the Sunni community acts as a vice-regent of Muhammad on earth, while the Shi'a Imam is the living spirit of Muhammad, and this is above all other authority, both religious and secular. To put it another way, "the prophet (Muhammad per Sunni Islam) *transmits* the Message of God, while the Imam (per Shi'a Islam) translates it for human beings" (p. 185).

Another way, again, that distinguishes Sunni from Shi'a Islam, is that in Sunni Islam, Muhammad reveals the message, while Ali executes it.

The Shi'a statement of faith then is: "There is no god but God, Muhammad is God's Messenger, and Ali is God's Executor."

Note: *Wali* is Arabic for executor.

Shi'a Islam believes that the Qur'an can only be properly understood by the Imam, and that the Qur'an contains both an obvious message—*zabir*—and a hidden message as well—*ta'wil*. Only the ayatollah, meaning "the sign of God," is able to fully know the hidden signs and thus alone can make binding decisions.

The sixth Imam of Shi'a Islam, Jafar, died in 757, and his son Ismail was designated by Jafar to be head of the community. However, Ismail died before his father and was then replaced by another son of Jafar, Musa al-Kazim. A faction of Shi'a Muslims refused to accept Musa, objecting that Jafar as Imam could not have made an error in choosing a successor and insisted that Ismail had not died but had gone into "occultation," or hiding, and would return as the seventh Mahdi at the end of history. Mahdi means one who guides rightly. This seventh "hidden Imam" will return at the end of history and usher in the Day of Judgment.

Thus was born the Seveners, also known as the Ismailis. The "Twelvers" refer to the rest of Shi'a Islam who are not Seveners and look forward to the twelfth and final Imam who will usher in the Day of Judgment.

Chapter Eight: "Stain Your Prayer Rug with Wine: The Sufi Way"

At the end of chapter seven Aslan makes a summary statement as to the very essence of Sufism:

> For Sufis, Islam is neither law nor theology, neither creed nor ritual. Islam, according to Sufism, is merely the means through which the believer can destroy his ego so as to become one with the creator of the heavens and the earth (p. 198).

Note: This description of Sufism can easily apply to many other religious practices, among which are Buddhism, Hinduism, Shamanism, Santeria, Wicca, various forms of contemplative or meditative Christianity, and worship practices found in extreme charismatic/Pentecostalism. These all depend upon the passive or altered state of mind. See *The Soul Journey: How Shamanism, Santeria, Wicca, and Charisma are Connected*, at www.evpbooks.com.

The term "Sufi" may be derived from *suf*, meaning wool garment, indicating poverty and a desire to be detached from the world. Sufism is connected, similarly but not organically, to Christian monasticism, the Hindu and Buddhist ascetic, Islamic Gnosticism, Neo-Platonism, some elements of Shi'a Islam, Manichaeism, and assorted other esoteric religious practices. The closest relationship with a spiritual practice came with Shi'a Islam, due to the goals of uncovering the hidden spiritual meanings of the Qur'an and, far more than Sunni Islam, having a devotional relationship with Muhammad. In this sense then, Sufism moved away from merely intellectual achievements and right practice.

The destruction, bypassing, or subjection of the ego is a main emphasis of Sufism, which is commonly found in most forms of mysticism. However, Sufism is different from common forms of mystical movements, in that Sufism does not embrace monasticism but is communal in nature; the Sufi is thoroughly engaged with the world.

Sufism, emerging out of Islam, did not attempt to remain within it. In fact, Sufism intends to break from Islam as from an empty shell. Islam, it is thought, points toward Allah while Sufism thrusts to Allah.

Sufism was also a reaction against the all-consuming goal of right practice and ritual that characterizes mainstream Islam, which lacked an actual spiritual dimension and desire to experience the divine. At the same time, Sufis are Muslims in all aspects of prayer, ritual, creed, and symbol while maintaining that all of these, even practiced to perfection, will not result in a true experience of the divine.

The journey of the Sufi then begins with Islam, the "outer shell," but pushes past it to the goal of "self-annihilation." For the Sufi, ritual and reason, creeds and law must be replaced by the one supreme virtue, love.

The greatest of all Sufi poets was Jalal ad-Din Rumi (died 1273), whose poem about a Persian, a Turk, an Arab, and a Greek pointed out that all were seeking the same thing though the religions were different. And of course, that which they all sought was what Sufism is.

As Aslan puts it, "Sufism is to Islam what the heart is to the human being: its vital center, the seat of its essence"(p. 209). The mystical journey toward that essence cares not for the externals of religion, and this journey is known by the Sufi as *tariqah*. This is the destruction of the ego and the merging with the divine. And there are stages on the way to reaching tariqah. It is little by little. The final stage is where a person is stripped of ego and becomes one with the Universal Spirit and is joined with the Divine.

The journey must be under the strict direction of a *pir*, someone who has reached the end of the journey and has drunk the "fifth cup," who can therefore assist others along the path. The pir is essential due to the reality that one can get lost on the journey. The pir is the friend of God and has much authority, sometimes referred to as "the cosmic pole," which is the axis around which the universe rotates.

Note: The above description of the pir is reminiscent of how shamans are described; the similarities in the religious traditions are abundant.

Iblis, or Satan, in mainstream Islam, was cast out of the presence of God when he would not bow to Adam. But Rumi, the great Sufi poet, puts a spin on this. He said it was not envy of Adam that prevented Satan from honoring God's creation but love, love for God. Rumi changed the mainline Muslim view into something quit different and which expresses a central truth of Sufism.

For the Sufi, one can attain a state of god-likeness though such is not expressly spoken of or written. However, Aslan says, "the Sufi enters fully into the qualities and attributes of God" (p. 219).

Sufis, long ago as well as today, are rarely welcomed into mosques. They were forced to develop their own structures. *Dhikr* is the physical act of remembering God, though this varies amongst the sects of Sufism. The most followed dhikr is the vocal dhikr. This involves chanting of phrases, rapid movements of the body, breathing techniques and more, all of which are designed to bring the Sufi into a state of trance.

Note: There is an essay on Sufism in appendix A.

Chapter Nine: "An Awakening in the East: The Response to Colonialism"

European nations have played a large role in deciding political and national boundaries in the Middle East and North Africa, among other places in the world. Much of this was without consideration for tribal and religious identities. The result of this miscalculation and the usual exploitation that followed led to some of the extreme forms of Islam we see today.

The Sepoy Mutiny, or Indian Revolt of 1857, was one of the first reactions of subjected peoples to colonialism. Certainly not all of European activity was harmful, but much of it was and would not be sustainable.

It was in Egypt, where British control was complete but veiled under the cover of an impotent monarchy, that the modern era of Islamic assertiveness began. It was the influence of Hasan al-Banna, who was much influenced by Sufism and who came to Cairo in 1923, that began the modern Islamic quest to be a dominant world religion. His leadership paved the way for the establishment of The Egyptian Muslim Brotherhood, which led the way in rejecting colonial repression and the effort to establish a truly Islamic society. What began in Egypt spread to Syria, Jordan, Algeria, Tunisia, Palestine, Sudan, Iran, and Yemen. Aslan describes the agenda of the Muslim Brotherhood this way:

> The Muslim Brothers vigorously tackled issues that no one else would address. Matters such as the increase in Christian missionary activity in the Middle East, the rise of Zionism in Palestine, the poverty and political inferiority of Muslim peoples, and the opulence and autocracy of Arab monarchies, were common themes in the Brothers' preaching (p. 241).

Sayyid Qutb (1906–1966) became the father of modern Islamic radicalism. Pursuing education in America he became outraged at what he saw of Western civilization. His desire was to establish a Muslin socialistic society. In 1950 he aligned himself with the Muslim Brotherhood, having come to identify himself with the thinking of al-Banna. Qutb saw that the recovery and health of Islam could only be achieved through radical means. The kingdom of man would have to be supplanted by the kingdom of God by force, politically and militarily. He saw himself as on a mission from God.

The story continues with the beginning of the Saud dynasty and the creation of Saudi Arabia in the early twentieth century. In a complex manner, a radical named Abd al-Wahbab (1703–1766) rose in influence as he preached a hard line return to the principles of seventh century Islam. Saud and al-Wahbab joined political and religious power forces, and an Islamic state was created. The Sufis and the Shi'a did not share in al-Wahbab's vision, and as a result, they were put to the sword.

The followers of al-Wahbab, known as Wahbabists, identified with the Kharijites, those fundamentalists who wanted to live and be just like Muhammad and the early companions of the prophet. They forced their "revival" upon the morally lax by banning music and flowers at the sacred places. They made tobacco, coffee, and alcohol *haram*, or forbidden, and under the penalty of death demanded men grow beards and women veil and seclude themselves. And so it remains to a large extent in Saudi Arabia today.

Note: It is Saudi Arabia that is responsible for so much of the extremism in Islam today, and thanks to their seemingly endless supply of oil money, they are able to pour millions of dollars a day into promoting their vision of Sunni Islam. Shi'a Islam must then counter, prompting Iran to commit millions to the cause of advancing their version of Islam.

A further development was jihadism, which emerged out of the defense of Afghanistan against the Russian invasion in 1979. Saudi Arabia took up a leading role in the battle against the Russians, being finally able to put their warriors to work. These warriors became known as freedom fighters and were celebrated around the world. Even Ronald Reagan approved and likened them to America's founding fathers.

Once the Russians were turned back, a whole new entity now existed—the jihadists who sought to rid the world of political boundaries and governments and establish a global Islamic State. There would be just one ummah worldwide, just as Muhammad had intended.

Here now was ultra-conservative Islam. Muslims became the "People of Heaven" and everyone else became the "People of Hell." Simple and clear-cut, and the jihadists' mission is to usher this into fruition. Their puritanical version of Islam is solely acceptable, and all Muslims who are weak and do not embrace it fully are to be eliminated from true Islam or forced into compliance.

Note: In this form of Islam, it is not necessary to "believe in your heart and mind." It is enough to declare compliance and follow through with the rituals. Real heart and head faith is not required.

At the conclusion of the chapter Aslan moves to the essential point of the book: Islam must experience genuine democratic reform. The jihadists can only be defeated in this way, and it must be through the existence of "genuine, homegrown, and indigenous democratic societies. Indeed, the very future of Islam depends on it" (p. 254).

Chapter Ten: "Slouching Toward Medina: The Quest for Islamic Democracy"

Can Islam realize an actual liberal democracy in the Middle East? Can traditionalists and rationalists exist side by side? Can the Muslim community come together and form a society like that which Muhammad developed in Medina?

These questions haunt the entire world. While he considers himself a Muslim—though in the Sufi expression of Islam—Aslan knows that the answers must be yes, or eventually Islam will be sidelined as a failed religion.

He notes that progress is being made, referring to the Arab Spring perhaps. He states that the majority of the world's Muslims already accept democratic institutions.

Note: Aslan's second edition was published in 2011, and so it does not take into account the declaration of the Islamic State in Syria and Iraq, the Syrian civil war, the rapid spread of extremist attacks in the West, the turmoil in Turkey led by those who want a more serious Islam in place, and more.

Can Muslims become religiously tolerant while maintaining their own Islamic identity? Must all differences be crushed?

Are the Jihadists correct? Must all opposition be smashed? Must morality be something that is demanded and enforced? Must all that is the West be wiped out and replaced with seventh century Arabianism?

The adoption of pluralism—toleration for differences in almost everything—is something that Muslims must move toward. And this struggle exists today amongst Muslims. The jihadists are not the majority, not even close. It is the moderates and the progressives with whom the future of Islam lies.

Note: My contention is that Islam's intolerance of the West is indicative of a severe weakness that lies at the very heart of the religion. To despise, hate, and quest to eliminate all that does not conform to one's own religion is an indication of fear, fear that one has committed oneself to that which is false. There is no peace for the Muslim who must crush all opposition. There is no maturity in those who demand that all believe and live alike. Islam has a long way to go to reach a place of self-assurance and confidence. Clearly, Islam's very acts of violence reveal it cannot compete in the global spiritual marketplace.

Chapter Eleven: "Welcome to the Islamic Reformation: The Future of Islam"

Islamic authorities known as the ulama are in many ways and places being set-aside by a growing number of self-styled and educated Muslims. Amr Khaled, the Egyptian televangelist, is an accountant with no special training or education, yet millions around the Muslim world look to him for counsel and advice. No longer are Muslims limited to the scholars, the jurists, the imams, the muftis, and so on. This is the heart and soul of the Islamic reformation.

Note: A few years ago I spent four days in Istanbul. There I saw a modern and westernized country where especially the youth were enjoying their lives. The mosques were lightly attended, the streets were filled each night with people living their lives freely and with exuberance. I was shocked at this Muslim city and wondered if this celebratory lifestyle could be found in other parts of Turkey. Will we now, in the winter of 2016/17, begin to see a resurgence of the hard liners there also? It remains to be seen.

Reform. Reformation. It is not as though Islam as a religion must be reformed. The basic doctrines are not the issue. All religions have their belief systems, and within them exist the usual sects and cults, but there is something in Islam that prevents reform.

The ulama-dominating, traditionalist legal scholars of Islam, those who insist the Qur'an in Arabic is uncreated and as eternal as Allah, are virtually the only ones who know the key documents of the religion. The Qur'an, the Islamic scholars maintain, cannot even be translated into other languages, thus any discussion of the Qur'an using anything but the original Arabic simply will not do. Other versions than Arabic are considered merely "interpretations;" thus any issue that is uncomfortable to Muslim scholars is easily dismissed. Indeed, only the ulama may make definitive and authoritative statements on the meaning of the Qur'an.

Note: Over the years, whenever I found myself in an informal debate with Muslims and things got dicey, I would be asked if I knew Arabic and whether I had memorized the Qur'an. With my negative reply, the issue was settled—I knew nothing about Islam.

Currently, however, the Qur'an is published in many languages, and Muslims are becoming more and more involved in determining what it means. In brief, the authority of the ulama is being challenged. And the process is too widespread for it to be controlled. The times are starting to change in Islam, but we cannot expect major changes in the short run.

This process of spiritual decentralization is defined by two terms: *tajdid* refers to renewal, and *islah* means reform. Those who dare to be active in this process are called Qur'anists.

Within the reform movements is the idea that no one acts as a mediator between Allah and the individual Muslim. It is here where those who favor pluralism, individualism, modernism, and democracy are found in place of "intolerance, bigotry, militancy, and perpetual war" (p. 286).

Aslan boldly asserts that the potential or power for reform "now belongs to every single Muslim in the world" (p. 286). However, one scary fact found in the very last chapter is that in Muslim-dominated countries, the ruling governing authority controls the ulama. This brings up the issue for Muslims moving to a more Western point of view of whether the ulama can be trusted. Younger Muslims, the Westernized in particular, gravitate to "garage mosques" and not to the establishment mosques.

Note: Reza Aslan gives a website, islam-online.net, which, at the time of the writing of his second edition, was receiving more than one million visits per day and mostly from people eighteen to twenty-four years of age. This may be a measure of the reform movement in Islam. I have to wonder, if and when it does come, will non-Muslims really value it? Or will the West and other non-Muslims be by then too traumatized by what is presently going on, what has gone on, and what will go on until the very last day? Will Christians welcome reform amongst Muslims and embrace those who are trying to embrace us?

In the last pages of *No god but God* Aslan reminds the reader of the messiness of the Protestant Reformation in the sixteenth century lead by Martin Luther and others. That reformation was long in the making. So should it be expected to be otherwise with an Islamic reformation?

The last two sentences in the book should be read loud and clear:
"The Islamic Reformation is already here. We are all living in it."

10

A Response to the Call for Reform by Ayaan Hirsi Ali and Reza Aslan

Reform may come to Islam, and this hope I share with Ali, Aslan, The Clarion Project's REFORM (for more on this go to change.org), and hosts of other Muslims and non-Muslims.

However, my instincts tell me that a significant minority of Muslims will resist any kind of reform or innovation. A daring and courageous effort to resist the radical hardliners must come then from within Islam itself.

My view and experience is that most Muslims want to live and let live. This alone, however, will not be decisive in bringing about real change whereby freedom of religion and speech prevail.

If only moderates, which some believe make up the majority of Muslims, push for genuine change, then real and lasting reform will fail, because the traditionalist radical element in Islam who want to bring back the seventh century of the Arabian Peninsula, dominate Islamic communities. They view any form of innovation, any kind of reform, any deviation from the path of the "pious ones" as heretical. And they will not tolerate heresy.

Why is this so? At the root of resistance to reformation lies a devastating weakness—fear that the religion itself cannot compete in the worldwide spiritual marketplace. To put it another way, knowledgeable Muslims understand that Islam's message is lacking. And more than lacking, it essentially offers only fear and despair.

Following is a short list of reasons why this is true:

» Life according to Islam is dominated by a cruel fatalism. Allah orders everything, and Allah directly determines any and every event and action.
» The only way to reach Islamic paradise is to die in violent jihad or build a mosque. Yes, there are hints in the Qur'an that the scales may be tipped in one's favor, but this is a faint hope.
» Allah is a deceiver and will lead his followers astray. One never really knows.
» That the real enemy of Muslims are other Muslims who happen to adhere to a slightly different interpretation of Islam points to an obvious flaw in the religion itself.
» Muslim evangelism is built on coercion and domination every bit as much as any

attempt at persuasion. This misguided directive creates a "we/they" cultic mentality that makes people of other religions enemies who are to be feared and opposed. Islam must dominate the globe, even if it means genocide.

» Leaving Islam is apostasy, and according to the doctrines of the religion traceable directly to Muhammad, it can only be rewarded with death.

Despite the obstacles, the call to reform must be made and much is owed to Ali, Aslan, and all those who have the insight and courage to challenge the Muslim hardliners. Insight, because few see what goes into creating and maintaining the cultic mindset. Courage, because the hardliners, radicals, and traditionalists are deeply threatened by any suggestion there is error at the heart of their creed.

Certainly this is true of Christianity, as well as most every other religion in which the fundamentalists, usually the loudest voices, are rigid and defensive to the point they cannot tolerate, in any form, deviation from what they hold to be authentic Christianity. I know, because I was in that camp for a long period.

Such a mindset prevents honest enquiry and critical analysis. I have found that faith grows and convictions are strengthened by an honest approach to foundational documents and the doctrines based thereupon.

11

BASICS OF THE QUR'ANIC CHAPTERS

There are 114 chapters, or suras, in the Qur'an. Of these, eighty-eight were received in Mecca and twenty-six in Medina. Except for the first, the chapters are mixed between the earlier and the latter suras. In general, the chapters are arranged according to their length, the longer to the shorter.

Sura Number	Sura Name	Revealed in Mecca or Medina
1	The Exordium or Introduction	Mecca
2	The Cow	Medina
3	The Family of Imran	Medina
4	The Woman	Medina
5	The Table	Medina
6	The Cattle	Mecca
7	The Heights	Mecca
8	The Spoils	Medina
9	The Repentance	Medina
10	Jonah	Mecca
11	Hud	Mecca
12	Joseph	Mecca
13	Thunder	Medina
14	Abraham	Mecca
15	The Rocky Tract (Hijr)	Mecca
16	The Bee	Mecca
17	The Night Journey	Mecca
18	The Cave	Mecca
19	Mary	Mecca

Sura Number	Sura Name	Revealed in Mecca or Medina
20	Ta Ha	Mecca
21	The Prophets	Mecca
22	The Pilgrimage	Medina
23	The Believers	Mecca
24	Light	Medina
25	The Criterion	Mecca
26	The Poets	Mecca
27	The Ants	Mecca
28	Narration	Mecca
29	The Spider	Mecca
30	The Romans	Mecca
31	Luqman	Mecca
32	Adoration	Mecca
33	The Confederates	Medina
34	Saba	Mecca
35	The Creator	Mecca
36	Ya Sin	Mecca
37	The Banks	Mecca
38	Sad	Mecca
39	The Crowds	Mecca
40	The Believer	Mecca
41	Fussilat	Mecca
42	Consultation	Mecca
43	Gold Ornaments	Mecca
44	Smoke	Mecca
45	Kneeling	Mecca
46	Sand Tracts (Ajqal)	Mecca
47	Muhammad	Medina
48	Victory	Medina
49	Chambers	Medina
50	Oaf	Mecca
51	The Winds	Mecca
52	The Mountain	Mecca
53	The Star	Mecca

Basic Details of the Qur'anic Chapters

Sura Number	Sura Name	Revealed in Mecca or Medina
54	The Moon	Mecca
55	Merciful	Mecca
56	The Inevitable Event	Mecca
57	The Iron	Medina
58	She who pleaded	Medina
59	The Banishment	Medina
60	She who is tested	Medina
61	The Battle Array	Medina
62	Friday	Medina
63	The Hypocrites	Medina
64	Cheating	Medina
65	Divorce	Medina
66	The Prohibition	Medina
67	Dominion	Mecca
68	The Pen	Medina
69	The Sure Reality	Mecca
70	The Ways of Ascent	Mecca
71	Noah	Mecca
72	The Jinns	Mecca
73	The Mantled One	Mecca
74	The Cloaked One	Mecca
75	The Resurrection	Mecca
76	Man	Mecca
77	Those sent forth	Mecca
78	Tidings	Mecca
79	The Soul-Snatchers	Mecca
80	He Frowned	Mecca
81	The Folding Up	Mecca
82	The Cataclysm	Mecca
83	The Just	Mecca
84	The Rending Asunder	Mecca
85	The Constellation	Mecca
86	The Night Visitor	Mecca
87	The Most High	Mecca

Sura Number	Sura Name	Revealed in Mecca or Medina
88	The Overwhelming Event	Mecca
89	The Break of Day	Mecca
90	The City	Mecca
91	The Sun	Mecca
92	The Night	Mecca
93	Daylight	Mecca
94	The expansion	Mecca
95	The Fig	Mecca
96	The Blood Clot	Mecca
97	The Night of Power	Mecca
98	The Clear Evidence	Mecca
99	The Convulsion	Mecca
100	The War Steeds	Mecca
101	The day of Noise and Clamour	Mecca
102	Piling Up	Mecca
103	The Declining Day	Mecca
104	The Scandal-Monger	Mecca
105	The Elephant	Mecca
106	The Quraysh	Mecca
107	Alms	Mecca
108	Abundance	Mecca
109	The Unbelievers	Mecca
110	Help	Medina
111	Lahab	Mecca
112	Purity of Faith	Mecca
113	The Dawn	Mecca
114	Mankind	Mecca

12

A Biographic timeline of Muhammad's Life

Scholars are not in complete agreement as to the major dates and events of Muhammad's life. There are some who insist that Muhammad never lived; others contend times and dates were developed as needed. With all the attention now being given Islam and the life of the Muslim Prophet, doubtless the debate will continue long into the future.

Here now however, are the details of Muhammad's life as commonly understood by most Muslims.

The Meccan Period

Birth	Born Monday, April 22, AD 571. Father, Abdullah, had died before Muhammad was born. Some give the date of 570 as his birth year.
Age 6	Mother, Aminah, dies.
Age 8	Abdul Mutalib, Muhammad's grandfather, dies. Muhammad is now cared for by his uncle Abu Talib, who becomes an exceedingly important person in his life. Muhammad is taught how to care for camels. At this point, a Christian monk named Bahira declared that Muhammad would be a prophet and that he was to be protected.
Age 12	Due to his skills with animals, Muhammad is hired by traders to care for the camels. He works for a business woman named Khadijah.
Age 25	Khadijah, impressed with the young man 15 years her junior, marries Muhammad in 595. Now with time on his hands, he begins to practice meditation among the mystics on Mt. Hirah near Mecca.
Age 40	In 610, Muhammad receives his first revelation from a being he first suspects is a jinn. With his wife's help he overcomes his objections to the visitations of Gabriel. Being illiterate, Muhammad recites the sayings to others.
Age 41	Muhammad is instructed by the being who revealed itself as the angel Gabriel and is given instructions on prayer.

Age 42–43	Muhammad preaches against polytheism at the Kaaba in Mecca.
Ages 44–46	Muhammad preaches to submit to the teaching of Allah that is given via Gabriel. At this point he begins to receive hostility from Arab tribes in and around Mecca.
Age 46	Some of the early Muslims flee to Ethiopia-Abyssinia after trouble with the Quraysh, Muhammad's own tribe.
Age 49	Khadija dies. Muhammad has no other wives at this time.
Age 50	Muhammad reports a "night journey" whereby he is transported to Paradise and meets other prophets. Aisha, his favorite and youngest wife would report that the journey occurred in his head.
Age 52	The Hijra occurs and the Muslims immigrate to Medina. At this point he marries Aisha when she is nine years old. The move to Medina from Mecca marks the beginning of the Islamic calendar.

The Medina Period

Age 54	The early Muslims begin battles with unbelievers by attacking the Nakhla tribe.
Age 54	The Muslim army defeats the pagans of Mecca in what is known as the Battle of Badr.
Age 54	The Jewish tribe, Qaynuqa in the Medina area, are dispersed.
Age 55	Battle of Uhud, when the Meccans who opposed submission to Islam defeat the Muslim army.
Age 55	The Nadir tribe from Medina are besieged by the Muslim army and exiled.
Age 57	Battle of the Trench, when the Jewish Qurayzah tribe breaks an alliance with Muhammad and is defeated.
Age 57	Muhammad beheads, or observes the beheading, of all the males of the Qurayzah and enslaves the women and children. He does select one of the women to be a wife.
Age 58	Treaty of Hudaybiyya is created with the remaining pagans of the Meccan region.
Age 58	An attempt is made on Muhammad's life by means of poison.
Age 60	The Muslim army completes the defeat of Mecca. Muhammad becomes the conqueror of all of Arabia.
Age 60	Muhammad begins to conquer outside of Arabia and comes into conflict with Christian tribes.
Age 61	Arab tribes, outside of the Arabian Peninsula, submit to Islam.
Age 62	Muhammad dies in Medina, on the bed of wife Aisha, on June 8.

13

THE CRESCENT AND STAR SYMBOL

At the Islamic Center of Mill Valley, California, on the front ornamental structure with the "pulpit" or lectern on the right, are two crescent and star symbols. Prominently displayed, the one on the left shows the crescent moon facing left, with a star within the waning moon, and the one on the right shows the crescent moon facing right, again with a star within the waxing moon. The same will be true for Sunni and Shi'a mosques anywhere.

Why they are there at all is curious, since Islam has long been adverse to the use or display of "holy symbols." It is thought that the use of the crescent and star symbol is in reaction to the Menorah of the Jews and the Cross of the Christians. Sunni Islam rejects images of Muhammad, while Shi'a Islam has no such problem with artwork featuring Ali.

Early Islamic coins had no symbols on them, only Arabic writing. What happened?

Sassanid Empire

Researchers look to the pre-Islamic Sassanid Empire of Persia to explain the Crescent and Star symbol that is found on some flags of Muslim-dominated countries and that appear in mosques.[1]

Ardashir I founded the Sassanid Empire in AD 224 (died 241), for in that year he and his army overwhelmed the Parthian Empire. The new empire went on to occupy what is now Iran, Iraq, parts of eastern Arabia, including Bahrain, Kuwait, Oman, Qatar, Syria, Palestine, Lebanon, Israel, Jordan, Armenia, Georgia, Azerbaijan, Dagestan, Egypt, much of Turkey, and more. The subjects of the empire were known as Eranshahr.

The new power warred against Rome from 229–232 and achieved independence. This empire ruled from 224 to 651, more than four hundred years, and was the regions greatest power alongside the Roman-Byzantine Empire.

The Sassanid Empire became the center of the greatest pre-Islamic Iranian civilization, with its high and advanced art, architecture, music, and science (which Muslims retained and claimed for their own). The impact of the empire stretched into Europe, Africa, China, and India.

In 636 the Sassanid Empire was invaded by Islamic forces and decisively defeated at

---

1   Other titles for the Sassanid Empire are Sasanian, Sassanian, and Neo-Persian.

the Battle of Al-Qadeseyyah, though the empire struggled on until 651. At that point it was completely submerged under the new Islamic power.

Sassanid Coinage

Much of the coinage of the Sassanid Empire featured the crescent and the star. In fact, the symbol of that empire was the crescent moon. In the twelfth century, the crescent began to be used by the Ottomans and became a symbol of Turkey. The use of the crescent on flags, with or without the star, became common in the Middle East from that time on.

At first the crescent on Muslim flags was secular not religious, but that changed over time.

On the Ottoman flag, as early as the sixteenth century and extending to the eighteenth century, were usually displayed three white crescents. In 1793 the three were reduced to one crescent with a nine-pointed star added. This usage by the dominant power in the region influenced the adoption of the crescent and star on flags and as a symbol of Islam.

In 1805, the Pasha of Egypt, Muhammad Ali, introduced a red flag with three white crescents, and each had a star with it. These represented the peaceful co-existence of the Jews, Christians, and Muslims.

Today many Muslim countries display the crescent and the star on their national flags. Neither Muhammad nor the early companions of Muhammad used a crescent or a crescent and a star as a symbol.

The Sword and Colors

Particularly among Shi'a Muslims, the sword is a frequently used symbol. The sword is that of Ali, the fourth caliph and founder of the Shi'a branch of Islam. Ali is pictured as a warrior, astride a charger with sword raised.

Colors have significance in Islam: Green is a dominant color due to Surah 18:31: "Those who inhabit paradise will wear fine silk garments of green." Covers of the Qur'an often are green in color, and there is often green on the exterior and interior of mosques.

White signifies purity and peace. Black, a symbol of mourning and also modesty, is the reason many of women's coverings, such as the hijab, are black.

Red is also a color found on Muslim flags.

14

THE SIRA: THE BIOGRAPHY OF MUHAMMAD

The full title of the biography is *Sirat Rasul Allah* or Biography (life) of the Apostle of Allah. The author of the Sira is Ibn Ishaq.

Ibn Ishaq, meaning son of Isaac, was born in Medina in AD 704 and died in 761 or 767.

His family was engaged in collecting stories of the life and times of Muhammad, known as hadith, and also in recording the chain of transmission of such stories, known as the isnad. Ibn Ishaq followed in the family footsteps.

He travelled to Alexandria, Egypt, when he was thirty years of age and studied under Yazid ibn Abi Habib. After his studies he returned to Medina. In Medina he was acquainted with Malik ibn Anas, the founder of the School of Maliki, one of the principle Sunni schools of Sharia Law.

Forced to leave Medina due to questions about his story collecting techniques, it is supposed he settled in Baghdad where he found patrons for the work that was about to commence—the writing of the story of Muhammad, which ibn Ishaq entitled, "In the beginning, the mission of Muhammad."

He set out to collect oral stories about what Muhammad said and did, much like the process used for the hadith. These oral renderings he dictated to his pupils, who then committed them to writing.

The original document has not survived, only an edited copy. This was reworked and then reworked again by students al-Bakka and Ibn Hisham. Fragments of other copies have been discovered.

Oxford University Press published the most respected edition of the Sira by Ibn Ishaq in 1955, with an introduction and notes by A. Guillaume. It runs 815 pages and is available through online book sites.

Note: The A. Guillaume edition is fascinating reading and, in my thinking, presents a realistic view of Islam in the early period.

There is considerable controversy surrounding the Sira, in both attempts to publish it and speak authoritatively on it. One of the main reasons for this is that the Sira is far more favorable to Shi'a Islam than the Sunni branch. For instance, Ali is presented as

Muhammad's choice to succeed him. And then Ali is assigned a prominent place in the life of Muhammad; indeed, Ali is presented as being the first male convert to Islam.

Selections from A. Guillaume's Introduction

These selections will be far from complete. Presented here is a series of quotes with only the page number noted:

"Occasionally he (Ibn Ishaq) inserted verses in his narrative, and sometimes gave his own opinion" (p. xv).

"The impression one gets from this section is of hazy memories" (p. xviii).

"While the Medinan period is well documented, and events there are chronologically arranged, no such accuracy, indeed no such attempt at it, can be claimed for the Meccan period. We do not know Muhammad's age when he first came forth publicly as a religious reformer: some say he was forty others say forty-five" (pp. xviii–xix).

Speaking of the accounts of the Medinan years, "The story of those years is filled out with legends and stories of miraculous events which inevitably undermine the modern reader's confidence in the history of this period as a whole" (p. xix).

Ibn Ishaq presented introductions to many of the narratives. One example is what happened to Muhammad at the hands of the Meccans. "When the Quraysh became distressed by the trouble caused by the enmity between them and the apostle and those of their people who accepted his teaching, they stirred up against him foolish fellows who called him a liar, insulted him, and accused him of being a poet, a sorcerer, a diviner, and of being possessed" (p. xix).

"A word that very frequently precedes a statement is *za'ama* or *za'amii*, 'he (they) alleged'" (p. xix).

"Very seldom does Ibn Ishaq make any comment of his own on the traditions he records except for mental reservations he expressed in various ways. In the account of Muhammad's night journey to Jerusalem and the ascent into heaven he allows us to see the working of his mind. The story is everywhere hedged with reservations and terms suggesting caution to the reader (pp. xix–xx).

After the account of the night journey and the ascent to heaven, Ibn Ishaq reports that "A'isha's statement, reported by one of her father's family, that is was only the apostle's spirit that was transported; his body remained where it was in Mecca" (p. xxi).

The actual account in the Sira is found on page 183: "One of Abu Bakr's family told me that A'isha the prophet's wife used to say: 'The apostle's body remained where it was but God removed his spirit by night.'"

From one of the companions of Muhammad is yet another account of the night journey. "I have heard that the apostle used to say, 'My eyes sleep while my heart is awake.' Only God knows how revelation came and he saw what he saw. But whether he was asleep or awake, it was all true and actually happened" (p. 183).

In various places, I.I. refers to stories of the events of Muhammad's life as, "only God knows what really happened" (e.g., p. xxi).

A. Guillaume in speaking of the eighth-century Middle East, states that miracles were commonly performed by religious figures, and the inference is that miracles would be done by Muhammad as well. However, in the Qur'an and hadith, Muhammad is not recorded as performing any miracles. Today Islam holds that Muhammad's miracle is the Qur'an itself. But the Sira reports many miracles done at the hands of Muhammad, some that are absolutely incredible. For example, Muhammad "summoned a tree to him and it stood before him. He told it to go back again and back it went. It is interesting to notice that the person for whose benefit this miracle was wrought regarded it as sorcery (p. xxiii).

***

The following is a break down of the table of contents of the Sira with some chapters mentioned:

Part I The Genealogy of Muhammad; Traditions From the Pre-Islamic Era; Muhammad's Childhood and early Manhood

- Arab Taboos
- Internal Dissensions
- The wells of Mecca
- His birth and foster mother
- His mother's death
- Rebuilding the Ka'ba
- Jews, Christians, and Arabs predict Muhammad's mission
- The Gospel prophesy of the sending of "the Comforter"

Part II Muhammad's Call and Preaching in Mecca

- His call and the beginning of the Qur'an
- Khadija accepts Islam
- Prayer prescribed
- Persecution of Muhammad
- 'Umar accepts Islam
- Some Christians accept Islam
- The night journey and the ascent into heaven
- Muhammad preaches to the Beduin
- Allah orders Muhammad to fight

Part III Muhammad's Migration to Medina, His Wars, Triumph, and Death

- Muhammad's Hijra
- The call to prayer
- Jewish opponents
- The first raid: on Waddan
- Raid on Buwat
- Raid on Safawan
- Fighting in the sacred month
- The change in the qibla
- Battle of Badr

- The chapter of "The Spoils"
- The willing homage
- Those left helpless
- Raid on Mu'ta
- Raid on Tubuk
- The farewell pilgrimage
- His raid on al-Ghaba
- Beginning of Muhammad's illness
- His death
- Preparations for burial

Note: Far less than a third of the chapters are listed above.

Final note

Even for the evangelical witness, knowledge of the Sira is not essential. Most Muslims know little about it, and those who do will shy away from it, especially Sunnis.

That said, though long and quite boring, it is nevertheless a document with which to be at least somewhat familiar. It can help round out one's knowledge about Islam in order to bring a credible witness to Muslims. And please understand that Muslim apologists generally know more about Christian documents than most Christians do. This can make for an embarrassing experience!

While engaging in a witness, debate, or conversation, it is never proper to catch someone with a zinger, meaning something from an Islamic authoritative writing or even an event from a news report, that makes Muslims look bad. This does not advance our cause. The evangelical witness does not depend upon one-upmanship. The goal is to present Jesus, His cross, resurrection, ascension, and soon return and reign as King of kings—not to embarrass or win an argument or debate. As someone once said, Gospel work is "one beggar telling another beggar where to find bread."

15

THE MIRACLES OF MUHAMMAD AND JESUS: A COMPARISON

Miracles Attributed to Muhammad

Imam Al-Bukhari's book *Sahih Al-Bukhari* is the most trusted and reliable collection of the words and actions of Muhammad compiled after the completion of the Qur'an. Concerning the piety of Imam Al-Bukhari, Dr. Muhammad Muhsin Khan, who summarized and translated Al-Bukhari's collection of hadith, writes: "It is for this reason, they (*Islamic scholars*) unanimously agreed that the most authentic book after the Book of Allah is *Sahih Al-Bukhari*."[1]

It is said that Imam Al-Bukhari collected 300,000 hadiths and memorized 200,000 of them. In the collection of hadith, however, he published only 7,275 of them. Al-Bukhari was born in the year 194 AH (meaning 194 years after the migration of the early Muslims from Mecca to Medina) and died in the year 256 AH (AD 879). His collection of the sayings and doings of Muhammad, then, began more than two hundred years after Muhammad's death.

Islam Credits Muhammad with the Following Twelve Miracles:

Miracle 1: The Qur'an itself. The entire book was revealed to Muhammad through Gabriel. Dr. Khan states: "Today 1400 years have passed and nobody has been able to change a single letter or produce its imitation, as it is said in the Qur'an" (see *Surah Hijr*, V. 15:9).

The Qur'an is, then, the revealed message from Allah and is considered perfect. This is Muhammad's first miracle.

Note: It is not claimed that Muhammad wrote the Qur'an or is responsible for anything contained in it. He received from Allah that which was spoken to Gabriel, who then recited the message to Muhammad, who in turn recited the words to others. One wonders, where is the miracle, and if there is one, to whom should it be credited?

Miracle 2: Muhammad split the moon when he was challenged by Meccans to show them a miracle.

---

1 Dr. Muhammad Muhsin Khan, *Sahih Al-Bukhari* (Riyadh, Saudi Arabia: Darussalam, 1994), 18.

Miracle 3: In Muhammad's mosque was a date-palm tree that he leaned upon when he preached. When a pulpit was made for Muhammad, meaning that he no longer leaned against the tree, the stem, or trunk, of the tree began to cry. Muhammad then went to it and rubbed the tree with his hand, and the tree ceased crying.

Miracle 4: At a time when water was needed for ablutions, water began to flow from between Muhammad's fingers, and there was enough water for 1,400 men to perform ablutions and satisfy their thirst.

Miracle 5: "The prophet's meals used to glorify Allah while he ate, and this glorification was heard by the companions of the Prophet" (p. 16).

Miracle 6: "Stones used to greet the Prophet whenever he passed by through the lanes of Makka" (p. 16).

Miracle 7: Once, when the body of a Christian was buried, the earth threw the body out of its burial place. This Christian had converted to Islam then later returned to Christianity. Over and over the Christian was buried, only to have the earth throw the body out of the ground. It was said to have been a deed of Muhammad. Eventually the body was simply left on top of the ground.

Miracle 8: Trees would screen or shade the Prophet whenever he answered the call of nature.

Miracle 9: A well at Hudaibiya gave water again after it had dried up. This miracle is attributed to Muhammad.

Miracle 10: "An increase in the amount of dates in the garden of Jabir bin 'Abdullah after the Prophet went round the heaps of dates and invoked Allah for His Blessings" (p. 16).

Miracle 11: The miracle of a wolf speaking. "It has been written that a wolf also spoke to one of the companions of the Prophet near Al-Madina. A shepherd prevented a wolf from attacking one of his sheep. Later, the wolf scolded the shepherd since it was Allah who had provided the sheep for the wolf to eat. The shepherd then travelled to see Muhammad and told him what had happened. Muhammad asked the shepherd to repeat the story to others. Muhammad stated that the day of resurrection would not occur until beasts of prey would speak to human beings. Even the stick lash[2] and the shoe laces of a person speak to him and his thigh informs him about his family as to what happened to them after him" (p. 17).

Miracle 12: "The ascent of the prophet to the heavens" (p. 17).

Note: At age fifty Muhammad reported that he had been transported to Paradise, where he met with other prophets. This event is termed the "night journey." Perhaps it is not mentioned as a miracle since Aisha, Muhammad's favorite wife, said the journey occurred in his head only.

Christianity Credits Jesus with the Following Miracles, and Many More:

Jesus did far more miracles—or "signs and wonders," as is the common phrase used for His miracles in the New Testament—than are recorded in the Gospel accounts of

---

2   The meaning of "the stick lash" is unknown.

Matthew, Mark, Luke, and John. He performed healing miracles, resurrections from the dead, the casting out of demons, the control of nature, and the multiplication of food. None of these was for show or to demonstrate Jesus' power and authority. They were centered on meeting the needs of ordinary people who came to Him.[3]

Here are some examples of miracles attributed to Jesus.

Jesus cleanses a leper, Matthew 8:1–4:

> When He came down from the mountain, great crowds followed Him. And behold, a leper came to Him and knelt before Him, saying, "Lord, if You will, You can make me clean." And Jesus stretched out His hand and touched him, saying, "I will; be clean." And immediately his leprosy was cleansed. And Jesus said to him, "See that you say nothing to anyone, but go, show yourself to the priest and offer the gift that Moses commanded, for a proof to them."

A leper was an outcast due to the danger of transmitting the disease to others. We note Jesus touches the man and does not fear to do so. Jesus does not want any notoriety about the healing and requests the former leper to do what is required according to the Law of Moses (see Leviticus chapters 13 and 14), so that the man now free of leprosy is able to enter into society once again.

The man had a genuine organic disease and not anything akin to a psychosomatic illness.

In Matthew 8:14–17 we find the story of the healing of Peter's mother-in-law, which may have occurred on the same day as the healing of the leper.

> And when Jesus entered Peter's house, He saw his mother-in-law sick with a fever. He touched her hand, and the fever left her, and she rose and began to serve Him. That evening they brought to Him many who were oppressed by demons, and He cast out the spirits with a word and healed all who were sick. This was to fulfill what was spoken by the prophet Isaiah: "He took our illnesses and bore our diseases."

In this passage are two miracles: one the healing of an illness, the other an account of many freed from demonic possession.

Continuing in Matthew 8, we come to a story illustrating Jesus' authority over nature. Matthew 8:23–27:

> And when He got into the boat, His disciples followed Him. And behold, there arose a great storm on the sea, so that the boat was being swamped by the waves; but He was asleep. And they went and woke Him, saying, "Save us, Lord; we are perishing." And He said to them, "Why are you afraid, O you of little faith?" Then He rose and rebuked the winds and the sea, and there was a great calm. And the men marveled, saying, "What sort of man is this, that even winds and sea obey Him?"

In Matthew 9:18–26 is an account of a resurrection.

The story is that a ruler of the Jewish people comes to Jesus and tells Him his daughter has just died. He says to Jesus, "But come and lay Your hand on her, and she will live." While Jesus is on His way to the girl, a woman who has had a long-

---

[3] When referring to Jesus with the use of him or he or his, I capitalize, as in Him, He, and His. The *English Standard Version* that I use does not do so.

term discharge of blood comes up behind Jesus, touches the hem of His garment, and is immediately made well.

Jesus arrives at the ruler's house at the time that the official mourners are present. He tells them all to go away, goes into the house, grasps the hand of the dead girl, and she arises. Matthew states, "And the report of this went through all that district" (Matthew 9:26).

An even more dramatic resurrection appears in John's Gospel, chapter 11—the raising of Lazarus. Lazarus lives in Bethany, a village about two miles from Jerusalem, with his two sisters, Mary and Martha. It is apparent that Jesus and His disciples would stay with this family from time to time. Lazarus is not well, and after the sisters have done all they can, they send for Jesus. Jesus does not come right away, even seeming to disregard the diagnosis. Meanwhile, Lazarus dies. Four days later, Jesus reaches Bethany. Upon His arrival, Martha seems to scold Jesus for being late. Lazarus has been dead for four days. Jesus nevertheless calls Lazarus out of the grave. A great celebration follows.

This resurrection from the dead is no small irritant for the Jewish leaders. Here is John's account of it:

> When the large crowd of the Jews learned that Jesus was there, they came, not only on account of Him but also to see Lazarus, whom He had raised from the dead. So the chief priests made plans to put Lazarus to death as well, because on account of him many of the Jews were going away and believing in Jesus. (John 12:9–11)

Jesus' enemies could not refute the miracle. In Jewish thought, it was possible for a person to revive after three days, though it was common that a corpse was buried the same day death occurred. The four-day delay made it plain Jesus had performed an incredible and undeniable miracle. Here even Jesus' enemies attest to the miracle.

Matthew 14:13–21 records the feeding of the five thousand. Jesus, teaching in a desolate place, finds that a large crowd has converged upon Him. He has compassion upon them and "healed their sick."

Toward evening, Jesus' disciples come to Him and say, "This is a desolate place, and the day is now over; send the crowds away to go into the villages and buy food for themselves."

Jesus replies, "They need not go away; you give them something to eat." The disciples state they have only five loaves and two fish, certainly not enough to feed the thousands. Jesus asks for the bread and the fish, has the disciples arrange for the crowd to sit on the grass, and proceeds to break into pieces the bread and the fish, after offering thanksgiving to the Father. The disciples are instructed to hand these out to the people. All are satisfied. The disciples then collect what food remains, which fills twelve baskets. Matthew concludes the event by stating, "And those who ate were about five thousand men, besides women and children."

In Matthew 15:32–39 we read the account of the miracle of the feeding of the four thousand. The two miracle feedings are quite similar but quite distinct at the same time. The miracles of feeding the thousands have to do with the multiplication of matter, which is a violation of basic physics. Tremendous energy is required to create matter, thus we see in a different light the miracle power that accompanied Jesus' ministry.

Matthew 14:22–33 has the account of Jesus walking on the water.

The disciples are in a boat on the Sea of Galilee, while Jesus remains on shore in order to pray. A storm comes up suddenly, which happens in that place, and eventually the boat is a long way from shore.

Suddenly, the disciples see Jesus walking toward them, and Matthew says they are "terrified." They think they are seeing a ghost—but no, it is indeed Jesus. He says to them, "Take heart; it is I. Do not be afraid."

In Matthew 15:29–31 we read the account of Jesus healing many.

> Jesus went on from there and walked beside the Sea of Galilee. And He went up on the mountain and sat down there. And great crowds came to Him, bringing with them the lame, the blind, the crippled, the mute, and many others, and they put them at His feet, and He healed them, so that the crowd wondered, when they saw the mute speaking, the crippled healthy, the lame walking, and the blind seeing. And they glorified the God of Israel.

There is nothing in the accounts of Jesus' healings indicating the use of magical manipulations, employing the power of suggestion, or the inducing of trance states. Nor are the illnesses due to psychosomatic suggestion. Nothing of the kind—these are actual organic, real diseases from which people were healed.

John 2:1–12 is the account of the wedding feast at Cana, a village in the region of Galilee, not far from where Jesus and His family lived. In this story, Jesus and His disciples are present at the wedding, along with His mother Mary and His brothers.

At some point in the wedding, the supply of wine is exhausted. Mary, upon learning of this, informs her son of the situation. At the site of the wedding are six stone water jars used for storing water used in Jewish rites of purification. Jars such as those described in this story have been archaeologically excavated. They are made of a single stone and are capable of containing many gallons of liquid.

Jesus tells the host's servants to fill the six jars with water. Once they are filled, He asks the servants to go back to the source of the water, likely a well, and draw some out. This liquid is taken to the master of the feast, who marvels at the excellence of the wine he is drinking.

John's conclusion to this, perhaps the first, miracle of Jesus is: "After this He went down to Capernaum, with His mother and His brothers and His disciples, and they stayed there for a few days" (verse 12). A rather ordinary finish to an incredible miracle.

John 4:46–58 demonstrates a healing of another kind—healing at a distance.

At Capernaum, an official (of what type or kind is not explained) comes to Jesus to inform Him his son is ill, probably dying, and asks Jesus to come and heal the boy. Surprisingly, or so it seems, Jesus replies, "Unless you see signs and wonders you will not believe."

To illustrate, perhaps, that Jesus need not be present in the flesh to perform miracles, Jesus says to the father, "Go; your son will live." The father believes Jesus' words and finds upon returning home that his son is well.

There Were Many More Miracles that Went Unrecorded in the New Testament.

Near the end of John's Gospel, the apostle John explains his reason for writing his account of Jesus' ministry.

> Now Jesus did many other signs in the presence of the disciples, which are not written in this book; but these are written so that you may believe that Jesus is the Christ, the Son of God, and that by believing you may have life in His name. (John 20:30–31)

Turning to the Book of Acts, chapter 2 verse 22, we find mention by Peter, in his Pentecost sermon, of the signs and wonders Jesus performed.

> Men of Israel, hear these words: Jesus of Nazareth, a man attested to you by God with mighty works and wonders and signs that God did through Him in your midst, as you yourselves know...

Then, in the same chapter is a description of signs and wonders seen in the ministry of the apostles. "And awe came upon every soul, and many wonders and signs were being done through the apostles" (Acts 2:43).

In chapter 3 of Acts is the account of a lame beggar healed through the ministry of Peter and John. Going to the temple at the hour of prayer, the two encounter a lame man begging of those coming into the temple.

Peter and John have no money to give him, so Peter says, "I have no silver and gold, but what I do have I give to you. In the name of Jesus Christ of Nazareth, rise up and walk!" (Acts 3:6).

The lame man leaps up and praises God. And the reaction:

> And all the people saw him walking and praising God, and recognized him as the one who sat at the Beautiful Gate of the temple, asking for alms. And they were filled with wonder and amazement at what had happened to him. (Acts 3:9–10)

Luke reports that signs and wonders were common in those early days. "Now many signs and wonders were regularly done among the people by the hands of the apostles" (Acts 5:12).[4]

As one reads through the Book of Acts by Luke, we find the continuation of miracles performed by Jesus' apostles, and it is plain that the power of these miracles belongs to Jesus Christ. And still to this day, we witness the same.

---

4 Signs and wonders, healings, and many other miracles are common in times of awakening and revival down through the history of the Church. During America's Fourth Awakening, called the Jesus People Movement, which occurred from 1967 to 1975, I personally witnessed hundreds of these miracles up close and personal.

16

ESSAYS ON ISLAM

Introduction

Any, all, or parts of the following essays may be used by anyone for whatever purpose, freely, without any consideration or money changing hands. If desired, references may be made without mentioning the articles or author.

The reader will notice differences in my orientation or feelings toward Islam in the essays. The tenth essay was written in late 2016, while the seventh is from 2002. I did not include the earliest essay, because when I wrote it I was quite angry toward Muslims and Islam in general. The more I learned about Islam and especially the more I engaged with Muslim people directly, my views softened, in that I realized Muslims were caught in the vice grip of an exceedingly unhealthy religious system.

The Islam of the extremists is purer, more traditional, and more radical than that practiced and understood by moderates. Only a small percentage of Muslims know much about their religion; the zealous Muslim knows much more about Islam and understands that if he or she has a chance of going to paradise rather than hellfire, it is necessary to move to a more fervent following of Islam.

Most Muslims want to live and let live. But their entire identity, their worldview, is Muslim. They cannot imagine being anything but Muslim. Outreach to Muslims is then dependent on the miracle working of God; the new birth is from above.

To be clear, I see Islam as wrongly oriented and founded. I no more accept Islam as a revelation from God than I do Hinduism, Buddhism, Shamanism, and the belief systems of many neo-pagan groups.

All organized religions are flawed, including Christianity. I am a Baptist pastor who understands that Baptists are flawed as well. Any and every institution with humans involved will be corrupt to some measure, some more than others. I definitely believe that God was in Christ reconciling the world to Himself and that God sent His only Son to take our sin upon Himself—to die, be buried, and be resurrected. He will come again to judge the living and the dead. There is salvation in no one but Jesus Christ of Nazareth.

A challenge to the reader: Which essay would be appropriate to give to a Muslim and which would not? All of the essays are written for Christians who have an interest in understanding Islam. Some are "softer" than others and may be used as a Gospel tract, so to speak, and given to Muslim people. Some are "harder" and would likely repel a Muslim reader. As Christians, we do not "pull punches." At the same time we are wise as serpents and harmless as doves. Our goal is to present the message of Jesus Christ to all people of the world including Muslims.

A note to readers who are feeling a bit overwhelmed at this point. There is so much to learn about Islam and all that goes with it. There is indeed a steep learning curve, and the journey up the initial curve is painful and frustrating. I not only have been there, but in many ways I am yet struggling up the incline. It is little by little for sure. And I must confess that when I speak with Muslims I find I really don't have to know all that much about Islam; this is necessary only when dealing with the imams and scholars. A good grasp of the essentials of Biblical Christianity is what counts the most. We simply present the message of the person and work of Jesus Christ. That is it, the basic evangel. And you will be surprised how many Muslims are eager to hear it.

Essay One

A Follower of Muhammad? A Follower of Jesus?

Average Muslims are caught in a very difficult predicament—they must be followers of Muhammad and attempt to do what he did in his lifetime, if they have any chance of entering paradise. A Muslim is required to live out a very rigorous commitment to the principles and practices of Islam.

The question, "What did Muhammad do during his lifetime?" therefore becomes a very large issue for Muslim people. The following is only a short list of those things that Muhammad did and highlights the most commonly known aspects of his life.

» Once he began preaching Islam, he is not known to have earned a living other than through acquiring the spoils of conquest.
» He forced people to convert to Islam or die, or, become enslaved to Muslims and submit to them.
» He gained converts by force, some by persuasion.
» He had at least twelve wives, plus concubines, and married at least one girl under the age of ten and did have sexual relations with her while she was under ten.
» He wore a beard.
» He ate only with his right hand.
» He slept only upon his right side.

To be a true follower of Muhammad and live like he did—not easily imitated. How might a faithful Muslim then live?

To be a follower of Muhammad you would:

» Live off a welfare system. This is extremely common in Europe, for example, where those Muslims on welfare are, comparatively speaking, a very high percentage of the Muslim population. After all, how can a faithful Muslim be employed with the requirement to pray five times a day, and three of the prayers coming during normal business hours?
» View others who were not Muslims as infidels and who may then be treated in any manner necessary to secure their submission including murdering them whether

man, woman, or child.

» Use force of whatever kind necessary to secure the advancement of the religion. (Every day in our newspapers this fact is highlighted and the television news broadcasts are choked with the gory details most every evening.)

» Satisfy your sexual needs as Muhammad did by having many wives, including children.

Note: Child brides are a staple in countries where Islam predominates. Very recently, in Gaza, the terrorist organization Hamas put on a large wedding celebration for 450 couples and the brides were all little girls under ten years of age. It must be pointed out that the usual cover-ups were made to a credulous Western population that such horrific behavior is only a cultural means of providing for poor families or suggesting there is no sex until at least puberty—none of which is close to the truth. No, it is pedophilia, which is sanctioned by the Muslim culture. There are estimates that there are 51 million child brides now living on the planet and almost all are in Muslim countries. Pedophilia was not only practiced by Muhammad but is also sanctioned by the Qur'an (see Surah 65:4).

The most famous Muslim cleric of the 20th Century, Ayatollah Khomeini, said that a man can have sexual pleasure from a child as young as a baby. However, the holy man said, he should not penetrate a female; rather, sodomizing a male child was permitted. The revered ayatollah further announced that a father who gives his child for such pleasure would earn a permanent place in paradise.

Yes, this is horrific, and I will stop here with descriptions. The Ayatollah wrote a book about his views on sex with infants, animals, and more. Here is the title of the book: *Ayatollah Khomeini's Book on Sex: For Shias*, by LagoShia. The Ayatollah is the leading scholar and jurist for Shi'a Islam and therefore his word is law. A Wikipedia search on the subject will yield all one needs to know.

A Follower of Jesus?

Make a comparison between Jesus and Muhammad. Read one of the gospels for yourself and you will find the difference to be as different as darkness is from light, as hate is from love, and death is from life.

The Muslim, especially if born in countries with a Muslim majority, is trapped into something he or she is virtually unable to escape from. They are caught in a religious culture that, I am convinced, they would renounce if they could.

Closing Comment

Behind and beneath and within Islam lurks that which is evil. Wish it were not so, wish that Islam was actually simply another of the world's great religions as it is so often portrayed.

Why is it that mostly only Biblically-oriented Christians understand the real nature of the religion? is a question to be pondered. It would seem that all the people of the earth would be alarmed at the core teachings and practices of Islam. And it is this fact that leads me to the conclusion that there is a hideous evil strength that runs through all of that which is claimed to be a religion and which demands proper respect and acceptance.

Essay Two

WERE THE CRUSADERS AND INQUISITORS CHRISTIANS? YES, NO, MAYBE

PART ONE: The Crusaders

"Crusader" is a negative word to many, and maybe deservedly so, but we may have to reconsider the negative position. Following is a brief summary and examination of the history of the crusades themselves.

There were eight crusades in all, from 1095 to 1294. Oddly enough, no Arab tribes played much of a role, if any, in fighting the crusaders. This is not to say that Muslim armies were not involved, but exactly who within Islam actually participated is another issue.

The French initiated the first crusade led by Godfrey of Bouillon. The purpose was to wrest control of Jerusalem away from the Muslim Seljuk Turks, who had taken it in 1070. Jerusalem had previously been part of the Fatimid Empire, composed mostly of Shi'a Berbers from North Africa, and during their control of the Holy City, Christians were allowed to visit their special religious sites. But such was not the case with the Seljuks, who violently persecuted the Christians and desecrated and destroyed churches. After a time, Pope Urban II called for the rescue of the Holy City from the Islamic infidels.

Bouillon, certainly a member of the Roman Catholic Church, managed to murder 70,000 Muslims and even burned down synagogues crowded with Jewish people hoping to escape the violence around them. Despite the slaughter, many of the European soldiers married local Muslim and Jewish women; they settled down, and for at least forty years, the Christians and Muslims lived peacefully side-by-side. The fact remains, however, that Crusaders slaughtered a host of people.

The second crusade in 1144 was undertaken when a Kurdish army from Mosul (now in the modern state of Iraq) attacked a Christian fortress in Edessa (now in the modern state of Turkey). As a result, Pope Eugenius III called for a crusade. Two Christian armies, one French, the other German, were completely decimated by the Seljuk armies while on their way to join the battle at Edessa. A monk named Bernard of Clairvoux was engaged in this one. Following the crusade nearly forty more years of peace ensued.

The third crusade was called in 1189 by the Holy Roman Emperor Frederick Barbarossa after the army of Saladin (1137–1193), the famous Kurd who became the Sultan of Egypt, defeated the crusader army on July 4, 1187, at the Horns of Hittin, a site just above the Sea of Galilee. It proved to be the most famous of all the battles during the crusade period. Jerusalem surrendered, and Saladin dealt humanely with the survivors; there was no sacking or murdering, and the city was kept open to Christian pilgrims. But Jerusalem's fall inspired Barbarossa to lead a French army into Turkey, where he died crossing a creek. The Seljuks quickly destroyed his army.

There was, however, more to the third crusade. King Richard the Third of England (the "Lion Heart") gathered an army of Norman Knights, set off for the Holy Land, and proceeded to capture Acre and Jaffa on the Mediterranean Coast, even defeating Saladin at the battle of Arsuf.

The two commanders treated each other with respect and signed a peace treaty on September 2, 1192, the terms of which left Jerusalem in the hands of the Muslims, while the Christians retained the coastal areas where Acre, Caesarea, and Jaffa are located.

Pope Innocent III in and around 1195 called the fourth crusade. This one had nothing to do with the Holy Land or Muslims, but the goal was to liberate Jerusalem. The French crusaders entered Constantinople, home of the Greek Orthodox Church, who resented the presence of the Roman Catholics and rose up against the crusaders. In the battle that resulted, the crusader "Western" Christians did not kill many Greek "Eastern" Christians, but they did completely pillage the city. After a short period, the crusaders made off with their loot and headed for home. Nothing was accomplished.

Pope Honorius III, Innocent's successor, could not accept the results of the fourth crusade and called for a fifth crusade. This time mainly Germans and Hungarians marched off to Jerusalem by way of Egypt in 1217. The army spent three years in skirmishes with the Kurdish Ayyubids in Egypt. They failed to make headway and finally called it quits and sailed home.

The sixth crusade's outstanding personality was the Holy Roman Emperor Frederick II, who was the grandson of the famous Barbarossa. Frederick II's daughter was married to John of Brienne, who now ruled Jerusalem. Thinking that marriage gave him authority over Jerusalem, he called for the sixth crusade in 1225. Due to the knowledge and negotiating skills of the remarkable Frederick, the crusade was peacefully conducted without one battle or casualty.

Frederick had studied a great deal about Islamic literature, science, and philosophy, which gave him a solid platform for interaction with the leader of the Islamic army, Malik al-Kamil, who was the nephew of the great Saladin. The two leaders resolved the confrontation by signing a ten-year treaty in 1229. (Ten years was the maximum time allowed for a treaty according to Sharia Law.) Christians and Muslims alike welcomed the terms of the treaty. Unhappily, the new pope, Pope Gregory IX, hated Frederick and refused to ratify the treaty, denouncing it vigorously.

Things went from bad to worse after Sultan Kamil's death in 1238, when a maverick Turk from Russia named Baibars led a Mameluk (Muslim) army against Jerusalem, sacking it and slaughtering the citizens in 1244.

King Louis IX of France called the seventh crusade. In 1250 King Louis brought an army to Egypt and sailed up the Nile to Cairo, where Baibars demolished that army. Baibars warred against everyone, Christian and Muslim alike, in an effort to establish his power and authority. His hate and murderous anger was mostly directed toward Christians, and he attacked one city after the other along the Mediterranean coast—Caesarea, Safad, Jaffa, and Antioch. He killed and enslaved thousands of Christians. Jerusalem was now firmly in the hands of Muslims, and the seventh crusade came to an end.

The eighth crusade flowed out of the outrage perpetrated against Christians in the seventh crusade. Louis IX demanded a new crusade in the year 1270. His plan was to come through Tunis on the way to Egypt, but a few days after landing in Tunis he died of dysentery.

Baibars died in 1277 (these crusades could last for years), and his successor, Sultan Khalil, managed to finally defeat the crusaders at Acre in 1291, killing or enslaving some 60,000 Christians there.

IMPACT OF THE CRUSADES

The crusades deepened the divide between the Eastern and Western wings of the Catholic Church, a rift that was already well underway centuries earlier.

Related to that, the crusades greatly weakened the Byzantine Empire, which succeeded the Holy Roman Empire.

The crusades also permanently embittered relations between Christians and Muslims, and they are used to this day to rationalize a continuing hatred that often erupts into violence. The fact that both Christians and Muslims committed horrible atrocities is often forgotten or conveniently submerged. Muslims have cited Christian crusader actions as justification for their own brutality. This is not a surmise, but openly declared by contemporary Islamic jihadists, whose portfolio of rallying cries includes something close to, "Remember the crusades." They legitimize their call for revenge by pointing to what the Christians did in the crusades. This is, of course, completely disingenuous but nevertheless effective.

Promotion of religion by force of arms demonstrates the weakness of Muslim ideals, ethics, and message. To spread the faith by means of intimidation is the worst possible program, one that no one can respect. Not only the Muslims but also Christians have been guilty here. (This topic will be explored in greater detail in the second section of this essay, "The Inquisitors.")

As early as the fifth century, and many say long before, becoming a Christian required baptism by an ordained priest of the one Catholic and Apostolic Church. Faith and grace now abandoned, the Church became a power structure and fell into the same tactics employed by many other secular institutions. Some use the word "Christendom" to describe the Church as empire, combining religion with the state.

The crusades marked a departure from the Church's mission to preach the Gospel to all nations. By picking up the sword, it was giving in to the barbaric culture of that day. The Church was intertwined with the state, the state using the Church and the Church using the state to advance goals and consolidate power.

As a result, the core doctrine of conversion was severely compromised. To coerce a person into leaving one faith for another is absolutely unbiblical. Requiring a choice of whether to convert, die, or pay the tax is not exactly proper evangelism, but the Church was guilty of this just as were the Muslims, and contemporary Muslims still employ these means. It cannot be said today that the Christian Church advances by means of force and fear. (Note: Instances of wrongly motivated attempts to convert so-called "primitive" people groups were occurring well into the nineteenth century, e.g., the forcing of Western/Christian culture and religion on Native Americans on reservations and similar activities by Britaish missionaries in India. Broadening the argument to include these examples or others is not possible in the space allowed, but we acknowledge needing to discuss this elsewhere.)

The same mentality that was seen in the crusades also resulted in the persecution of those we today call evangelical Christians, especially those who reject infant baptism, transubstantiation (Jesus being actually present in the Bread and the Cup), and the necessity of receiving other sacraments in order to go to heaven—in other words, those who adhere to salvation by grace alone, faith alone, and Christ alone.

***

The story of two ancestors of mine might be of interest now. The first concerns Sir John Philpott.

John Philpott was a "Salter and Pepperer" (a grocer) who lived in the latter part of the fourteenth century in London, England, while the One Hundred Years War with France was underway. He relied on his merchant fleet to bring foodstuffs into England from the Continent, but a combination of a weak English king and an aggressive French king meant Philpott's business was faltering. He was able, however, to convince the English king to allow him to outfit his ships into a navy and be crewed by convicts from London's prisons, of which there were plenty. The result was a series of victories by Philpott's navy, and on the strength of that he was elected Lord Mayor of London in 1388 and 1389. He was a faithful Christian, and in his will he left 100 pounds to be distributed amongst the poor of London at Christmas time each year. In the old city of London there is still Philpott Lane where a plaque commemorating this faithful Catholic and Christian man has been installed.

Then there was another Englishman, again named John Philpott, this time living in the sixteenth century. He was a Puritan, meaning he hoped that the newly founded Church of England that broke away from the Roman Church, precipitated by King Henry VIII, would be purified—that is, would conform more closely to what we see of the church in the New Testament. Philpott was forced into the Court of the Inquisitors and found guilty. Refusing to recant, he was burned at the stake in 1555. (Burning at the stake was desirable form of execution because it was thought the destruction of the body made resurrection impossible.)

PART TWO: The Inquisition

Although the story of the development of the Church in the centuries leading up to the "Dark Ages" (stretching from approximately AD 500 to 1500) is not so easy to uncover, there is evidence that the faith of Jesus and the early disciples was not extinguished. That it was diverted, perverted, and undermined, especially toward the end of the third century, is fairly plain history, at least as evangelicals read it.

During that dark time, the vibrant faith we see in the New Testament gradually shifted to a more formalized, mechanical, ritualistic, even magical understanding of what it meant to be a follower of Jesus. Especially after the so-called conversion of Constantine in the early fourth century, people became members of the Church and were counted among the faithful, despite their never hearing the real Gospel message or knowing much of anything about the core doctrines of Scripture.

The power of the Church over salvation, the only really important issue in life, was under the control of an ecclesiastical hierarchy. Those who rebelled against this were the targets of the Inquisition, the first court of which was formed around the year 1231 and continued for some three or four centuries. From the Church's point of view, the Inquisition was necessary, because many good Catholics were turning away from the doctrines of the Church, especially after publication of the Bible in common languages, which allowed people to see what the Bible actually taught. For nearly a thousand years it had been hidden in a dark covering of non-intelligible Latin, Greek, or Hebrew.

The renaissance of Biblical understanding forced the established Church to react, and energetically; heresy became the most heinous of all crimes. There is evidence that many were troubled by the means used to keep the Church pure. Ecclesiastical leaders would often plead with secular authorities for sentences to be carried out mercifully. In the early days of the persecution, Roman Church officials acted ruthlessly. For instance, the Cathari (or Albigenses) and the Waldenses were persecuted, sometimes to death, during the 1220s by the order of Pope Gregory IX.

Fringe Christian groups were not the only ones to be sought out by the Inquisitors. As with John Philpott in 1555, the point at the center of the trials had to do with the elements of the Mass, otherwise known as Communion, Eucharist, or the Lord's Supper. Along with the Reformers (i.e., Martin Luther and John Calvin), Philpott believed the bread of the Eucharist was just bread and the juice in the cup just juice. But the Church had developed the concept that the bread was transformed by an act of the priest into the actual body, the flesh, of Jesus. Likewise, the juice invisibly, magically, became the actual blood of Jesus.

Two Latin words were actually pronounced by the priest before the Mass began—*hocus pocus*—and when the words were pronounced, the magical power inherited from Peter and passed down through the properly ordained priesthood transformed the substances, shazam!

How this came to be is not possible to describe here, but there is an actual history to it. The short version is this: The Church had become far too Western in its understanding of the Middle-Eastern document we call the Bible, both Old and New Testaments. And when Jesus said, "Truly, truly, I say to you, unless you eat the flesh of the Son of Man and drink his blood, you have no life in you. Whoever feeds on my flesh and drinks my blood has eternal life, and I will raise him up on the last day. For my flesh is true food, and my blood is true drink" (John 6:53-55), the Roman Church took His words literally.

To take Jesus' words literally, however, would have been ludicrous for a Jewish person in the first century. And the early history of the Church clearly reveals that the passage was taken metaphorically—after all, the Church was composed mostly of Jews for the first generation. The point was that the disciples were to trust in and believe in Jesus as the Savior and that His death on the cross, with His broken body and shed blood, was the once-forever sacrifice for sin. Therefore, long after the "Eastern" sense of things was lost, the "Western" mindset misunderstood much of the nature and means of salvation.

The Inquisition was aimed at Christians, but Muslims and Jews were also tried, and many were executed. It is only natural that Muslims and Jews would have a negative reaction to this, and it is certainly possible that it yet lingers as something else horrible that Christendom perpetrated and thus could be avenged in whatever era.

During the period of the Inquisition there were undoubtedly thousands of bishops, priests, and regular members of the Roman Church who sincerely thought they were being faithful Christians to support and participate in what they perceived as a cleansing of their Church from heretical doctrine and practice. Undoubtedly, there were thousands of Christians who were horrified at what was being done in the name of Jesus Christ. And during the period of history when the Church and state were wed, significant resistance was virtually out of the question. Such resistance finally came in 1517 under the inspiration of a Catholic monk named Martin Luther.

PART THREE: Yes, No, Maybe

Were those who conducted the Inquisition real Christians?
Were the crusaders real Christians?
Were the Muslims who fought against the crusaders real Muslims? Or, to put it another way, are those Muslims who engage in violent jihad today the real Muslims?
To these questions the answers are, Yes, No, and Maybe.

LOOKING AT CHRISTIANS

It must be said that no one could possibly know for sure whether real and actual born-again Christians committed atrocities against Muslims and Jews, in that day or in this. If a group of careful observers had watched the murder of Muslims and Jews at the hands of people known as Christians during the crusades and at other times, would they have know for certain which was the right conclusion? The proper answer would have to be, No!

Why is this so? The core of the answer lies in the mystery of conversion. While one can be baptized, join a church, and even reform his or her life, this is far from genuine Christian conversion. Being a part of a church does not mean one is a Christian. Conversion means that the Holy Spirit indwells the one believing in Jesus, the one who has had all sin removed and forgiven. It is a profound spiritual experience not an intellectual or emotional one. It is something God does completely apart from anything an individual can do. It is miracle and mystery. Every pastor who has ministered to a congregation for ten or more years knows that in that congregation are those who have truly been born again and those who have not.

Not that every real Christian does right and lives right. The Christian life is a growing up into the fullness of Christ, little by little—first as an infant, then a toddler, young child, older child, adolescent, teenager, young adult, adult, older adult, and senior. Still after a lifetime of maturing, the Christian is not anywhere perfect until in heaven and in the presence of our holy God.

Is it possible that a Christian could be deceived into thinking that killing and persecuting others because they believed differently is justified? Yes, it is possible.

Might Christians commit horrific acts, because they were told to do so by powerful religious authorities? Maybe. Might Muslims? Maybe.

Would a Biblically literate Christian believe he or she was serving God by persecuting or even killing "infidels"? No, unless there was some unknown source of intimidation going on behind the scenes and/or such Christian had his or her mind bent to the point that they became merely tools of evil.

Perhaps the right answer for all of these questions is, Maybe!

Would persecuting or killing a non-Christian win approval with God? Would it ensure a place in heaven? To both of these, the answer is an unequivocal, No!

Would defending the cause of Christianity, the Church, a Christian leader, or anything else in all creation by harming others merit the favor of God? Certainly not! Would dying in defense of the God of Scripture assure a place in paradise? In no way!

This is my solemn opinion as a follower of Jesus.

Essay Three

LOOKING AT MUSLIMS

It is declared by a growing number of Christians and non-Christians alike that what is observed in the Islamic State (IS, also called *Daesh* from an Arabic acronym) and with all those who practice violent jihad does not represent true Islam. This, however, is debatable.

Muhammad did force non-Muslims into submission and made them pay a tax to stay alive. Muhammad did behead captured enemies, or at least ordered such and then observed the process. He did cut off the hands of thieves. He did arrange that captured women and children be sold as slaves. He did permit captured women to be taken as concubines; in fact, his last wife was a beauty he had rescued from a Jewish tribe that the Muslim army had defeated. Muhammad authorized lying if and when the cause of Islam was being defended or advanced. He did practice forced conversions. Whatever Muhammad did in his lifetime, as spelled out in the Qur'an, found in the hadith, or seen in the biography of Muhammad (called the Sira, written by Ibn Ishaq), are being imitated by the Islamic State now. And this Caliphate does not deny but proudly embraces this fact.

Not only do they not deny they are imitating Muhammad's tactics, but IS would view non-compliance to be at minimum weakness bordering on apostasy. This is the present state of affairs. Muhammad taught that Islam should be global and that Shar'ia Law be universal, which would result in the entire world then being at peace. It is the task of Muslims to bring this about. Anything less than this is un-Islamic.

Then there is Salafism. This term describes Muslims who practice a conservative, even radical form of their faith. They attempt to imitate Muhammad and hope to live under Shar'ia Law. It is just that they cannot do so except in a place where it is politically and culturally possible. "Most Salafis are not jihadists, and most adhere to sects that reject the Islamic State," writes Graeme Wood in his March, 2015, article in Atlantic entitled, "What ISIS Really Wants." They might, however, if given the chance, be every bit as strict as violent jihadists. Wood states that Salafis might implement "monstrous practices such as slavery and amputation – but at some future point." The Salafis' stated agenda is to purify their personal lives, including personal hygiene, and to be faithful in prayer and observance of all standard forms of the main rituals of Islam.[1]

Are all those who promote and/or engage in violent jihad real Muslims? If the answer is No, then it must be asked, "How could this be?"

There are many reasons why one would turn to violent jihad other than wanting to live like Muhammad. Is it possible that young men and women living in very poor circumstances, without much of a future, could be recruited into something they would later regret? Perhaps peer pressure overcomes them. Perhaps boredom, hopelessness, or a strong sense of inferiority might trigger the desire for a radical change in living. By means of the Internet, which jihadists use but detest at the same time, they recruit these vulnerable youth.

Not only those who grow up in less than ideal circumstances are attracted to violence and murder. It is enough that Muhammad both sanctioned and participated in such. The desire for a wonderful eternal future is a powerful magnet and may be the strongest motivator for a violent defense or advance of Islam.

The Internet also shows clearly what is available in the Western world; could envy be an instigating element that plays on the Muslim mind? Or, might a motivation be a chance for a quick ticket to paradise and seventy-two virgins, which may appear to be the only way to get love? Might young men and women be driven to distraction, to a cultic or toxic state of mind and made willing to do almost anything to lift themselves out of depression and despair?

Since Islam is both religion and state, which predominates? Or is there such a blending that there is no religion or state, just Islam? Islam is yet very much tribally oriented, one tribe against another, which is plain to see in daily news stories. Is the Muslim fighting for Muhammad, the imam, the umma (Muslim community), the political boundary, or what? This question might receive a hundred different answers, and silence as an answer could be expected.

Are all fighters with al-Qaeda, the Taliban, the various Shia and Sunni militias, even with ISIS, true Muslims? Yes, No, and Maybe! Only God knows.

---

1 By "Personal hygiene" is meant the intent to properly observe and avoid the many ways that Muslims might defile themselves before prayer. A chief instance of this is to avoid splashing oneself with urine in the toilet. Proper techniques for washing feet, arms, hands, and face before prayer is critical in the Muslim mind. This little section could continue for many pages describing the means of coping with and defending against the evil jinn (demons), since hygiene in the Muslim world is not what non-Muslim Westerners understand but is more concerned with superstitions about the supernatural.

Essay Four

A Fundamental Error of Islam

When visiting a local Sunni mosque, I was given a booklet entitled *A Brief Illustrated Guide to Understanding Islam*. The anonymous author states:

> Muslims believe that Jesus was not crucified. It was the plan of Jesus' enemies to crucify him, but God saved him and raised him up to Him. And the likeness of Jesus was put over another man. Jesus' enemies took this man and crucified him, thinking that he was Jesus.

The author backed up his contention with a quote from the Qur'an:

> ...They said: "We killed the Messiah Jesus, son of Mary, the messenger of God." They did not kill him, nor did they crucify him, but the likeness of him was put on another man (and they killed that man)...Qur'an 4:157

A fundamental error of Islam is this denying of the crucifixion of Jesus Christ while saying another man who looked like Jesus was actually placed on the cross. This is essentially a form of Gnosticism called Docetism.

Gnostics existed prior to the Christian era and were able to incorporate varying religious thought into their system. The Gnostics viewed matter as evil and mind or thought as good. The Christian incarnation, that is, God become flesh in Jesus of Nazareth, ran counter to their core doctrine. Therefore they developed the idea that Jesus did not actually die on a cross, rather someone who looked like Jesus did. This belief system is called Docetism, based on the Greek dokeo, meaning "to seem like."

The basic principle of Docetism was refuted by the Apostle John in 1 John 4:2-3:

> By this you know the Spirit of God: every spirit that confesses that Jesus Christ has come in the flesh is from God; and every spirit that does not confess Jesus is not from God; and this is the spirit of the antichrist, of which you have heard that it is coming, and now it is already in the world.

Also, 2 John 7, "For many deceivers have gone out into the world, those who do not acknowledge Jesus Christ as coming in the flesh. This is the deceiver and the antichrist."

Ignatius of Antioch (AD 98–117), Irenaeus (115–190), and Hippolatus (170-235) wrote against the Gnostic error in the early part of the second century.

Docetism was condemned at the Council of Chalcedon in 451.

Many sects and cults over the centuries have taken a Gnostic stance and thus substitute their own teaching as the means of salvation. This is precisely what Islam has done.

And Islam must do so. If salvation is based solely on Christ's death on the cross, where our sin was atoned for, then Islam has nothing to offer but is in fact a conduit for false salvation.

Islam is agonizingly focused on attaining eternity in paradise, or heaven, which is really the same thing. Heaven is fellowship with a holy God, and is made possible only through the cleansing blood of Jesus shed on the cross.

Islam and Christianity are polar opposites. Both cannot be right at the same time. This reality must be squarely faced.

The purest, most religious Muslim or the filthiest, most hypocritical Christian. Which would I prefer to be?

Which am I? I am the latter, and due to the utter holiness of the Triune God, I remain the filthy, hypocritical Christian until that day I stand before the Judgment of God on the Last Day and hear my Lord say, "Well done, good and faithful servant, enter into the joy of your rest."

Essay Five

THE WEAKNESS OF ISLAM

In nearly every edition of major American newspapers are stories of Muslims somewhere, east or west, engaged in acts of violence—in the name of Allah. Suicide bombing, kidnapping, killing Christians, Jews, and Hindus, burning churches and temples, destroying ancient religious relics, protesting free expressions of religion and the press—such terrorist reports are routine. What does this indicate about the very fabric of Islam?

I say it demonstrates a core weakness.

By weakness, I mean Islam is not able to compete in the spiritual marketplace of ideas. It must instead resort to repression, intimidation, and violence. Perhaps there is a sense of inferiority in that Muslims are gripped by the fear that Islam is not able to stand alongside Christianity, which does not seek to gain influence and converts by dependence on questionable, cultic methods.

I am reminded of Paul who, prior to his conversion, vigorously persecuted the Church. Many Bible scholars think he was motivated by a fear that his religious beliefs were inadequate or even erroneous. Paul was a terrorist while he was still known as Saul, according to the Biblical account in Acts. Yet after Jesus appeared to him on the road to Damascus, Paul no longer threw men, women, and children in prison merely because they believed in Jesus. Rather, he himself became a simple preacher of the gospel armed only with the message of a crucified and risen Savior.

Paul learned from Jesus, who taught His disciples to turn the other cheek, to pray for their enemies, and to do good to those who treated them shamefully. Jesus taught that His followers were to love their neighbors as themselves and to do to others as they would have done to them. Jesus said nothing of killing infidels or repressing religious teachings. He did warn of false prophets whose aim would be to deceive and corrupt. Clearly, however, He did not advocate imprisoning or killing them. In one instance, Jesus taught His disciples to simply go on to the next town when opposition arose. Jesus Himself practiced this, as did Paul throughout his missionary journeys.

Consider a society like Saudi Arabia where even the simple recounting of the Christian message to a Muslim is a capital offense. That is weakness in the extreme.

Islamic evangelistic strategy, known as da'wa, is so very often fueled by intimidation and violence. "Convert or die" has too often been the Muslim message. Am I exaggerating here? I don't think so, since sufficient historical data supports my claim, both ancient and modern. In fact, I think that the Islamic means of spreading the faith are held in check only by fear of retaliation from target peoples.

Biblical Christianity has entirely different weapons of warfare. Paul wrote, "For though we walk in the flesh, we are not waging war according to the flesh. For the weapons of our warfare are not of the flesh but have divine power to destroy strongholds" (2 Corinthians 10:3-4). Such is the power of the message of Jesus.

Evangelical Christians proclaim the message of the Cross of Jesus and His resurrection. The Holy Spirit of God then convicts individuals of their rebellion against God and draws them to the Savior, Jesus Christ, who has completely provided for their salvation. No one can be forced to become a Christian; no one can even "join" Christianity or apply for membership. It is a work of God and not of man. One of the great weaknesses of Islam is that it arose and continues to exist as the work of man. Few voluntarily choose to join Islam, especially in recent years now that the religion was been partially unmasked. It is usually by birth and community attachments that one becomes a Muslim. And especially in Muslim-dominated countries it is nearly impossible to leave it. This again is a great weakness. There is no religious freedom for Muslims to come and go, to be faithful or not; there is only fear of the community, of hellfire, and peer pressure. To be an apostate Muslim, that is one who has declared faith in Jesus rather than Muhammad, is to be classified worse than an infidel. The result is often death.

Paul trusted in the work of the Holy Spirit and did not revert to his old ways of violence and imprisonment—*fleshly* warfare. In Ephesians, Chapter 6, he describes the "armor of God"— which is the belt of truth, the breastplate of righteousness, for the feet the gospel of peace, the shield of faith, the helmet of salvation, and the sword of the Spirit, which is the word of God (see Ephesians 6: 10-20).

This is strength. This is confidence. This is peace. This is actual dependence on and submission to God.

Essay Six

Islam's Cultic Connection

Islam is rarely critiqued by journalists, because it can be dangerous to do so. This has been less true since September 11, 2001, because people are interested in Islam and are searching for answers.

However, it is still risky to write anything that may impugn Islam and especially the founder, Muhammad. This is one reason why I call Islam a cult. Muslims often treat opponents with something less than kindness as they seek to defend the honor of "Allah."

What Is a Cult?

My working definition of a cult is non-theological. Traditionally, Christians apply the term to Bible-based groups that have departed significantly from the mainstream and historical creeds. Such cults frequently deny the full deity and humanity of Jesus; His atoning work on the cross; His bodily resurrection; and His return at the end of the age to judge the living and the dead.

However, here I employ a secular definition of a cult: "any group that uses psychological or sociological techniques to recruit, motivate, and retain adherents."

Cults are not necessarily religious; they may be political, commercial, educational/therapeutic, or economic in nature. They may be large or small, named or unnamed, known or unknown.

Cults may have a leader or be without a leader. The common feature is the use of control mechanisms that violate the individuality of participants in the three areas stated above: recruitment, motivation, and retention.

Is Islam Cultic?

Many would deny that Islam has the characteristics of a cult. But why is Islam not a cult when in many Muslim-dominated countries it is a capital offense to hand Muslims a Bible or explain Christianity (or any other religion) to them?

Saudi Arabia, the guardian of Islam's most holy shrines at Mecca and Medina, is a highly restricted society where Christians are not allowed any public expression of their faith.

Why is Islam not a cult when it is virtually impossible for a Muslim to leave the religion, even if he merely wishes to become an atheist or agnostic?

Why is Islam not a cult when Muslim warriors force their religion on people? The history of Islam is full of that kind of "proselytization."

It is true that the Roman Catholic Church has in the past forced "pagans" to adopt Catholicism. However, that church has acknowledged that it was both wrong-headed and anti-Christian to do so and has terminated the practice.

As a Baptist, I can say that in 500 years of our history we have not engaged in such tactics and neither have any of the traditionally Evangelical, Protestant denominations.

SATANIC VERSES

A vivid illustration of the cultic nature of Islam is the case involving the novelist Salman Rushdie. Rushdie had a death contract issued against him for writing his book, *The Satanic Verses* and supposedly impugning the character of Muhammad. Yet novelists, journalists, commentators, filmmakers, and television producers routinely blaspheme Jesus of Christianity and the Creator God without reprisals made against them by Christians.

Of course, the fatwa against Salman Rushdie is blamed on "fundamentalists" and "extremists," exonerating most Muslims who live in Western countries as peace-loving citizens. But the loyalty inculcated by Islam runs deeper than allegiance to any nation. Muslims will change political affiliations if needed, but their commitment to the defense of Islam easily becomes fanatical.

A CONTRAST

How insecure and weak must Islam be when Muslims threaten those who oppose it with violence rather than use reasoned defense. Such paranoid behavior renders Islam resistant to self-evaluation and exposes its internal deficiencies.

Biblical Christianity thrives in a free, pluralistic, and democratic society. It neither needs nor benefits from the support of a nation state. By contrast, Islamic control in many countries is totalitarian, dictatorial, and oppressive.

In countries ruled by Sharia Law, minor infractions may be punished by the loss of a hand, a foot, or life itself. Muslim women have been stoned to death for inadvertently exposing an ankle or forearm in public. The much-touted "mercy" of Islam is hard to detect.

Disillusionment with the religion simmers under the surface in Islamic societies. Many Muslim immigrants to Western countries, if not pressured by the local Muslim community to tow the line, either moderate or abandon Islam altogether. Others go through the religious motions, but their hearts are not in it.

THE COST OF DEFECTION

Today there is a "rallying to the cause," as many Muslims believe the war against terrorism is between "Christian America" and Islam. But many Muslims would prefer to be free of such influences if they could. Of course, Muslim clerics in the West realize this and do not hesitate to isolate their constituents from non-Muslim influence. Isolation is a typical cultic mechanism—defections are treated most seriously.

In lands dominated by Islam, the rule is "once a Muslim, always a Muslim." Like the Mafia, Islam is difficult to leave, and any who defect do so at a great price. Most cults ostracize defecting people, cutting them off from family, friends, and even employment. Muslims sometimes assassinate people who leave their religion. How very cultic!

World Rule

Cults are dangerous—they control and manipulate those under their sway. Islamic leaders may issue a declaration (fatwa) or call for a holy war (jihad). Muslims are expected to obey these calls despite their individual feelings. As with the fatwa against Rushdie, Muslims remained under a theoretical obligation to kill him even though restrained from doing so by the law of the land.

If Islam were not so fractured into sects and splinter movements, the non-Muslim world would face a more serious enemy than it does today. Islam sanctions the murder of infidels and, of course, I am one, and so is anyone who is not a Muslim. It is no secret that Islam's goal is world rule. This is not some right-wing conspiracy theory; it is the stated aim of Islam.

On the other hand, while Christians seek to share the Good News of Christ worldwide, they are not intent on forcing people to accept Christianity, much less eliminating those who reject the message.

Spiritual Process

Conversion to Christ is a spiritual process, not the recitation of a formula such as, "There is no god but Allah and Muhammad is his prophet." Biblical Christianity is about grace, which is God's gift of faith and forgiveness.

Christianity is grounded both in the sacrifice Jesus offered for sin on the cross, and upon His resurrection that declares that those for whom He died are "justified." No one becomes a Christian on the basis of his or her works or actions. Rather, conversion is something God brings about. This is why the New Testament uses the term "new birth" to describe it (see John 3: 1-15). Humans do not control their physical birth, and with the new (spiritual) birth it is the same. Salvation is accomplished through God's power, not man's. No public or private declaration will ever make a Christian out of anyone.

Revised Religion

Islam is classed with those religious groups that have "revised" Christianity. Some of these are The Church of Latter Day Saints (Mormons) and Jehovah's Witnesses.

In these groups, including Islam, Jesus is acknowledged and honored as a prophet. He may even be worshipped to some degree. Yet Jesus' teachings are declared to be incomplete and outdated. They must therefore be replaced or superseded by the teachings of _____ (insert name of group or prophet).

The Christianity Muhammad knew in the sixth and seventh centuries in the Arabian Peninsula was far different from New Testament Christianity—which had radically deteriorated. Observing the deficiencies in Judaism and a degenerate Christianity, Muhammad replaced them with his own concepts. This is understandable. The result, however, is not an improvement; it is simply another failed revisionist effort.

Downgrade

It is patronizing, too, for Islam to say it respects Jesus as a prophet while denying or altering what He said about himself and what the New Testament writers said concerning Him. I am thinking of such Scriptures as John 1:1-3 and Colossians 1:15-20 among many others. Of course, the Mormons and Jehovah's Witnesses do the same. Revisionist cults must downgrade Jesus so that the "new, improved prophet" (or "truth") can be presented as a replacement.

If Jesus is God in the flesh—Emmanuel, as the Christian Scripture proclaims; and if Jesus is the Messiah prophesied by the great Hebrew prophets; and if Jesus is the only Lord and Savior who will return to judge the living and the dead, then it is impossible to replace him.

Revelation and Misunderstanding

The Qur'an declares that the Bible, both Old and New Testaments, is a revelation from God. But it then proceeds to reject the clear message of the Bible! If the Bible is accurate about Jesus, there is no need for the Qur'an or Muhammad.

So, was Muhammad using flattery or attempting to patronize Christians when he seemed to honor Jesus? Or did he simply not understand? Essentially, Muhammad rejected a Christianity vastly different from the teaching of the New Testament.

Another sign of a cult is the way it keeps its adherents in the dark about other faiths. I doubt whether Muslims today know much about the message of Jesus and His Gospel. They know only what they have been told by their religious teachers. How accurate would we expect this information to be considering that the Qur'an is their authority?

To make it even worse, there is a general misunderstanding of what Christianity is. One misconception, for example, is that the West is Christian and that America is a Christian nation. Obviously, all that goes by the name of Christian is not Christian. To grasp what is the true essence of Jesus' teachings, we must examine the primary source, the Bible.

Christians reject the belief that Muhammad is the prophet of God. Christians reject the Qur'an as a revelation from God. At least this is an honest position, innocent of any effort to mislead, flatter, confuse, or patronize.

What about the Crusades?

Muslims often ask, "What about the Crusades?" The intention of this question is often to deflect attention from the violence and oppression displayed by Muslims worldwide in the name of Allah.

Yes, there were the Crusades, and historians debate the complex tangle of religion and politics that gave rise to them. The Church of that era did not always pursue a true Christian and Biblical agenda. And this same authoritarian organization persecuted Jews and Protestants also. This same medieval church persecuted to the death those who believed the truths that I, as a Christian today, hold precious.

Is it therefore accurate for Muslims to blame all that goes by the name Christian for the Crusades? Would it not be fairer and wiser to discriminate amongst Christians? After all, most people do not blame all Muslims for the actions of some extremists.

Women in Islam

Another cultic aspect of Islam is the oppression of women in countries under Islamic rule. It is shocking, deviant, and evil.

Why is this frightful treatment tolerated? Why is there such an exaggerated fear and mistrust of women? Islamic spokesmen say the women are merely being protected. The women themselves generally resent their treatment and lowly status, but are seemingly powerless to bring about change.

The plight of young men and women in Islamic countries is sad indeed. Their isolation from one another distorts normal social relationships between the sexes. Wealthy (and usually older) men can have four wives and as many concubines as they can afford, while younger, poorer men, are deprived. This deplorable situation stems directly from the nature and traditions of Islam itself as well as the tribal culture from which it sprang.

Women are denied education in countries ruled by strict Sharia law. Why? Is it to keep women in their place? Why must women cover themselves so that not even an ankle can be seen in public? These are twisted gender mores.

Moderate Muslims claim that these practices are only enforced by extremists. The "extremists" claim they are only interpreting Islam in the purest manner possible! Who is right?

Fruit of Islam

Islamic political control has prevented social progress and economic development. For example, does anyone own a car made in an Islamic country? How about a television set, a computer, an alarm clock, an airplane, or a boat? Why are many Islamic countries among the poorest in the world even while their oil reserves are vast?

Where do wealthy Muslims send their young people to be educated? To Western countries, for the most part, since those countries freely entertain examination of all points of view for the widest number of topics using the latest discoveries and thinking.

The cultic nature of Islam prevents Muslim-dominated countries from developing middle class wealth, which would require an ever-increasing importation of Western ways, and this is feared and condemned by Muslim clerics. The shot callers in Islam fear the rise of a middle class.

Muslims have undoubtedly contributed to the world's storehouse of achievements. But if we look at the Islamic nations today, we see they are something less than wonderful. Except for Afghan refugees trying to enter Pakistan, I haven't read about people lining up at their borders waiting to get in. Islam is sometimes described as the "beautiful religion," but where can this beauty be seen? What Islamic country practices Islam in such a way that someone might be motivated to move there?

It is one thing for Muslim leaders to disown the September 11 terrorists as extremists. It is another to demonstrate peaceful moderation and tolerance.

Please understand I am not saying that Muslim people are not as capable, intelligent, and worthy as any other people. Rather, it is the toxic and repressive nature of recruitment, retention, and motivation that is cultic.

Muslims are born into a religious heritage they did not choose and cannot walk away from. They are molded by their environment into dedicated Muslims; there is essentially no choice available for them—they are stuck.

The Major Difference

Islam is a religion based on performance, whereas Biblical Christianity is grounded on God's grace. The Islamic deity rewards obedience. Muslim heaven, or paradise, must be earned, either by martyrdom or by carefully keeping rules and regulations.

And since Allah is depicted as remote and detached from the individual Muslim, there is no assurance of salvation nor any confidence that even the faithful Muslim will achieve paradise.

Works-based religion can and does inspire fear and extremism in those who take it seriously. It is not surprising that some go to extremes to curry the favor of the deity and their religious leaders, especially when a favorable eternity is at stake.

The Qur'an assures martyrs that they will attain paradise, and it is this very promise that attracts and motivates suicide bombers, including those who turned commercial airliners into missiles on September 11. Since that day, the Qur'anic command to "strike terror into the heart" of the infidel has been obeyed more and more often by young men and women recruited by watching on the Internet horrific violence against innocent civilians in dozens of filmed executions and other gruesome attacks.

Biblical Christianity, on the other hand, emphasizes grace, which signifies "God's giving". Through Jesus Christ, God imparts forgiveness and salvation as a free gift, apart from any good work. Salvation is by grace, not by works (Ephesians 2:4-10). Even extreme devotion, sacrifice, and obedience will never secure God's favor.

Furthermore, Christians have assurance of salvation by the inner witness of the Holy Spirit, so they are not left in doubt and insecurity (Romans 8:15-17). Everlasting life with God in heaven is given to the Christian through the work of God the Son. It cannot be lost, since God the Father keeps the believer by His great power (John 10:27-30).

An Absurdity

Cults employ mind-bending techniques to induce their followers to be obedient—this has long been understood.

What about the mind-boggling promise of seventy-two virgins available for the pleasures of every martyred Islamic warrior? This is as extreme an example as can be found even in the strangest cult sects!

Certainly, for poor, young, love-starved men, whose future is clouded at best, the promise of unlimited fleshly pleasure in the hereafter might be an inducement to die for the sake of Allah. But is this obscene and sexist doctrine true? Moderate Islamic interpreters say no; the sexually oriented promises are unfounded. Yet, this perverse promise is constantly embraced. Many a mind-bent warrior has killed and died to acquire his virgins.

A Challenge

Harassment of Muslims is unacceptable, and this essay is not an attempt to bring grief to Muslim people.

However, I would challenge Muslims to examine their religion—indeed, their hearts and minds, and ask themselves these questions:

- Why am I a Muslim? Is my commitment to Islam based on a free decision apart from family influences?
- What is my attitude towards those of other religions, particularly Jews and Christians?
- Are my attitudes cultic in any way?
- Do I honestly think that killing Jews and Christians serves Allah?
- Do I believe it is a Muslim's duty to defend Islam by martyrdom or suicide?
- Should I support religious tolerance for people of other faiths in Muslim-dominated countries like Saudi Arabia?

Many Muslims are seekers after God, and this is good. The Hebrew prophet Jeremiah wrote: "You will seek me and find me; when you seek me with all your heart" (Jeremiah 29:13).

Whether Muslim, Hindu, Buddhist, Jew, nominal Christian, or nothing at all—the challenge is to seek God because He can be found. Jesus said, "Seek first his kingdom and his righteousness, and all these things shall be yours as well" (Matthew 6:33).

Knowing God

Regardless of our religious background, we are created in the image of God. We have been made by and for Him, and we will never be satisfied until we know Him personally. The Creator God sent His Son, Jesus, to break down the walls of separation between men and reconcile all kinds of people to Himself (Ephesians 2:14-18).

The challenge is to make up your own mind about Jesus Christ. Learn about Him yourself and do not merely accept the opinions of others.

Find a New Testament, read the story of His life, and see if you find anything amiss with Him. Is there any sin, or anything false, in the one who came from God? Find an Old Testament and read the prophecies of the Messiah (which is Hebrew for "Christ"), passages like Psalm 22 and Isaiah 53. Are these passages not about Jesus?

If you seek Him, He will be found.

Essay Seven

My First Essay on Islam

I am sixty years old, born in Portland, Oregon, and now live in Mill Valley, California. I became a Christian at age twenty-one. I am married with five children and eight grandchildren. I was ordained in 1966; most of the time my denomination has been Baptist.

The first spiritual truth I knew was that I was a lost and hopeless sinner. This is while I was in the military. My life was ordinary, no crises, but after hearing the message of Jesus and the cross, I understood for the first time that He died in my place, taking my sin upon Himself. The second truth I learned was that Jesus is the Savior, raised from the dead, who loves me and would give me the gift of eternal life.

I have been in the ministry ever since my ordination, most of that as a pastor, and have seen many hundreds become followers of Jesus. For Christians this means conversion, or the new birth, one and the same thing. We are not born Christian, though we might be born into a culture heavily influenced by Christianity. But this can be problematic since we can mistakenly believe that we are Christian due to our physical birth.

Now, as to the issue of Christianity, Islam, and Judaism worshipping the same God—yes and no. Certainly Judaism and Christianity see the God of Abraham, Isaac, and Jacob as the Creator God. Islam, however, worships Allah, and Allah was a local deity worshipped by people of a particular area, the area where Mohammed lived.

Mohammed was born in Arabia and lived in Mecca. He belonged to the Quraysh tribe that controlled the worship at the Ka'bah shrine, which contains the "black stone." This shrine was the center of idol worship with more than 360 idols being honored. The Arabic word for idol is "ilah" and "al" is Arabic for god. Allah, a combination of these two, and was the name for the primary god worshipped in Mecca. In addition, Allah was the name pre-Islamic Arabs used for the moon god, which was represented by the crescent moon. This symbol, the crescent moon, was used for many idols in pre-Islamic Arabia. Indeed, it was common among pre-Islamic Arabs to pray facing Mecca and to observe a fast one month a year. Mohammed incorporated many pre-Islamic religious concepts into the Qur'an. Mohammed merely declared that only Allah would be worshipped to the exclusion of all other idols. Allah was essentially then the name of a local moon god.[2]

The claim that Islam worships the same God as Judaism and Christianity is false. This is not to say that Muslims are not people of good will who are seeking peace. Some may and some may not. My concern is spiritual not political. If I had a merely political agenda I might overlook the theological differences between the religions. However, the issue that transcends all others is a personal relationship with God. Error here is ultimate, the greatest of all enemies.

Now Judaism, in rejecting Jesus as Messiah and Savior, makes a mistake. To worship the Son of God, Jesus, is to worship God the Father. He who has the Son has the Father, but he who does not have the Son does not have the Father. To love one is to love the other. The Scripture is plain on this point. Many Jewish people do trust in Jesus, however. And Muslims may also trust in Jesus—anyone may. The names of the various religions are merely man-made designations. The fact is there is one God and we are all made in His image. I am not personally concerned about religious labels, but I am a follower of Jesus Christ, He is my Lord and Savior. He is not God of the Christians, He is the Lord of heaven and earth.

Many groups claim the God of the Bible as their God—groups like the Mormons, the Jehovah's Witnesses, and so on. But they reject or deny what the Bible says about the Messiah in both the Old and New Testaments. Are we Christians bound to accept the picture of Jesus that the Jehovah's Witnesses, for example, give us? They say Jesus is the archangel Michael and not Emmanuel, God with us, despite, for example, what the prophet Isaiah wrote (see Isaiah 7:14). Am I bound to accept the pronouncements of the Jehovah's Witnesses? Because groups like the Mormons say their prophet is the latest prophet superseding all others, am I bound to believe this? The Mormons say their Book of Mormon is the final truth and all that came before is good but not the final revelation of God. Do I have to believe this?

Mohammed claimed to be the final prophet and the Qur'an to be the final revelation. Am I bound to believe this? Numerous so-called prophets have come along with new versions of truth—so what! They each diminish or do a re-make on Jesus so they can insert into the place of the Lord Jesus Christ their own prophet, revelation, or holy book. No, we are wise to this in America; these prophets and angelic revelations—they are a dime a dozen.

I live in a free society that has freedom of religion. My faith is personal, and I don't care what anyone else thinks about it. I did not choose God anyway, He chose me. He called me and gave me faith in Jesus, His only begotten Son. I am not a Christian because I was born one, I did not even want to be a Christian. But when God, by His Holy Spirit, showed me that Jesus, the perfect lamb of God, had died in my place, had taken all my sin upon Himself, and through His resurrection gives me the gift of eternal life, well, that was enough for me. I did not figure anything out, I did no good religious work; no, God

---

2 On this point I have altered my opinion. Christians will see things differently and on this point there are definite differences. My new book is entitled, If Allah Wills. I have found that even many Muslims who have converted to Christianity still call God Allah. Allah was the term for God among Christians and Jews who lived in the Arabian Peninsula before, during, and after the time of Muhammad. Let us determine to agree to disagree on this point.

changed my heart, helped me repent, and gave me faith.

This is the Gospel. Please know that I wish all the people of the world would live in peace and harmony. I have no anger or resentment toward Muslims. For what it is worth, I am also the manager of a baseball team, and I just appointed as my primary coach a Muslim man. And my leadoff hitter and second baseman is also a Muslim.

Would you be a Muslim if you did not have to be? Could you walk away from Islam? What might happen if you decided to be an atheist or even a Christian? You made no choice in the beginning—you were born Muslim. Where is free will involved in who you are and what you believe?

America is my country, though I do not think all we do is correct. I am a Christian first, an American second. Being an American does not commend me to God in any way. Christian does not equal American and vice versa. Wherever I live the Scripture commands me to be a good citizen. We do stand for freedom and an open society, and these are great things. I hate war, as anyone would, and I wish there weren't a reason for a war on terrorism. But there is, and we can pray that it will end soon and we can all live in peace.

Would the destruction of America solve Islam's problems? Would the destruction of Israel solve Islam's problems? Is not the problem sin and rebellion in the human heart? Isn't the human heart deceitful and desperately wicked, as the prophet said (see Jeremiah 17:9). Perhaps Muslims might feel superior and vindicated, if America and/or Israel should fall, but would that stop the warfare that constantly goes on within the "Muslim brotherhood"? The problem is a proud spirit and evil that lurks within—and it was for all this that Jesus died on the cross. Jesus died in our place, taking the death and judgment and hell upon Himself that we would have to bear, if we were to die unforgiven. Jesus was sacrificed instead of us; He atoned for the transgressions of those who believe in Him.

Over and above all that goes on in this crazy world, there is the reality of God. Let us seek Him, let us honor Him, let us worship Him, let us love Him. He has made this possible through our Lord Jesus Christ. Jesus said, "Come to me, all who labor and are heavy laden, and I will give you rest. Take my yoke upon you, and learn from me; for I am gentle and lowly in heart, and you will find rest for your souls. For my yoke is easy, and my burden is light" (Matthew 11:28-30).

Kent Philpott
March 2002
Mill Valley, CA

Essay Eight

SHAME VERSUS GUILT

There is a world of difference between a shamed-based culture and a guilt-based culture.

"Culture" can mean a whole nation, religion, tribe, clan, family, church, or any other similar entity.

Let us say a Christian leader is found to be guilty of a sin that is publicly revealed.

The shame-based church, of which there are many, particularly among churches that tend toward legalism, could be either a works-oriented or a grace-oriented church. The fallen Christian leader is an embarrassment to the church, maybe a wider grouping of churches, perhaps a whole denomination. This leader may be cast aside, fired, shunned, or any number of things might happen. This is known as "shooting the wounded" and is demonstrative of a shame orientation.

The guilt-based church with a fallen leader will not shoot the wounded but will take steps to bring healing and reconciliation. And this will work when the Christian leader acknowledges the sin and moves away from it, confesses his sin to God and man, and repents. If treatment or therapy is required, very well, but the fallen leader is restored.

The difference between a shame-based and a guilt-based church could not be greater.

Now then, let us change the scenario. Islam is founded on and produces a shame-based culture. For instance, if a young woman rejects an arranged marriage, she dishonors her family, clan, and tribe, indeed the religion of Islam itself. It falls to the family to restore honor, and this is very often accomplished by the killing of the young woman. The father, a brother, even a mother, will carry out this act. The young woman brought shame, and the only way to restore honor is murder. The murderer is not shamed but honored.

Or, to site another example, a member of the family or clan converts to another religious faith. Knowledge of this might be discovered and become widely known. In order to restore honor, the apostate must be killed. The murder covers the shame, and again, the murderer(s) are honored.

Or again, let us say a starving ten year old boy steals a loaf of bread at the town's market, is caught, and has his hand chopped off without anesthetic in the public square (common in Saudi Arabia), in order for honor to be restored to the community.

The above are examples of what may happen in a shame-based culture.

So too, in shame-based cultures there is a great deal of secrecy and silence. For instance, homosexuality is harshly condemned among Muslims, and a homosexual caught in the act may well be killed, depending on the country. At the same time, homosexuality is widely practiced, especially in Muslim-dominated countries, but it is concealed from public view. Shame only comes when forbidden acts are exposed. The sin of the act itself it not what brings shame; it is the exposure of the act that brings shame.

Consider a guilt-based culture, say an evangelical Bible-based church, which will probably view homosexual behavior to be sinful. If a case comes up in such a church, the sin does not tarnish the entire church community. The individual involved hopefully will receive appropriate ministry aimed at restoration and recovery.

THE BIBLE WAY

Most readers of the New Testament know that when Jesus was arrested and taken away to trial, Peter denied Jesus three times. Jesus even told Peter and the rest of the disciples that such would be the case (see Mark 14:26–31). It turned out just as Jesus had foretold (see Mark 14:66–72).

Peter thought he was so strong, but fear got the better of him. When the pressure came, Peter crumbled completely. After the third denial, Peter finally came to himself: "And he broke down and wept" (Mark 14:72).

The early church was not a shamed-based culture but a guilt-based culture. The chief apostle fell and did so publicly, and everyone who has ever read a Gospel knows this. Peter was not shunned and did not suffer violence; rather, he continued on to be the one who preached the first Christian sermon, which we find in Acts, chapter two, and upon whose name the Roman church claimed to be founded.

Jesus Himself demonstrated for His Church the way things ought to be. We find a gripping and amazing story in the twenty-first chapter of John's Gospel. The scene is a beach beside the Sea of Galilee after Jesus' resurrection. It was a spring morning, and Peter, along with six other apostles, went out in a boat to fish but without success. Then at dawn the fishermen saw on the shore a stranger who told them where to cast their net. Immediately, the net was nearly bursting with fish. It was then Peter realized who the stranger was, so he jumped into the water and rushed to Jesus. Later on after the breakfast, which Jesus had prepared for the seven, Peter and Jesus took a stroll along the beach. As they walked, Jesus asked Peter three times if he loved Him. Three times Peter answered, "yes" and three times Jesus responded with, "Feed my sheep."

Peter denied Jesus three times. Jesus gave Peter the blessed opportunity to affirm his love for his Master three times. Jesus did not bring Peter's sin up to him; there was no need, since the Holy Spirit does this far better, and Peter was encouraged to continue to follow Him.

This is the great model for a guilt-based culture, which the Church must be if it is to be healthy. The legalists get in the way, however, and twist things to shame-based. This is what Islam has done, along with so many other religions, and certainly most of the Bible-based cults in Christianity have followed this pattern.

And it is to the legalists, those who are sinners as we all are, to whom I am reaching out with this essay—whether Muslim, Christian, or whatever.

Jesus died on the cross to cover sin, not shame. Biblical Christianity is guilt-based and thankfully so, since sin may be forgiven. The healthy church is not shamed by the acts of an individual. And most importantly, God delights in redeeming guilty sinners and erring Christians.

The Real Problem

The real problem with a shame-based culture is that guilt is never dealt with but persists and often resurfaces as depression, anger, or self-hatred—maybe all of these.

Imagine the father who is forced to kill his daughter who refuses to marry a man she neither knows nor loves. The shame may be covered by the murder of the girl, or so it is assumed, but what about the conscience, the heart, or the mind of the family members? Guilt, a natural occurring brain function, remains. And there is no forgiveness.

A young boy or girl steals a loaf of bread, is caught, and brings shame upon the family and clan. Sharia Law demands a public amputation of a hand and/or a foot. What about the boy or girl, the family, the friends? What about the observers of the event or those who have the responsibility of carrying out the punishment? Everyone is traumatized, unless all of these people are inoculated against such atrocities, which I suspect might be the case when a person is brought up in a shame-based culture.

I was a medic with the U.S. Air Force from 1961 to 1965. My unit was 2nd Casualty Staging Flight, which is based at Travis Air Force Base in Fairfield, California. For years my duty hours were from 5 PM to 8 PM. Many a green beret or ranger who had been wounded in Vietnam (starting in1963) would wonder down to my office late at night, and we would spend hours talking about what happened to them. It was known then as combat fatigue, and it was real. Not all had suffered actual bodily wounds. Many were listed as psychiatric on the flight manifest. Some had killed, raped, and maimed innocent civilians. They knew horrors such as I had never heard. My own brother, a combat engineer in Vietnam, came back emotionally wounded from experiences there and eventually committed suicide. With my college background in psychology and my newfound faith in Jesus, I was able to talk about forgiveness with traumatized young men. And for some, not many, the forgiveness found in Jesus Christ and His cross made all the difference.

Post Traumatic Stress Disorder, or PTSD, can be deadly. Those who have experienced it have a high rate of suicide, become psychotic, and sometimes go off on murderous rampages. (The statistics are available by means of a Google search.)

I cannot help but wonder about the wrenching struggles many experience in Muslim cultures where the covering of shame is virtually mandated. Guilt does not go away. There it sits, eating away like a cancer deep in the interior. And this is why I emphasize the shed blood of Jesus in my witness to Muslim people.

At the conclusion of every morning service at our small Miller Avenue Baptist Church in Mill Valley, California, we observe the Lord's Supper. We do it because Jesus directed His Church, the Body of Christ, to do so. (There is no set frequency of observance.) We also do it because it is a wonderful presentation of the forgiveness that we have in the finished work of Jesus, the Son of God. I conclude this essay with some of the passages we recite just prior to receiving the Bread and the Cup.

The Confessional:

"For there is no distinction: for all have sinned and fall short of the glory of God." Romans 3:23

The Jesus Prayer:

"Lord Jesus Christ, Son of God, have mercy on me, a sinner."

The Promise of acceptance and forgiveness

"If we confess our sins, he is faithful and just to forgive us our sins and to cleanse us from all unrighteousness." 1 John 1:9

Individual, silent prayer of confession

The Confirmation:

"There is therefore now no condemnation for those who are in Christ Jesus." Romans 8:1

The Assurance:

"Those whom he predestined he also called, and those whom he called he also justified, and those whom he justified he also glorified." Romans 8:30

Essay Nine

ABROGATION OR PROGRESSIVE REVELATION?

Surah 2:106 of the Qur'an reads:

> Such of Our revelations as We abrogate or cause to be forgotten, we bring (in place) one better or the like thereof. Knowest thou not that Allah is Able to do all things?" (from The Glorious Qur'an translation)

Another edition of the Qur'an, *The Holy Qur'an*, translated by Abdullah Yusuf Ali, reads slightly differently:

> None of our revelations
> Do We abrogate
> Or cause to be forgotten,
> But We substitute
> Something better or similar:
> Knowest thou not that God
> Hath power over all things?

Though the renderings differ, the meaning is obvious; earlier verses received by Muhammad were replaced by later verses. And abrogation, the replacing of doctrines, is of great interest.

ABROGATION

Very early Muhammad received from Gabriel the message that the Jews and Christians, people of the Book as they were known, and who shared a similar origin with Muslims, were not counted as disbelievers.[3]

First, from *The Glorious Qur'an*:

---

[3] The exact process by which Muhammad received the recitations from Allah that eventually became the Qur'an, through the angel Gabriel, is unclear. Allah did not appear to Muhammad nor did Muhammad hear directly from Allah. The intermediary, Gabriel, was either physically present, or Muhammad heard the angel's voice, or Muhammad's mind was "impressed" and such impressions were passed on to others. This last idea is more probable, since it appears that Muhammad would enter a trance state to receive the revelations from Gabriel.

Lo! Those who believe (in that which is revealed unto thee, Muhammad), and those who are Jews, and Christians, and Sabaeans[4] – whoever believeth in Allah and the Last Day and doeth right – surely their reward is with their Lord, and there shall no fear come upon them neither shall they grieve.

Then from the Ali translation:

> Those who believe (in the Qur'an)
> And those who follow the Jewish (scriptures),
> And the Christians and the Sabians,
> Any who believe in God
> And the Last day,
> And work righteousness,
> Shall have their reward
> With their Lord: on them
> Shall be no fear, nor shall they grieve.

Despite the differences in the two editions of the Qur'an, it is plain that the Jews and Christians—People of the Book—were not counted as disbelievers by Muhammad.

But things changed, due to any number of reasons, but mostly because of opposition to Muhammad's preaching from both Jews and Christians. Thus was born the concept of abrogation, that is, the later truths replaced or superseded the earlier truths.

There are many examples of abrogation in the Qur'an. One is the oft-quoted axiom that there is no compulsion in religion. The first sentence of Surah 2:256 reads: "Let there be no compulsion in religion." But this was abrogated or changed such that Islam would later be required to be forced upon disbelievers. It is interesting to note that Islam means submission, and originally it was by choice not compulsion. That changed with the opposition Muhammad received, even in Mecca, and especially so in Medina. It became normative that disbelievers would either be forced to convert or pay taxes to their Muslim overlords. If not, only death remained as an option. This is clearly stated in Surah 47:4 (The Ali translation):

> Therefore, when ye meet
> The Unbelievers (in fight),
> Smite at their necks;[5]
> At length, when ye have
> Thoroughly subdued them,
> Bind a bond
> Firmly (on them): thereafter
> (Is the time for) either
> Generosity or ransom:

From *The Glorious Qur'an* is Surah 5:33:

The only reward of those who make war upon Allah and His messenger and strive after corruption in the land will be that they will be killed or crucified, or have their hands and feet on alternate sides cut off, or will be expelled out

---

4 There is no nation or tribe known today as the Sabaeans. Little is know of their history.
5 "Smite at their necks" came to mean beheading.

of the land. Such will be their degradation in the world, and in the Hereafter theirs will be an awful doom.

Of course, there are the Satanic Verses (about which Salmon Rushdie wrote), where Muhammad at first conceded that a particular Arab tribe's god and goddesses would be honored, but later on, after receiving significant negative reaction from Muslim faithful, Muhammad reversed course and condemned the worship of the pagan deities. At one point Muhammad had compromised with a pagan Arab tribe, the Quraish, regarding their deities, Al Lat, Al Uzza, and Manat, and had said that he had received from Allah that these idols could be worshipped. While this news thrilled the Quraish, the Muslim faithful were quite unhappy about it. In time, the verses acknowledging the efficacy of the gods and goddess of the Quraish tribe were abrogated. Passages to look to on this matter are: Surahs 17:19–20, 22:52–53, and 53:19–20.

Muslims do not deny the practice of abrogation, but uphold it.

Muslims also see their religion as superseding or replacing Judaism and Christianity, as an intentional and natural progression ordained by Allah. Islam, Muslims believe, is the culmination of what is revealed in the Scripture, meaning the Old and New Testaments. Certainly, Christians claim the Old Testament to be inspired by the Creator God, while official Judaism rejects the New Testament in terms of it being revealed by the God of Abraham, Isaac, and Jacob.

Islam is not the only religion to regard their revelations to be the final message from God. This approach has been copied by many over the years, including the Mormons; in fact, Islam and Mormonism share an uncanny resemblance. In Mormonism you have an angel giving the book of Mormon on golden plates that present a new and improved truth that abrogates all that went before, especially referring to Biblical Christianity.

Progressive Revelation

Christians hold that the New Testament does not make much sense apart from the Old Testament. We see the prophecies of the Messiah sprinkled throughout the Hebrew Scripture, starting with Genesis 3:15:

> I will put enmity between you and the woman,
> and between your offspring and her offspring;
> he shall bruise your head,
> and you shall bruise his heel.

The woman Eve was a type extending on and pointing to Israel the nation, then Mary the mother of Jesus, then the Church. These entities are the "woman" of Genesis 3:15, and it has been understood in this manner down through the centuries. The offspring of the woman delivers a deathblow to Satan, the serpent, while the serpent merely bruises the offspring's heel. And that is how it worked out, just as Genesis said. The Apostle John much later wrote, "The reason the Son of God appeared was to destroy the works of the devil" (1 John 3:8b).

Then there is Psalm 22 where King David describes a man dying on a cross, and he wrote it around 1,000 years before the actual event took place. Not only that, but history tells us that the Greeks did not use crucifixion as a means of execution until many centuries after David wrote his Psalm. Then the Romans picked it up from the Greeks some centuries later.

The 22nd Psalm begins with words Jesus spoke while on the cross: "My God, my God, why have you forsaken me?" This forsakenness is the subject of Jesus' prayer in Gethsemane (see Mark 14:32–42). In verses 16 to 18 of Psalm 22 we find,

> For dogs encompass me, a company of evil doers encircles me, they have pierced my hands and feet – I can count all my bones – they stare and gloat over me; they divide my garments among them, and for my clothing they cast lots.

There is more from this Psalm that makes it clear David is depicting a man dying on a cross.

In the eighth century before Christ, the prophet Isaiah described the suffering servant of Israel who dies for sin as an atoning sacrifice to the holy God of Israel. Following are just a few verses from Isaiah, but the whole of the chapter, even parts of chapters 52 and 54, could be presented as well. Here is Isaiah 53:5–6:

> But he was wounded for our transgressions; he was crushed for our iniquities, upon him was the chastisement that brought us peace, and with his stripes we are healed. All we like sheep have gone astray; we have turned every on to his own way; and the LORD has laid on him the iniquity of us all.

Verse 9 of Isaiah 53 describes exactly what happened after Jesus' death on the cross: "And they made his grave with the wicked and with a rich man in his death, although he had done no violence, and there was no deceit in his mouth." Jesus died as a criminal yet was buried in a rich man's grave, that of one of the members of the elite Sanhedrin, Joseph of Arimathea.

Isaiah did more than speak of the suffering servant of Israel; he prophesied that the Messiah would be born of a virgin. The key verse is Isaiah 7:14: "Therefore the Lord himself will give you a sign. Behold, the virgin shall conceive and bear a son, and shall call his name Immanuel." Two key points are made in the verse. One, a virgin would conceive and give birth—"offspring"—(remember Genesis 3:15 and the offspring of the woman). And two, the child would be God. Immanuel means "God with us." There it is, the child is actually God become flesh. Here is how the Apostle John put it: "And the Word became flesh and dwelt among us" (John 1:14a). We note that in verse one of chapter one of John's Gospel he makes it clear that the "Word" is God.

Then the prophet Micah, long centuries before Jesus' day, described His birthplace. "But you, O Bethlehem Ephrathah, who are too little to be among the clans of Judah, from you shall come forth for me, one who is to be ruler in Israel, whose origin is from of old, from ancient days" (Micah 5-2). And that is just where Jesus was born—Bethlehem. Almost hidden in the prophecy is the idea that the one born is from ancient days, meaning one with a long history.

There is Daniel's prophecy that actually describes the period of time when the Son of Man would appear. And also the prophet Malachi stating that there would be a forerunner announcing the coming of the Messiah, one crying in the wilderness to prepare the way for the arrival of that long promised Messiah. And it would be fulfilled when John the Baptist saw Jesus coming to be baptized in the Jordan River. John cried out, "Behold, the

Lamb of God, who takes away the sin of the world" (John 1:29).

The point is that everything about Jesus, from who He is, what He did, when He did it, and what it meant was all outlined centuries before the events took place in real time.

THE DISTINCTION

Abrogation is utterly different from progressive revelation. In the Qur'an, changes in policy and understanding forced Gabriel, Allah, Muhammad, or someone, to change their mind. The Jews and Christians would be tolerated for only a few short years, until suddenly not tolerated anymore.

Progressive revelation is God beginning at one point and moving throughout history toward the end goal, His ultimate intention, which is to bring those made in His image, those whom He called to be His chosen people, to once again have perfect fellowship with Him in paradise.

The difference between Islam and Biblical Christianity could not be greater.

TWO MORE LITTLE THINGS:

*Works and Grace

Muslims depend on getting lots of points by performing rites and rituals so that they have a chance of going to paradise when they die. Stated another way, Islam is works-based. It all depends on what one does. The sure way to get to paradise is to die in violent jihad or maybe to build a mosque. In any case, it is chancy, since Allah is a deceiver and might just lead one astray. Interestingly, one of the 99 names of Allah is Deceiver.

Going to heaven to be with Jesus forever depends on the grace of God that is freely given to lost sinners like me. I cannot earn it, achieve it, or work so very hard, even die a martyr—no, nothing at all I do will make it happen, as it all depends on God's love. "For God so loved the world, the he gave his only Son, that whoever believes in him should not perish but have eternal life" (John 3:16). And even the "believes" part is a gift, as Paul points out in Ephesians 2:8-9: "For by grace you have been saved through faith. And this is not your own doing, it is the gift of God, not a result of works, so that no one my boast."

*World Views

I do have to mention a second major difference between Islam and Christianity that involves the fundamental goals of the two religious systems.

Islam intends, as commanded by Allah in the Qur'an, to dominate the world. The state and the religion will be one under Shar'ia Law—this is the Muslim worldview. This is why Muslims claim Islam is the "religion of peace." Because, when Islam dominates, all enemies will be subdued, and there will be peace. This will be accomplished by whatever means necessary and is the reason for the horrors perpetrated by Muslims who take the Qur'an seriously.

Christianity has one goal this side of the return of Messiah Jesus, and that is summed up by Jesus Himself in Acts 1:8: "But you will receive power when the Holy Spirit has come upon you, and you will be my witnesses in Jerusalem and in all Judea and Samaria, and to the end of the earth."

Although there have been times when Christendom got it wrong and allied itself with military and political power —and forced conversions, as if such a thing were possible, Biblical Christianity is evangelical. True Christianity has always had its evangelicals from day one. By evangelical I mean all those, regardless of what group they belong to, who go about presenting the gospel of Jesus. Christians are to present the message of Christ, and the Holy Spirit does the rest. It is as Paul says in Romans 10:17: "So faith comes from hearing, and hearing through the word of Christ." Jesus, both who He is and what He did on the cross, is offered, simply preached, and those whom God has called will be convicted of their sin, the Holy Spirit will reveal Jesus as the Savior, and the miracle of conversion will take place.

The contrasts between Islam and Christianity are nearly endless, but this essay at least points out some of the more dramatic ones.

Essay Ten

Eid Al-Adha: Who Has it Right?

Eid al-Adha, the great feast of Islam, also called the Day of the Sacrifice, falls on the 10th day of the last month of the lunar calendar. It comes during the Hajj pilgrimage festival, the fifth pillar of Islam, and is essentially a reenactment of Abraham's near-sacrifice of his son, the Biblical account of which is found in Genesis chapter 22.

The essential Qur'anic story is found in the 37th chapter and verses 99 to 109. Quoted now from The Noble Qur'an:

» 99   He said, 'I am going towards my Lord; He will be my guide.
» 100   My Lord, bestow on me a right-acting child!'
» 101   And We gave him the good news of a forbearing boy.
» 102   When he was of an age to work with him he said, 'My son, I have seen in a dream that I must sacrifice you. What do you think about this?' He said, 'Do as you are ordered, father. Allah willing, you will find me resolute.'
» 103   Then when they had both submitted and he had laid him face down on the ground,
» 104   We called out to him, 'Ibrahim!
» 105   You have fulfilled your vision. That is how We recompense good-doers.
» 106   This was indeed a most manifest trial.
» 107   We ransomed him with a mighty sacrifice
» 108   and let the later people say of him.
» 109   'Peace be upon Ibrahim.'

It is plain that neither the names Isaac or Ishmael are in the text. Only Islamic sources and tradition provides names, some Ishmael and some Isaac.

Abraham, the true Muslim, in absolute obedience and submission to Allah, intends to sacrifice his son—Ishmael or Isaac. (To reiterate: Islamic scholars are divided on just who was to be sacrificed.) God intervenes and provides an animal to be sacrificed in place of the son. For Muslims the bottom line is that they are to be like Abraham and fully submit to Allah's commands.

THE BINDING OF ISAAC

In Genesis 22:1-19 of the Hebrew Scripture is the story of the sacrifice of Isaac. God instructs His obedient servant Abraham to take his son to the region of Moriah and there sacrifice him. Abraham called the place of the sacrifice "the LORD will provide" (verse 14). The writer in that same verse adds, "On the mountain of the LORD, it will be provided." Later on in the Hebrew Scripture—Isaiah 2:3 and 30:29, Zechariah 8:3, and 2 Chronicles 3:1—we read that the temple is built on the "mountain of the LORD" or Moriah, the very mountain where Isaac was to be sacrificed.

For Judaism, the story of the obedience of Abraham is not much different from that of Islam, except that Islam does not focus on sacrifice but on obedience and submission to the will of Allah. For Judaism, much has to do with the actual location of the sacrifice, the temple mount where the temple of Solomon would be built and which therefore lays the ground for the whole sacrificial system we find in the Torah, especially Exodus and Leviticus.

THE RAM AS SUBSTITUTE

One of the areas on which Christians tend to agree is the reason for the Binding of Isaac (Abraham bound Isaac before placing him on the make-shift altar—Genesis 22:9). While Abraham was indeed obedient to God, and yes, the location was likely Jerusalem and maybe even where the temple was built more than a thousand years later, the real storyline for Christians has to do with what we call "substitutionary atonement."

What happened in our Genesis account? God told Abraham to take his son, his "only son Isaac" by the way, to a place far away and there kill him as a sacrifice. Abraham would have been familiar with animal sacrifice, as various forms of evidence demonstrate such was part of religious customs in Abraham's world. He did not hesitate and was about to go through with it, when he was stopped cold. Here now is Genesis 22:11-14:

> But the angel of the LORD called out to him from heaven and said, "Abraham, Abraham!" And he said, "Here I am."
>
> He said, "Do not lay your hand on the boy or do anything to him, for now I know that you fear God, seeing you have not withheld your son, your only son, from me."
>
> And Abraham lifted up his eyes and looked, and behold, behind him was a ram, caught in a thicket by his horns. And Abraham went and took the ram and offered it up as a burnt offering instead of his son.
>
> So Abraham called the name of that place, "The LORD will provide"; as it is said to this day, "On the mount of the LORD it shall be provided."

In place of Isaac a substitute was provided for the sacrifice. The spilled blood and death of an animal was acceptable to God, and Isaac did not die.

It was a burnt offering, which meant that after the sacrificial animal was killed the remains were burned. A burnt offering is for covering or atoning for sin—**substitutionary atonement**.

God Did Not Spare His Own Son

The New Testament is essentially about, perhaps only about, substitutionary atonement. Here God does not spare His only Son. The two verses below explain what I am trying to say.

> For God so loved the world, that he gave his only son, that whoever believes in him should not perish but have eternal life (John 3:16).

> He who did not spare his own Son but gave him up for us all… (Romans 8:32a).

"Gave" means giving up to death, and in the case of Jesus the Son, it is death on a cross, which is exactly what King David spoke of in Psalm 22, and also the Prophet Isaiah recounted in Isaiah 53. From the point of view of a Bible-believing Christian, it cannot be missed.

Who would or should have been given up to death? You and I, is the plain answer.

> For the wages of sin in death, but the free gift of God is eternal life in Christ Jesus our Lord (Romans 6:23).

The God of the Bible, both Old and New Testaments, is a holy God who will not tolerate sin in His presence; thus the necessity for hell. And I testify that I would not want to bring my load of sin into the presence of God, even if I could. No, I would much prefer hell.

But for reasons I do not fully understand, my Creator God loves me, and it is His desire that I should enjoy His fellowship forever. (Wow, it is beyond comprehension that He should act on my behalf, since I helped send His only Son to die horribly on a criminal's cross!) Since I am a rotten sinner unable to do anything to atone for it myself, God provided "a ram caught in a thicket" (and rams do not get caught in thickets) to be bound and sacrificed in my place. This is the essence and the totality of it. We must then depend solely on the grace of a loving God.

How Could Islam and Judaism Get it Wrong?

Islam has no choice but to get it wrong, because the religion denies that Jesus even died on the cross. Salvation for Muslims is based on obedience to Allah, hopefully doing more good than bad.

Islam, as I mentioned above, is divided as to who was bound, Isaac or Ishmael. Many Muslims say Ishmael, because Arab tribes are thought to descend through Ishmael and Jews through Isaac, making Ishmael more of a father to the original Muslim world.[6] The reason some Muslims say Isaac is because the Qur'an is not clear on the subject (see Qur'an 37:107).

Judaism sticks with Isaac, since that is clearly attested in the Hebrew Bible. Christians stand with the same choice, but the Christian position of substitutionary atonement pointing to the ultimate substitute, Jesus, is unacceptable to official Judaism.

---

6 It should be noted that Islam, or most of Islam, says Abraham and Ishmael built the Ka'ba, though some say it was built in heaven. Ishmael plays a relatively minor part in the whole Biblical story, so perhaps there is a need to artificially enlarge his role?

An Appeal

Let me state emphatically that one's position on this issue has eternal consequences. I know this is complex and mystifying, and the emotion of fear looms large, as one's whole identity is also placed into the mix. But we must see the larger picture, the only one that counts. Is Jesus our substitute, the One who took our sin upon Himself and freely and completely wipes out all our sin forever? This is the one and only true thing that counts, ultimately.

My appeal then is this: Find a time to be alone. Get on you knees and bow your head. Address God, Allah if you like, and ask Him whether Jesus died in your place. It is okay to do so; it is only reasonable that you do so. You have nothing to fear, nothing to lose, and everything to gain.

When you find yourself trusting solely in Jesus for salvation, I suggest you do the following:

1. Obtain a Bible and begin reading the Gospel of John, the fourth book in the New Testament.
2. Make a prayer list of concerns you have on your heart and in your mind. Find time to read your Bible and pray every day.
3. Find a group of those who believe in Jesus Christ as Lord and Savior and be in fellowship with them.
4. This group may be an organized church or not, but the main thing is that the Bible is taught and preached and that the Gospel message is proclaimed regularly and clearly.
5. This gathering of believers in Jesus may be large or small, the people may be young or old, rich or poor, educated or not.
6. This group should have an interest in communicating Jesus and His cross to others and be concerned about the poor and vulnerable around them.
7. This group, to be healthy and strong, should be able to disagree among themselves but keep focused on Jesus.
8. This group should identify with other Christians of whatever denomination and not see itself as the only correct and legitimate people of God.
9. It may take some time to find a Christian group with whom you will be comfortable, but keep trying.
10. Please email me if you have questions: philpott.kent@yahoo.com

Essay Eleven

THE MAKING OF AN EXTREMIST

This essay is prompted by Patrick T. Dunleavy's book, *The Fertile Soil of Jihad: Terrorism's Prison Connection* (Washington D.C.: Potomac Books, 2011). In striking if not startling terms, Dunleavy describes how Islam in prison spreads in its many forms, including the Nation of Islam, the Dar-ul-Islam movement, and Prislam, a cultic form of Islam that sees its flock more as gang members than fervent converts. Muslim evangelism in prisons is growing, sponsored by both international and grass roots Islamic organizations. Its expansion over the years has been both phenomenal and disturbing. I am a firsthand witness to this.

My Prison Experience

During my thirty years as a volunteer at San Quentin State Prison in Marin County, California, I saw Islamic Da'wa (evangelism/recruitment) in action. While coaching the baseball team there for seventeen years, I sometimes arrived early and sat by a garden-type fountain (usually broken) that faced the building housing both the Jewish synagogue and the Muslim mosque. Yes, a strange combination, but that is how it was and still is.

Over the course of five years I listened to many sermons in English (unlike the sermons given in Arabic at the local mosque that I often visit), and I could easily follow along with the message. The messages by the imams were most often angry tirades about the persecution Muslims received over the centuries. Their hate speech frightened me from time to time, and I was tempted to speak to prison authorities about it, but I never did. (During that time, I did not understand as much about Islam as I should have.) In total, I probably heard ten or fifteen hours of outright expressions of rage and calls for revenge aimed at all that was non-Muslim.

Muslims began showing up to try out for the baseball team and the eight-man flag football team I formed. Every one of the Muslims were African Americans, and they were generally good players and reliable. One of them was my most trusted team member, a person I could rely on to tell what was going on with the team, if anything. We became friends, and the week after he was released from prison he came to our Sunday morning church service, stood before the congregation, and spoke to us for ten minutes; what he said was completely appropriate—and from a kind and generous spirit.

I correspond frequently on Facebook with this man who converted to Islam in prison, but I still do not know much about his background or how he became a Muslim. Recently, he dropped his Muslim name acquired in prison when he made his profession of faith, and he has gone back to his given name; I am not sure what that means, but I intend to speak with him about it.

Many African Americans have taken the path to Islam for several reasons. They find the doctrine compelling and the close-knit community welcoming, but there are also material benefits: they and their families on the outside often receive financial assistance, and a job and maybe a car will be waiting for the convert upon release from prison.

Dunleavy speaks about the selection of Islamic clergy for chaplain positions and the inadequate vetting process that allows imams with extremist views to enter the prison environment. Muslim evangelists able to find their way into prisons are almost always on the radical fringe.

The radicals begin their work little by little, and it is not just African Americans who are targeted. Hispanic and Anglo-American inmates are also pursued in Islam's prison outreach movement. To be counted as a Muslim in prison can be advantageous. There is a certain safety and special handling that often accompanies being in the prison's Muslim brotherhood. After all it is part of human nature to want to belong to a group that gives both purpose and meaning to one's life, no matter how misdirected that purpose is. Dunleavy's book speaks of the role of religion in the fertile soil of prison. They say there are no atheists in foxholes or prison cells, but theology and doctrine play a very minor role in conversions of convicts.

The irresistible draw is to be part of a world-wide brotherhood of like-minded people who have a compelling mission. And this Muslims certainly have. Here is a young convict with a messed up past and not much hope for the future, and along comes a group that offers great enticements and a sense of meaning. I am not surprised that many African Americans and other people in our world jump at the chance to be a part of it all.

THE WHYS

John Grisham, in his book, Rogue Lawyer (New York: Dell Books, 2015), gives a brief but accurate rendition of what drives African Americans, among others, into Islam. In the story line of the book the rogue lawyer is visiting his bodyguard's son who is in prison. Reading from page 109: "Young and black . . . in for nonviolent drug offenses . . . average sentence seven years . . . three years later 60% are back . . . convicted felons a branding they will never be able to shake . . . ."

These are Grisham's words, but there is more, and my summary of the felon's situation is this: Filled with anger and a desire for revenge, with no job skills, no real education to build upon, no family to lean on for support, and no sense of wanting to build his own family; his only friends are ex-cons or partners in crime; he finds peace only in drugs and lives with an expectation that his life will be short. Grisham sums up with, "One million young black men now warehoused in decaying prisons, idling away the days at taxpayer expense."

I might add that now there are far more than just young blacks who fit this narration;

growing numbers of Hispanics and whites are mixed in, and these numbers are growing. This is not an indictment, but it clears up any mystery of why Islam is growing in our prisons. If radical Islam feeds on the emotions of hate, anger, revenge, and alienation, this is a perfect storm condition for recruiting converts.

Recruitment and Motivation

Anyone can be radicalized and end up committing horrible crimes as a result—and not only born Muslims. By radicalized I mean someone who goes to prison for burglary and ends up willing to die in violent jihad for the sake of Allah. This is far different from someone who goes to prison for burglary and learns how to perfect the art thereof. Anyone who kills in the name of God is an ideologue and has been radicalized.

If you are in one group, members of another group will likely be viewed as an enemy. It is safe to say that religion and politics are prime categories of people groupings and identity that have traditionally and historically produced real trouble. The Irish Republican Army is an example of political terrorism. ISIS and Al Qaeda are examples of religious terrorism.

Fighting back and getting revenge are compelling reasons for joining a group, though they may not be in the conscious mind at the point of recruitment. Almost all of us have these emotions in us, sometimes buried deep, and they are powerful motivators driving some to ignore or disregard the consequences of their actions. The promises made by the group for security, power, belonging, and meaning, even material wealth or outlandish notions such as seventy-two virgins awaiting the jihadist martyr hero, are all enough to blind the eye and stop the thinking.

It is nearly an everyday event now that some extremist blows himself or herself up in the hope of killing and maiming as many as possible; and is it all for the glory of Allah!

Haram and other Motivators

Haram is Arabic for prohibited or forbidden.

There are two distinct world systems in the Muslim mind. There is Dar ul Islam (the world of Islam) and Dar-ul-Haram (the forbidden world). Much of the Western lifestyle is forbidden and seen as threatening the faith of a Muslim, particularly the young, through it's seductions and enticement to things forbidden in the Qur'an. For the pious Muslim, it is a duty to attack the degradation of the West, especially American style degradation, now that most of the country has embraced homosexuality. The excesses of contemporary civilizations are a motivator for those who want to live in the seventh century with Muhammad and his early companions.[7]

In my time, I have known Christians who were seduced by the immorality around them. This is the reality of our world, and it is unlikely to change much despite efforts to sanitize the culture. It is not a simple task to live for Jesus when all those around us demean it. (I live in the San Francisco Bay Area of California, so I know whereof I speak.) My experience is that Christians learn how to keep their footing regardless of the culture

---

[7] Those Muslims who want to return to the time when Islam first began are called Salafists. It comes from the Arabic word *salafi* meaning forefathers or the time of the forefathers.

in which they are embedded. We understand that we are "in the world but not of the world." While not always easy, it is doable, since Christians have the indwelling Holy Spirit, the written Word of God, and hopefully a supportive church community.

What about the crusades? They were far away and long ago, and it is far from clear if the crusaders were "crusading" to lift up the name of Jesus. Mostly not. Nevertheless, Muslims use the battle cry "Crusades" to build anger toward Christians that will directed to acts of revenge; the charge need not be historically accurate.

What about colonialism? This is a major motivator for those who do not understand the development and expansion of nation states, most of which were not motivated by solid Christian and Biblical directives.

Oppression comes to mind. Muslims have been repressed; although, what people group has not been oppressed or repressed at some time in their history? This is too big a topic for this essay, but simply saying Muslims are being oppressed is enough of a trigger to set hearts and minds yearning for revenge. As I understand it, domination over Muslim countries, especially following World War I, flowed from the Western democracies.

But there is something else that may be a major if not the most important reason for Islam to be what it is today.

Fear of Failure in the Spiritual Marketplace

Extremists can be born out of a fear that Islam itself is inadequate to compete with other world religions, particularly Christianity.

One of the great contrasts with Christianity and Islam is that Islam's ultimate goal is to dominate the world—Dar ul Islam—to see to it that all people live under Sharia Law. No Muslim who really knows the Qur'an would deny this in private, yet some do publicly.

The goal of Christianity is to present the message of Jesus to all peoples on the planet. As I have heard it said, Christian evangelism is "one beggar telling another beggar where to find bread." And we know some will be convinced of their need of a Savior and turn to Jesus to save them from their sins. We also know that no amount of coercion, even slick persuasion, will yield a genuine new birth.

My sense of it is that only a small percentage of Muslims know much of what their religion teaches beyond the rituals, rites, pillars, and attendant cultural traditions. (This is also true of many in Christian churches. There is a difference between being religious and having true faith in Jesus as Savior and Lord.) I have met so many people who identify with Islam but are practical, if not actual, atheists. They will go through the motions, but their heads and hearts are empty. These people may be in danger, because the honor brigades in the mosques, the zealous and pious musclemen, will know who they are and will label them as "weak." Please note, I am not implying that this phenomenon exits only Muslim-dominated cultures. This exists wherever there is a mosque.

The message of Islam is not a comforting one. I am writing this essay after completing the basic content of this present book. A person, whether in prison or not, has a void in his or her life, a hunger and thirst, and will unconsciously attempt to fill it with something, somehow. Islam seeks to draw the thirsty with a false promise of water. I have pointed out the horrors that Allah has in store for non-Muslims and for Muslims as well. The Qur'an states that all Muslims will enter hellfire and will maybe escape it after a time.

Allah is, after all, a deceiver and may lead even a faithful Muslim astray. Even those who die in violent jihad or who build a mosque have no real assurance of making it to paradise or escaping a temporary stay in hellfire. Allah's mercy and compassion are quite fickle, making the true message of Islam rather unattractive after all.

With any awareness of this reality, Muslims must fear that Islam is unable to compete in the spiritual marketplace of life. Today there are numerous former Muslims busy presenting Jesus and the message of the cross to Muslim communities. The Gospel is inescapable, and the draw is a Creator God who loves us and sent His Son to die in our place. Many Muslims are converting to Christ when Jesus is revealed through the faithful witness of believers and the drawing of the Holy Spirit. God chases down those whom He will. Conversion to Jesus is an event not a decision.

Death, and this is not merely physical but eternal death, is the end result of sin, yet the Christian has gone from death to life. Everyone dies, and then comes the judgment. On the cross, Jesus has taken our judgment upon Himself. We call this grace. We pray for it for our Muslim friends and neighbors. We do not pray for revenge or retaliation.

Essay Twelve

But . . . It *Is* Warfare!

War it is and of two kinds.

One Kind of War

Sadly, the killings go on daily. Who is waging this war? The jihadists—not all of Islam—are at war, or so we say. But some say we are in a real war with Islam itself. That is both accurate and inaccurate at the same time.

Islam's core doctrine is that Sharia Law must rule the world. There is no question about it, and any knowledgeable Muslim would concede this. While many if not most Muslims care little about Islam being the only true religion in the world, these moderates or progressives are not the shot-callers and have little real authority or power. We must therefore recognize to whom we are referring when we speak of war.

According to Islam, from the super pious to the moderates, the West is corrupt. What is to be done? While most Muslims want to live and let live, there is a sizable faction, perhaps as much as 5%, who are willing to go to battle. This 5% equates to around 500,000 dedicated warriors.

Another Kind of War

Christians are at war, too. In fact, we are called to take up the armor of God.

Finally, be strong in the Lord and in the strength of his might. Put on the whole armor of God, that you may be able to stand against the schemes of the devil (Ephesians 6:10–11).

For we do not wrestle against flesh and blood, but against the rulers, against the authorities, against the cosmic powers of this present darkness, against the spiritual forces of evil in the heavenly places (Ephesians 6:12).

Paul admits the existence of a war, but it is a spiritual war fought against an army mightier than any that humans could raise. He is referring to Satan and his minions. Fallen angels are the troops, and they possess spiritual power. C.S. Lewis used the term "hideous strength" in speaking of the ungodly power arrayed against the people who profess Jesus as Lord. If Christians think about this too long, we can become fearful, except that we recall 1 John 3:8: "The reason the Son of God appeared was to destroy the works of the devil."

John the Apostle wrote about the works of the devil and points out that the devil has been defeated—active yes, but nonetheless defeated, and in at least two ways. One, our sin—that which screams at us that we are no good and destined to live in hell forever—has been utterly removed, not in part but the whole, and it has been nailed to the cross. So our sin—all of it, past, present, and future—is wiped out, cleansed, washed away by the blood of the Lamb. Incredible, but a fact.

Then two, the enemy called death has been conquered. Not physical death, because we will all die unless Jesus returns before we actually physically die, but the real death is the eternal death.

Hellfire is very frequently found in the Qur'an, most often used as a threat and a warning, and thus hellfire is very present in the Muslim mind. On this point there is a connection with Biblical Christianity. There is a hell, most definitely, and it was created for the devil and his angels, for there must be a place apart for that which is unholy.

Physical death is but a moment in time; spiritual death, however, is eternal. It is plain which is the real enemy. It is no wonder why John 3:16 has for so many centuries been the one verse most Christians have memorized: "For God so loved the world, that he gave his only Son, that whoever believes in him should not perish but have eternal life."

It should be noted here, that in Islam Allah determines the moment and means of death. If a Muslim dies, it is the will of Allah. Biblical Christianity is far different. That we all die is plain enough, as we find in Hebrews 9:27-28:

"And just as it is appointed for man to die once, and after that comes the judgment, so Christ, having been offered once to bear the sins of many, will appear a second time, not to deal with sin but to save those who are eagerly waiting for him."

It is not the moment or means of death that God appoints but that death is a reality that comes with being human. Muslims may take comfort that death is in the hands of Allah, but Christians have the promise of being forgiven and having everlasting life based on what Jesus has already accomplished.

Still Another Kind of War-Game

A convict told me years ago that to make it in prison you have to have a mission. A mission, a cause, a reason for living, without which one might go crazy. Could it be that jihad becomes not just the means to accomplish the mission but the mission itself?

War-games are exciting to play. The secrecy, the codes, the manipulations, extortions, intimidations—war-games. And the stakes are extremely high, making life all the more interesting.

When one has nothing or next to nothing, and the future looks bleak, and so many others seem to be living the good life, one stops caring and will bet everything on a cause, and Allah is the highest of all causes for pious Muslims. As General Patton is reported to have said, "Compared to war all else pales."

My point in this little aside is, maybe it is not religion that draws a religionist to the war.

THE WEAPONS OF OUR WARFARE

Back now to Ephesians chapter six and the weapons of the Christian's warfare, which are not bombs, knives, swords, or guns. Here is the list:

- "Stand therefore having fastened on the belt of truth" (6:14a). Here truth is not a "what" but a "Who," and that Who is Jesus, who is the way, the truth and the life (see John 14:6).
- "Having put on the breastplate of righteousness" (6:14b). Jesus Himself is our righteousness, we have none of our own but have His as a free gift.
- "As shoes for your feet, having put on the readiness given by the gospel of peace" (6:15). The soldier stands secure knowing that he has no battle with God but is settled in the finished work of Jesus Christ on the cross. That war is over and there is peace.
- "In all circumstances take up the shield of faith, with which you can extinguish all the flaming darts of the evil one" (6:16). Since Satan's power over us has been nullified though the work of Jesus, we stand behind Him trusting in the triumphant Lamb of God.
- "And take the helmet of salvation" (17a). The head, the most vulnerable part of the body, is totally protected in the salvation we have in Jesus, which cannot under any circumstance be taken from us. Our position in Christ is secure to all eternity, and even we ourselves cannot change that.
- "And the sword of the Spirit, which is the word of God" (6:17b). "Word" is both the living and written word of God, Jesus Himself and the Scripture, the Bible from Genesis to Revelation. It is a sword, a spiritual sword, and it is sharper than any two-edged blade. The word is truth and there is great power in truth.
- "Praying at all times in the Spirit with all prayer and supplication" (6:18a). We pray, not necessarily by rote, which is acceptable and a Biblical way to pray—I am thinking of the Lord's Prayer here—but saying to our heavenly Father what is on our heart and mind. The Christian is never alone; always walking with us is the Triune God, Father, Son, and Holy Spirit.

Oddly, or not, the equipment is not heavy and may be borne by the young and old, weak and strong.

This is our kind of war, one that has already been won. The only blow struck was inflicted a long time ago while Jesus was on Calvary.

17

WHO IS GABRIEL?

This essay will examine three questions. First, Who is Gabriel? The answer prompts a second question: Who is Allah? The answers to these provoke a third question: Who is Muhammad? All that is Islam hangs on the answers to these three questions.

GABRIEL OF THE BIBLE

The name Gabriel is found in four places in the Bible: Daniel 8:16 and 9:21, and Luke 1:19 and 1:26. The name *Gabriel* means "God is mighty."

The Two Passages from the Hebrew Bible Book of Daniel

> When I, Daniel, had seen the vision, I sought to understand it. And behold, there stood before me one having the appearance of a man. And I heard a man's voice between the banks of the Ulai, and it called "Gabriel, make this man understand the vision." (Daniel 8:15–16)

> While I was speaking and praying, confessing my sin and the sin of my people Israel, and presenting my plea before the Lord my God for the holy hill of my God, while I was speaking in prayer, the man Gabriel, whom I had seen in the vision at the first, came to me in swift flight at the time of the evening sacrifice. (Daniel 9:20–21)

Gabriel is thus introduced in the book of Daniel, and we see more of him in the New Testament.

The Two Passages from the New Testament Gospel of Luke

While the priest Zechariah is on duty at the temple in Jerusalem, an angel of the Lord appears to him. The angel announces to Zechariah that the prayers of him and his wife Elizabeth have been answered, to the effect that Elizabeth will bear a son and his name will be John. We pick up the story in Luke chapter 1:

> And Zechariah said to the angel, "How shall I know this? For I am an old man,

and my wife is advanced in years." And the angel answered him, "I am Gabriel. I stand in the presence of God, and I was sent to speak to you and to bring you this good news." (Luke 1:18–19)

In the sixth month the angel Gabriel was sent from God to a city of Galilee named Nazareth, to a virgin betrothed to a man whose name was Joseph, of the house of David. And the virgin's name was Mary. (Luke 1:26–27)

Now we look at the words of Gabriel to Mary in verse 28: "Greetings, O favored one, the Lord is with you!" Mary, greatly troubled at the greeting, tries to understand what the angel means. Gabriel continues:

"Do not be afraid, Mary, for you have found favor with God. And behold, you will conceive in your womb and bear a son, and you shall call His name Jesus. He will be great and will be called the Son of the Most High. And the Lord God will give to Him the throne of His father David, and He will reign over the house of Jacob forever, and of His kingdom there will be no end." (Luke 1:30–33)

Is the Angel in Matthew Also Gabriel?

Joseph, engaged to and about to marry Mary, is troubled when he learns she is pregnant. Thinking to divorce her quietly, he receives a visit from an angel in a dream. The angel (*no name given*) says to him:

"Joseph, son of David, do not fear to take Mary as your wife, for that which is conceived in her is from the Holy Spirit. She will bear a son, and you shall call His name Jesus, for He will save His people from their sins." All this took place to fulfill what the Lord had spoken by the prophet: "Behold, the virgin shall conceive and bear a Son, and they shall call His name Immanuel" (which means, God with us). When Joseph woke from sleep, he did as the angel of the Lord commanded him: he took his wife, but knew her not until she had given birth to a Son. And he called His name Jesus. (Matthew 1:20–25)

Is the angel who spoke to Joseph the same one who spoke to Zechariah and Mary? We cannot be completely sure, but it seems as though it must be the case. However, the argument I am about to make does not depend on the answer to that question, as both angels in Luke and in Matthew are clearly angels of the Lord.

What have we learned so far? The angelic appearances have to do with the birth of Jesus, the one who would save His people from sin. The birth was miraculous, accomplished by the Holy Spirit, and this is all the explanation for the pregnancy we have. The point is clear: no human being had sex with Mary. Neither God the Father nor God the Holy Spirit had sex with Mary. The birth was miraculous, and this fits perfectly with the word God revealed to Isaiah six hundred years earlier:

There the Lord Himself will give you a sign. Behold, the virgin shall conceive and bear a son, and shall call His name Immanuel. (Isaiah 7:14)

The passage is referred to as "The Sign of Immanuel," meaning that the virgin's child is God, come to be with us in a miraculous manner—thus a sign. God actually became flesh, which the Creator of the universe could do. And He did.

The child born to Mary is not called Immanuel, but Jesus. Immanuel, in traditional Jewish understanding, is what He *is*, which is God become man. The name Jesus refers to what He would *do*. *Jesus* is a name derived from the Hebrew name *Joshua*. It means "God saves." Joshua was the one who brought the chosen people across the Jordan River into the promised land of Canaan. Moses was not allowed to do this, and the concept demonstrated by that is that the law of Moses cannot in itself bring salvation. No, salvation is a gift of God and is not by works of the law. In His dying for sin, Jesus became the Savior, and this is proven by His resurrection. Jesus is Immanuel, God with us.

One Last Word from Gabriel, the Angel of the Lord

Gabriel says to Mary in reference to the child she will bear: "He will be great and will be called the Son of the Most High" (Luke 1:32). This virgin birth, not the result of sexual intercourse, will be miraculous. The child will be of the same nature as the Father.

Then Gabriel says, "He will reign over the house of Jacob forever, and of His kingdom there will be no end" (Luke 1:33). The meaning is obvious: the child will be the reigning King forever, just as Isaiah had announced: "For to us a child is born, to us a Son is given; and the government shall be upon His shoulder, and His name shall be called Wonderful Counselor, Mighty God, Everlasting Father, Prince of Peace" (Isaiah 9:6). Without question, the prophet Isaiah states that the child born is God Himself.

This takes us into the mystery of the Trinity. We will never fully comprehend how the Father, the Son, and the Holy Spirit are one and complete God all at once. Christian historians and theologians simply note what the evidence reveals.

The point is plain enough—the child born is God in the flesh. He is Jesus, born of the virgin in Bethlehem, the one who will die in our place, taking our sin upon Himself. Then, on the third day, He will be raised from the dead. He is alive now in heaven, one day to return to receive His own.

Nearly six hundred years later, however, there appeared another "Gabriel."

GABRIEL OF ISLAM

The majority of Muslims today hold that the Qur'an is eternal (eternal as Allah is eternal), was brought down to earth by an angel, and was then recited by the angel Gabriel to Muhammad. Allah spoke each and every verse to the angel, who then recited them, piecemeal, over the course of about twenty-two years, to Muhammad. Muhammad, unable to write, memorized the recitations and spoke them to others, who then wrote them down. (Qur'an means "recitation," or "that which is recited.")

The angel that appeared to Muhammad at a cave on the slopes of Mount Hira near Mecca, about AD 610, also had the name Gabriel. It was the custom of many Jews, Christians, Zoroastrians, and Gnostics to retire to secluded places in hopes of receiving spiritual dreams and visions and thereby experience a direct connection with deity. Muhammad was one of these.

Ascetics would fast, meditate, and stay awake for days in order to empty the mind and receive dreams and visions. Muhammad, after a time, achieved trance-like states during which the angel Gabriel, as the angel announced himself to Muhammad, spoke to him. We find a hint of this in the hadith of Abu Dawud, Book 12, No. 2247a, which reads, "When the Apostle of Allah (peace be upon him) came to himself (after the revelation ended)…"

Muhammad reported his visits by Gabriel to his wife Khadija, who supported the idea that it was indeed an angel speaking to her husband. Muhammad, however, was not sure of the nature of the vision he had, but he eventually adopted his wife's opinion.

At the very beginning of Muhammad's encounter with Gabriel, he wondered if he was actually in contact with a jinn (demon) rather than an angel. This is stunningly apparent based on a hadith reported by Aisha (the mother of the faithful believers and favorite wife of Muhammad) as found in the most trusted of all hadiths, *Sahih Al-Bukhari*, Vol. 1, Book 1, No. 3:

> The commencement of the Divine Inspiration to Allah's Apostle was in the form of good dreams, which came true like bright day light, and then the love of seclusion was bestowed upon him. He used to go in seclusion in the cave of Hira where he used to worship (Allah alone) continuously for many days before his desire to see his family. He used to take with him the journey food for the stay and then come back to (his wife) Khadija to take his food like-wise again till suddenly the Truth descended upon him while he was in the cave of Hira. The angel came to him and asked him to read. The Prophet replied, "I do not know how to read."
>
> The Prophet added, "The angel caught me (forcefully) and pressed me so hard that I could not bear it any more. He then released me and again asked me to read and I replied, 'I do not know how to read.' Thereupon he caught me again and pressed me a second time till I could not bear it any more. He then released me and again asked me to read but again I replied, 'I do not know how to read (or what shall I read)?' Thereupon he caught me for a third time and pressed me, and then released me and said, 'Read in the name of your Lord, who has created (all that exists) has created man from a clot. Read! And your Lord is the Most Generous.

Muhammad was so harshly treated by what he thought was the angel Gabriel that he doubted it was an angel from Allah at all. He became depressed and considered throwing himself off the mountain of Hira. It was only through the intervention and convincing of Khadija, his first wife, that Muhammad was prevented from doing so.

We find an interesting account referred to as "The Lap." The story is that Muhammad continued to believe the being that appeared to him was a jinn, a demon. Khadija, in the midst of Muhammad's fears and doubts, asked him to sit on her lap, first one side then the other. When he did she asked him if he saw the angel. He responded yes. Then she asked him to sit on her lap and once again asked if he saw the angel. Again, yes. Then she disrobed and asked Muhammad to sit on her lap again. She asked if he saw the angel and Muhammad said no. With that Khadija convinced Muhammad it was indeed the angel Gabriel by saying that only a good angel would not look upon a woman's nakedness.

The above account is a paraphrase from the *Sira*, the official biography of Muhammad. Below now is the account, called "The Lap" as reported by Ibn Ishaq, Muhammad's biographer:

Ibn Ishaq recorded that when the spirit came to Muhammad another time, Khadija tested him:

Ishma'il b. Abu Hakim, a freedman of the family of al-Zubayr, told me on Khadija's authority that she said to the apostle of Allah, "O son of my uncle, are you able to tell me about your visitant, when he comes to you? "He replied that he could, and she asked him to tell her when he came.

So when Gabriel came to him, as he was wont, the apostle said to Khadija, "This is Gabriel who has just come to me." "Get up, O son of my uncle," she said, "and sit by my left thigh."

The apostle did so, and she said, "Can you see him?" "Yes," he said. She said, "Then turn around and sit on my right thigh." He did so, and she said, "Can you see him?" When he said that he could she asked him to move and sit in her lap.

When he had done this she again asked if he could see him, and he said yes, she disclosed her form and cast aside her veil while the apostle was sitting in her lap. Then she said, "Can you see him?" And he replied, "No." She said, "O son of my uncle, rejoice and be of good heart, by Allah he is an angel and not a satan."[1]

Gabriel in the Qur'an and Hadith

Gabriel appears in only three verses in the Qur'an: Sura 2:97–98 and Sura 66:4.

Say, (O Muhammad, to mankind)[2]: Who is an enemy to Gabriel! For he it is who hath revealed (this Scripture) to thy heart by Allah's leave, confirming that which was (revealed) before it and a guidance and glad tidings to believers. (Sura 2:97)

Who is an enemy to Allah, and His angels and His messengers, and Gabriel and Michael! Then, lo! Allah (Himself) is an enemy to the disbelievers. (Sura 2:98)

If ye twain turn unto Allah repentant, (ye have cause to do so) for your hearts desired (the ban); and if ye aid one another against him (Muhammad) the lo! Allah, even He, is his protecting Friend, and Gabriel and the righteous among the believers; and furthermore the angels are his helpers. (Sura 66:4)

---

1 Ibn Ishaq, *The Life of Muhammad*, trans. A. Guillaume (Oxford: Oxford University Press, 1967), 107. The *Sira* has for centuries been linked with the Qur'an and hadith as authoritative on the life of Muhammad. In more recent years, the *Sira* has been largely neglected, as the accounts of what Muhammad said and did are rather fantastic, problematic, and embarrassing.

2 Words in parentheses indicate explanatory notes made by editors of the Qur'an. Without them, many passages of the Qur'an would be unintelligible.

The Two Gabriels: The Same or Different?

Are the Gabriel of the Bible and the Gabriel of Islam one and the same?

I am going to make the case that the two are different—in fact, very different. However, it is easy to be fooled. The apostle Paul warned the church at Corinth that demons could disguise themselves as angels.

> For such men are false apostles, deceitful workmen, disguising themselves as apostles of Christ. And no wonder, for even Satan disguises himself as an angel of light. So it is no surprise if his servants, also, disguise themselves as servants of righteousness. Their end will correspond to their deeds. (2 Corinthians 11:13–15)

Note: An apostle is a messenger, one sent with a message.

Let me be clear at once: both Gabriels are angels. One is an angel of the Lord; the other is a fallen angel, a demon. My contention is that a fallen angel—a jinn or demon—appeared to Muhammad on Mount Hira. Muhammad was right in his first assessment.

The Ultimate Offense

Stating that Islam's Gabriel is a jinn, or demon, is the ultimate offense for Muslims, since it utterly invalidates the three most important elements of the Islamic faith: Allah, the Qur'an, and Muhammad. This is because Allah relays to Gabriel what is in the Qur'an, and Muhammad is merely passing along what a demon recited to him. Islam is then based upon absolute error and nothing more.

Such accusations, let alone suggestions, can earn one the death penalty in Muslim-majority societies. Religions or governments that forcefully, even ruthlessly, stifle dissent show their weakness. This is true of Islam, even in countries where the Muslim population is small. If a Muslim abandons Islam, which is called *apostasy*, he or she may be punished by death, though this is not clearly spelled out in the Qur'an. Therefore, to consider this assertion that Islam's Gabriel is a jinn can be a life and death matter.

The Christian's Obligation

With the understanding of this enormous deception, what must a Christian do? Must we remain silent and not voice even the possibility that the whole of Islam is based on demonic deception? To refrain from speaking out is immoral and unethical.

Writers of Scripture were known for denouncing false religion and the behaviors they spawn. Many paid the ultimate price for standing with the truth. Many are dying even today in Muslim-dominated nations for speaking their hearts and minds.

In the face of terror and in light of the Great Commission given Christians by Jesus Himself (see Matthew 28:19–20, among others), we must stand up to the murderous lies of the chief demon, Satan. Jesus, while countering the attacks of religious opponents, was clear. Jesus said:

> You are of your father the devil, and your will is to do your father's desires. He was a murderer from the beginning, and does not stand in the truth, because there is no truth in him. When he lies, he speaks out of his own character, for he is a liar and the father of lies. (John 8:44)

Challenging error is not disrespectful, especially when what is at stake is heaven or hell, both of which are eternal.

Another Islamic Teaching about Gabriel

Some spokesmen for Islam identify Gabriel as the Holy Spirit in both the Bible and the Qur'an. Where in Islam's authoritative texts do they find this? In Sura 2:87 and Sura 2:253, where, without the word *Gabriel* appearing, we find, "We supported him with the Holy Spirit." Islamic interpreters say this "We" is the angel Gabriel. But the plain text of the Qur'an does not state this.

Not only does the Qur'an not identify Gabriel with the Holy Spirit, the hadith does not either. Instead, we find just the opposite, as illustrated by *Sahih Muslim*, in book 30: "Gabriel, the Apostle of Allah is among us, and the Holy Spirit who has no match." Gabriel is not the Holy Spirit.

THE HOLY SPIRIT IN THE BIBLE

The Hebrew Bible

Both the Hebrew Bible and the New Testament show the nature and identity of the Holy Spirit. The Holy Spirit is deity, often referred to as the Spirit of God, in that the Holy Spirit is holy, and only God is holy. The Holy Spirit is omnipresent, is referred to as a "He" and thus is personal, and is omnipotent, meaning all powerful. And the Holy Spirit can only be God, as are the Father and the Son.

The second verse of Genesis speaks of the Holy Spirit being involved at the moment of the creation of the universe. "The earth was without form and void, and darkness was over the face of the deep. And the Spirit of God was hovering over the face of the waters."

Second Samuel 23:2–3 identifies the God of Israel with the Spirit of the LORD.[3]

> The Spirit of the LORD speaks by me; His word is on my tongue. The God of Israel has spoken; the Rock of Israel has said to me: When one rules justly over men, ruling in the fear of God...

Isaiah 40:13 reads, "Who has measured the Spirit of the LORD, or what man shows Him his counsel?" We notice "LORD" in the phrase "Spirit of the LORD," clearly identifying the Holy Spirit with God.

The New Testament

We could examine many more verses dealing with the Holy Spirit in the Hebrew Bible, but now we turn to the New Testament—first to the third chapter of the Gospel of John.

A leader of the Jewish people named Nicodemus approaches Jesus at night, presumably to speak with Him in private. He says he knows Jesus is from God because of the miracles Jesus performs. Jesus, however, redirects the conversation by saying, "Unless one is born again he cannot see the kingdom of God" (v. 3). Of course, the elder statesman does not understand how a person can be reborn. Jesus replies, "Unless one is born of water and the Spirit, he cannot enter the kingdom of God" (v. 5). To be born of the flesh

---

3   In the Hebrew Bible, when "LORD" is written in capital letters, it refers to Yahweh, that name of God revealed to Moses in the burning bush incident. See Exodus 3:14.

is one thing, but to be born of the Spirit is quite another. And we must be clear: Jesus is not talking about any angel, much less one named Gabriel. Only God brings life, both physical and spiritual.

The Holy Spirit works the new birth, or conversion. This is clear in the passage in John 3, and we find the same in Acts 8:14–20. Also in Acts 3:1–4, the Holy Spirit is directly referred to as God. The writer of Hebrews also declares that the Holy Spirit is eternal, in reference to the power of the shed blood of Jesus: "How much more will the blood of Christ, who through the eternal Spirit offered himself without blemish to God, purify our conscience from dead works to serve the living God" (Hebrews 9:14).

Looking back to the birth passages in Luke's Gospel, we find an answer to Mary's question of the angel Gabriel as to how she will have a baby, when Gabriel replies, "The Holy Spirit will come upon you" (Luke 1:35). It is obvious that the angel Gabriel separates himself from the Holy Spirit. Certainly, the Holy Spirit and Gabriel are not the same at all.

It is clear that neither the Qur'an nor the Bible anywhere identifies Gabriel with the Holy Spirit.

Angel or Holy Spirit?

The goal of Islamic scholars who claim that Gabriel is the Holy Spirit is to contaminate the Christian doctrine of the Trinity. Which is it then? Is Gabriel an angel or the Holy Spirit, or maybe both at once, at least from an Islamic point of view? Our arguments above show that Gabriel is actually a jinn or demon, thus further clouding an already murky subject.

Who Is Allah?

The Name "Allah"

"Allah" was the name used by Christians and Jews in the Arabian Peninsula for centuries before the Islamic era. Indeed, the word *Allah* was used by Jews in the Arabian Peninsula for the God of Abraham, Isaac, and Jacob before the Christian era.

To put it another way: Neither Muhammad, Abu Bakr, Umar, nor Uthman invented the word *Allah*. They would have known the word *Allah* from childhood.

It is not the word that counts; it is the content or meaning of the word. To the Jew of the period when Islam was born, Allah would be the creator, the lawgiver, and the one who led the family of the patriarchs out of Egypt and gave them the promised land, the land of Canaan.

To the Christian of that period, Allah would be the God and Father of the Lord Jesus Christ, in addition to all that the Jewish people believed about God. It would be only natural for Muhammad to also use the term *Allah* in reference to the creator God. Clearly, however, Muhammad gave new definition to who or what Allah is.

Islam's Allah

Islam claims that Allah spoke to Gabriel, who then spoke to Muhammad, who then recited the revelations that originated with Allah by way of Gabriel to other people, who at some point committed them to writing.

The narrative of the collecting of the Qur'an is fascinating. There were so many variations going about that Uthman, the third caliph after Muhammad, ordered all the renditions be gathered together in order to make a uniform document. All the other manuscripts were then burned. But the picture of Allah in the Qur'an is interesting.

Allah is distant, speaks through an angel, loves those who love him, and hates those who do not believe in him. Allah is called the greatest of deceivers and might lead astray even the best of Muslims. Though Allah repeatedly refers to himself as the most beneficent, the most merciful, the most forgiving, and so on, evidence of this is lacking or scant other than what he says of himself.

It is not unfair nor a misrepresentation to say that the God of the Qur'an is far different from the God spoken of in the Bible, both the Hebrew Bible and the New Testament.

Transcendence Versus Immanence

One of the major differences between the Bible's God and Islam's Allah has to do with whether or not he is present with his creation. From what we find in the Qur'an and hadith about Allah, he is transcendent and not immanent.

In contrast, the God of the Hebrew Bible is transcendent but is also immanent, in that He interacts personally with His people. He walks and talks with Adam and Eve in the garden of Eden, otherwise known as Paradise. He does so until the Fall, the moment that God's single law is broken, which we read about in Genesis chapter 3. The terrible consequence of that event is that God's human creation is sent east of Eden. But God never leaves them entirely alone; He does not abandon them.

God once again speaks with a human being out of a burning bush in the Arabian desert, when He appears to Moses and tells him His name: Yahweh (YHWH, known as the Tetragrammaton). God commands and directs Moses to supervise the erection of a tabernacle, which contains a special place within it—the Holy of Holies—where God will dwell with His people.

This is a foreshadowing of what will come later. The prophets point to a time when God will arrive in person. This is what the name Immanuel means—"God with us." We can see this in the word itself, even if we are not Hebrew literate. The last two letters of Immanuel, "el" is the English transliteration of the Hebrew word for God: El. *Imma* means "with," and *nu* means "us." Simply put, "God with us."

This is who Jesus is.

Is Allah a Fiction?

Again, my premise is that Gabriel is indeed an angel in reference to Islam, but a fallen angel. Muhammad was correct when he thought the being that presented itself at the cave on Mount Hira was a jinn, which is an Arabic word meaning "demon." It was only his wife Khadija who convinced him otherwise.

The question that must follow this reasoning, then, is, If Gabriel is a demon, and Gabriel is reciting to Muhammad what is supposedly spoken by Allah, then just who or what is Allah?

It is clear from the Hebrew Bible and the New Testament that Satan and his demons are surely angels—but fallen angels who became the enemies of God. And Satan is a **god**, too.

And even if our Gospel is veiled, it is veiled to those who are perishing. In their case the **god** of this world has blinded the minds of the unbelievers, to keep them from seeing the light of the Gospel of the glory of Christ, who is the image of God. (2 Corinthians 4:3–4, emphasis added)

There is an Allah, but it is Satan in disguise who directed an underling demon to approach Muhammad while Muhammad was in a trance state and therefore open to demonic invasion.

In saying this, have I committed blasphemy, and of the worst sort, against the Islamic trinity? Yes, indeed I have, but not out of meanness or an attempt to deceive. Rather, I have presented the truth from a heart of love for the Muslim people, in the hopes that the veil of deception will be removed from their eyes.

The only possible conclusion given the evidence and arguments above is to say that Allah is a demon (Shayton or Satan), that Islam's Gabriel is also a demon (jinn), and therefore that Muhammad was very cleverly deceived. And this is what most Christians do believe, but it is a fearful endeavor to put these ideas into public view, given the retribution we have seen from Islam in these past few decades.

Who Is Muhammad?

Is Muhammad a true prophet of God? Was he duped into thinking he was hearing words from Allah? Did he make the whole thing up? Was it all a dream? Was it a scheme to acquire power and prestige? Is Muhammad a prophet to be trusted? Is he to be obeyed? Is he to be believed? Is he a false prophet?

We cannot be afraid to ask these questions. Too much hinges on the answers, for Muslims especially. Muslim people are sincere seekers after God. Even the most radical among them are only following through on what has been communicated to them from the cradle. Muslim people, in my experience, are more "religious" than most Christians, Buddhists, Hindus, and so on.

Few desire to be with God in Paradise as much as Muslims. And many will do anything to assure being there. After all, no Muslim can be sure they will be in Paradise after death, since Allah is a great deceiver and will lead astray any he chooses. Unlike the Christian who will experience assurance of salvation, the Muslim can only hope and work hard to earn Allah's favor.

Some commentators doubt Muhammad even existed. I am not one of these. As to whether there were those who embellished the story, especially in the latter part of the seventh and into the eighteenth century, this is a possibility. We are aware that gnostics in the second and third centuries also made Jesus into a superhero and magician.

It is well established that Muhammad was not certain in his own mind as to the nature of the entity he encountered on Mount Hira. At first he thought the "angel" was a jinn, a demon; his wife Khadija convinced him it was an angel of God.

What Is the Truth?

That which was revealed to Muhammad differs utterly from what we see of God in the Bible. Which account is the true one? Islam, of course, says that the revelation to Muhammad supersedes or replaces what is found in the Bible—and in a number of significant ways. For instance, Jesus is not God who has come to be with us and die on a cross for our sin. Jesus is a prophet, but not of the rank of Muhammad. Jesus plays a role in the last days, but dies and ends up being buried next to Muhammad. It is rather complex, but the Jesus of the Qur'an is not even close to the Jesus of Christian Scripture.

Then, God in the Qur'an is separated from humans and speaks through an angel. In the Bible, God becomes flesh and dwells among us. Also, being in Paradise/heaven in the Qur'an depends upon believing that Allah alone is God and that Muhammad is his messenger. But that is only the beginning. Mostly, heaven is earned by doing good deeds, working for salvation. In the Bible, forgiveness, salvation, and being assured of heaven depend upon God's gift alone.

Closing Statement

Who is Allah? Allah is either a chief demon—perhaps Satan himself—or a fantasy figure invented by Muhammad. At minimum, Allah is not God.

Who is Gabriel? Gabriel is either a jinn, meaning a demon, or a fantasy figure invented by Muhammad. Gabriel is not an angel of the Lord God.

Who is Muhammad? He is a seventh-century man living in Arabia who was either deceived by a demonic entity or who developed a fictional account about communications he received from God. Muhammad is not a prophet of God; he is a false prophet.

Another Contradiction Within Islam:

There is a cascading danger for Islam in its claim that Gabriel is the Holy Spirit. Islam is supposed to be monotheistic, meaning that Allah has no partners. If Gabriel is the Holy Spirit, then Gabriel is deity as well—Allah has a partner. Add to that the doctrine held by the traditionalists in Islam that the Qur'an is eternal in heaven. Another partner? Consider also the reverence shown to Muhammad. Is it so complete that he is actually lifted to the status of deity as well? One more partner for Allah?

Muhammad is not God and never claimed to be, despite how Muslims tend to view him, and neither is Gabriel. If Gabriel is the Holy Spirit and the Qur'an is eternal alongside Allah, and if every Muslim must model his own life after the "perfect man" Muhammad, it is not a stretch to say that Islam has a fourfold divinity: Allah, Gabriel, the Qur'an, and Muhammad.

The list of contradictions emanating from Islam is long, and this essay only introduces some of them.

18

DEBATING WITH MUSLIMS

Introduction

Following this introduction to debating with Muslims are examinations of two books by the deceased Ahmed Deedat, a Muslim missionary who frequently debated Christians.

At first I thought it best to present various styles associated with formal debate events and then suggest winning strategies. But, regarding winning strategies, one of my old jokes is, "No Christian wins a debate with a Muslim scholar."[1] This statement is not 100 percent true, but apologists for Islam are often trained to be such from early childhood. Plus, combined with the tendency by Muslims to resort to taqiyya, or sacred deception, winning a debate may not be either possible or desired.

For example, earlier today in a television debate/discussion in which I participated, I brought up that Allah is the great deceiver or schemer (see Quran 3:54) and that he will lead astray (see Qur'an 18:17). In reply I was told that without knowing Arabic one is unable to determine what Allah actually recited to Muhammad through Gabriel. He went on to say that the English translations of the Qur'an I rely upon do not always give the right translation. And, "No, Allah is not a deceiver nor will he lead astray, but he will allow a person to be deceived and/or be lead astray." It is proper to bring such points up, but the Muslim scholar will do his best to confuse the audience.

Yes, one can win and lose at the same time. The Christian apologist's goal is not so much to win as to witness. In the filming of the television series "The Imam and the Pastor," I decided not to confront each and every distortion, embellishment, and confusion of issues presented by the imam. It was often a better strategy to let things go, since I suspected viewers would be able to work though the misrepresentations and fallacies.

However, in order to equip a Christian witness to Muslims, it seemed best to provide material that would suit casual as well as formal encounters with Muslims, whether with Muslim clerics or everyday Muslim folk. It soon became apparent to me that I could only provide a "starter kit." My suggestion is that the reader uses what he or she finds here as a foundation for building a framework that can be added to as new information comes in.

---

1 Without exaggeration let me say that I am not a good debater. Indeed, even in general discussion, I am often bested. It is nice to *win well*, but it may be even better to *lose well*.

Fortunately for me, I like Muslim people. It was not always so, as I had a hard time getting over the wanton killing of innocents in the name of Allah. Over time, it seems as if the Holy Spirit of God has softened my heart to the point I enjoy spending time with Muslim people.[2] And I love filming the broadcasts with Imam Abu Qadir Al-Amin of the San Francisco Islamic Center. We have become friends.[3]

I have a short story on how I was stumped by a young Muslim named Omar. He is a passionate Muslim and well trained as an apologist. Born in Africa, educated in America, I met him at the local mosque in Mill Valley. We had lunch together one day about two years ago, and I was impressed with him to the point that I invited him to attend my Islamic Studies class at the church I pastor. About midway into the class he said to me something like the following: "You only know Islam from the outside looking in. To know the heart of Islam you have to be in it, experience its wonder and grandeur. And you have to know Arabic and have read the Qur'an."

This, I discovered later, is a typical approach Muslims will take. They know, of course, that very few would qualify. (The late Nabeel Qureshi, amongst a growing number of others, was one who qualified.)

I replied that I had been studying and writing about Islam for fifteen years and attending the local mosque as well. In addition, I mentioned several imams that I had spoken with at length about Islam. This was not enough for Omar, however. My point is that the above tactic will be employed when a Muslim person feels threatened and perhaps feels inadequate to the task of defending or promoting Islam.

For a moment, I was stumped by Omar. I simply admitted that I was an outsider looking in, and the same was true of him. Therefore, I pointed out, we were on equal footing.

Fear of Muslims, hatred of Muslims, and even generalized dislike of Muslims will undermine interaction with both Islamic scholars and everyday Muslims. Therefore, we must see that Muslim people are desperately hoping to win favor with God, yet never finding either joy or peace. Works-based faith is empty and futile. This is the way we all were before God broke into our lives and by His Spirit revealed Jesus to us.

Perhaps the best way to prepare to debate with and or witness to Muslims is to be acquainted with certain concepts Muslims of all stripes understand and employ in conversation with Christians. It is essential that one must have a solid understanding of Scripture and Christian doctrine. No, this does not require a seminary degree, but there is real work to be done. The sole reason for this book is to equip the Christian witness to Muslims.

So then, let's go to work.

Elementary Study for Witnessing to Muslims through Debate

Key subjects that often come up in debate or discussion with Muslims are presented here in alphabetical order. This is intended to serve only as a starter kit. Direct evangelical encounters with Muslims will necessitate expanded study.

---

2 I intend to be at the Friday prayers two hours from now at the Mill Valley Islamic Center.

3 Yes, I know Muslims are warned about making friends with non-believers, but sometimes they cannot help it.

The following is a list of translations of the Qur'an:

1. The Qur'an by Abdullah Yusufali
2. The Qur'an by M. H. Shakir
3. The Glorious Qur'an by Muhammed Marmaduke Pickthall
4. The Holy Qur'an by S. V. Mir Ahmed Ali
5. The Glorious Qur'an by S. V. Ahamed
6. El Coran by Julio Cortes
7. The Qur'an by 'Ali Quli Qara'l

For this section I am using *The Glorious Qur'an* by Muhammed Marmaduke Pickthall.[4]

Abrogation[5]

While he was still alive, Muhammad would tell his followers that certain portions of the Qur'an he had recited before were no longer to be recited. This was met with resistance, as people asked him how the Word of God could be cancelled. The response is recorded in Q 2:106, where it says Allah can substitute verses in his divine scripture because "he has power over all things."

On this issue, some Muslims say some verses are to be recited but not practiced, while others say some are to be practiced but not recited. So then, hadith is needed to determine the actual practice of Muhammad. This is why Muslims use the Qur'an mostly for memorization, liturgy, and prayers.

Q 2:256 is the "no compulsion" verse and is abrogated by Q 9:29, and Q 9 is said to be the last revelation received by Muhammad.[6]

Qur'an 3:84 reads: "Say: (O Muhammad)[7] We believe in Allah and that which is revealed unto us and that which was revealed unto Abraham and Ishmael and Isaac and Jacob and the tribes, and that which was vouchsafed unto Moses and Jesus and the prophets from their Lord. We make no distinction between any of them, and unto Him we have surrendered."

Qur'an 3:84 is a difficult verse for Muslims to deal with and so the necessity of making it sound different than it actually reads. The Holy Qur'an version's editor quite unclearly remarks that to reject the final revelation to Muhammad is to "renounce guidance."

Is there any indication of abrogation in the Bible? There are two examples that quickly come to mind. In the Hebrew Bible, the Old Testament, if someone drew an Israelite away from the worship of God, or into apostasy, that person was to be stoned to death. See

---

4 Muhammad Marmaduke Pickthall, The Glorious Qur'an (Elmhurst, NY: Tahrike Tarsile Qur'an, Inc., 2000).

5 See my essay "Abrogation or Progressive Revelation?" in regard to this issue.

6 Not all Qur'ans are identical in terms of citations, and this can cause confusion. Different Muslim scholars prefer different versions.

7 The Holy Qur'an version lacks the parenthetical phrase, but in a footnote makes sure the reader understands that only those who embrace Islam have true religion. This verse, 3:84, quite clearly indicates that no distinction is made between the books given to Moses and Jesus, and that which was revealed from Allah.

Deuteronomy 13:10 on this point. There is nothing similar in the New Testament.

Also, in Leviticus 20:10-21, there is mention of the stoning of adulterers. But in the New Testament—John's Gospel, chapter 8—is the account of a woman taken in adultery. Jesus prevents the carrying out of the Old Testament requirement. And nothing else in the New Testament suggests that we are to obey the strictures of Leviticus 20.

Christians have traditionally understood that the purpose of the law is to show humans their sinfulness, and that salvation is not to be found in the keeping of the law. It is plain that Jesus fulfills and completes the law in His death and resurrection. My approach is to explain that what might seem like abrogation is really fulfillment, a forward-looking prophetic word.

Allah, the Great Schemer Who Will Lead Astray

Muslims may be driven to religious compulsions by the fear of hellfire, since Allah is a schemer—even the best of schemers—and may even lead one astray. There is no assurance of salvation in Islam. One never knows how the scales might appear on the Last Day.

Qur'an 3:54 states: "And they (the disbelievers) schemed, and Allah schemed (against them): and Allah is the best of schemers." Qur'an 18:17, "He whom Allah guideth, he indeed is led aright, and he whom He sendeth astray for him thou wilt not find a guiding friend."

Believing in Jesus Results in Hellfire

Qur'an 5:72 reads: "They surely disbelieve who say: 'Lo! Allah is the Messiah, son of Mary.' The Messiah (himself) said: 'O Children of Israel, worship Allah, my Lord and your Lord.' Lo! Whoso ascribeth partners unto Allah, for him Allah hath forbidden Paradise. His abode is the Fire. For evil-doers there will be no helpers."

Believing that Jesus is deity, as God the Father is deity, means ascribing a partner to Allah. Muhammad thought the Christian Trinity was God the Father (Allah), Jesus, and Mary. In that part of the world and at that period, Muhammad would not have been the only one with that understanding. Muhammad saw himself as battling against pagan idolatry—and this prior to the visits with "Gabriel" on Mount Hira. (That encounter was not with an angel, but with a jinn—a demon—that changed and perverted Muhammad's life. Please see the essay "Who is Muhammad's Gabriel?")

It is plain to see that the author of all that is Islam has but one goal and that is to prevent a person from turning to Jesus Christ for salvation. This is, of course, the strategy of the chief demon, Satan. This is the bottom line.

Christians Worship a Man

Muslims say that it is wrong to worship Jesus since He is a man. Though they are aware of passages in Scripture that clearly show that Jesus is both God and man, they will ignore this or insist it is error.

Passages in Scripture that point to the deity of Jesus are: Isaiah 7:14, where the one born of the virgin is called Immanuel, which means "God with us." Then Isaiah 9:6, where the "Son" is "Wonderful Counselor, Mighty God, Everlasting Father, Prince of Peace."

In the New Testament, the following passages clearly point to the deity of Jesus: John 1:1, 14; 5:18; 10:30, 33; 12:45; 14:6, 9; 2 Corinthians 4:4; Colossians 1:15; Hebrews 1:3; and 1 John 5:20.

Contradictions in the Qur'an

It is said there are 120 contradictions in the Qur'an. Only a few will be listed here.

- Moses and the burning bush: compare Q 20:9–24 with Q 27:7–14 and Q 28:19–33
- Moses' childhood: compare Q 20:35–40 with Q 28:7; 11:13
- Israel's obedience: compare Q 2:38–59 with Q 7:161–162
- Moses and the sorcerers, or magicians, of Egypt: compare Q 20:65–73 with Q 26:41–52
- Do Muslims and Christians worship the same God? compare Q 109:1–6 with Q 2:139
- Allah's forgiveness, or non-forgiveness, of adultery: compare Q 4:48 with Q 4:153

Note: The verses immediately above are from the same *surah*, or chapter, yet differ significantly. This is because the Qur'an has been pasted together—and that early on—and it does not run consecutively. It is a jumble of segments patched together. When many variant recitations of the Qur'an were causing dissension among Muslims, Uthman (644–655), the third caliph, or successor, to Muhammad, gathered or recalled all Qur'anic manuscripts and destroyed them by fire. He then issued an official, standardized version. Many Muslims protested, and the history of this remains. And no attempts are made by Muslims to hide this fact.

- Compulsion, or no compulsion, in religion: compare Q 2:256 with Q 9:29. This ninth surah is said to be the last revelation of Allah through Gabriel to Muhammad.
- Number of creation days: compare Q 7:54; 10:3; 11:7 (six days) with Q 41:9–12 (two days)
- Order of Allah's creation of earth and the heavens: compare Q 2:29 with Q 79:29–30
- Materials Allah used to create man: compare Q 15:26 (clay and black mud) with Q 25:54 (water), Q 30:20 (dust), and Q 96:2 (a clot of blood)

Caution: Many Islamic scholars are aware of contradictions in the Qur'an; most Muslims are not. The scholars may shrug off a mention of a contradiction with something like, "There are contradictions in the Bible," or, "You are not using the best translation of the Qur'an," or, "You have to know Arabic to get the full and accurate recitations." Or, you may simply get a smile and, "Only Allah knows, and He is all knowing." At this point it is best to move on.

The average Muslim will either not know how to respond when presented with something they know nothing about, or stop communicating at all. Others may say they will have to research the issue. Once again, for the Christian, the objective is to plant a Gospel seed. Presenting something that goes to the credibility of the Qur'an or questions the authority of Muhammad, and thus Allah, may trigger a fear response from a Muslim. The Christian apologist/evangelist will want to pray for the gift of humility when speaking with Muslims.

Crucifixion Is Pagan

Muslims believe that Jesus' crucifixion is paganistic. They will speak of ancient cults where children were sacrificed to various gods and goddesses, which is in fact historical. And they will point to the sacrificial system in the law of Moses.

The death of Jesus on the cross is, in fact, God dying in place of the sinner. His death is not a sacrifice to appease God. The distinction is crucial. "Sin when it is fully grown brings forth death" (James 1:15). Rather than the sinner dying, Jesus dies in the sinner's place.

Muslims categorically deny that Jesus died on a cross or that He died at all. This is perhaps the key point with Muslims as they know the death of Jesus on the cross is the core of Christianity. On this point, examine my treatment of Ahmed Deedat's book on the crucifixion.

The Crusades[8]

For the most part, the Crusades were launched in defense of European nations after two-thirds of the Christian world had been conquered, over a period of several centuries, by Muslim armies. For centuries after the Crusades, Muslims understood this and held no grudge against Crusaders, until modern times. Islamic terrorists like to protest that their murder is in retaliation for what the Crusaders did.

The actions of some Christians do not necessarily say anything about Christianity, just as the actions of some Muslims do not necessarily say anything about Islam. "All have sinned"—we know this, and simply because someone is a Christian does not mean they are without sin. That said, it is only right to recognize that the Crusades were conducted during the Dark Ages, during which genuine biblical Christianity was hard to find.

Historically, Augustine developed the "just war" concept, which essentially taught that Christians could defend themselves when attacked. Then, during the Crusades, the concept of "holy war" emerged, which taught that Christians could go on the offensive. Indeed, Crusaders were promised blessing from God if they fought in the wars against Islam. It must be made clear that nowhere in the New Testament or in the words and deeds of Jesus is there anything like a just or holy war. To this day, there are Christians who will embrace, at least, the "just war" concept.

Difference between the Bible and the Qur'an

Burning of the Qur'an is a major sin, since the Qur'an is thought to be eternal, according to the traditionalists. The Bible is not so considered. The Bible is not deity; it is a book, though containing inspired writing. The Bible is *rhema*, Greek for "a written word," and

---

8 See my essay "Were the Crusaders and Inquisitors Christians? Yes, No, Maybe" for a fuller discussion of the important issue of the Crusades.

not *logos*, or deity. The eternal Word, or Logos, is Jesus. As it is said in John 1:14, "And the Word [logos] became flesh and dwelt among us, and we have seen his glory, glory as of the only Son from the Father, full of grace and truth."

The Qur'an is revealed; the Bible is inspired. Muhammad supposedly received the Qur'an from Gabriel, who got the revelation from Allah. Muhammad, it is claimed by Islam, did nothing to shape the message; he only relayed it.

The Qur'an, then, has no other corroboration than a seventh-century Arabian male—the witness of one person. The Scripture, both the Hebrew and Greek portions—Old and New Testaments, has many authors living in vastly different cultures—prophets, kings, apostles—inspired by God over a period of not less than fifteen hundred years. And throughout, the same essential message is consistently told, that God would send His servant, the Messiah, to establish His kingdom forever.

Forgiveness

One problem Muslims have involves a misunderstanding about the grace of God freely given. For the Muslim this means that no Christian goes to hell. The question becomes, Why should any Christian do good? Isn't it better to earn God's favor by obeying laws?

Essentially, this reflects a lack of understanding about the nature of forgiveness. God's love and grace produce a desire to please Him and be a faithful follower of Jesus, doing what He commanded. It has nothing to do with pleasing God to earn salvation, but living a thankful life for the gift of forgiveness. We forgive because of Jesus' example of forgiveness, and we treasure His forgiveness because it is at the heart of our salvation.

Grace

Muslims misunderstand grace. They will say that Christians are free to sin since they are going to heaven regardless. They do not see that grace leads one to obedience, but instead believe that Christians are free to sin because of salvation by grace. Paul speaks to this issue in Romans 6:1-14. Though Christians still sin, Jesus took all our sin—past, present, and future—upon Himself on the cross. John points out in 1 John 1:8-2:2, that Christians are to confess sin. The paradox is all our sin is removed and forever, yet it is important to daily confess our sin. Grace is not a cover for continual sinning. Islam's salvation is based upon works, thus God's grace to sinners is unacceptable.

The "Holy" Spirit in the Qur'an

In Qur'an 5:110 we find: "Then Allah saith: O Jesus, son of Mary! Remember My favour unto thee and unto thy mother; how I strengthened thee with the holy Spirit, so that thou spakest unto mankind in the cradle as in maturity; and how I taught thee the Scripture and Wisdom and the Torah and the Gospel, and how thou didst shape of clay as it were the likeness of a bird by My permission, and didst blow upon it and it was a bird by My permission, and thou didst heal him who was born blind and the leper by My permission; and how thou didst raise the dead by My permission; and how I restrained the children of Israel from (harming) thee when thou camest unto them with clear proofs, and those of them who disbelieved exclaimed: This is naught else than mere magic."

Note: This mention of the "holy Spirit" (notice the lower case "h") is problematic for Muslims. In every case when I have asked, "Who is this referring to—the angel Gabriel, Allah, Muhammad, or someone else?" the answer I receive is, "I will have to do some research on this matter." No answer is ever forthcoming.

The content of the verse above is obviously coming from the Gospel of Thomas, a non-biblical writing that depicts Jesus according to gnostic understanding. It is also a thorny issue for Muslims, who will try to quickly move to another topic.

Jesus Ascended, Not Resurrected

Quran 4:158 says, "But Allah took him up unto himself." This verse comes after verse 157, which argues that Jesus did not die on the cross. Thus, Islam teaches that Jesus did not die, but ascended, and thus He was not resurrected.

In Q 3:52–55, the disciples righteously follow Allah, and Allah promises to exalt Jesus' followers, making them superior to others until the Day of Resurrection.

Jesus Not Crucified

The Qur'an teaches that Jesus was not killed or crucified. Q 4:157 reads: "And because of their saying: We slew the Messiah Jesus son of Mary, Allah's messenger—They slew him not nor crucified, but it appeared so unto them; and lo! Those who disagree concerning it are in doubt thereof; they have no knowledge thereof save pursuit of a conjecture; they slew him not for certain." Another version of the Qur'an puts it thus: "He was not killed, nor was he crucified, but so it was made to appear."

Note: This is a core issue for both Muslims and Christians. Either Jesus died by crucifixion or He did not. Either Islam or Christianity is in error, and every Muslim is fully aware of this.

Islam will appeal to three different views. One is the swoon theory—that he appeared to have died, much like some gnostics claim, but was revived later. A second view is substitution, that Simon of Cyrene, or even Judas Iscariot, died instead of Jesus. A third variation of this theme is that Jesus' face appeared on someone else who was dying on the cross.

In his very wonderful book *No God but One: Allah or Jesus?*, Nabeel Qureshi shows that Qur'an 4:157 reflects the teaching of Basilides, a second-century gnostic leader whose ideas survived for centuries, even into this present age. "Irenaeus, 130–202 AD, records the following concerning Basilides teaching about Jesus' death on the cross: 'He (Christ) did not himself suffer death, but Simon, a certain man of Cyrene, being compelled, bore the cross in his stead; so that this later being transfigured by him, that he might be thought to be Jesus, was crucified, through ignorance and error, while Jesus himself received the form of Simon, and standing by, laughed at them.'"[9] This is from Irenaeus book, *Against Heresies*. Nabeel states that the Muslim belief that Jesus did not die on a cross is based on faith in Islam, not on historical fact.

Basilides taught that Jesus was the *nous*, or mind, from God and could not have had a material body—so then, He could not be crucified. So the Qur'anic teaching that Jesus

---

9 Nabeel Qureshi, *No God but One: Allah or Jesus?* (Grand Rapids, MI: Zondervan, 2016), p.179.

was not crucified is traceable back to the second century. The Arabian Peninsula was inhabited by gnostic groups and monks for centuries before the days of Muhammad, and it was from these people that Muhammad likely learned.

The Romans and the Jews saw crucifixion as a tremendous stigma. Deuteronomy 21:23 states that to die on a tree is to be cursed of God. For the Jew, it would be impossible for the Messiah to die in such a way. To the Roman, only the worst of the worst would be put to death by crucifixion. For the Muslim, the one Christian doctrine they hate almost as much as associating partners with Allah is Jesus' death on the cross for our sin. This doctrine alone is enough to invalidate Islam's reward system of salvation by works.

A telling point is that there is no record of anyone surviving a Roman crucifixion. If Jesus had survived, for whatever reason, it would have been considered a huge miracle by early believers and Romans alike. Early on, the crucifixion was problematic for the evangelists and missionaries, but the core Gospel message was never altered because our salvation was won at the cross. The early followers of Jesus, having been told on at least three occasions by Jesus that He would be crucified, did not or could not believe it.

Not only are there many passages in the New Testament describing encounters with the crucified and risen Messiah Jesus, there are also extra-biblical accounts. For instance, Josephus, the Jewish historian writing a history of the Jewish people for a Roman audience in the latter third of the first century, speaks of Jesus' crucifixion. So does Tacitus, another Roman historian. Pliny the Younger does as well while writing to Trajan (98–117). Reporting about Christians, he said, "Where Nero's scapegoats for the fire of 64 AD are those people loathed for their vices, who were commonly styled Christians, a name derived from the word, "Christ," who was executed by the procurator Pontius Pilate when Tiberius was emperor..."

Note: There are many passages in the New Testament, especially in the letters of Paul, that speak of the crucifixion and resurrection of Jesus. The apologist and witness for Christ will want to be aware of these passages.

It is often argued that Paul never knew Jesus during His earthly ministry, and was not present at the crucifixion or at any of the resurrection appearances. But, at minimum, he knew many who witnessed both. In addition, Jesus appeared to him on the Damascus Road; thus Paul both saw Jesus and heard His voice.)

Muhammad: The Final Prophet?

Islam claims that all who followed prophets like Adam, Noah, Abraham, Moses, David, and so on are also considered Muslims, even if they were born ages before Muhammad.

Since so many did not follow these prophets, Islam claims Allah sent Muhammad, and in Allah's mercy he gave us the Qur'an and Islam. Thus Muhammad is the final prophet.

Note: Islam is not the only religion to claim to be founded by the "final prophet." We think of Mormonism's Joseph Smith, but there are many other, lesser final prophets.

The parallels between Islam and Mormonism, by the way, are staggering and very revealing. Muslims can be very much aware of this, too. Both have a last prophet, the last revelation in a book, plenty of laws, and plural marriage (most Mormons have abandoned or were forced to abandon polygamy), and both attempt to live their lives under the laws of their religion. In both, the early years saw persecution and the development of a cadre of elders who refined the religion. And I could go on.

Paul: The Inventor of Christianity?

The issue of the place of Paul is a major consideration. Muslim scholars particularly attack Paul, saying it was Paul who created Christianity. For example, Muslim scholars argue that Paul disregarded the law, but that Jesus meant to fulfill it. This is a misunderstanding of Matthew 5:17: "Do not think that I have come to abolish the Law or the Prophets; I have not come to abolish them but to fulfill them."

Jesus says essentially that the law and prophets point to Him. The law shows that we are lawbreakers, thus sinners, who cannot be with the Creator God in heaven. The prophets point to the coming and triumph of the Messiah. So then, Jesus does fulfill the law and the prophets by taking our transgressions upon Himself on the cross and fulfilling all the prophets said about the coming King and kingdom.

Muslims will argue that Paul never saw Jesus, and that Paul does not comment much on the life of Jesus. It is not absolutely certain that Paul did not see Jesus during His ministry. He would have heard much about Him while persecuting His followers in the very early stages of the Church in Jerusalem.

The Qur'an does not mention Paul or refer to him in any way.

Predestination

One of Islam's Six Articles of Belief is predestination. For Islam, the idea of predestination is linked to fatalism, in that everything has been determined. Whatever happens is the will of Allah.

It must be noted that the Sunni branch of Islam has a belief in Allah's unlimited power, while Shia Islam speaks of Allah's power as limited. Most Muslims believe, however, that Allah knows all and nothing happens outside of his will. Again, this may be termed predestination, or fatalism, but it boils down to the idea that Allah determines all. (Read much more on predestination in our chapter "A Summary of *Understanding Islamic Theology*.")

Islamic scholars often accuse Christians of being predestinarians, while insisting they are not. This is another area where it is difficult to score a point. My approach is to simply point out that God is sovereign and Lord of all. But that all that happens is not the direct will of God. There is a demonic force and sinful behavior produces results.

The Qur'an: Is It Eternal?

A conflict developed in the ninth century, termed the "Islamic Inquisition." Mihna is the Arabic term used to describe this. It was an Islamic inquisition over *tawhid* imposed during the reign of the seventh Abbasid caliph, Al-Mammun in AD 813. He established a dynasty that lasted for 750 years. He stated that the Qur'an is a created book and thus not eternal. He was one of the so-called "rationalists."

On the other hand, the "traditionalists" hold that the Qur'an is eternal. If eternal, then tawhid is compromised, as there are two that are eternal, Allah and the Qur'an. The rationalists quote Qur'an 43:2–3, "By the Book, That makes things clear, We have made it A Qur'an in Arabic, That ye may be able To understand (and learn wisdom)." Then, if it is "made," it cannot be eternal. The inquisition went on for fifteen years when Al-Mammun forced the issue. He said that the worst of Muslims are those who say the Qur'an is eternal, which makes them "the tongue of the devil."

The traditionalists dominate Islam today and hold that the Qur'an is eternal and exists in Paradise now. But at the same time, they will resort to saying, "Bila Kayb," meaning something like, "Who knows these things!" The idea being that both concepts are true at once, despite the irrationality of it.

Note: The Qur'an is the eternal word of God for Muslims. Jesus is the eternal Word of God for Christians.

Salvation

Islam teaches that the real problem for people is ignorance, and so one must be guided to live the good life. The core teaching of Islam, then, is that people must learn what to believe, *aqeeda*, and how to live, Shariah, so they can earn the pleasure of Allah.

In Islam, the way to life is conformity to a code of laws. In Christianity the way to life is a Person.

Islam sees the world living in ignorance and thus is compelled to dispel that ignorance and darkness by teaching Shariah and enforcing its laws. Christianity sees the world as broken and proclaims that God Himself is the only means of reconciliation and forgiveness, based on the work of Jesus the Messiah dying in the sinner's place on the cross.

It is obvious that Muhammad—and/or whoever or whatever was Muhammad's prime mover (see the essay "Who Is Muhammad's Gabriel?")—knew that Christianity stood directly in opposition to Muhammad's message. For instance, Qur'an 5:72 says, "They surely disbelieve who say: Lo! Allah is the Messiah, son of Mary. The Messiah (himself) said: O Children of Israel, worship Allah, my Lord and your Lord. Lo! Whoso ascribeth partners unto Allah, for him Allah hath forbidden Paradise. His abode is the fire. For evil-doers there will be no helpers."

For Muslim people, the above passage is a most effective tool to keep them away from salvation in Jesus Christ. It is only the power of the Holy Spirit that can bring a Muslim to faith in Jesus.

Sexual Relations

Men can have sex with female captives, or participate in sex slavery, and this comes from Q 4:24: "And all married women (are forbidden unto you)[10] save those (captives) whom your right hands possess. It is a decree of Allah for you." This is also supported in the Sunnah: *Sahih Muslim* 3432, 3371; *Sunan abi Dawud* 11.2150, and *Bukhari* 3:46, 718. Q 4:24 sanctions having a number of wives.

---

10   Words or phrases in parentheses are not original to the Qur'an but have been added by various Muslim scholars/editors over the centuries.

Muta marriage, or temporary marriage—maybe for an hour, a day, or a week—is found in many hadith. This is found mostly with Shia Islam.

The Qur'an sanctions women being beaten (scourged). "Men are in charge of women, because Allah hath made the one of them to excel the other, and because they spend of their property (for the support of women). So good women are the obedient, guarding in secret what Allah hath guarded. As for those from whom ye fear rebellion, admonish them and banish them to beds apart, and scourge them. Then if they obey you, seek not a way against them. Lo! Allah is ever High Exalted. Great" (Q 4:34).

(**Caution**: Many Muslims know that the New Testament, especially in Paul's letters, teaches that the husband is to be the head of the wife. Muslims will not understand the teaching that Christ is the head of the Church, as the Bridegroom, and that the Church is the Bride. It is an area that can be mentioned but has the potential for confusion and misunderstanding.)

Shariah Law

Shariah law is based on four sources: the Qur'an, hadith, *ijma*, or consensus explained by imams, and *qiyas*, or analogous reasoning. (See the chapters on Shariah law for a fuller examination of Shariah law for both Shia and Sunni Islam.)

The Trinity

Qur'an 4:171 reads: "O People of the Scripture! Do not exaggerate in your religion nor utter aught concerning Allah save the truth. The Messiah, Jesus son of Mary, was only a messenger of Allah, and His word which he conveyed unto Mary, and a spirit from Him. So believe in Allah and His messengers, and say not 'Three'—Cease! (it is) better for you!—Allah is only One God. Far is it removed from His Transcendant Majesty that he should have a son. His is all that is in the heavens and Allah that is in the earth. And Allah is sufficient as Defender."

In Qur'an 5:116, Allah accuses Jesus, son of Mary, of saying that He and His mother are gods beside Allah.

Note: Islam rejects polytheism, as do Christianity and Judaism. In ways that are not crystal clear, Muhammad thought the Christians worshipped three gods, the *Transcendant Majesty*, Jesus, and Mary. This is not the proper understanding of the Christian Trinity, however. Indeed, Muhammad thought that the Creator God had sex with the god Mary and birthed Jesus. This was repugnant to Muhammad, and so it should have been. Muhammad was, in many ways, a victim of the period and place where he lived.

It was some time, perhaps as long as two centuries, before the Church was able to come to grips with the mystery that is the Trinity. From many passages in Scripture it is clear that the Creator God (Father) is indeed deity. Further, that Jesus is Immanuel, God with us, is clear. The Spirit of God, a person and not some sort of ghost or apparition, is also God. So, then, we have three, but an echad, a unity of plurality—unified in mind, purpose, essence, and being—a three in one or one in three. This is illustrated in Genesis 2:24, where a man and wife are an echad—two, yet one.)

Unusual Passages in the Qur'an

It is probable that most Muslims, even trained Muslim apologists, will not be aware of these interesting passages in the Qur'an. Using them in debate or discussion might not be appropriate—then again, they just might.

Child killing: The Qur'an teaches that Allah allowed idol worshippers to kill their children. This is found in Qur'an 6:137–140. Qur'an 6:137 reads: "Thus have their (so-called) partners (of Allah) made the killing of their children to seem fair unto many of the idolaters, that they may ruin them and make their faith obscure for them. Had Allah willed (it otherwise), they had not done so. So leave them alone with their devices."

The sleepers: In Qur'an 18:9–25 is the story of a certain number of youths and their dog who escaped the persecution of idol worshipers that wanted to punish them for their belief in monotheism. They were directed by Allah to a cave where they went to sleep for many years. The sun altered its course to help them. No one but Allah knows how many youths there were, but some say seven. With the addition of their dog, there were eight. No one but Allah knows how long they slept, but in verse 25 it is given that they slept for 309 years.

A peculiar resurrection story: Qur'an 2:259 relates the story of a person who observed a ruined city and wondered how Allah would raise the bodies of its ancient inhabitants. Allah caused this skeptic to die and after one hundred years brought him back to life. Allah asked him, "How long hast thou tarried?" He thought only one day. He was told that he was gone for one hundred years. His food and drink were still fresh, but his donkey had turned to dry bones.

Superman: In Qur'an 18:83–99 is the story of a man Allah created who could do anything. His name was Dhu'l-Qarneyn. Among other things, he traveled on a road so far west that he saw where the sun landed in a pool of black mud. He traveled on another road so far to the east that he saw a kind of people who were close to the rising sun as it started its journey. They had been left without any protection against the nearness of the sun's burning rays. Another of his exploits was to construct a huge dam, which completely filled the space between two steep mountains. The dam was made of iron blocks coated with molten lead, which was so massive that the people of Gog and Magog could not scale it or dig through it to disturb their neighbors. It is said the great dam will survive until the Judgment Day.

Elephants and birds: In Qur'an 105:1–5 is the story of an army that used elephants and was once defeated by Allah. Allah caused swarms of flying creatures (birds?) to pelt the elephants with stones of baked clay. The elephants were utterly destroyed, being made like green crops devoured by cattle (maybe cow pies?).

Jinn are converted. In Qur'an 72:1–15 is the story of jinn flying up to heaven, the edge thereof, and listening to the reading of the Qur'an. They saw the meteors and other protectors, which were thrown at the jinn to keep them away from hearing what was taking place around Allah's throne. They heard the message that Allah is one and that he has no wife or children, and they believed the message. Some became believers—Muslims—but some did not and are the fuel for the fires of hell.

Killing of Allah's camel: In Qur'an 11:61–68 is the story of the tribe Thamud, who were warned by their brother Salih to serve Allah and worship him. But they took issue with him, saying they had doubts. Salih presented them with the "camel" of Allah, a she-camel, and he warned them she must not be harmed. But they hamstrung her. Salih prophesied that they would be punished after three days. On the morning of the predicted day they were all found "prostrate" (dead?) in their dwellings.

Sabbath breakers turned into apes: In Qur'an 2:65–66 is the story of Jews (those who broke the Sabbath). They were made an example by being turned into apes, "despised and hated." This is intended to be an example for future generations.

Violent Jihad in the Qur'an and Hadith

Q 2:256 says there is to be no compulsion in religion. Muslims typically say this is abrogated by Q 9:29, which tells Muslims to fight Jews and Christians. This last chapter of the Qur'an to be revealed by Gabriel to Muhammad reads: "Fight against such of those who have been given the Scripture as believe not in Allah not the Last Day, and forbid not that which Allah hath forbidden by His messenger, and follow not the religion of truth, until they pay the tribute readily, being brought low" (Qur'an 9:29).

Q 28:59 teaches Muslims to kill wrongdoers.

Q 3:151 reads: "We shall cast terror into the hearts of those who disbelieve because they ascribe unto Allah partners, for which not warrant hath been revealed. Their habitation is the Fire, and hapless the abode of the wrong-doers."

Note: Casting terror into the hearts of people is a core goal of violent jihad, and is a tactic used by Islamic terrorist groups in this present era. One reason for this is that Muslims think that by blowing up innocents, their cause will triumph. It is largely the only tactic they are left with. Their error is they misunderstand the power and will of non-Muslim countries, especially those with a democratically based political system.

In hadith are stories where Muhammad orders the slaughter of innocents in order to encourage other enemies to surrender and submit to Islam by becoming either Muslim or dhimmis.

Muhammad thought so much of fighting in jihad that it is reported that he said there was nothing equal to it in this world (*Bukhari* 4:56.2924, 4:52.50).

Muslims use Matthew 10:34, "I have not come to bring peace, but a sword," to say Jesus supported war. But the biblical context has to do with inter-family difficulties and not warfare.

The verses promoting violence against Jews, Christians, and polytheists are all found in chapter 9 of the Qur'an—the last major revelation according to the Islamic records. It is noteworthy that the Qur'an's last words, the last revelation from Allah to Muhammad through Gabriel, are among the most violent words of all. Q 47:4: "Now when you meet in battle those who disbelieve, then it is smiting of the necks until, when ye have routed them, then making fast of bonds; and afterward either grace or ransom till the war lay down its burdens."

"Smiting of the necks" in the above verse came to be interpreted by jihadists as cutting off heads back in the seventh century and in this present century. It was also interpreted as a "chop" by a Muslim leader, with the hand to the neck to demonstrate that the non-believer was in submission. It was intended to humiliate.

Allah also orders crucifixion for those who make war against Allah's Islam, and this when the armies of Islam are in either a defensive or offensive mode. From Q 5:33 we read: "The only reward of those who make war upon Allah and His messenger and strive after corruption in the land will be that they will be killed or crucified, or have their hands and feet on alternate sides cut off, or will be expelled out of the land. Such will be their degradation in the world, and in the Hereafter theirs will be an awful doom."

Q 8:67: "It is not for any Prophet to have captives until he hath made slaughter in the land."

Caution: The hadith are replete with references to Muhammad's orders that apostates or enemies be killed. He did engage in killing, even beheading captives. Only Islamic scholars would be equipped to discuss relevant hadith passages on the subject, but for the most part any discussion would not be welcome. It is enough to know of this and it is appropriate to state such. Then the topic, perhaps the entire debate or discussion, would come to a conclusion. And it is right here where debates and discussions are won or lost. I have gotten angry more than once in such circumstances, and it certainly did not enhance my witness.

Other important verses from the Qur'an on jihad are Q 2:190, 193, 216.

A Final Word

There are many excellent websites and books available today that will be of great help to those who desire to share the message of Jesus with Muslims. The books by Nabeel Qureshi are especially helpful.[11] I suggest the teachings and videos of David Wood.[12] The *Answering Islam* site is so wonderful.[13] There are so many solid Christians that God has called into reaching out to Muslims; we are indeed blessed here.[14]

This section on equipping Christians in debating and witnessing to Muslims, formally or informally, is a mere starter kit—a place to start and something that can be built upon. Though I have been writing on Islam since 2002, I consider myself to be just a beginner. It is a lifelong pursuit, but a valuable one, since I have been able to grow in my understanding of the Bible and study ways to communicate the Gospel I had never thought of before.

Expect spiritual warfare to come your way as you pursue Muslim evangelism. It is highly likely that anyone who desires to reach out to Muslims with the Gospel will encounter attacks from the enemy. This enemy is not from Muslims, but from the prince of demons—Satan. But He who is with us and in us is greater than he who is in the world.

---

11 nabeelqureshi.com/.

12 acts17.net/.

13 answering-islam.org/.

14 We suggest jesustomuslims.org, itl-usa.org, afshinjavid.com, koomeministries.com, aishamydaughter.org, answeringmuslims.com, and many more.

19

WAS JESUS CRUCIFIED?

This will be an answer to Ahmed Deedat's book of the above name. From Wikipedia's introduction to Ahmed Deedat we find:

> **Ahmed Hoosen Deedat** (1 July 1918–8 August 2005) was a South African writer and public speaker of Indian descent. He was best known as a Muslim missionary, who held numerous inter-religious public debates with evangelical Christians, as well as video lectures on Islam, Christianity, and the Bible. Deedat established the IPCI, an international Islamic missionary organization, and wrote several widely distributed booklets on Islam and Christianity. He was awarded the King Faisal International Prize in 1986 for his fifty years of missionary work. He wrote and lectured in English.[1]

Introduction

Muslims must strongly and aggressively attack the crucifixion and death of Jesus. Deedat is fully aware that without the cross and death of Jesus there is no Christianity. If salvation is found in the atoning death of Jesus on the cross, there is no reason or need for Muhammad, the Qur'an, and Islam.

One of the principle tenets of Islam is that Jesus ascended to heaven and did not suffer death. He is to return on the day of judgment and declare His allegiance to Muhammad, whereupon, Jesus will suffer death.

Mr. Deedat does seem to agree that Jesus was crucified on a cross. However, he argues that Jesus did not die on the cross. He relies on articles by some who claim to be Christians that support his arguments. I will make no attempt to examine each and every distortion and conclusion made by Ahmed Deedat. Mostly, I will mention key arguments of his and present counter arguments.

Mr. Deedat uses the King James Version of the Bible in his book, while I will quote from the English Standard Version.

Point 1

On the opening page (p. 3), Mr. Deedat cites Deuteronomy 18:20: "But the prophet who

---

1 wikipedia.com.

presumes to speak a word in My name that I have not commanded him to speak, or who speaks in the name of other gods, that same prophet shall die."

He means that if Jesus did die, then it would be because He[2] was a false prophet. The Deuteronomy passage, however, is not a prophetic word about the coming Messiah, thus does not apply to Jesus, but a reference to a common event—people stating they were prophets and giving prophecies.

He then proceeds to make it clear in the most emphatic terms that "the Jews did not kill Jesus nor crucify him." In fact, Mr. Deedat states, "The Muslims love and revere Jesus Christ to such an extent that even the thought of him being led to the cross is repugnant to them. How could God allow His Chosen Messenger—Jesus Christ—to bear the ignominy and nakedness of the Cross?"

Mr. Deedat denies that Jesus died on the cross and comes close to saying Jesus was not crucified. It is apparent that Mr. Deedat does not expect his readers to look too deeply.

Mr. Deedat notes Basilides, an early gnostic Christian who taught in Alexandria, Egypt, from AD 117 to 138. The Gnostics, an esoteric religious group, developed some centuries before the time of Christ and incorporated aspects of Christianity into their system. They devised a method to fit Jesus into their views. They denied that deity could have any contact with sinful human flesh and taught that Jesus only appeared to be an actual man. This philosophy is known as Docetism. The idea that someone other than Jesus died on the cross is known as *adoptionism*.

Here Mr. Deedat depends on his readers' unfamiliarity with Basilides to insinuate that he was a Christian. He wants the readers to think that even Christians doubted that Jesus died on the cross.

Point 2

Mr. Deedat mentions a document known as the Gospel of Barnabas (p. 4). Islamic scholars claim that the author of the Gospel of Barnabas was the partner of the apostle Paul, as we read in the book of Acts.

Two copies of the gospel are known. Both were written during the late sixteenth century, one in Spanish and one in Italian. Muslims believe it was an original gospel account of Jesus' ministry but was suppressed due to its view of Jesus, much of which is shared by Islam.

The Gospel of Barnabas denies the deity of Jesus, rejects the Trinity, and denies that Jesus was crucified.[3] Mr. Deedat states: "It is inconceivable that the Gospel of such a great Apostle should have been denied the honour of inclusion in the Canon of the New Testament."

Such a gospel was not known to the Church until the sixteenth century. If it had been known, it would have been noted by scholars, especially those who compare manuscripts.

Mr. Deedat states that three councils of the Church denied the inclusion of the Gospel into the canon of the New Testament, that of the decree of the Western Church, 382 C.E., the decree of Innocent the First, 465 C.E., and the decree of the Council of Gelasius, 496 C.E. He is surprised Barnabas' gospel was rejected, since Barnabas was such

---

2   I will capitalize pronouns referring to Jesus, while Mr. Deedat and the ESV do not.

3   Go to: y-Jesus.com for a detailed account of the Gospel of Barnabas.

a noted apostle. What Mr. Deedat does not say is that the Gospel of Barnabas was not known to the attendees of the three councils mentioned above because it simply did not exist. It hadn't been written yet at the time of these councils. He assumes the reader will not investigate further.

Point 3

Mr. Deedat states, "I propose to advance evidence from the Bible itself, to prove that Christ Jesus was **NEITHER KILLED NOR CRUCIFIED** as the Jews boasted and the Christians believed" (p. 5).

Mr. Deedat, in speaking of the Last Supper, states that it was a somber time since Jesus had just found out that "his own mother and brethren" were in collaboration with the temple authorities in order to betray Him.

Jesus does know of the betrayal by Judas and says so during the supper. He now advises His followers to arm themselves with swords, or so reasons Mr. Deedat based on Luke 22:38—especially the reaction of the disciples, "Look, Lord, here are two swords." Jesus responds with, "It is enough."

In verse 36 of Luke 22, Jesus says, "Let the one who has no sword sell his cloak and buy one." The insinuation is that Jesus is preparing His followers for war against the authorities, which would include the Roman garrison in Jerusalem.

Mr. Deedat bases much on the statements quoted above from Luke 22:35–38. Mr. Deedat argues that Jesus is ready to fight the authorities and avoid arrest and thus, avoid being crucified.

"Two swords" is hardly enough to battle against the hundreds of heavily armed and trained troops. Jesus' words are ironic at best. It would take a legion with thousands of swords, for behind the temple guard stood the legion of soldiers at the Fortress of Antonio in Jerusalem.

Mr. Deedat is a literalist when it suits his purposes.

Point 4

Mr. Deedat speaks of the incarnation of Jesus (p. 7), and quotes passages such as John 5:30, where Jesus says, "I can of Mine own self do nothing," and Mark 10:18, "Why callest thou Me good? there is none good but one, that is, God," and Mark 13:32, where Jesus states only the Father knows of "that day," referring to the coming of the kingdom.

Mr. Deedat then surmises that Jesus does not worry about His followers having only two swords, since He will rely upon God and miracles.

Mr. Deedat apparently does not grasp the extent of the incarnation—the Living Word of God become flesh. Jesus emptied Himself of His deity, as we read in Philippians 2:1–11, for the very purpose of dying a real death on the cross and thus atoning for sin.

Point 5

Mr. Deedat moves to the account of the garden of Gethsemane on the night of Jesus' betrayal. Jesus leaves eight at the edge of the garden, while taking only three with Him—Peter, James, and John—while He prays.

Later, Mr. Deedat will state that the three disciples are "armed to the hilt," while an outer guard, meaning the eight other followers, remain at the entrance to the garden. And, at least Peter, one of the inner three, has a sword. He states: "It is inconceivable that he should now beseech the Head of the Trinity to let him off from his obligation which he had voluntarily (?) undertaken" (p. 9).

Here again we see the failure of Mr. Deedat to grasp the meaning of the incarnation, the Word become flesh. And this is not surprising, since who of us could do so without the help of the Holy Spirit? We have the words of David in Psalm 22:1, "My God, my God, why have You forsaken me?" We know, of course, Jesus uttered these very words while hanging on the cross (Matthew 27:46). What Jesus dreaded most was being separated from the Father. Certainly we cannot even approach understanding such love as that between the Father and the Son.

Jesus knew without doubt what would be the result of taking our sin upon Himself— He must be forsaken by the Father. God is holy; no sin can come before Him or into His presence.

At the sixth hour, high noon, after Jesus had been on the cross three hours, the sky suddenly turned dark. This cosmic symbol of the Father turning from the Son as our sin was placed upon Him was what prompted Jesus to quote Psalm 22:1. Hell is spoken of as "outer darkness" in Matthew 8:12, 22:13, and 25:30. The darkness of hell Jesus then experienced.

Jesus would be on the cross three more hours, and shockingly, these six hours on the cross, as plainly indicated in the Gospel accounts of the crucifixion, are sharply denied by Mr. Deedat. The reason for this denial will be revealed later.

Point 6

Mr. Deedat refers to Luke 22:44 and the account of Jesus praying in the garden, that "His sweat became like great drops of blood falling down on the ground." Mr. Deedat then asks, "Has anyone ever seen anyone sweating blood?" (p. 10). He states that this very question was asked of ten thousand Christians and twenty thousand Muslims at a symposium on the subject, "Was Christ Crucified?" at Cape Town, South Africa. And Mr. Deedat testifies that not even one had seen such.

An examination of the text, Luke 22:44, reveals that Jesus' sweating reminded one of blood but was not blood, but only human sweat. It is a literary device used to say that Jesus was in great agony of spirit. The point is that Mr. Deedat wants to use what he sees as an absurdity as a way of discrediting the Gospel account—and if Luke is tinged, then all the other Gospel accounts are tinged as well. All this is intended to feed into the idea there was no actual crucifixion. But for those who are willing to consider that Jesus did actually sweat blood, medical science has identified a condition called *hematidrosis*, in which the capillaries that supply blood to the sweat glands tear and leak into the sweat ducts in high stress situations, resulting in bloody sweat.[4]

It is noted that there is continual confusion going on here. On the one hand, Jesus'

---

4 W. D. Edwards, W. J. Gabel, and F. E. Hosmer, "On the Physical Death of Jesus Christ," *Journal of the American Medical Association*, 1986 [255:1455–1463].

crucifixion is denied, and on the other, it is admitted. The one issue for Mr. Deedat is that Jesus did not die on the cross. The Qur'an does clearly state, however, that Jesus was neither crucified on the cross nor did He die, but rather ascended into heaven without experiencing death.

Point 7

Mr. Deedat looks to Deuteronomy 21:23, where it says, "A hanged man is cursed by God." The insinuation is that if Jesus was crucified it would show that He was therefore "cursed by God." He follows with the concept that Jesus supposedly did not want to die on the cross, quoting Jesus' statement, "If it be possible, let this cup pass from Me" (Matthew 26:39). The reason Deedat gives for Jesus not wanting to die on the cross is that the Jewish people would then lose "THEIR PROMISED MESSIAH" (p. 11).

Very clever really, but understandable, are Mr. Deedat's manipulations and misunderstandings. I am reminded of what Paul said in 1 Corinthians 1:18: "For the word of the cross is folly to those who are perishing, but to us who are being saved it is the power of God," and 1 Corinthians 2:14: "The natural person does not accept the things of the Spirit of God, for they are folly to him, and he is not able to understand them because they are spiritually discerned." We must remember that this was true of us all prior to our conversions; it was certainly true of me.

Point 8

Mr. Deedat quotes Hebrews 5:7, which reads: "Who in the days of His flesh, when He had offered up prayers and supplications with strong crying and tears unto Him that was able to save Him from death, and was heard in that He feared." His point is that it was not Jesus' intention or goal to die on a cross. Mr. Deedat focuses on "was heard in that He feared." He then wonders what "He feared" means and concludes that the Father heard Jesus' prayers and did not allow Him to die on the cross.

Mr. Deedat attacks the doctrine of "substitutionary atonement," whereby Jesus died as a substitute for sinners, which was determined "before the foundation of the world."[5] His point is that if Jesus' death on the cross was predetermined, it would be akin to suicide.

Then Mr. Deedat says, "If this was the scheme of God for the redemption of mankind then obviously He had made the wrong choice" (p. 13).

Point 9

Going back to the events at the garden of Gethsemane, Mr. Deedat writes: "The manner in which Jesus had deployed his disciples—EIGHT AT THE GATE and an INNER LINE OF DEFENSE, armed to the hilt—shows that Jesus was not prepared to be made a scapegoat for his followers. He had prepared to fight to the bitter end" (p. 13).

When the soldiers guided by Judas arrive at the scene, Mr. Deedat says the three disciples are caught napping. But when Peter, James, and John realize what is happening, they ask Jesus if they should fight. Peter pulls out his sword and cuts the right ear off of the

---

5 See Matthew 25:34; Luke 11:50; Ephesians 1:4; Hebrews 4:3; 1 Peter 1:20; Revelation 13:8.

servant of the high priest. Jesus, according to Mr. Deedat, seeing there is no chance, orders the swords be put away. He does not mention that Jesus heals the man with the ear cut off.

"Armed to the hilt" is a bit over the top. Mr. Deedat desires to reinforce his argument that Jesus did not intend to allow Himself to be crucified, but that He intended to fight. Two swords—even one hundred swords wielded by trained soldiers—would not nearly be sufficient. Mr. Deedat's reach is a mile too long.

It must be pointed out that on three occasions Jesus warns His disciples that He will be crucified. See Matthew 16:21-23, 17:22-23, and 20:17-19. Following the first time Jesus tells His disciples about what is coming, He follows it up with: "If anyone would come after Me, let him deny himself and take up his cross and follow Me" (Matthew 16:24).

To suggest that Jesus does not know He will be crucified is beyond imagination. Mr. Deedat is desperate to deny the crucifixion, but he does so since God dying in our place absolutely nullifies all that is Islam.

Point 10

Mr. Deedat paints the apostles as fearful turncoats by quoting Mark 14:50, where the disciples are depicted as forsaking Jesus and running away, which they do. He says, "In the history of the world, there is no parallel of such dastardly betrayal and despicable desertion" (p. 14).

That the disciples are fearful is plain. They doubted their relationship with Jesus would ever include such a tragic circumstance. They know what will likely be their lot, so they flee. They do not understand that Jesus is heading straight to the cross, as He has already told them three times. They know Jesus is the Messiah, they witnessed His miracles, and they want to reign with Him in the coming kingdom. But they are human beings and do not want to die.

It is not clear to me why Mr. Deedat brings up the point about the fear the apostles experienced, except perhaps to cast disparagement on them, as they are primary witnesses to Jesus' ministry. However, these same apostles include their embarrassing flight to safety in the biblical accounts of the crucifixion, since it is exactly what happened. This also shows they were not ready for, nor were even anticipating, an armed fight with real soldiers.

Point 11

Mr. Deedat moves next to the trial before Pilate and records Pilate's disposition of the case: "HE DELIVERED JESUS UNTO THEM TO BE CRUCIFIED." Then he mentions the dream Pilate's wife has, and also that she says Jesus is a "just man."

Point 12

Mr. Deedat states that the Phoenicians developed the practice of crucifixion. He does not provide any historical data to support this.

This method of execution, Mr. Deedat wants his readers to understand, was specifically designed to inflict maximum pain over a long period of time. Other means of execution, being quickly applied, did not allow for enough suffering.

His point is that Jesus is only on the cross a short time—only three hours—and few would have expired in so short a time. Therefore, the conclusion is: Jesus did not die and was likely not crucified either.

Based on a number of Internet searches, no one mentions the Phoenicians inventing crucifixion. One source credits the Persians doing so around 300 to 400 BC. The Romans then reportedly adopted it themselves.

Another source says the Greeks are credited with developing crucifixion. The Greek historian Herodotus describes the execution of a Persian general by crucifixion close to or during the year 479 BC. Again, the Romans are said to have adopted the practice.

Perhaps the biggest argument Mr. Deedat launches is that Jesus, according to the Gospel accounts, dies too quickly, and thus the story of the cross in the Bible is errant. For reasons not explained, Mr. Deedat does not state where he comes up with the three-hour time frame for Jesus being on the cross. It is plain He is crucified at 9 a.m., or the third hour; then the sky darkens at noon, the sixth hour; and death comes at the ninth hour, 3 p.m. Here are the details:

The third hour:[6]

"And it was the third hour when they crucified Him" (Mark 15:25).

The sixth hour:

"Now from the sixth hour there was darkness over all the land until the ninth hour" (Matthew 27:45).

And when the sixth hour had come, there was darkness over the whole land until the ninth hour" (Mark 15:33).

"It was now about the sixth hour, and there was darkness over the whole land until the ninth hour" (Luke 23:44).

The ninth hour:

"And about the ninth hour Jesus cried out with a loud voice, saying, 'Eli, Eli, lema sabachthani?' that is, 'My God, My God, why have You forsaken Me?'" (Matthew 27:46).

"And at the ninth hour Jesus cried with a loud voice, 'Eloi, Eloi, lema sabachthani?' which means, 'My God, My God, why have You forsaken Me?'" (Mark 15:34).

Point 13

Mr. Deedat finds it impossible for Jesus to have been crucified because He was only on the cross three hours. He states, "The victim INVARIABLY survived the first day, GENERALLY lived up to the second day, and SOMETIMES even up to the fourth and fifth day" (p. 18).

He says the *sadile* (body support) on the cross allowed victims to rest their weight and thus survive longer. Three hours, and dead already! It was impossible, then, for Jesus to have been crucified.

---

6   The day for the Jews began at 6 a.m.—sunrise—so the third hour would be 9 a.m., the sixth hour would be 12 noon, and the ninth hour would be 3 p.m.

Mr. Deedat neglects the fact that Jesus had been scourged, which often killed the victim. The terrible whipping with the long leather straps embedded with pieces of bone and metal at the ends ripped the flesh and left the victim bloody and torn. Also, we know that Jesus stumbled carrying the cross, and Simon of Cyrene, a passerby, was forced to carry Jesus' cross to the execution site. Six hours might be considered a long time to survive under such circumstances.

One other point is that we have no idea of whether or not the cross Jesus was crucified on had a sadile.

How Mr. Deedat calculates that Jesus is on the cross for only three hours is a complete mystery, as he never makes any attempt to prove that assertion.

Point 14

Mr. Deedat talks about the *crurifragium*, which is the process of breaking the legs of a person hung on a cross, to hasten death. When the Roman soldiers, who were likely skilled at conducting executions, came to break Jesus' legs after doing so to the two others hanging beside Jesus, they found they did not need to do so in His case, since Jesus was already dead.

Deedat's insinuation is that Jesus was not dead at all, but unconscious and merely appearing to be dead. The soldiers were fooled. Thus the possibility is opened up that a comatose Jesus could have survived, and would not have had His legs broken.

It is curious that Mr. Deedat goes to the trouble of presenting the possibility that Jesus *survived* being crucified when Islam claims Jesus was *never* crucified. It appears that Mr. Deedat is closing the door to any possibility of Jesus' actual death, at minimum, by suggesting He survived after all. Islam declares that Jesus ascended into heaven without having died.

Point 15

Pilate was surprised to hear that Jesus died so quickly and asked the soldiers to make sure He was really dead. Shortly thereafter, a soldier thrusted a spear into the side of Jesus, and a mixture of blood and water poured out. Mr. Deedat provides information from experts, without references, that Jesus is alive at the point of the spear thrust and survives it.

Deedat asserts that Jesus was then buried in an "airy" and large room. After He came to Himself, He disguised Himself when Mary Magdalene arrived on Sunday morn. Mary supposed she was talking to the gardener. Mr. Deedat describes the meeting of the two with, "Jesus addressed her, giggling beneath his breath, 'Why do you cry'" (p. 23).

Mr. Deedat continues by saying that Jesus warned Mary "TOUCH ME NOT; FOR I AM NOT YET ASCENDED TO MY FATHER." And by this Jesus meant, do not touch my wounds, as I am not yet healed. Jesus has to convince Mary that He is alive.

This changing of the obvious statements in the Gospels so that the reader may be assured that Jesus did not die is calculated to show that Jesus would be able to ascend to heaven, thus matching the scenario of Islam.

Point 16

Mr. Deedat discusses the account of Jesus walking with two disciples who are traveling to

Emmaus. His theory is that Jesus was careful with them, as He was thinking that if they knew who He was, they would attempt to kill Him. Jesus' "effective disguise" was working up to a point, but once the three broke bread together, Jesus might have been discovered, so He simply vanished. Mr. Deedat says, "Jesus felt unsafe in the company of these two disciples" (p. 24).

Luke's account of the incident (Luke 24:13-35) plainly shows that the two disciples are just that—disciples. They recognized who the stranger was at the meal where Jesus broke bread. It is no wild guess that these two had been with Jesus before, very possibly at the Last Supper in the upper room. It is a stretch too far to suggest they might have attacked Jesus, particularly considering how distraught they were thinking He had died.

Point 17

On pages 27-28, Mr. Deedat lists twenty-five reasons the death of Jesus did not occur:

1. That he was reluctant to die
2. He beseeched God for help
3. God "heard" his prayers
4. Angel strengthened him
5. Pilate finds him "not guilty" and
6. His wife sees a dream to save a "just man"
7. On the cross for only three hours
8. The other two were still alive
9. Encyclopaedia Biblica says – "was alive when spear thrust"
10. His legs not broken
11. Thunder, earthquake and eclipse within three hours
12. Pilate "marvels" on hearing about his death
13. Jews doubted his death
14. Placed in a roomy sepulcher
15. Stone had to be removed
16. Always in disguise
17. Forbade Mary to touch him
18. Said "not yet ascended"—not dead yet
19. Mary was not afraid on recognizing him
20. Disciples were terrified on seeing him
21. Ate food within their very sight
22. Never shown himself to the Jews
23. Took only short trips
24. Never said, " I was dead and now I am alive"
25. German scientists say: "Heart never stopped functioning"

I have dealt with most of the twenty-five items above in one form or another earlier. Mr. Deedat, as a Muslim missionary, must come to his conclusions, however preposterous they might be.

He does understand that if Jesus really was crucified, died, and was raised from the dead, Islam is a false religion. He recognizes, as do all knowledgeable Muslims, that Islam and Christianity are mutually exclusive. To "make nice" and suggest that all paths lead to God is disingenuous at best.

Point 18

Mr. Deedat calculates the days between the crucifixion and the resurrection, all while denying both altogether. Matthew 12:40 is quoted: "For just as Jonah was three days and three nights in the belly of the great fish, so will the Son of Man be three days and three nights in the heart of the earth."

Deedat asserts that Jesus died on a Friday, according to the Bible, was in the grave on Saturday, then raised either Saturday just before sunrise or Sunday, or after the sunrise—according to the Gospel accounts. Mr. Deedat reasons then that the total number of days would then be less than three, and the total number of nights would also be less than three. Thus, he sees a major biblical contradiction.

Two points must be made. First, the number three for Jewish people meant a short time, and thus the number three would not necessarily be taken literally. Second, the Jewish people counted even a single hour of a day as one day. For instance, 5 p.m., the last hour of the day in Jewish reckoning, counted as a full day. So then, either way, Jesus' statements about three days and three nights in the "heart of the earth" works fine—Friday, Saturday, and Sunday—three days.

20

ANSWERING A. DEEDAT'S COMBAT KIT AGAINST BIBLE THUMPERS

Mr. Deedat introduces his "kit"[1] thusly: "In the current crusade, the Christian world has launched their 'scud' (The Holy Bible) in two thousand different languages. For the Arabs alone they have published their Holy Scriptures in fifteen different scripts and dialects.... . This manual will enable you to convert the Christian scud into a 'Patriot Missile!'" (p. 2)

The "combat kit" consists of forty-four points. Each one will be presented with Mr. Deedat's subject stated, using his own spelling and formatting for titles and subtitles of sections, though I have rewritten some to make them more understandable. My remarks follow or are interspersed. Mr. Deedat uses the King James Bible as his source, so we will reflect that in our discussion, though I will also use the ESV for comparison.

Point 1: ARABS AND ARABIA: In the Christian Bible

Mr. Deedat shows that Arab lands are mentioned in the Bible by quoting Isaiah 22:13, 41:11, Ezekiel 27:21, and Deuteronomy 33:2. This last passage, according to Mr. Deedat, mentions the name of Muhammad, or something close to it. Upon examination, I cannot find anything in the Hebrew text that could possibly be mistaken for Muhammad. He states the passage speaks of the conquest of Makkah (an ancient spelling for modern day Mecca). The Paran in the text is a city in the tribal area south-southwest of Canaan and is far from Mecca.

Deedat also states that Deuteronomy 32:21 has a reference to Jews being angry with a "foolish nation," which Mr. Deedat takes as a reference to pre-Islamic Arabs.

Point 2: ABRAHAM: He wedded his own sister (Sarah.)

This references Genesis 12:19, where Pharaoh of Egypt scolds Abraham for not telling him that Sarah is his wife and not his sister, a lie he told not only in Genesis 12, but also Genesis 20:12.

Apparently Mr. Deedat cites this to show that Abraham lied to Pharaoh—either that or he wants to say that Abraham wedded his own sister, which is unseemly and suggestive

---

[1] (1992, reproduced 2015 by Faisal Fahim via Amazon's CreateSpace Independent Publishing Platform)

that the Bible is errant, or that the people of the Bible are not upstanding people. This is very interesting, since the passage in Genesis makes it clear that Abraham did lie to Pharaoh. He told a lie in order to protect his wife Sarah. As a beautiful woman, she might have been taken by force if Pharaoh thought she was Abraham's wife. But seen as his sister, she would be available. This is interesting in that Abraham is the father of the Arab nation through Hagar and their son Ishmael.

Then Mr. Deedat writes, "Hagar, Abraham's wife!" He quotes Genesis 16:3 to show that Sarah did give Hagar to Abraham to have children. Mr. Deedat surely knows that it was not an uncommon practice in the second millennium BC for a slave woman to bear children for the slave owner.

Under the heading, "Unfulfilled Prophecy," Mr. Deedat quotes Genesis 17:8, where God gives all of the land of Canaan to Abraham as an everlasting possession. In contradiction to this promise, Abraham never did receive even a single foot of land free, but God gave it to his offspring.

Mr. Deedat says that this promise was never fulfilled, but it may be he intends to say that the promise was fulfilled when Islam conquered the territory. Thus, he neglects the possession of the promised land under the leadership of Joshua forty years following the exodus from Egypt.

Point 3: ABSURDITIES in the Book of God, the Holy Bible

1. A TALKING ass, Numbers 22:22–28. This is the account of a donkey speaking to Balaam.
2. FOUR footed fowls, Leviticus 11:20, but the reference is to winged insects, which the passage says, "are detestable to you."
3. Birth of females a DOUBLE pollution, from Leviticus 12:1, 2, and 5, but the passage speaks of a time of uncleanness for the female, meaning she is not to engage in sexual relationships with her husband. Apparently Mr. Deedat is attempting to cast disparagement upon God or accuse God of treating women poorly who have just given birth.
4. Shamgar KILLS 600 with an ox goad.
5. Samson KILLS A THOUSAND with the jawbone of a donkey, as we read in Judges 15:15–16. The two items (d) and (e) are typical of hero stories that abounded in that and in earlier and later eras. We find these in the Hebrew Bible, and it is highly likely the people at the time did not take them literally.
6. A SEVEN HEADED leopard. Revelation 13:1–2. Mr. Deedat does not understand symbolic, apocalyptic language that involves words with double meanings. The readers of the book of Revelation would not have imagined John to be speaking of an actual leopard with seven heads. No absurdity at all.
7. To eat SHIT and drink PISS. 2 Kings 18:27 and Isaiah 36:12. This is again a situation where Mr. Deedat does not understand that the reference is to dire straits that occur during a time of siege.
8. DUNG on your faces, referencing Malachi 2:3. This is a reference to judgment falling upon a people and is not to be taken literally.

9. To eat cake with SHIT. The reference is to Ezekiel 4:12–15. The passage speaks of the necessity, during terrible times, to have to use dung instead of wood for fuel to cook a meal.
10. Samson has SEX with a whore in Gaza, referencing Judges 16:1. This is what is recorded of Samson, and no one doubts it happened. For some reason Mr. Deedat thinks it tarnishes the Bible to have major personages committing immoral acts. His purpose is plain: cast a shadow of illegitimacy on the Bible used by Jews and Christians.
11. Ruth COHABITS with Boaz in Ruth 3:4–15. The passage does not say that Ruth and Boaz had sex; it says the opposite. Another attempt to disparage the Bible?
12. David SLEEPS with a young virgin, 1 Kings 1:1 and 3. Yes, David did this. The Bible pulls no punches but states the good and the bad of those found therein. No one in the Bible is as pure as the wind-driven snow. "For all have sinned" is the message throughout. Only Jesus Christ is without sin.

Point 4: ALCOHOL: A devilish advice in God's Book?

Mr. Deedat says alcohol is only for people who are dying and are miserable. Yes, Islam condemns the use of alcohol, and also all other substances that would make one tipsy. He then goes on to show that in the New Testament alcohol is not forbidden, citing Paul in 1 Timothy 5:23, where Paul advises Timothy to take a little wine for the sake of his stomach.

What Paul does say is that Christians are not to be "drunk with wine," (Ephesians 5:18) for this is debauchery; he does not, nor does anyone else in the New Testament, say that all alcohol is forbidden. Yet we also find warnings against its abuse.

Point 5: APOSTASY

Quoting Deuteronomy 13:8–9, Mr. Deedat notes that the passage says to kill apostates—those who go after other gods. Here the attempt is not so much to show the murderous nature of the God of Israel, but to excuse their own relentless persecution and murder of those who deny Islam and Allah.

Point 6: BASTARD: This word occurs in the Bible THREE times.

Mr. Deedat quotes two passages from the Hebrew Bible where the word "bastard" is used: Deuteronomy 23:2 and Zechariah 9:6. The word means someone whose father is unknown. Then there is a reference to Hebrews 12:8, where we find the idea that God disciplines His sons and daughters, otherwise we would be like illegitimate children—which we are not.

Apparently, the goal for Mr. Deedat is to cast disparagement upon the Bible. Can you imagine, the Bible has within it this terrible swear word three times? Horrors!

Point 7: CIRCUMCISION: A perpetual pact with God

Genesis 17:13 is quoted to show that all males in Israel are to be circumcised. Then

Genesis 17:14 is quoted to show that the uncircumcised are "to be cut off." Mr. Deedat interprets this to mean the uncircumcised are to be killed, but this is not at all what the biblical text says. This misstatement is egregious and a lie, meant again to cast the Bible and Christianity into a false light.

Circumcision of the male child on the eighth day was a sign of the parents committing their children to the God of Israel and continues to be even now. Gentiles adopted this same practice, except for the eighth-day stricture.

Christians are not required to circumcise children; instead, circumcision is of the heart. This means that upon conversion, the believer is forgiven of sin and is now indwelt by the Holy Spirit; thus he belongs to the family of God.

Point 8: CONTRADICTIONS: In the Bible

1. The "Lord" tempted David (2 Samuel 24:1), or "Satan" provoked David (1 Chronicles 21:1)

2. In 2 Samuel 24:1 the ESV has the word "incited," not "tempted." God was responsible. And in 1 Chronicles 21:1, the same Hebrew word is used, translated here as "moved." We have long known that the KJV uses many out-of-date terms, which in this present era fail to communicate the intention of the author.

3. 700 or 7000?, 2 Samuel 10:18 vs. 1 Chronicles 19:18

4. Solomon had 2000 baths (1 Kings 7:26), or 3000 baths? (2 Chronicles 4:5)

5. Solomon had 4000 stalls of horses (2 Chronicles 9:25), or 40,000 stalls? (1 Kings 4:26)

6. Here we do find legitimate contradictions. This is often the case when 1 and 2 Chronicles are compared with 1 and 2 Samuel and 1 and 2 Kings, and such has been long noted. Commentators usually yield, but not always, to Samuel and Kings when there are discrepancies. The author(s) of Chronicles wrote centuries after the authors of Samuel and Kings and tended to exaggerate the numbers. This "ramping up" is typical of literature of the time. Numbers and reputations of leaders are heightened, even when the author(s) of Chronicles were aware that other documents were known. These things are interesting, but understood, and do not suggest the documents were forged.

7. Mr. Deedat is correct. However, the contradictions do not cast a shadow on the entire Bible, which is what he is attempting to do.

8. Did Saul enquire of the Lord or didn't he? (1 Samuel 28:6 vs. 1 Chronicles 10:13–14).

9. Mr. Deedat makes it appear as if there is a contradiction here. In 1 Chronicles 10:13–14, Saul consults with a medium, but not with the Lord. In 1 Samuel, Saul attempts to consult with the Lord, but the Lord does not comply, so Saul resorts to a medium instead (v. 7).

10. No man has ascended to heaven (John 3:13), contradicted by Enoch and Elijah ascended to heaven (Genesis 5:24; 2 Kings 2:11)

11. 2 Kings 2:11 says, "And Elijah went up by a whirlwind into heaven." Genesis 5:24 says, "Enoch walked with God: and he was not; for God took him." Indeed, only these two human beings did enter into God's presence without dying.

12. Jesus is unique in that only He, the Word become flesh, descended first and then ascended again into the presence of the Father. This is far different from what either Enoch or Elijah experienced. The follower of Jesus will, in fact, ascend to heaven at the second coming of Christ, as did Elijah and Enoch.

13. Jesus lost "none" of His disciples (John 18:9), or He lost "one" (John 17:12)

14. All those who were born again of the Holy Spirit were saved. Judas was not of the saved, which he proved with his betrayal. So both statements are true.

15. "ALL" are sinners (2 Chronicles 6:36), Contradicted by: or "Whosoever is born of God DOTH NOT commit sin" (1 John 3:9).

16. Here is the ESV translation of 1 John 3:9: "No one born of God makes a practice of sinning, for God's seed abides in him; and he cannot keep on sinning, because he has been born of God."

17. In chapter 1 and 2 of 1 John, John writes that Christians are to confess their sin, and sin they will indeed commit. The paradox having to do with sin is that all the believer's sin is gone—past, present, and future—but at the same time we continue to sin. But we grow up into the fullness of the stature of Christ and have a growing desire to understand what sin is and turn from it. This paradox is extraordinary, yet true.

18. Mr. Deedat almost has it right. "All" are sinners, but the saved sinner does not become sin free or perfected. Nowhere in Scripture is this taught.

Point 9: DAVID: "Man after God's own heart"

Mr. Deedat intends to tarnish both David and God. It is stated in Scripture that David was an adulterer and a murderer. This we see in 2 Samuel 11:4–25. Plus, reference is made to David dancing naked, and this by a prophet of God!

Is this an attempt to deflect attention away from the unseemly acts of Muhammad? Probably, but Deedat's main focus is to prove the Bible unreliable, and thus Christianity unreliable, by highlighting this as the manner of such a highly respected person as David.

The Bible depicts everyone, including those whom God favors with warts and all. David was not perfect, but God loved him in any case. David's sins were horrible, and no attempt is made to whitewash these.

However, God is not like David. The God of Scripture is holy, without sin, and it is no sin for God to love David.

Point 10: GOD: Qualities ill-befitting God

1. Mr. Deedat says God "hisses" in Zechariah 10:8.

2. Indeed, the JKV uses "hiss" in the passage, but the word means "whistle," as we find in the ESV.

3. God "roars" in Isaiah 42:13 and Jeremiah 25:30.

4. Once again, Mr. Deedat relies on the KJV, but other translations use "shout". The idea is that God is a mighty One who is in command. The Hebrew words in both places make it clear that shout or roar are acceptable, but Mr. Deedat implies that such loud commanding is not God-like.

5. In Isaiah 7:20 it is said that God is a "barber."

6. Again, the implication is that this is not God-like behavior. The passage says that God will shave the head and beard of the king of Assyria, meaning that God will humble the Assyrian king. It is not meant to be taken literally.

7. In Jeremiah 15:6 and Genesis 6:6, God is said to be penitent, which of course, is not God-like.

8. In the Jeremiah passage, the key word is "relenting" and in Genesis it is "regretted"—both describing God's sorrow. Attributing human-like emotions to God is referred to as anthropomorphism. Conveying the nature and character of the Creator God in human language is virtually impossible, thus the necessity of using words that humans can grasp.

9. Mr. Deedat is offended that God is pictured in 2 Samuel 22:11 as "riding" a cherub.

10. The passage is poetic, and poetic license is taken. The ESV for 2 Samuel 22:11 reads: "He rode on a cherub and flew; he was seen on the wings of the wind." Does Mr. Deedat not understand this use of genre? Or does he merely hope to disparage the Bible?. And, does not Islam view the Hebrew Bible as well as the New Testament, the Injil, as inspired?

11. In 1 Samuel 6:19 God murders 50,070 people for looking into a box.

12. The number killed as found in the KJV, 50,070, is considered to be a scribal error. In the ESV the number is seventy. The reason for God's judgment is that seventy opened the ark of the covenant that contained the Ten Commandment tablets, wanting to know what was inside. This was a gross violation of the command of the holy God of Israel.

Point 11: GOD WITH A SMALL "g"

Mr. Deedat's point here is that English translations of the Bible will capitalize words that refer to God. In other words, we read "God" and not "god."

He notes that in 2 Corinthians 4:4, in reference to the devil, "god" is used and not "God." Does he think that the devil should be referred to as God? Paul's intent is to show in the passage that Satan has a God-like hold on the people of the world.

Then, in Exodus 7:1, God says to Moses, "I have made thee a god to Pharaoh." Does Mr. Deedat suggest that Moses should be referred to as God? Apparently, whenever the word "god" appears in the Bible, Mr. Deedat believes it must be capitalized, regardless of the obvious context.

Most interesting is that at the same time, in referencing John 1:1, Mr. Deedat is disturbed that Christians brazenly capitalize *Logos*.

Point 12: GOD: His contradictory attributes

These Scriptures:

» "No man hath seen God at any time" (John 1:18).

» "[God], whom no man hath seen, nor can see…" (1 Timothy 6:16).

» "And He [God] said, Thou canst not see my face: for there shall no man see me, and live" (Exodus 33:20).

Contradicted by:

» Exodus 33:11 is quoted to show that God speaks to Moses face to face.

» Moses, Aaron, and seventy others see God (Exodus 24:10).

» Jacob says he has seen God and survived (Genesis 32:30).

» Moses sees God's back (Exodus 33:23).

Mr. Deedat must think that the whole glory of God can be seen by a human being. On occasions, people would observe a vision or a partial glimpse of God's glory. And, to see God's back is another instance of the use of anthropomorphism.

We will behold God only when we are with Him in heaven. Imagine—the God who created all the light that is in the universe surely cannot be observed by the human eye. To stare at the sun for even a short period is dangerous. No, Scripture says we will have a resurrection body, far different from what we experience now, and then we shall behold Him.

Point 13: GOD: Is not a fabricator of confusion

This Scripture:

» 1 Corinthians 14:33 states that God is not the author of confusion.

Contradicted by:

» "I make peace and create evil" (Isaiah 45:7).

» The ESV reads: "I form light and create darkness; I make well-being and create calamity; I am the Lord, who does all these things." This is a statement that means God is sovereign over all things, not that He is the author of evil. For reasons we will never comprehend, God allowed evil into His universe. Mr. Deedat apparently is unable to see the nuanced literary style and is compelled to take things literally when it serves his purpose.

» Saul was troubled by AN EVIL SPIRIT (1 Samuel 16:14).

» Again, this indicates God is sovereign, and for reasons not explained, God allows Saul to be troubled.

» "And for this cause God shall send them strong delusion, that they should BELIEVE A LIE" (2 Thessalonians 2:11).

Again, God is sovereign and allows those who wish to believe lies to be deceived. I would ask Mr. Deedat if Islam does not view Allah as sovereign. Does anything happen without his predestinating it? It might be asked whether God has sent a strong delusion upon Muslims.

Point 14: GOD: Further contradictory qualities

This Scripture:
» God as an omnipotent being: "And Jesus...saith,...for with God ALL THINGS are possible" (Mark 10:27, also Matthew 19:26,).

Contradicted by:
» In Judges 1:19 we find that though God drove out the mountain people, He could not drive out the people of the valley due to their "chariots of iron."

In Joshua 17:16–18, the problem was that the Israelites feared the valley people and did not take God at His word, thus they failed to drive out the people with chariots of iron.

This Scripture:
» God's anger abideth for a minute: "For his (God's) anger endureth but a MOMENT" (Psalm 30:5).

The full passage reads: "For his anger is but for a moment, and his favor is for a lifetime" (Psalm 30:5a ESV). It is difficult to know if Mr. Deedat expects his readers not to check on his citations for accuracy. The psalmist speaks in a most beautiful and poetic manner to the mercy of God, though for a season, life can be a burden.

Contradicted by:
» From Numbers 32:13 we find that God made Israel wander in the wilderness for FORTY YEARS.

Again, Mr. Deedat's objection shows a failure to understand differing genres of literature. God's "moment" for rebellious Israel lasted forty years.

This Scripture:
» God does not show any self-reproach: From Numbers 23:19 we see that God does not repent or change His mind.

Contradicted by:
» God REPENTED of making Saul king (1 Samuel 15:35), and God REPENTED of the evil He brought upon Israel (Exodus 32:14).

Here we encounter a Hebraism—a form of speech employed in biblical literature—which does not carry the New Testament weight of "repent." This latter use of the word *repent* means "to change the mind." In the Hebrew Bible, we find expressions that indicate God is perfectly able to allow something for a time and then move in another direction, which to observers might seem like a changing of the mind, or repentance.

This Scripture:
» God's mercy endureth for ever: Here Mr. Deedat quotes Psalm 100:5, "For the LORD is good; and his mercy is EVERLASTING."

Contradicted by:

» In 1 Samuel 15:2-3, God remembers what King Amalek's nation did to Israel when they came out of Egypt hundreds of years previously. He then instructs that the descendants of that nation be completely destroyed.

The reason for this is complex. Usually two answers are given. Firstly, God is clearing out Canaan, the promised land, of those who live there. Because of their pagan worship this is necessitated, lest Israel fall prey to their gods and goddesses. Secondly, God is judge and will judge completely.

We see severe judging abundantly in the Qur'an, in every chapter and in hundreds of verses. But here, the God of Israel is disparaged.

This Scripture:

» God dwells in light: 1 Timothy 6:16 has "(God) dwelling in the LIGHT which no man can approach unto; whom no man hath seen, nor can see."

Contradicted by:

» 1 Kings 8:12 speaks of God dwelling in "THICK DARKNESS."

God dwelling in unapproachable light and in thick darkness mean virtually the same thing. God is beyond finding out and will present Himself in any and every manner.

Also, to some He is light, while to others He is darkness. In the text Mr. Deedat refers to, 1 Kings 8:12, Solomon says God will dwell in thick darkness. And so it was in the inner sanctum of the temple Solomon was building. The Holy of Holies was without light and here God was pleased to dwell among His people.

This Scripture:

» God does not entice man: Mr. Deedat looks to James 1:13, where the KJV has "Let no man say when he is tempted, I am tempted of God: for God cannot be tempted with evil, neither tempteth He any man."

Contradicted by:

» James 1:13, Mr. Deedat says, is contradicted by Genesis 22:1, where the text says God tempted Abraham. This has to do with the sacrifice of Isaac. The idea of "tempt" in the passage means for Mr. Deedat that God intended to lure Abraham into sin. This is a far cry from the obvious objective of God. At the last moment, a substitute is found that Abraham is to sacrifice rather than his son Isaac. It is a vivid picture of Jesus, It is also a dramatic historical prophecy of the crucifixion and death of Jesus on the cross. Mr. Deedat knows this, and since his major goal on the part of Islam is to deny the crucifixion and death of Jesus, this particular passage must be discredited at all costs.

Point 15: HOLY GHOST: Every sect and denomination of Christian cults claim the "Gift" of the HOLY GHOST. This gift is so cheap that 75,000,000 'BORN AGAIN' Christians of America are also boasting this possession.

1. In Luke 1:15 we find, "And he [John the Baptist] shall be filled with the Holy

Ghost, even from his mother's womb." Mr. Deedat states he does not know what is meant by "mother's womb." He laments that "poor Jesus" had to wait thirty years before He got filled with the Holy Ghost.

2. "And Elizabeth was filled with the Holy Ghost" (Luke 1:41).
3. "And his father Zacharias was filled with the Holy Ghost" (Luke 1:67).
4. "He [Jesus] breathed on them, and saith unto them, Receive ye the Holy Ghost" (John 20:22).
5. "But he that shall blaspheme against the Holy Ghost hath never forgiveness, but is in danger of eternal damnation" (Mark 3:29).
6. It seems as though Mr. Deedat sees the Holy Spirit cheapened as a gift that many receive—women, apostles, John the Baptist—a common commodity.
7. Amongst Muslims, some believe Gabriel is the Holy Spirit, others Muhammad, and then it gets murky since amongst the twenty-some sects of Sunni Islam alone there are differences. I will assume here that Mr. Deedat believes Muhammad is the Holy Spirit, thus the natural successor to Jesus. And the question must be raised, Is this close to the blasphemy of the Holy Spirit?

Point 16: INCEST: "Sexual intercourse between two persons who are too closely related."

Incest in God's Book between a Father and His Daughters

» Mr. Deedat is looking at Genesis 19:33–35, where Lot's daughters get their father drunk then sleep with him hoping to become pregnant. And they succeed, according to the biblical account.

Apparently, Mr. Deedat is holding up this incestuous event to discredit the Bible as though God had engineered the incestuous affair. Casting a cloud over Judaism and Christianity must be the design of this section, which is not uncharacteristic of Mr. Deedat. Jewish and Christian scholars have long understood that the Scripture is merely recording events, nothing more.

Incest between Mother and Son

» Reuben, the firstborn son of Jacob (Israel), has intercourse with Bilhah, his father's concubine (Genesis 35:22). A rather cheap and uninformed smear tactic, just as above and following.

Incest between Father-in-Law and Daughter-in-Law

» Now comes the account of Judah having intercourse with Tamar, his daughter-in-law (Genesis 38:15–18). From this liaison, twins are born, and one of these, Perez, is part of the genealogy of Jesus.

Incest and Rape between Brother and Sister

» In 2 Samuel 13:11 is the account of Amnon raping his sister Tamar. Amnon is one of David's sons, and Mr. Deedat reminds the reader, David is a man after God's own heart.

Wholesale Rape between Son and His Mothers!

» In 2 Samuel 16:22 is the account of Absalom (another son of the man after God's own heart), who has intercourse with his father's concubines.

A common tactic of those who are desperate to harm someone or something is to tarnish, scandalize, and smear, when nothing better is at hand. It is a cheap trick which is not to Mr. Deedat's credit.

Mr. Deedat does not call attention to Muhammad's sexual adventures, beginning with the young girl Aisha. Muhammad managed to have twelve wives in all, plus unknown numbers of concubines.

The authenticity of the biblical accounts is heightened rather than discredited by mentioning unsavory and immoral events carried out by biblical personages. Tarnishing Amnon and Absalom, among others, advances Mr. Deedat's agenda.

Point 17: ISRAELITES: Insatiable whores

» Israel played the whore with the Assyrians and could not be satisfied (Ezekiel 16:28).

I'm not sure why Mr. Deedat does not inform the reader that this reference to playing the whore is meant to communicate that the Israelites bowed down to and worshipped Assyrian gods and goddesses. Is it possible he is not so aware?

Whoredoms of the 2 Sisters — Ahola and Aholiba

» Again, Ezekiel 23:1-19 has the story of lustful sisters, whose names are Oholah and Oholibah per the ESV.

Ezekiel 23:4 makes it plain that Oholah stands for the nation of Samaria, and Oholibah stands for Jerusalem. Again, it means that the two nations went after and worshipped false gods.

» In Hosea 4:12, 6:10, and 9:1, Israel has the spirit of whoredoms and goes whoring after other gods.

It is shocking that Mr. Deedat is preparing for Muslims to go into combat armed with the crazy ammunition provided in this book, and in this last section, the absurdity of his arguments seems to have reached a climax.

Point 18: JEREMIAH: Made a prophet before his birth

» Jeremiah 1:5 reads, "Before I formed you in the womb I knew you, and before you were born I consecrated you; I appointed you a prophet to the nations."

One of the six articles of belief for Muslims is predestination. Islam holds that Muhammad was predestined to be the great and final prophet before he was born. Yet Mr. Deedat makes this complaint about Jeremiah. My question is, Does Mr. Deedat see Jeremiah as a rival to Muhammad, or is he attempting to show the Bible as an unreliable, even absurd, document?

Jeremiah Deceived by God

» Jeremiah 20:7 reads: "O Lord, thou hast deceived me, and I was deceived."

Jeremiah confesses his limitations. He is an imperfect prophet. He is obedient to his call, but he does not know where it will all lead. At times the role Jeremiah plays causes others to hold him in derision. Jeremiah is up and down, elated then depressed—a hard calling indeed.

God did not deceive him—this again is a figure of speech, a lamenting form of communication that Jeremiah is adept at (see the book of Lamentations by Jeremiah at the conclusion of the book of Jeremiah). Just because he complains that God has deceived him, it is not necessarily a statement of fact that God deceived him. It may simply be an expression of Jeremiah's forlorn perspective.

Are the Hebraisms and other complex and subtle literary styles in Scripture over Mr. Deedat's head? He seems intent on taking everything absolutely literally, without any sense of nuance.

Point 19: JESUS (PBUH)[2]

His First Miracle in the Holy Bible and the Holy Qur'an

John 2:9 has the story of Jesus turning water into wine at the marriage feast at Cana. The Qur'an has as Jesus' first miracle His defense of His mother while Jesus Himself is an infant. This is found in Qur'an 19:30–33.[3]

This is indeed a problem for Mr. Deedat, and therefore, all of Islam. Either the Bible is correct, or the Qur'an is correct; there is no middle ground.

The New Testament with John's Gospel appears six centuries before the Qur'an. There are miracle stories about Jesus in the Gospel of Thomas and other gnostic writings, but these are clearly authored long after John was written.

His Invectives Against the Elders of His People

» "Hypocrites!" (Matthew 23:13); "Wicked and adulterous generation" (Matthew 16:4); "Whited sepulchres" (Matthew 23:27); "Ye generation of vipers" (Matthew 23:33)

Jesus speaks directly to the distortion of the religious leaders He encounters. He gives "full disclosure" and makes no attempt to flatter or deceive.

» Jesus refers to His mother Mary as "woman" in John 2:4 and uses the same word for a prostitute in John 8:10.

Mr. Deedat makes the unwarranted assumption that the term *woman* is used by Jesus in a derogatory manner. *Woman* is a perfectly appropriate, even dignified, appellation. Addressing a prostitute in this way shows Jesus' kindness and respect for someone who received little of this from others.

---

2 PBUH stands for "Peace Be Upon Him" and is intended to be similar to a prayer. Muslims will not mention the name of Muhammad, or write it, without a PBUH.

3 This comparison is discussed further in the chapter, "The Miracles of Muhammad and Jesus: A Comparison."

"The Prince of Peace"

Jesus boasts that He did not come to bring peace on earth but fire and division.

Mr. Deedat thinks the designation "Prince of Peace" is not an appropriate term for Jesus, since in Luke 12:49–50, Jesus Himself says that He comes to send judgment fire to the earth, and also that He came to bring division on earth and not peace.

Jesus observes the evil present in the world and the harm therefrom and so looks ahead to the Day of Judgment. Here we see an expression of grief and concern on Jesus' part.

He brings division, yes, and this has been so from the start. There are followers of Jesus and there are those, and by far the greater in number, who oppose Him. Yet He also brings peace, in that He has bridged the enmity between humankind and God, "making peace [between ourselves and God] by the blood of His cross" (Colossians 1:20).

(Jesus) NOT GOD!

Jesus, Mr. Deedat states, would not allow anyone to call Him "good," let alone call Him "God."

Mr. Deedat is thinking of the story of the rich young ruler, found in Matthew 19:16–22, Mark 10:17–27, and Luke 18:18–27. In Matthew's account, Jesus is addressed as "Teacher." In Mark and Luke, it is "Good Teacher."

In Mark and Luke, Jesus asks the young man why he calls Him good. In Matthew the young man approaches Jesus and asks Him what good thing he could do to obtain eternal life. Jesus wants to know why the young is asking Him this question. Then Jesus goes on to say that the young man must keep the commandments.

The young man says he has kept the commandments. Then Jesus says he must sell all he has and give the money to the poor. Whereupon, the young man walks away.

In Mark and Luke the story reads differently; the young man says, "Good Teacher." Jesus, perhaps aware of the insincerity or boasting, replies that there is only one who is good and that is God. Many commentators, including myself, think Jesus is forcing the young man to examine his own heart. Jesus, by this time, has performed countless miracles, including a resurrection, and cast out many demons. Jesus may have been coaxing the man to question just whom he was talking to.

These two seemingly different accounts are easily harmonized. Likely Jesus dealt with two separate issues.

Mr. Deedat wants his readers to think that Jesus rejected the idea that He is God. He presumes to know what was on Jesus' mind and uses this incident to defame Jesus, which many Muslims would not do.

Mr. Deedat has a warfare mindset, which comes through repeatedly.

(Jesus') Power Not His Own

Jesus says in Matthew 28:18 that all authority is given to Him. In John 5:30, He says that He can do nothing on His own. In Luke 11:20, Jesus says He casts out demons "by the finger of God."

Turning to the raising of Lazarus in John 11:41–43, Mr. Deedat points to Jesus saying in prayer, "Thou hast heard me," meaning that Jesus did nothing of Himself. After praying before the tomb of Lazarus, the man came forth alive. Mr. Deedat says that Jesus did not do this, but God did it.

One of the fundamental problems Mr. Deedat has, which most Muslims share, is not grasping the incarnation of Jesus—that is, God becoming human. In Philippians 2:5–11 (ESV), we read of this:

> Have this mind among yourselves, which is yours in Christ Jesus, who, though He was in the form of God, did not count equality with God a thing to be grasped, but emptied Himself, by taking the form of a servant, being born in the likeness of men. And being found in human form, He humbled Himself by becoming obedient to the point of death, even death on a cross. Therefore God has highly exalted Him and bestowed on Him the name that is above every name, so that at the name of Jesus every knee should bow, in heaven and on earth and under the earth, and every tongue confess that Jesus Christ is Lord, to the glory of God the Father.

In Hebrews 1:1–4 (ESV) we find evidence of the incarnation:

> Long ago, at many times and in many ways, God spoke to our fathers by the prophets, but in these last days He has spoken to us by His Son, whom He appointed the heir of all things, through whom also He created the world. He is the radiance of the glory of God and the exact imprint of His nature, and He upholds the universe by the word of His power. After making purification for sins, He sat down at the right hand of the Majesty on high, having become as much superior to angels as the name He has inherited is more excellent than theirs.

Then, in Paul's letter to the Colossians, chapter 1:15–20 (ESV), we see more of who Jesus is:

> He is the image of the invisible God, the firstborn of all creation. For by Him all things were created, in heaven and on earth, visible and invisible, whether thrones or dominions or rulers or authorities—all things were created through Him and for Him. And He is before all things, and in Him all things hold together. And He is the head of the body, the church. He is the beginning, the firstborn from the dead, that in everything He might be preeminent. For in Him all the fullness of God was pleased to dwell, and through Him to reconcile to Himself all things, whether on earth or in heaven, making peace by the blood of His cross.

It is abundantly clear that Jesus is God, and He became man to die as a real man on the cross. Of course, this is absolutely impossible to comprehend with the human mind. What we do have, however, is the Scripture and then the Holy Spirit of God, who reveals these truths to us, which we understand to some degree or another.

However darkly we see through a glass, we know Jesus is Immanuel, God with us.

Listen Now to Peter's Testimony

» "Ye men of Israel, (0 Jews!) hear these words; Jesus of Nazareth, A MAN approved of God (meaning a prophet) among you by miracles and wonders and signs, which GOD DID BY HIM in the midst of you, as ye yourselves also know..." (Acts 2:22, Deedat's emphasis retained).

Again we see the failure of Mr. Deedat's understanding of the incarnation. Jesus, indeed, on the planet with us—fully human—left aside His glory. Only God can do this.

Mr. Deedat then credits Jesus with being a prophet, but no more—a distortion nearly all non-Christian faiths employ.

Was Luke Inspired by God to Say that Jesus (PBUH) Was the Son of Joseph?

In Luke 3, Luke presents a genealogy of Jesus. In verse 23, Luke mentions Joseph as part of that lineage and adds, "(as was supposed)." Luke knows that some people think Jesus was born of Mary and Joseph. Interestingly, Jesus never attempts to correct this notion but always honors Joseph, without saying he was Jesus' father.

Mr. Deedat says that "(as was supposed)" is a gloss and thus not original to Luke's Gospel. To admit it would mean that Luke is saying that Joseph, though in the linage, was only "thought or supposed to be" the father of Jesus.

There is no textual or manuscript evidence for this. Mr. Deedat is depending on the hope that no one will check him on this point.

Jesus (PBUH), Too Self-Considerate

Mr. Deedat, presenting the story of a woman who anoints Jesus with precious, or costly, oil, prefers to see Jesus as overly proud of Himself. The passage is Matthew 26:6–13 (ESV):

> Now when Jesus was at Bethany in the house of Simon the leper, a woman came up to Him with an alabaster flask of very expensive ointment, and she poured it on His head as He reclined at table. And when the disciples saw it, they were indignant, saying, "Why this waste? For this could have been sold for a large sum and given to the poor." But Jesus, aware of this, said to them, "Why do you trouble the woman? For she has done a beautiful thing to Me. For you always have the poor with you, but you will not always have Me. In pouring this ointment on My body, she has done it to prepare Me for burial. Truly, I say to you, wherever this gospel is proclaimed in the whole world, what she has done will also be told in memory of her." (ESV)

Notice the word *woman* in verse 10 used as a title of respect by Jesus.

The disciples are indignant that the flask of ointment was wasted, and thus they are disrespectful of the woman. I'll make two points here: one, Jesus is looking ahead to His death; and two, Jesus defends the woman while honoring her. And indeed, this story has been told around the globe and in every language from that time to this.

Jesus also points out that the poor will always be with them; however, there is something far more important going on here.

Point 20: Jesus (PBUH) a "GOD"?: Powerless

Mr. Deedat is referring to John 5:30, where Jesus says, "I can of mine own self do nothing."

No Christian would be troubled at the statement, since we know Jesus depended upon the Holy Spirit of God for the miracles, healings, casting out of demons, multiplying food, and raisings from the dead.

For Mr. Deedat it means that Jesus is not God, but only human.

He Had No Knowledge of the Hereafter

Quoting Mark 13:32, where Jesus says that He does not know the day and the hour of the coming of the Kingdom, Mr. Deedat wants to again present evidence that Jesus is not God. And once again Mr. Deedat shows He does not understand the nature of the incarnation. Please reread Philippians 2:7 above, where we see that Jesus "emptied Himself," laying aside His full power and knowledge in order to dwell with us as a man.

He Was Ignorant of the Seasons

Mr. Deedat is quoting Mark 11:13, where Jesus approaches a fig tree, and expecting to find fruit, He finds only leaves. Mr. Deedat makes the deduction that "If He is God, He would know these things."

The fig tree passage, Mark 11:12–14, is a kind of lesson from nature, and very close to being a parable. The fig tree is likely a reference to Israel, past and present. Since the leaders of Israel rejected John the Baptist and his message, they were bound to reject Jesus. And in doing so, it could be said, metaphorically, there is no fruit; as the people of God, Israel is barren.

Jesus (PBUH) as a Thirsty "God"?

One of the seven statements from the cross that Jesus uttered is "I thirst" (John 19:28). For Mr. Deedat, it is inconceivable that God would thirst.

This Scripture passage provides a vivid illustration of the incarnation. Put in a folksy way, it can be said that the God-man, willingly setting aside His deity to become fully human, suffers the fully human frailties and limitations common to human beings, including being thirsty.

Psalm 22, written a thousand years before the crucifixion, depicts a man desperately thirsty. In Psalm 22:15 is an incredible portrait of a man dying on a cross: "My strength is dried up like a potsherd, and my tongue sticks to my jaws; you lay me in the dust of death." Indeed, Jesus was the thirsty God.

Jesus (PBUH) as a Weeping "God"?

The shortest verse in Scripture is John 11:35, "Jesus wept." For Mr. Deedat it gives further proof Jesus is not God. Again we find his failure to grasp the incarnation. But he must do so or quit being a Muslim.

Imagine a "God" Being Tempted by the Devil

Mr. Deedat is referring to the temptation in the desert, and he quotes from Mark 1:13. Satan must attack Jesus and does so soon after Jesus' baptism in the River Jordan. One would expect such a thing. Jesus faces the devil down and wins a decisive victory over the kingdom of evil.

Point 21: JESUS (PBUH) (A RACIST): Only came for the Jews

1. Matthew 10:5–6, where Jesus sends the apostles out to preach only to Jews—the House of Israel—brings Mr. Deedat to the idea that Jesus is a racist.
2. In Matthew 15:24–26, a non-Jew—a Canaanite woman—approaches Jesus to

ask Him to heal her daughter. Jesus then asks if it is right to help the "dogs," as Jews often called Gentiles. When the woman persists, Jesus heals her daughter from a distance.

Jesus was no racist, as Mr. Deedat makes Him out to be. Jesus' first agenda is to present Himself to the House of Israel, but He also reaches out to a number of non-Jews during His earthly ministry. Mr. Deedat's smear is disingenuous at minimum, besides being errant.

To know Jesus' full and ultimate intention, one need only read His commission to His followers: "Go therefore and make disciples of all nations, baptizing them in the name of the Father and of the Son and of the Holy Spirit" (Matthew 28:19). And this is precisely what has happened, from that day until this.

Point 22: Jesus (PBUH): (Sundry Tidbits)

Jesus' (PBUH) Second Coming, Never Materialized

Mr. Deedat quotes Matthew 10:23, where Jesus says the disciples will not have gone over all the cities of Israel before the Son of Man returns.

Since Jesus has not returned yet, in Mr. Deedat's understanding, it must point to a major failure coupled with a lack of knowledge. It is plain, however, from Matthew 28:19 quoted above and Acts 1:8 quoted below, that Jesus meant that the entire world was in view, not merely the Jewish nation. Here is what Jesus said to His disciples moments before the ascension: "But you will receive power when the Holy Spirit has come upon you, and you will be my witnesses in Jerusalem and in all Judea and Samaria, and to the end of the earth."

Paul, in Romans 1:16, echoes the command of Jesus when he writes: "For I am not ashamed of the gospel, for it is the power of God for salvation to everyone who believes, to the Jew first and also to the Greek." From Jesus' day to this, the Christian witness is to extend to Jews first and then to Gentiles.

As for the return of Jesus, there are growing indications that this is nearer than we might think. No one knows the day or hour.

Jesus Spoke in Parables to Deceive the Uninitiated.

Mark 4:11–12 is quoted to prove that Jesus' use of parables is intended to deceive non-Christians. Close, but not the case.

We find that the natural man, or the unconverted person not indwelt by the Holy Spirit, cannot understand the things of the Holy Spirit. Paul helps us understand this: "For the word of the cross is folly to those who are perishing, but to us who are being saved it is the power of God" (I Corinthians 1:18), followed by 1 Corinthians 2:14: "The natural person does not accept the things of the Spirit of God, for they are folly to him, and he is not able to understand them because they are spiritually discerned."

Paul knew full well this simple truth. Jesus—His person and message—are not understood until we are born anew. It was that way for Paul until he was suddenly converted. Not only that, but blindness to the truth of Jesus has another source as well. Paul, speaking of the unbelievers, wrote: "In their case the god of this world has blinded the minds of the unbelievers, to keep them from seeing the light of the gospel of the glory of Christ, who is the image of God" (2 Corinthians 4:4).

Is it unfair on my part to imagine that our dear Mr. Deedat could see the things of the Spirit of God? Certainly, without the Holy Spirit of God working in him, that will never happen.

Hate as Foundation of His (Jesus') Faith

Mr. Deedat quotes Luke 14:26: "If any man come to Me, and hate not his father, and mother, and wife, and children...he cannot be My disciple."

Mr. Deedat ignores Jesus' commands to love all, including enemies, and misunderstands Jesus' use of hyperbole, so often employed by Jesus. Christians have always understood this to mean that we are called to obey the first and greatest commandment, to love God with all we have. Everything else is important, but secondary.

Peter Contradicts Jesus (PBUH) Regarding Himself as "The Only Way"

Mr. Deedat quotes John 14:6, where Jesus says He is the way, the truth, and the life. The Muslim missionary then quotes Acts 10:34–35, where Peter is speaking to Cornelius, the Roman centurion. Peter says: "Truly I understand that God shows no partiality, but in every nation anyone who fears Him and does what is right is acceptable to Him."

Peter is preaching to Gentiles, and not just to any Gentiles, but to the hated Romans. God has opened Peter's mind to the fact that he is to accept Gentiles into the faith. These Gentiles then are converted, filled with the Holy Spirit, and baptized in the name of Jesus.

Mr. Deedat has it exactly backward.

Point 23: JEWS: A rebellious people

The missionary quotes Deuteronomy 9:24, where the Jews are spoken of as a rebellious people. Then they are called a stiff-necked people in Deuteronomy 31:27. Again, in Deuteronomy 28 God says that *if* Israel is unfaithful, they will be scattered into the nations and in constant distress, even being sent back into Egypt. As a result of Israel's rejection of the prophets sent to them, Hosea 8:13 indicates Israel will figuratively return to Egypt, meaning a return to the worship of those foreign and false gods.

In Matthew 21:43, Jesus states that the kingdom of God will be taken from the Jews and given to another nation.

This truth reveals God's slowly evolving plan, that people from the entire world will be drawn into the kingdom. We see this begin to occur in the pages of the New Testament.

Point 24: KETURAH: The third wife of Abraham

Abraham took a wife by the name of Keturah after the death of Sarah (Genesis 25:1).

But, Mr. Deedat says, this is a biblical contradiction, since 1 Chronicles 1:32 refers to Keturah as a concubine. He goes on, however, to note: "Here is an extra contradiction in the Bible, unless 'wife' and 'concubine' are synonymous terms."

And he hit it right on the head. It would be the same for Hagar, the second "wife" of Abraham, who bore him Ishmael, the supposed father of the Arab nation. Thus, Islam is considered an Abrahamic religion, as are Judaism and Christianity.

Point 25: MASSACRE: At the hands of the Jews

Mr. Deedat quotes Numbers 31:17-18: "Now therefore kill every male among the little ones, and kill every woman that hath known man by lying with him. But all the women children, that have not known a man by lying with him, keep alive for yourselves." Then the number of virgins taken is 32,000.

Mr. Deedat then cites Deuteronomy 20:16, Joshua 6:21, and Joshua 10:28, where God commands destruction of people and their cities.

Both Jewish and Christian scholars make attempts to soften such passages. Some say it is a historical picture of judgment happening in real time, or it is a prelude to what is coming at the end of history.

Others say such reports are embellishments—hero stories—designed to cover the atrocities inflicted by Israelites invading the land of Canaan.

Still others, like myself, do not know what to think. It must be noted, however, that there is nothing of the sort in the New Testament.

Point 26: MELCHISEDEK: This High Priest of Salem has qualities that outshine even Jesus Christ.

Hebrews 7:3, where Melchisedek is mentioned, is quoted: "Without father, without mother, without descent, having neither beginning of days, nor end of life..."

In Genesis 14:17-19 is the story of Abraham meeting a mysterious king named Melchizedek (Old and New Testament spellings in the KJV are different), who is referred to as "priest of the most high God" in Genesis 14:18. This priest blesses Abraham. The question is, Just who is this priest?

A number of answers have been given. One, he is a prefiguring of Jesus, a pre-incarnate Christ. Two, he is a legendary personage given an honorific title, but nothing more than that. Three, he is a powerful king who bestowed upon himself the grand title. Four, he is an angel of God sent to encourage Abraham.

I have no opinion on the matter.

From Hebrews 7:3, we see Melchisedek had no father or mother, or any lineage at all for that matter, but Jesus does have all of these. Having no beginning or end of life might be strong evidence that Melchisedek is a pre-incarnate Christ. This eternalness is indeed true of Jesus.

Mr. Deedat's statement that Melchisedek "outshines even Jesus Christ" is a stretch too far. Jesus is King of kings and Lord of lords, and this would include being King and Lord over Melchisedek, if he is an actual human being. To say the least, Melchisedek is an interesting, but minor, character.

Point 27: MESSIAH: Translated "Christ"

Mr. Deedat makes a case that the Hebrew word for "messiah" in the Hebrew Bible, *mashiach*, means "anointed," wherever found and in every context. He gives the following examples:

» In Genesis 31:13, a pillar is anointed by Jacob. So, the pillar is the Messiah?

» In Leviticus 8:10 Moses anoints the tabernacle with anointing oil. So is Jesus the oil

- and Jesus the tabernacle?
- » In 1 Samuel 2:10 are the words, "exalt the horn of His anointed." So, a horn is Messiah, Mr. Deedat wonders?
- » In Ezekiel 28:14 a cherub is anointed, but this cherub is king of Tyre. So now, is a cherub (angel) Messiah, or is the king of Tyre?
- » In Isaiah 45:1, the Persian king Cyrus is God's anointed. So, is Cyrus the Messiah?

Mr. Deedat wants to somehow compromise Jesus as Messiah, the anointed of God. This borders, maybe crosses the line, into that which is ludicrous.

Anointing was a common practice; it meant to set something aside for special use by God. So anointing oil was widely used, and of course, not everything that was anointed therefore became the Messiah.

Does not Islam teach that Jesus is Messiah? For, that is the meaning of the word "Christ," which is the Greek equivalent of Messiah.

Point 28: MUHUMMED[4] (PBUH): Is a true prophet of God according to the Bible.

1. Mr. Deedat references Qur'an 3:45, among other passages, where Jesus is referred to as the Christ. Then is quoted 1 John 4:2: "Every spirit that confesseth that Jesus Christ is come in the flesh is of God."

1 John 4:2 has to do with Jesus being God incarnate, the God-man. So then, every "person" who so confesses this is of God. The trouble is, Islam denies that Jesus is the incarnate God—that is, God become flesh.

But since Muhammad acknowledged Jesus as Messiah, that must mean Muhammad is a true prophet, which is a complete twisting of 1 John 4:2.

Muhummed (PBUH) Mentioned by Name in the Bible

1. This, Mr. Deedat says, is supported by Song of Solomon 5:16: "His mouth is most sweet, and he is altogether desirable. This is my beloved and this is my friend, O daughters of Jerusalem."

The words *sweet* and *desirable* are said to stand for Muhummed. The Hebrew words, when transliterated, do appear similar to "Muhummed." If the passage does speak of Muhammad, the passage would read: "His mouth is Muhammad and he is altogether Muhammad."

The passage is variously interpreted. Some see it as a love poem, an expression of love between a man and a woman. Others see it as depicting God's love for humans and human love for God.

If the author of Scripture wished to refer to Islam's prophet, why settle for an obscure reference in the Hebrew Bible, and in a book that may not be at all prophetic, but a love poem?

---

4 It is curious that Mr. Deedat uses the spelling "Muhummed" instead of the standard "Muhammad." Is this to make it easier to think that Song of Solomon 5:16 refers to the Muslim prophet?

Muhammed a "Comforter" Like Jesus, Peace Be Upon Them

John 14:16 is quoted by Mr. Deedat: "And I will pray the Father, and He shall give you another Comforter, that He may abide with you forever."

Mr. Deedat then says that Jesus was the first comforter and Muhammad is the second, a man and not a ghost. Here we find what many Muslims believe, that Muhammad is the Holy Spirit.

This "comforter," translated from the Greek of John 14:16, is *paraklete* and means one who comes alongside to counsel and comfort. This is the Holy Spirit, who descended upon and filled the early Christians on the day of Pentecost (see Acts 2).

In Isaiah 9:6, we find: "For to us a child is born, to us a son is given; and the government shall be upon His shoulder, and His name shall be called Wonderful Counselor, Might God, Everlasting Father, Prince of Peace." In the Septuagint, the Greek translation of the Hebrew Bible, "Counselor" is paraklete.

Again we have an attempt by Mr. Deedat to say the Bible points to Muhammad as the comforter, or counselor. But Jesus clearly, and simply, explains to His disciples in Acts 1 that they are to wait for the coming of this "promise of the Father" in Jerusalem. Jesus says, "You will be baptized with the Holy Spirit not many days from now" (Acts 1:5).

And in ten days, the words of Jesus are fulfilled when the Holy Spirit falls on the 120 people gathered. A crowd rushes together to find out what all the noise is about and then hear the first sermon Peter ever preached.

This Point 28 is a desperate attempt by Mr. Deedat to insert Muhammad into history as the Holy Spirit.

Point 29   ONANISM: "The withdrawal of the penis from the vagina before ejaculation."

The background to "Onanism" is found in Genesis 38:1–11. Onan was to have intercourse with a dead brother's wife so that the family line would continue. This was a practice not unheard of in that era, since the survival of the family line was vital. But Onan consistently withdrew his penis at the last moment. This was unacceptable, and verse 10 says the Lord put Onan to death as a result.

It is not clear why the Lord put Onan to death. In this very ancient strata of Scripture, most everything that occurred is said to be from the Lord. Christian commentators have long wondered about this, some reaching the conclusion that the composers of this material maintained that everything that happened was from God. As time goes on, this blanket awarding changes.

That said, Mr. Deedat does not provide a reason for including this item. I can only guess that he intended to suggest there is something amiss in the Bible's account or that it was unseemly.

Point 30: PAUL: On his own admittance being cunning, used deceit:

Mr. Deedat quotes 2 Corinthians 12:16, "But be it so, I did not burden you: nevertheless, being crafty, I caught you with guile."

Unfortunately, Mr. Deedat does not quote this passage correctly. Here is the full verse: "But granting that I myself did not burden you, I was crafty, **you say**, and got the better of you by deceit" (ESV, emphasis added). Mr. Deedat conveniently left out, "you say" in order to make it appear that Paul is acting deceitfully.

This is a flagrant twisting of the Scripture, and not at all uncommon for Mr. Deedat. It must be that he assumes few, if any, readers will investigate.

Point 31: PIGS: See "swine" in the index.

Mr. Deedat directs the reader ahead to Point 41, and thus I will combine Points 31 and 41 further on.

Point 32: POLYGAMY: Solomon the wise had a thousand wives and concubines:

Indeed, Solomon had seven hundred wives and three hundred concubines, based on 1 Kings 11:3. Additionally, Abraham, the friend of God, and Jacob (Israel), and David the king also had more than one wife. Mr. Deedat says, "There is not a single word of reproach in the "Book of God" the Holy Bible, against polygamous marriages." This, of course, is to defend polygamy amongst Muslims and as sanctioned in both the Qur'an and hadith.

hough many biblical characters had multiple wives, besides concubines, God does not endorse polygamy. From the days of Abraham to those of Solomon, having multiple wives and concubines was culturally accepted behavior. However, the opening material in Genesis endorses and sanctions one man married to one woman, these two becoming one flesh (Genesis 2:24). Furthermore, one doesn't have to look far in the Bible to find examples where polygamy caused a world of trouble for all involved.

In the New Testament era, and for many centuries before, there was no polygamy in Israel. Jewish men did not take more than one wife, and they had no concubines. Neither Jesus, nor any apostle, nor any author of a New Testament book ever endorsed polygamy. In the history of the Church, it is recorded that some took more than one wife, but this was rare and of no consequence and certainly not enough to say that Christianity endorses or approves of polygamy.

Again, Mr. Deedat is counting on the hope that few, if any, will check what he says.

Point 33: PROPHECIES: Empty threats

This Scripture:

» "But of the tree of the knowledge of good and evil thou [O Adam] shalt not eat of it: for IN THE DAY that thou eatest thereof thou shalt SURELY DIE" (Genesis 2:17, Deedat's emphasis).

Contradicted by:

» "And all the days that Adam lived were nine hundred and thirty years: and he died" (Genesis 5:5).

Mr. Deedat detects a contradiction between these two Scriptures. He even says that the serpent, Satan, was more truthful than God, when he said, "Ye shall not surely die" (Genesis 3:4).

Mr. Deedat demonstrates that he does not grasp the meaning of the passage. Adam and Eve did die; they were sent away from the presence of God—spiritual death. They did not die physically, at that point, though the Fall made them subject to death.

This understanding of death is core to the Bible. Physical death is one thing, and everyone does die, but the spiritual death is immeasurably more significant, since it means separation from God eternally.

The devil was deceitful. He lied, and Mr. Deedat does so here; it is a point that cannot be missed.

Point 34: PROPHETS (BUT NAKED): If such are the priests, God bless the congregation.

Here Mr. Deedat speaks of Noah, who, when drunk, lay naked in his tent (Genesis 9:21). Saul prophesied naked before Samuel (1 Samuel 19:24). Then King David danced naked (2 Samuel 6:20). Isaiah walked naked and barefoot three years (Isaiah 20:2), "Young and old, naked and barefoot, even with their buttocks uncovered, to the shame of Egypt" (Isaiah 20:4).

Starting with Isaiah, his nakedness was a form of dramatic prophecy, not uncommon in that era. Isaiah's prophecy was meant to demonstrate what the king of Assyria would do to the Egyptians after conquering them. It was certainly no endorsement of nakedness.

David danced naked, wild, and crazy, but not directed or sanctioned by God in this. Saul was also wild and crazy, and in a time when he was not walking in favor with God. Noah was drunk—not the Lord's doing, certainly.

Mr. Deedat attempts to say this is normal for all those who believe in the God of the Bible. He uses the word *priests*, a word not used in the New Testament to describe Christians. No priests existed in the early Church; this aberration came centuries later. Jesus is the Christians' great High Priest.

It is obvious that Mr. Deedat is hoping to scandalize both biblical personages and Christian leaders.

Point 35: RAPE: Brother rapes and commits incest with his sister.

Referring to the story of Amnon, a son of David, raping his sister Tamar, in 2 Samuel 13:14, as we discussed earlier in Point 16.

Son Commits Incest and Rapes His Mothers Wholesale!

The passage under consideration is 2 Samuel 16:22, where Absalom, another of David's sons, has sex with his father's concubines.

Mr. Deedat says the concubines are David's wives, which is not at all what the text says. The ancients clearly distinguished between a wife and a concubine, and Mr. Deedat must know this. He goes further, suggesting or insinuating that God ordains such behavior. Such behavior on the part of Amnon and Absalom is sinful. He also states, as seen above, that Absalom raped his mothers. This is an incredible departure from the text.

More incredible is that Muslims believe the God of the Hebrew Bible is Allah. So Mr. Deedat attributes moral improprieties to Allah?

Point 36: SABBATH: Sabbath as a standing insult to God in the Bible.

Exodus 31:17 reads, "For in six days the LORD made heaven and earth, and on the seventh day He rested, and WAS REFRESHED" (Deedat's emphasis).

On the Contrary, the Holy Qur'an States:

> "His throne doth extend
> Over the heavens
> And the earth, and He feeleth
> No fatigue in guarding
> And preserving them
> For He is the most High,
> The Supreme (in glory)."
> (Holy Qur'an 2:255)

Mr. Deedat's idea is that it is insulting to God to say that after creating the universe He had to be refreshed. Mr. Deedat points to the Qur'an verse that says God did not need to be refreshed, since the creating work did not exhaust him.

The Genesis parallel reads, "rest," and this is the meaning of Sabbath (see Genesis 2:1-2). The passage means that the work of God was complete or finished, and has nothing to do with resting after hard labor.

In the Exodus 31:17 passage, the word Sabbath is used, echoing Genesis 2:1-2, and another word for rest is also used. To distinguish the two words, "refresh" is used. But—and it must be known to Mr. Deedat—that "refresh" does not refer to recovering.

From the earliest times, there has been a Sabbath day—a day of rest, a day of peace. For Jews it is from sundown Friday to sundown Saturday. The tendency of Judaism has been to make Sabbath day rules burdensome.

The early Christians adopted Sunday for this day of rest, for differing reasons. The Christian emphasis is not so much on resting from work as resting in the finished work of Jesus. In Christ, who freely gives us forgiveness of sin and everlasting life, we can rest in His work. Here is how the writer of the book of Hebrews, addressing Jewish believers in Jesus, put it: "There remains a Sabbath rest for the people of God, for whoever has entered God's rest has also rested from his works as God did from His" (Hebrews 4:9-10).

The religions of the world focus on doing what is good and understanding mysteries, secrets, and knowledge. Biblical Christianity is far different: it is about relying upon our Savior, Jesus Christ, who died in our place and saved us by His grace. He did the work; we rest in it.

Point 37: SARAH: The Holy Bible does not even spare God from illicit sexual aspersions being ascribed to Him:

Mr. Deedat, speaking of the virgin birth of Mary, suggests that the coming upon Mary by the Holy Ghost is a kind of physical act, indeed a sexual act, in that it produces the baby Jesus.

Here is how Mr. Deedat quotes the key verse: "The Holy Ghost shall come upon thee. And the power of the most High shall overshadow thee (again, how?) (Luke 1:35).

Notice "(again, how?)"—this is added to the passage by Mr. Deedat. He is suggesting that God had sex, via the Holy Ghost, with Mary. Here indeed is a desperate attempt to scandalize the virgin birth and consequently, God Himself.

Mr. Deedat also refers to Sarah, who is beyond the years for a natural conception, but who miraculously conceives Isaac (Genesis 21:1–2). Here Abraham is the father, not an immaculate conception, but the conception is nevertheless miraculous.

Point 38: SLAVERY: Sanctioned by God:

Leviticus 25:46 is appealed to in order to support Mr. Deedat's position. "And ye shall take them **(the slaves)** as an inheritance for your children after you, to inherit them **(the slaves)** for a possession; they shall be your bondmen **(slaves)** forever" (Deedat's emphasis).

Slavery was of a different sort in that era. Instead of being slaughtered, captives were made slaves. This we understand. It can be viewed as an act of mercy. It must be noted that slavery was never enshrined by the Jewish people, and in later times was abandoned. Slavery is spoken of in the New Testament, in that a Christian belongs to Christ. Also, there are slaves mentioned in the early Church—actual slaves who acted as preachers and pastors.

It is rather curious that Mr. Deedat raises the point of slavery, since such was widely practiced by Muslims during the time of Muhammad and for centuries afterward and was sanctioned by him.

Point 39: SODOMY: The Bible's reason why human beings become lesbians and homosexuals.

Mr. Deedat quotes, in pieces, Romans 1:24–27, which depicts the human race crumbling into impurity. Here is the complete presentation:

> Therefore God gave them up to the lusts of their hearts to impurity, to the dishonoring of their bodies among themselves, because they exchanged the truth about God for a lie and worshipped and served the creature rather than the creator, who is blessed forever! Amen. For this reason God gave them up to dishonorable passions. For their women exchanged natural relations for those that are contrary to nature, and the men likewise gave up natural relations with women and were consumed with passion for one another, men committing shameless acts with men and receiving in themselves the due penalty for their error.

Mr. Deedat does not go further than this, indicating, I assume, that Islam has a different understanding of how and why people move into homosexuality.

My research and direct engagement with Muslims over the course of sixteen years shows that Islam rejects homosexuality among men and women, on paper at least, but excuses it wholesale, especially in Muslim-dominated countries. Among women, it is kept on the down-low.

Point 40: SONS OF GOD: The Bible ascribes sons by the tons to God.

Mr. Deedat points out that:
Enos, the son of Seth, was the **Son** of God (Luke 3:38).

1. The "**SONS OF GOD** saw the daughters of men that they were fair..." (Genesis 6:2).
2. "Thus saith the Lord, Israel is **MY SON** even **MY FIRSTBORN**" (Exodus 4:22)
3. "And Ephraim is my **FIRSTBORN**" (Jeremiah 31:9)
4. "Thou (O David) **ART MY SON**; this day have I (God) **BEGOTTEN** thee" (Psalm 2:7)
5. "For as many as are led by the Spirit of God, they are the **SONS OF GOD**" (Romans 8:14)

First, the words capitalized in bold above notify the reader that they are not capitalized in the Bible. The words in parentheses were added by Mr. Deedat. Then, Mr. Deedat seems to misunderstand that God continues to have sons. Does he mean to suggest that this is immoral behavior on the part of God?

The Scripture is clear that a son or daughter of God belongs to God and has a personal relationship with Him due to the new birth.

The metaphorical form of language cannot be lost on Mr. Deedat. He desires to tarnish the God of the Bible by means of gross misinterpretation and insinuation.

Point 41: SWINE: The flesh of the swine forbidden.

» Leviticus 11:8 states that the meat of swine, or pigs, is not to be eaten or even touched. The flesh of pigs is declared unclean.

For reasons that are unclear, at least to me, the Bible contains many commands having to do with certain animals that are not to be eaten. There may have been dietary and hygienic reasons behind the prohibitions. Some commentators suggest the food restrictions kept the Israelites from mingling with pagans, who ate meat sacrificed to idols.

In the New Testament, these commands are not continued, even for Jewish believers. There is an account of a vision Peter has that greatly impacts the Christian community, prior to his encounter with the Roman centurion Cornelius. While taking a nap on a rooftop at a home in Joppa, Peter sees a great sheet lowered from the sky with all manner of animals, including reptiles and birds. Then he hears a voice, "Rise, Peter; kill and eat" (Acts 10:13). Peter says he won't do so. Then the command is given a second time, with the addition of, "What God has made clean, do not call common" (v. 15).

The gist of the vision from God is that Gentiles are not unclean, but clean. This sets the stage for Peter's ministry to the Gentile Cornelius. This event changes Peter's position, and that of the whole Church, to accept Gentiles into the Church. As a byproduct, many food prohibitions also fall by the wayside.

Jesus (PBUH) Destroyed 2,000 Pigs to Heal One Man

Mr. Deedat brings up the story of Jesus casting a legion of demons out of a man, and the demons pleading with Jesus to be sent into a large herd of pigs grazing nearby. The pigs, now possessed by demons, stampede over a cliff into the sea and drown. This is found in Mark 5:1–20.

It is not clear to me what Mr. Deedat's point is. His issue could be that Jesus would allow two thousand pigs to be destroyed, as if to say, "What a waste!" If so, he assumes Jesus intended the destruction of the pigs, which is not evident from the account itself. Ironically, Muslims absolutely will not touch the flesh of a pig.

Point 42: WHORRING (sic): See under "Israelites" in the index.

Looking at the index under "Israelites" is found only Point 17, previously covered.

Point 43: WOMEN: Forbidden to open their mouths in the Church.

Mr. Deedat quotes from 1 Corinthians 14:35, "For it is a shame for women to speak in the church."

1 Corinthians 14 is a complex passage, and some parts of it, such as that quoted above, have generated much debate and discussion. There are a number of positions on the issue of what it means that women are not to speak in church services and meetings.

First of all, we note that women do so speak, from that day to this, though there are some who forbid it. By "speak" may be meant preaching, teaching, prophecy, and so on. But it may not. I am of the opinion that spiritual gifts, such as speaking in tongues, were getting out of hand and causing confusion in the Corinthian church specifically. Paul was all for order and sensibility.

On this point, I could go on and on. The reality is that some take it literally, but most do not. Let me point out that about half the churches in the world are pastored by women.

Point 44: WORSHIP:

Mr. Deedat points out that in Mark 5:6, part of the account of the man who had a legion of demons cast out of him by Jesus—which demons then invaded two thousand pigs—the word meaning "worship" is found. Some translations of the Mark 5 passage, such as the ESV, read "fell down before Him." The person who "fell down before Him" is the demon-possessed man, and the "Him" is Jesus.

It is unclear, at least to me, what Mr. Deedat's point is. He could be alarmed that a demon-possessed man worshipped Jesus. It must be noted that the demons did not worship Jesus, the possessed man did. When this desperate and tormented man saw Jesus, he ran to Him. Moments later, the devilish demons were gone, and the man so very much wanted to follow Jesus wherever He went. Jesus urged him to remain where he was, and said to him, "Go home to your friends and tell them how much the Lord has done for you, and how He has had mercy on you" (Mark 5:19).

Whereupon, we have the twentieth verse: "And he went away and began to proclaim in the Decapolis how much Jesus had done for him, and everyone marveled."

21

ISLAMIC HYGIENE

Information about Islamic hygiene is not abundant. The information for this essay is derived from three sources: One, personal conversations with Muslims and observations made over a three-year period during which I attended Friday prayers at a Sunni mosque. Often, sermons that precede the *adhan* (call to worship) and the imam's two sermons (units) in Arabic are in English and have to do with hygiene issues. Two, the booklet by Muhammad Vandestra, "The Etiquette of Eating & Personal Hygiene from Islamic Perspective."[1] Three, a book on Islamic prayer entitled *The Prescribed Prayer Made Simple* by Tajuddin B. Shu'aib.[2] You will find additional material on Islamic hygiene in the section covering Shariah law.

Based upon my understanding of Islamic hygiene, it seems that Muhammad Vandestra's work is written for a Western audience, meaning that some of the more unusual—shall we say—mechanisms of Islamic hygiene are softened and made less strange. It may be stated that some of the more bizarre means of achieving cleanliness have been deleted altogether.

One example of such omission is the role hygiene plays in coping with jinn and other demons. Perhaps the blowing of the nose three times every morning to rid oneself of jinn that have entered the body via the nostrils during the night is omitted since it is not a strictly hygienic process.

Also missing from the booklet are the extensive precautions designed to avoid splashing urine on clothing and what to do if this should occur. Indeed, there are many requirements concerning the use of the toilet that are missing from the book.

Following is a section by section summary of Muhammad Vandestra's booklet.

Prologue

The opening statement is: "The religion of Islam is a holistic way of life" (p. 5). This means

---

[1] Muhammad Vandestra, "The Etiquette of Eating & Personal Hygiene from Islamic Perspective" (2017; no publisher provided).

[2] Tajuddin B. Shu'aib, *The Prescribed Prayer Made Simple* (Los Angeles: Da'awah Enterprises International, Inc., 1993).

that everything about life comes under the purview of Islamic law.

Food and cleanliness are central, then, and Islam has complete guidelines on these subjects to make it easy for a Muslim to be rightly guided. The author states that the Prophet "reminded us that our body has certain rights and one of those rights is that it should be maintained with cleanliness" (p. 5).

The Etiquette of Eating in Islam

The Islamic guidelines about preparing food and the hands that touch the food are complete. The name of God must be mentioned before eating anything and everything. Muslims are not to over- or under-eat but always be moderate, even if the food is very delicious. The Prophet said it is not good to be overweight.

It is obligatory for Muslims to eat with the right hand. If the right hand is missing or disabled, the left hand may be used. However, the left hand is used to clean the body. "Prophet Muhammad also advised his companions that Satan eats with his left hand and that the believers should disassociate themselves from anything that resembles Satan" (p. 8).

Eating should be a worship activity for Muslims, being thankful and grateful to Allah. Uneaten food is not to be left for Satan. It is important to eat with three fingers, to lick the remains of the food off the fingers at the conclusion of the meal, to not recline while eating, and to refrain from spitting or blowing the nose while eating. It is good also to praise the food; one should not criticize food, but rather refrain from eating that which one does not like. Observing all of this will bring rewards from Allah.

The first thing a Muslim does before eating is say "Bismillah" (I begin with the name of God); after eating one is to say, "Alhamdulillah" (all praises and thanks are due to God). Qur'an 11:6 is quoted at this point: "And no moving (living) creature is there on earth but its provision is due from God."

Why it is that pork is absolutely outlawed in Islam? This would seem to be a question needing an answer, given the Qur'anic quote above.[3]

Cleanliness Is Part of Faith

"Islam places great emphasis on cleanliness" (p. 11). One must not even pray unless the body is clean. In Qur'an 2:222, we find that God "loves those who turn to Him in repentance and He loves those who keep themselves pure and clean" (p. 11). And it is important that after eating, the hands, mouth, and teeth be cleaned. Muhammad recommended using a tooth stick.

Good Advice Is a Mercy

"Prophet Muhammad was sent to the world as a mercy, he came to complete God's only religion and to teach us in practical ways how to please and worship God" (p. 11).

The prophet also taught about drinking water. He advised that "water should be

---

3   It is likely that Muhammad, knowing of the Jewish rejection of pork, followed suit to please the Jewish tribes in Mecca. Leviticus 11:7 and Deuteronomy 14:8 condemn eating pigs.

drunk in three breaths rather than gulping the water in one mouthful, and he cautioned against breathing into the vessel because it contaminates the water with spittle" (p. 11).

Personal Hygiene in Islam

Islam does not merely give advice about personal hygiene, it insists upon it and makes it obligatory or compulsory. Indeed, "cleanliness is half of faith" (p. 11).

It is especially important to remove "the dirt or grime that collects in the various parts of the body, such as teeth, nostrils, under the nails, in the armpits and around the pubic area" (p. 13).

Ritual Washing

Purity is the key to prayer. Before one prays, he must be sure that his heart is free from sin, arrogance, and hypocrisy. Once this is accomplished, he is then able to clean himself from physical impurities, and this is usually done using water.

The problem with this instruction is that we are unable to purify our own hearts of sin, arrogance, and hypocrisy without the help of God. According to Jesus, we can be as clean as a whitewashed tomb on the outside and still filthy on the inside. His concern is with our hearts.

Qur'an 5:6 instructs: "O you who believe! When you intend to offer the prayer, wash your faces and your hands (forearms) up to the elbows, wipe your heads, and (wash) your feet up to the ankles. If you are in a state of Janaha (i.e., had a sexual discharge) purify yourself" (p. 14).

In Shariah law, a great deal of attention is given to the contaminating effect of bodily fluids coming into contact with skin and clothing. This is in sharp contrast to the New Testament, which treats sexual love between a husband and wife as a gift from the Creator.

Ritual purification is either by *wudu*, or ablution of only a part of the body (i.e., the hands or feet), or by *ghusl*, a full bath. Wudu rids the body of minor impurities and ghusl rids it of major impurities. "Ghusl must be performed after sexual intercourse or any sexual activity that releases bodily fluids" (p. 14).

"Ritual cleansing of the body by performing wudu includes washing the hands, rinsing the mouth and nose, washing the face, washing the arms up to the elbows, wiping the head (and beard), washing the ears, including behind the ears and washing the feet up to and including the ankle. A person does not have to repeat this ablution for every prayer unless he has broken his wudu by one of the following methods; urinating or defecating, breaking wind, eating camel meat, falling asleep while lying down, losing consciousness, directly touching the genital area or becoming sexually excited sufficiently to emit a discharge" (p. 14).

Ritual purity can be achieved without water. This is called *tayammum*, or dry ablution. This is done by striking the hands lightly over clean earth and then passing the palm of each hand on the back of the other, the dust is then blown off and the hands are passed across the face. (p. 15)

If it is not possible to work wudu or ghusl due to circumstances, Allah is merciful.

Then there is the concept of *fitrah*. It means causing a thing to exist for the first time, and that is what Allah did in creating the world. Muhammad said "that every child was born in a state of fitrah, with the correct understanding of God" (p. 15).

Included in this innate understanding, this fitrah, are five things: shaving the pubic hair, circumcision, trimming the moustache, plucking the armpit hairs, and cutting the nails" (p. 16). These are now examined below.

Shaving the Pubic Hair

Shaving the pubic hair makes it easier to maintain purity, as urine and feces may be trapped in the pubic hair or on the skin. So Muslims are advised to keep their genital area and underwear as clean as possible. Muhammad advised use of the left hand for this cleaning. He also advised plucking the hair out, but other methods can now be used. The use of toilet paper is not enough either. Water must also be applied. "Muslim homes often have water hoses installed next to the toilet or have water jugs available to facilitate cleanliness" (p. 17).

Circumcision

This is obligatory for Muslim men, which makes it easier to keep the genital area clean. "Female circumcision is not part of the obligatory rites of Islam" (p. 17).

(The above statement about female circumcision is what is usually presented to a Western audience, disguising the fact that in many places in the Muslim world, including Muslim enclaves in Western nations, female circumcision (female genital mutilation of FGM) is widely practiced.

Trimming the Moustache

The Prophet made it clear that a Muslim male should have a beard, but shave the moustache. There are some differences of opinion on this issue. Mainly, the hairs of the moustache are not to get into the mouth.

Plucking the Armpit Hairs

Though plucking would be the best way to remove armpit hair, other methods may be used. The reason for the removal of this hair is that sweat and grime can accumulate there, and thus one is not in a ritual state of purity. This applies for both men and women.

Cutting the Nails

As above, dirt, grime, and bacteria can be found under the nails of both hands and feet, thus rendering one ritually impure. Such impurity would mean no rewards from Allah, despite carefully performing acts of prayer and worship.

The Prophet Muhammad, it is stated by the author, advised this cleaning be done at least every forty days. After all, physical purity is as important as spiritual purity. "Pleasing God is the ultimate goal and God reminds us in Quran that cleanliness is pleasing to Him" (p. 18).

Visiting the Sick

"Visiting the sick is an obligation rewarded by the Most Merciful God, and was the practice of his merciful Prophet Muhammad" (p. 19). Visiting the sick is a sign of mutual love.

Summary of *The Prescribed Prayer Made Simple* by Tajuddin B. Shu'aib

"Purification can be achieved using pure water. Pure water is that which is pure in itself and can purify anything else" (p. 26). Pure water must be rainwater, ice water, rivers, or water from melted snow. According to a hadith, seawater is also pure, as is water from wells and fountains.

Relieving Oneself

In regard to relieving oneself, there is a prayer to be said before entering the toilet: "In the name of Allah, O Allah! I seek refuge with You from all offensive and wicked things (evil deeds and evil spirits)."

It is haram, or forbidden, to enter the toilet carrying anything that has the name Allah on it, including the Qur'an, and jewelry such as bracelets or necklaces.

One should be silent while in the toilet. If one sneezes, then it is necessary to say, Allamdu Lillaah. From a hadith from Ibn 'Ubar is: "The Prophet was urinating when a man passed by and greeted him, but the Prophet did not answer him."

If a person, driven by necessity, has to relieve himself in an open place, he should not face the Qiblah or turn his back to it.

One must be out of sight, so the doors of the toilet should be closed.

One should avoid urinating in any hole around shade trees or fruit trees, or riverbanks near water tanks, or where people perform ablution, or any place that people gather.

After using the toilet, one should clean oneself with water. One can use water and paper. After relieving oneself and cleaning oneself, one should say, "Praise be to Allah who relieved me of the filth and gave me relief" (p. 28).

Shaving the pubic hairs and plucking the hair under the armpits can be performed by either cutting or trimming the hair. The nails of both hands and feet must be cut and the moustache clipped. A hadith from *Sahih Muslim* reads: "Five are the acts of Fitrah, circumcision, cutting the nails, shaving, clipping the moustache, and plucking the hair under the armpits" (pp. 28–29).

These acts are best done once a week. Other hadith say these should be done at least every forty days.

Having gray hair on the head or in the beard is okay, but dye can be used.

"Using perfume is recommended, as it gives one a good feeling. The Prophet used to like Musk more than any other kind of perfume" (p. 29).

22

Christian Hygiene?

Are Christians interested in hygiene? Yes, of course. But not for spiritual reasons.

There are Levitical law codes found in the book of Leviticus and other books of the Torah as well, especially in Deuteronomy, that have a focus on hygiene. The reason for these laws is variously understood. Some say it has to do with keeping the people of Israel healthy; both Jewish and Christian scholars will hold to this. Orthodox Jews, to this very day, attempt to follow these law codes, but most Christians do not.

There are exceptions. Messianic Christians may practice some of the Levitical laws regarding foods and their preparation. However, Christians traditionally see the law code of the Torah as *prophetic*.

Christian expositors have for centuries seen the regulations in the law of Moses as depicting the age of the Messiah. These scholars see in the Hebrew Bible a thread of prophetic material that runs straight to Jesus and the cross. The fine-tuned decorations of the temple, the way sacrifices are regulated in the temple, small details in terms of colors, measurements, and much more, are there to point toward the sinless Lamb of God, bearing as the ultimate sacrifice the sin of God's people upon Himself.

Examining the instructions for the exodus from Egypt—the selection of the Passover Lamb, the placing of the blood on the doorposts and lintel—we see the story of Jesus. During the Last Supper, a Passover meal, Jesus makes it clear the unleavened bread is His broken body, and the wine is His blood. Jesus is the Passover Lamb. The story in Exodus 12 is seen by most Christians as prophetic. This is my view as well.

Matthew 5:17

The Christian "law code"—if there is such a thing—is thought to be the Sermon on the Mount, found in Matthew chapters 5, 6, and 7. Perhaps the key verse in the sermon is Matthew 5:17: "Do not think that I have come to abolish the Law or the Prophets; I have not come to abolish them but to fulfill them."

Jesus, clearly, did not instruct His followers to obey the law of Moses found in the Torah. Jesus did not conform to many of the regulations that the Pharisees observed. Regularly then, He got into plenty of trouble with the Pharisees for this neglect. Jesus, as seen in Matthew 5:17, states He will fulfill them.

Jesus completes or fulfills the prophetic thread that runs through Scripture. All of the minute regulations point to the Messianic ministry Jesus established. No longer would God's presence be in the Holy of Holies part of the temple. No, God became flesh and dwelt among His people. And He continues to do so through the ministry of the indwelling Holy Spirit.

There is a law that Jesus left us: We are to love the Lord our God with all we are and have, and we are to love our neighbor as ourselves (Matthew 22:34–40). We are to do to others as we would have done to us. We are to love our enemies. This law of love is one that every Christian breaks, without wanting to, all day long. (As a young Christian, I boasted to myself that I was right on track, but in later years I saw how spiritually immature I really am.)

In Islam, the many rules of Shariah law are kept in order to please Allah and tip the scales of judgment in our favor. We Christians, despite our weaknesses, still desire to follow the law of love—not to earn points with God but because we want to be like Jesus. This distinction makes all the difference.

Close

We humans would rather do than be. It is easier to do than to be, especially when we learn to lie to ourselves and repress the unclean, selfish thoughts in the process. Doing allows us to take some credit for our imagined goodness.

Yes, we like to be good people and help people and be nice—and we do and can to some degree. There are those who are more altruistic than others—than I am—but how wonderful do you have to be to earn favor with God?

The follower of Jesus comes to the reality that he or she is not good enough, cannot be good enough, will not ever be good enough, and so then must rely upon the mercy and grace of our Lord Jesus Christ.

The best hygiene is the cleansing power of the blood of the Passover Lamb. "But if we walk in the light, as He is in the light, we have fellowship with one another, and the blood of Jesus His Son cleanses us from all sin" (1 John 1:7).

23

NAMES GIVEN TO MUHAMMAD IN THE QUR'AN AND HADITH

The Prophet	Of Perfect Character
The Messenger of Allah	Gifted With Every Merit
The Beloved	The Remover of Disbelief
The Chosen One	The One of Primordial Religion
The Trustworthy	The Prophet of Penitence
The Honest	The Strengthened One
The Kind	The One Made Invulnerable
The Model of Conduct	Held in Awe
The Perfect Man	The Opener
The Best of Mankind	The Gatherer (First to be Resurrected) on the Day of Judgment
The Seal (Last) of the Prophets	The Intercessor
Love, Mercy and Compassion to the Worlds (all creation)	The One Whose Intercession Shall be Granted
The Witness	The Comforter
The Bearer of Good Tidings	Father of Al-Qasim
The Warner	Father of the Pure
The Reminder	Father of the Pleasant
The One Who Calls (unto God)	Father of Abd Allah
The Announcer	Father of Ibrahim
The Light Personified	Grand Son of Abd al-Muttalib
The Light-Giving Lamp	Most Deserving of Praise
The Noble and Generous One	Praiser of God

The Divine Favor	Praiseworthy
The Unlettered Prophet	Servant of Allah
The Universal Prophet	Last Prophet
The Enwrapped	Last Messenger
The Shrouded	Final Prophet
The Last Prophet	Final Messenger
The One who Puts his Trust in God	The Walking Qur'an

Comments: Muslims must not attribute deity to Muhammad, and to do so would be to make Muhammad a partner with Allah. Many of the names above, and there are said to be 201 names, are titles that would seem should be reserved for God alone.

Go to http://www.netuse.co.uk/clients/salawaat/Asma-un-Nabi.htm for a complete list of the 201 names.

24

TWENTY-FIVE WAYS

"Twenty-Five Ways to Enter Jannah (Paradise)" is a traditional Islamic text. It conforms to this topic since proper eating and hygiene have primarily to do with earning the favor of Allah and thus securing a place in Paradise.

The source is given in brackets at the conclusion of each of the twenty-five ways. Most of them are from the hadith.[1]

1. Whoever meets Allah without ascribing anything to Him will enter Jannah. (Sahih al-Bukhari)

2. Whoever believes (has Iman) in Allah and His messenger (peace be upon him), and establishes the prayer and the fasts in the month of Ramadan, it is incumbent upon Allah that He enters him in Jannah. (Sahih al-Bukhari)

3. Whoever says: "I am pleased with Allah as my Rabb, and with Islam as my Deen, and with Muhammad (peace be upon him) as my Prophet, Jannah would be mandatory for him. (Sunan Abu Dawud)

4. Whoever asks Allah for Jannah three times, Jannah will say: "O Allah, enter him into Jannah." (Jami'al-Timidhi)

5. Whoever says "SubhanAllah al-adthim wa Bihamdhi (Glorified and exalted is Allah, The Great, and with His Praise), a date-palm tree will be planted for him in Jannah. (Jami'al-Tirmidhi)

6. Allah has Ninety Nine Names, one hundred minus one, and whoever believes in their meanings and acts accordingly, will enter Jannah. (Sahih al-Bukhari)

7. Indeed, truthfulness leads to righteousness and indeed righteousness leads to Jannah. (Sahih al-Bukhari)

8. Whoever builds a masjid seeking by it the Pleasure of Allah, Allah will build for him a similar place in Jannah. (Sahih al-Bukhari)

9. Whoever repeats after the Mu'adthin (the caller to prayer) from his heart (i.e., sincerely) will enter Jannah. (Sunan an-Nasa'i)

---

1 Rather than editing obvious flaws in the "25 Ways," the text is presented verbatim.

10. Whoever calls the Adhan for 12 years, Jannah will become mandatory for him. (Sunan Ibn Majah)

11. Whoever prays the two cool prayers (Asr and Fajr) will go to Paradise. (Sahih al-Bukhari)

12. Allah will prepare for him who goes to the mosque (every) morning and in the afternoon (for the congregational prayer) an honorable place in Paradise with good hospitality for (what he has done) every morning and afternoon goings. (Sahih al-Bukhari)

13. Any one who performs the ablution perfectly and then offers 2 rak'ahs of prayers concentrating on them with his heart and face, Paradise will necessarily fall to his lot. (Sunan Abu Dawud)

14. Whoever prays 12 Rak'ah in the day and night, a house in Jannah will be built for him. (Sunan an-Nasa'i)

15. Whoever takes a path in search of knowledge, Allah will make easy for him the path to Jannah. (Jami' at-Tirmidhi)

16. I saw a man going about in Jannah (and enjoying himself) as a reward for cutting from the middle of the road, a tree which was causing inconvenience to the Muslims. (Muslim)

17. Whoever can guarantee (the chastity of) what is between his two jawbones and what is between his two legs (i.e., his tongue and his private parts), I guarantee Paradise for him. (Sahih al-Bukhari)

18. Anyone whose soul leaves his body and he is free of three things, will enter Jannah: Arrogance, stealing from the spoils of war, and debt. (Sunan Ibn Majah)

19. Whoever raises two girls then I and he will enter Jannah like these two (Prophet indicated with his two fingers). (Jami' at-Tirmidhi)

20. Whoever visits an ailing person or a brother of his to seek the Pleasure of Allah, an announcer (angel) calls out: "May you be happy, may your walking be blessed, and may you be awarded a dignified position in Jannah". (Jami' at-Tirmidhi)

21. Allah guarantees him who strives in His Cause and whose motivation for going out is nothing but Jihad in His Cause and belief in His Word, that He will admit him into Jannah. (Sahih al-Bukhari)

22. O people, spread the Salaam (greetings), feed the hungry, and pray while the people are asleep, you will enter Jannah in peace. (Sunan Ibn Majah)

23. (The performance of) Umrah is an expiation for the sins committed between it and the previous Umrah; and the reward of Hajj Mabrur (i.e., one accepted) is nothing but Jannah. (Sahih al-Bukhari)

24. Whosoever's last words are: La ilaha illa Allah, will enter Paradise. (Sunan abu dawud)

25. O Allah, You are my Lord, none has the right to be worshipped except

you, You created me and I am Your servant and I abide to Your covenant and promise as best I can, I take refuge in You from the evil of which I committed. I acknowledge Your favor upon me and I acknowledge my sin, so forgive me, for verily none can forgive sin except You (Allahumma anta rbbi la ilaha illa ant, khalaqtani wa ana 'abduka, wa ana 'ala ahdika wa wa'dika ma-stata 'tu. A'udhu bika min sharri ma sana 'tu wa abu'u ilayka bini'matika 'alayya wa a'tarfu bidhunubi faghfirli dhunubi innahu la yagh-firudy-dhununba illa ant). If somebody recites this invocation during the day, and if he should die then, he will be from the people of Jannah. And if he recites it in the night, and if he should die on the same day, he will be from the people of Jannah." (Jami' at-Tirmidhi)

May Allah SWT forgive all our sins, help us to stay on the right path and unite us in His Jannat-ul-Firasue. Ameen.

Concluding note:

These Twenty-Five ways a Muslim can enter Paradise most graphically reveals Islam to be a works-based religion, which is characteristic of most of the world's religions. Of course, unhappily, much of Christianity conforms to this same view.

We speak of "works versus grace" and grace meaning that the God of Scripture freely gives forgiveness of sin and eternal life to all those who are born again. And there is absolutely nothing a person can due to achieve or acquire grace. No one can birth themselves. (see John 3:1-15)

28

SIGNIFICANT MUSLIM POPULATIONS

Map showing percent of population being Muslim worldwide[1]

Afghanistan

Islam is the official religion of Afghanistan, accounting for 99.8% of the population. About 80% are Sunni with the rest being Shi'a. Most of the Shi'a belong to the Twelver sect.

Africa

Most Muslims in Africa are Sunni, but country by country there will be different schools on how to interpret Sharia Law. Muslims constitute about 45% of the population of Africa.

Algeria

The vast majority of Algerians are Sunni Muslim. There is a small population of

---

1 Map image by M. Tracy Hunter (Own work) [CC BY-SA 3.0 (http://creativecommons.org/licenses/by-sa/3.0)], via Wikimedia Commons

Ibadis and Sufis. Islam came to the country in the latter part of the seventh century.

Egypt

Nearly 90% of the population of Egypt is Muslim, and most of these are Sunni. There is a small minority of Shi'a and Ahmadi Muslims. There is also a Christian minority, numbering anywhere from 3 to 20%. Islam is the state religion of Egypt.

India

The Muslim population of India is 15%, second only to Hinduism, which means the Muslims total about 176 million people. There are Sunni, Shi'a, and a number of other Muslim sects in India.

Indonesia

Islam is the dominant religion in Indonesia and has the highest Muslim population, about 200 million, of any country in the world. Officially Indonesia is a secular state. Most are Sunni, at least on paper, and large numbers are moderate as opposed to being traditional hardliners.

Iran

Islam is the official religion of Iran since the Islamic Revolution of 1979, at 99.5%. Of the Muslim population, about 93% are Shi'a and the rest Sunni. Most of the Shi'a are Twelvers. Iran's population is mostly Persian.

Iraq

The Shi'a branch of Islam is estimated at about 65% with the rest Sunni. The Kurds, who occupy much of northern Iraq are about 90% Sunni with the rest Shi'a. Iraq's population is mostly Arab.

Israel

The Muslims in Israel are mostly Arab and represent about 18% of the population. Jerusalem is Islam's third holiest location, and the temple mount is where Mohammad is said to have ascended to Paradise.

Jordan

Jordan is a majority Muslim country, 95% of whom are Sunni. There are also Salafi and Druze, with various Christian denominations making up about 4% or the population.

Kenya

Approximately 11% of the population of Kenya identifies as Muslim, most of whom live near the coast of the Indian Ocean. Most Muslims in Kenya are Sunni, but there are also Shi'a and Ahmadi followers.

Kuwait

Islam is the state religion of Kuwait. It is estimated that 63% are Sunni and the rest Shi'a. There are also small numbers of Christians, Hindu, Buddhist, and Bahai.

Lebanon

Lebanon is the most religiously diverse country in the Middle East. Muslims represent the majority of the population, with about 27% being Sunni and 27% being Shi'a. There are about 16 other religions represented, however, among which are the Greek Orthodox Church, the Protestant Church, the Armenian Apostolic Church, and Druze. The various Christian groups make up about 40% of the rest of Lebanon's population.

Libya

The majority of Muslims in Libya are Sunni. Islam arrived in the late seventh century to North Africa. For much of its history, there was no separation of church and state.

Malaysia

Islam makes up about 62% of the population, which is mostly Sunni. Malaysia identifies itself as a Muslim nation.

Morocco

The vast majority of Muslims in Morocco are of the Sunni branch. And as with other North African countries, Islam arrived in the late seventh century.

Nigeria

Of the countries of West Africa, Nigeria has the largest number of Muslims, which amounts to about 50% of the population. Muslims in Nigeria are mostly Sunni, but there are Shi'a and Ahmadi minorities.

Oman

The population of Oman is considered to be 100% Muslim and belong to the Ibadi sect of Islam, which is close to Sunni Islam. Oman's Muslims are considered moderate and tolerant.

Pakistan

Islam is the state religion of Pakistan, yet it is religiously diverse, with about 80% Sunni, 18% Shi'a, and 2% Ahmadi, but also with Hindu, Christian, Bahai, Sikh, Zoroastrian, and Kalash religious groupings.

Qatar

Qatar's state religion is Islam with 80% of the population being Muslim of a strict version of Islam. Along with Saudi Arabia, they are the only two Muslim countries following this strict practice of Salafi or Wahhabist Islam. There is a Christian minority that accounts for nearly 9% of the population, many or most of which are foreign workers living and employed in Qatar.

Saudi Arabia

Sunnis make up about 85% of the Muslim population, with Shi'a Muslims making up the rest. The nation was founded by the House of Saud in 1932, and Islam is the state religion.

What is now Saudi Arabia is the original home of Islam, with both Mecca and Medina in it's borders. It is also the birth and burial place of Mohammad. Saudi Arabia is also where the Arab language was born and where the Qur'an was compiled.

Somalia

1,400 years ago Islam came to Somalia, and the vast majority of population belongs to the Sunni branch. Salafism, the more strict and traditional view and practice of Islam, is present within the Muslim population.

Sudan

The vast majority of the population of Sudan is Muslim which has dominated the country since 1956. About 3% of Sudanese are Christians or animists. Sufism also has a presence in Sudan, which has made the country more moderate and tolerant than it otherwise might be.

Syria

Some 90% of Syrians are Muslims, and Sunnis make up 74% of this number, while Shi'a Muslims are about 13%. Among the Shi'a Muslims are the smaller sects of the Alawites, Twelvers, and Ismailis. There are also several large Sufi orders present in Syria as well. Druze, not really Muslims, make up about 3% of the population. President Assad is from the Alawite tribe.

Tunisia

Islam is the official state religion of Tunisia, of which the vast majority are Sunnis, and the constitution demands the president must be a Muslim. As in most of the North African countries of Algeria, Libya, and Morocco, Tunisia's Muslims are not all practicing the religion, and the percentage of the faithful is not easily determined.

Turkey

Muslims make up about 98% of the population of Turkey, with the rest being non-religious. 78% of Muslims in Turkey are of the Sunni branch, with the Shi'a branch accounting for about 20%. Urban Muslims in Turkey are quite moderate, diverse, and tolerant.

United Arab Emirates

Islam is the state religion of the United Arab Emirates, with about 85% being Sunni Muslim and the remainder Shi'a. There are also Ismaili Shi'a and Ahmadi Muslims.

Yemen

The vast majority of Yemenis are Muslim, with 56% being Sunni and 44% Shi'a, and this 44% is largely of the Zaidi order of Shi'a Islam. It is said that Ali established Islam in Yemen while Mohammad was still living.

26

THREE RELIGIOUS MOVEMENTS ASSOCIATED WITH ISLAM

Bahai'i, Subud, and Sufism

Bahai

Primary Beliefs

The religion is generally known as Baha'i Faith. It is monotheistic, that is, believing in one God. Central to Baha'i is that all the major religions come from the one and same God who is creator of all, and thus all religions are united whether they know it or not. The main doctrines of Baha'i are the unity of God, the unity of religion, and the unity of humankind. The goal is for all human beings to know who God is and to love him. The methods to achieve this are prayer, reflection, and being of service to others. Human spirituality is evolutionary, such that, with each messenger God sends, progress toward ultimate spirituality is accomplished.

To achieve ultimate spirituality, God sends divine messengers from time to time, about every 1,000 years, including Abraham, Krishna, Zoroaster, Moses, Buddha, Jesus, and Muhammad. The most recent messengers are the Bab and Baha'u'llah. Baha'u'llah is said to have been prophesied by the other religions and fulfills the expectations of a Messiah. Others who made such claims, Joseph Smith of Mormonism, Sung Young Moon of the Unification Church, and other claimants, would not be considered as legitimate messengers of God.

Brief History

Baha'u'llah (In Arabic the name means "The Glory of God") was born on November 12, 1817, in Tehran, Iran (Persia), which was dominated by Islam. The last part of Baha'u'llah's name is derived from Allah. He married in October, 1835. He died on May 29, 1892.
On Mary 23, 1844, Siyyid'Ali-Muhammad of Shiraz, Iran, declared he was the Bab, meaning "the Gate." He was claiming to be the Madhi, the Twelfth and last Imam of the Shiite branch of Islam. The Bab announced the coming of "He who God shall make mani-

fest." His followers became known as Babis. The religious leaders of Iran then persecuted the Bab and his followers. The Bab was executed in 1850.

In 1852, Baha'u'llah was first imprisoned due to his identification with the Babis. While in prison he claimed to receive a vision of God's will for the people of the entire world.

In 1863, Baha'u'llah announced he was the divine revelation the Bab had prophesied was to come. Baha'u'llah, having become the figurehead of the movement, was arrested and thrown into a notorious prison, the "Black Pit."

It was in Baha'u'llah's long years in prison that he wrote a number of books that would become the "scripture" of the Baha'is.

After the death of Baha'u'llah in 1892, Abdu'l-Baha succeeded him as leader of the religion. In 1921, Abdu'l-Baha died and Shoghi Effendi took over as "Guardian." Shoghi Effendi died in 1957, and in 1963 the Universal House of Justice in Jerusalem was created to serve as the headquarters for Baha'i.

Source Of Authority

The writings that are considered to be of divine origin are authored by the Bab and Baha'u'llah. The writings and talks of Abdu'l-Baha and Shoghi Effendi are considered authoritative interpretation of the Baha'is scripture. The writings of the Universal House of Justice are looked upon as "authoritative legislation and elucidation."

Baha'u'llah's teachings dealt with social and ethical themes, but he wrote a number of books that were of a mystical nature. Chief of these is *The Seven Valleys*, which speaks of the soul's journey towards God. Another of Baha'u'llah's books, *The Hidden Words*, also speaks of mystical concepts.

Baha'u'llah developed a teaching involving a "Greater Covenant" which set forth the appearance of a Messenger of God to all of humankind around every 1,000 years at a time of chaos and confusion. The "Lesser Covenant" is an agreement between the Messenger of God, Baha'u'llah, and his followers in this "dispensation." Followers are expected to abide by this Lesser Covenant. There have been a number of schisms in Baha'i over the years, and covenant breakers are usually shunned and excommunicated.

Islam And Baha'i

Both the Bab and Baha'u'llah were Muslims of the Shiite branch, and Baha'u'llah considered himself to be the successor to Muhammad. Due to this, Baha'i continues to be persecuted in Islamic countries, especially in Iran, Afghanistan, Egypt, Indonesia, and Iraq.

Trends

There are approximately six million members of the religion worldwide. Statistics on Baha'i are difficult to come by, but indications are that its membership is declining.

Subud

Primary Beliefs

Subud, an international spiritual movement, began in Indonesia in the 1920s and claims to have no doctrinal beliefs. It is centered on a spiritual event experienced during the initiation ceremony to Subud. Though the founder of Subud was Muslim, Subud is not steeped in Islamic doctrine and practice.

Subud is a spiritual practice centered on the Latihan Kejiwaan, described as a vivid encounter with the divine, where an individual surrenders to the divine force within each person. The initiate surrenders to the "power of God" or the "Great Life Force."

The core of Subud is the personal experience of the Latihan. The word Latihan generally means "opening" as in opening up to divine presence or reality.

The word "Subud" is an acronym that incorporates three Sanskrit words - *susila*, *budhi*, and dharma. Suzila means "well-disposed," and "good-tempered." Budhi refers to the mindset or outlook of a Buddha and an enlightening as to the nature of things. Dharma refers to the basic laws that regulate the universe. These terms reveal a co-mingling of Jainism, Buddhism, Sikhism, and Hinduism.

Brief History

Muhammad Subuh Sumohadiwidjojo, also referred to as Pak Subuh and Bapak, the originator of Subud, was born in Indonesia in 1901 and died in 1987. Bapak (the name most commonly used) describes an event in 1925 when he received an unusual experience. He said that while on a late night walk he found himself enveloped in a brilliant light. He said it was like the sun falling directly onto his body. Frightened and thinking he was having a heart attack, he went home to rest, but the experience was so strong that he surrendered himself to it.

After resting for some time, he rose and began performing movements similar to the Muslim prayer practices he had grown up with. He did not seem to be moving on his own accord but rather the experience was one of being involuntarily manipulated. He thought the force moving him was the power of God. He reported that this same experience continued for 1,000 days during which he experienced "inner teaching" and was given the ability to understand a variety of things spontaneously. Bapak said he gained insight into people and their situations.

In 1933 he "received" the assurance that other people could gain the same spiritual experiences if they were physically near him while he was in a state of "latihan" or opening. The term "opened" is what was said then to happen to people—they were opened up as he had been and could, in turn, open others. The core of Subud then is the latihan or opening experience.

Source Of Authority

Bapak himself and the recounting of his experience of being opened is the sole source of authority for Subud. Subud is not a religion or a teaching, or so their literature contends, but is a spiritual experience of being "awakened" by the Power of God. Such enlightenment is intended to free a person from the passions of desiring and thinking.

Bapak's book, *Susila Budhi Dharma*, written in 1952, is looked upon as Subud's chief authority. In addition, guidance and direction for Subud is also derived from the many talks Bapak made.

Though there are no formal rules, Bapak advised at least two practices that should be observed: one, men and women are not included in the latihan together; and two, a person must be "opened" before attending a latihan.

The World Subud Association directs Subud.

Latihan Kejiwaan

The latihan is a spiritual exercise or training of the spirit. Men and women go separately, about twice a week, to a center for a latihan.

After sitting and receiving "helpers" instructions, the members stand and act on the basis of what comes from within them. They will make involuntary movements, some quiet, others dramatic. There will be dancing, crying, jumping, skipping, laughing, the making of strange sounds, and so on. It is said that such phenomenon were observed in the wild camp meetings that were experienced in the second awakening in America during the early 1800s. Appeal is also made to ecstatic events that accompanied the "Laughing Revival" at the Toronto Vineyard Church during the 1980s and 90s.

Participants in the latihan report they experience purifying, cleansing, or a sense that they are energized and reaching greater peace.

The latihan can be experienced alone, but the group event is preferred.

Islam And Subud

Though Bapak was Muslim, probably a moderate, there is no clear Muslim teaching in Subud. There may be a Muslim connection through Sufism, however, which is an Islamic offshoot that incorporates activities similar to the latihan and brings participants into an ecstatic state of mind. In some ways, Subud has more connection with Buddhism and Hinduism than Islam.

Fasting

Bapak recommended fasting during a period of time that lines up with the Muslim fast of Ramadan. Some fast during Lent or at other times. It is thought that fasting can be spiritually edifying.

Trends

There are Subud members in 83 countries with more than 10,000 members worldwide. The focus of the work of Subud is directly helping people in third world countries in a variety of ways. There is little focus on bringing in new members. That religious doctrines are virtually absent from Subud attracts those who are generally anti-religious but pro-spirituality. The process towards membership requires a person attend classes twice a week for three months and then attend a latihan with the hope of being "opened." Due to the simplicity of the process and the fact it is open to anyone of whatever belief, the movement will continue to grow albeit slowly. It is a viable option in the spiritual marketplace.

Sufism

Sufism is the mystical side of Islam. The one who so practices is called a Sufi. There are many "orders" in Sufism that are likened to the denominations in Christianity. The orders are formed around meeting places known as a tekke. Except for Western forms of Sufism, Sufis are expected to be observant Muslims and adhere to Islamic law, but this is not always observed, especially in its Western versions.

The origin of the word "sufi" is variously understood. One tradition is that it comes from the Arabic word which means "purity." Another suggests it is derived from the Arabic word for "wool," indicating the rough dress of the Sufi ascetic. There is also the combination of the two: the Sufi wears wool on top of purity. Tradition says that Sufi comes from the Greek word for wisdom—*sofia*. Still another tradition is that Sufi comes from the Arabic word *ahl as-suffah* used to describe poor followers of Muhammad who practiced *dhikr*. Dhikr refers to the practice of repeating the names of God following traditional prayers, and/or a form of asceticism—practicing self-denial.

Basic Beliefs

Traditionally, Sufi scholars believe their teachings and practices are the pure and original form of Islam. Sufism is claimed to be "a science whose objective is the reparation of the heart and turning it away from all else but God." Sufism is likened to a vehicle in which one can travel or journey into the presence of the Divine by purifying the mind and inner self from the corruption of the world and thus acquiring exemplary ways of living.

Muslims hold that they have, due to Muhammad and the Qur'an, the right path to God, and by following the teaching of the Qur'an they will come close to God in paradise. Historic Sufism embraces these doctrinal tenants but goes further, believing it is possible to come closer to God in this lifetime rather than waiting for death and Paradise. It is through mystical experiences that this closeness to God is achieved. It is generally thought that Sufism was influenced by mystical forms of Hinduism and Buddhism, including practices of Christian monks living the ascetic life in the deserts of Arabia during the early Muslim period.

The core of Sufism may be expressed in this way: By following self-discipline, focusing on God, suppressing the self, and having sincere adoration for God, it is possible to enter into a union with God where the self disappears; and thus the connection with Hinduism and Buddhism. Further it must be noted that the goal of the Sufi is very similar to and connected with the goal of the shaman—a direct spiritual contact with the divine.

"The Perfect Man" is a core concept of Sufism. This Perfect Man is the perfect channel of grace from God to human beings. This Perfect Man is in a state of sanctity, or perfection. The Perfect Man is like a supposed "axis" of the universe where the divine intersects with the non-divine. The axis or pole in Arabic is Qutb and the Sufi Qutb is equivalent to Shi'as Imam and forms one of the basic points of conflict between Sufism and Islam.

Brief History

Sufism emerged out of Islam during the ninth and tenth centuries or about two hundred years after the time of Muhammad. It was a reaction against the corruption, the materialism, and the political goals of the victorious Islamic armies. Sufi orders claim their origins go back to the Prophet Muhammad through his son-in-law (and cousin) Ali. (The Sufi order Naqshbandi, however, trace their origin to the first Caliph, Abu Bakr.)

The traditional history is that Muhammad gave his disciples who had the ability to grasp it a direct experience with God. Those who were able to receive the teaching then passed it down to others and so on through the centuries.

Becoming A Sufi

To become a Sufi, one must first find a teacher with proper standing and authority, which has been passed down from "masters of the way" going directly back to Muhammad.

Al-Ghazali taught that the one seeking to be a Sufi had to become a broken person, divested of all earthly habits through the processes of solitude, silence, sleeplessness, and hunger.

Sufis believe it is necessary to live with and serve a teacher for many years, since Sufism cannot be learned through books.

In Western countries like America, the path is far simpler. One does not ordinarily need to either be a Muslim or seek a teacher connecting all the way back to Muhammad.

Source Of Authority

Muhammad and the Qur'an, plus the hadith, which are traditions related to Muhammad, form the foundation for Sufism. During the tenth century, however, writings of Sufi teachers began to appear that shaped the basic teachings of Sufism and helped differentiate it from mainline Islam. One of the great writers of Sufism was Al-Ghazali, who argued in his books, *Revival of Religious Sciences* and *Alchemy of Happiness*, that Sufism emerged directly from the Qur'an and was compatible with Islamic Law. To be a proper Sufi, Al-Ghazali believed, one must be a faithful Muslim. Al-Ghazali's work cemented Sufism within the Islamic faith.

Several centuries later, a growing body of Sufi literature appeared that shaped what would become modern Sufism. This material helped move Sufism away from standard Islamic thought and traditional practices. Sufism began to stand on its own but seemingly without an intention to do so.

Three Branches Of Sufism

There are generally three branches of Sufism. The first two are opposites of each other. The first is the order from the "signs of the Signifier" (the Signifier being the creator God). This is also described as moving from the arts to the Artisan and means a cleansing or purifying of the self from corruption, which prevents one from seeing that God has created all. Al-Ghazali and most of the Sufis identify with this order.

The second is the order from the "Signifier of His signs." This order reverses the order of the first and is a moving from the Artisan to His works, and involves an attraction to the works of the creator God and an experience of the Divine Presence.

Some recognize a third branch called the Risale-I-Nur, which is an embracing of the way of Muhammad and an ignoring of the first two orders. It is a kind of Sufism outside of Sufism.

It must be noted that the spiritual practices of Sufis vary widely.

Dhikr

Muslims engage in Dhikr in order to remember God as directed in the Qur'an. This is done by practicing a specific devotional act that includes the repetition of the divine names and short statements of faith taken from or based on the hadith or the Qur'an. Dhikr is doing that which maintains an awareness of God or a consciousness of the Divine Presence and love. Muhammad was said to be in a constant state of Dhikr.

Sufi Dhikr may involve singing, recitations, music, dance (the Whirling Dervishes or better known as Sufi whirling), incense, meditation (known as Muraqaba), ecstasy, and trance. Some Sufi orders practice what is called Khikr-e-Qulb or "remembrance of Allah by Heartbeats." The point is to visualize the Arabic name of God, Allah, as though it were written on one's heart.

The Sufi "goes inside" through the various practices spoken of above to reach into the Divine Presence. These practices connect it with many other forms of religion including that of the shamans and Wiccans and their trances that make soul journeys possible.

Sufis will speak of their experience of entering into the Divine Presence as intoxication or by means of intoxication, which makes it unacceptable to Muslims, alluding to the use of alcohol. However, the Sufis are referring to the altered states achieved through song, dance, meditation, and so on. Sufis understand that the consciousness of God is elusive.

Persecution Of Sufism

Sufism emerged out of Islam and over the course of centuries developed its distinct forms and practices. Sufism is a mystical form of Islam, but while embracing Islam to a more or less degree, it developed differently than traditional Islam and drew persecution from traditional Muslims.

Sufis have been systematically persecuted in Muslim countries, the very countries where most Sufis live. Sufis are seen as too moderate. Sufism, unlike mainstream Islam, builds shrines for its saints, which is not pleasing to Muslim hardliners who consider the traditional mystical school of Islam heretical. In recent times, Sufi shrines and mosques have been vandalized, even destroyed and Sufis have been killed as well. These events have been most notable in Pakistan, Kashmir, Somalia, Mali, Egypt, Libya, Tunisia, Russia, Dagestan, and Iran.

Sufism In The West and Neo-Sufism

The poet and philosopher Rumi, who has become well known in Western nations, has drawn many to Sufism. In America in particular, Sufism is seen as an alternative form of Islam free from Islam's political agendas. It holds a fascination similar to that of Zen Buddhism and Yoga, and some American Sufis blend into churches like Unitarianism and Unity School of Christianity, to name a few.

The terms Universal Sufism or Neo-Sufism refer to forms of Sufism that do not demand a person be a Muslim and accept Islamic Law. The Western forms of Sufism do not require the genders be separated in meetings and there is less reliance on the Qur'an. Sufism is gaining a foothold with the "all paths lead to God" folk. Increasingly, there are Sufi groups that are open to all other faiths.

Trends

The openness of Western Sufism, especially as it disconnects from or soft-pedals Islam, will mean spiritually oriented people will find their way into Sufi gatherings. The fact that groups that seek ecstatic states of consciousness are making surprising comebacks in recent years may portend an upswing in Western style Sufism. Since shamanism, Christian-oriented contemplative prayer, charismatic ecstatic worship, and the soul journeys popular with Wiccans and other neo-pagans have gained in popularity, it would not be surprising if Sufism would benefit as well.

27

MINISTRIES TO MUSLIMS

This list was developed by means of a Google search. There were pages more of outreaches to Muslims that I did not look at. It is apparent that the Lord is working to bring Muslims to faith. The ministries here are not in alphabetical order but appear in the order I found them.

Answering Islam

Crescent Project

The Clarion Project

Ministry to Muslims Network

Team: A Global Alliance of Churches and Missionaries

Ravi Zacharias, RZIM Ministries

Every Muslim for Christ Initiative

2 Ministries

Jesus to Muslims Ministries

Network

Comma

International Project

SEND International

Global Initiative: Reaching Muslim Peoples

Christian Aid Mission

Arabic Bible Outreach Ministry

Say Hello: Serving Muslim Women

Touch of Christ Ministries

Global Opportunities

WELS: Christ's Love, Our Calling

SEND International

International Project

Ligonier Ministries

Canadian Network of Ministries to Muslims

Encountering the World of Islam

Christian Answers

IHOPE Ministries

Frontiers USA

The Gospel Coalition

Glad News for Muslims

Persian Ministries International

Living Oasis Ministries

Global Catalytic Ministries

ABWE Muslim Ministries

Call of Hope: Reach Muslims For Christ

Engaging Islam: Horizons International

Billy Graham Evangelistic Association

GO Ministries

InTouch Ministries

CARM: Christian Apologetics & Research Ministry

Persecution Blog

Glossary

Terms Related to Islam

Abd   Arabic for slave, and forms the first syllable of many Islamic names, i.e., Abdullah, meaning slave of Allah.

Abrogation   The idea Muslims hold that early teachings and verses in the Qur'an have been reealed or replaced by later Qur'anic revelations. Primarily the recitations received by Muhammad at Mecca will yield to the later recitations given in Medina.

Abu   Arabic for "father of" as in the entry below.

Abu Bakr   570–634, the first caliph and the father of Aisha, wife of Muhammad. A merchant and first male convert to Islam. A close friend of Muhammad's and buried next to him after his assassination.

Adhabal-qabr   The torments of the grave.

Adhan or **Azan**   The general call to prayer recited at the beginning of the prayer time and has the power or ability to drive away jinn. It is repeated three times: "Allah Akbar, I bear witness that there is no God but Allah. I bear witness that Muhammad is the apostle of God. Come to prayer. Come to prayer. Come to divine service. Come to divine service. Allah Akbar. Allah Akbar. There is no God but Allah." The Mu'adhan, Mu'azzin, or "Mu'ezzin" is the person who recites the adhan. "(Also see Iqamah.)

Ahl al-Injil   The Qur'anic identification of Christians and means, "the People of the Gospel." See Surah 5:47

Ahl al-Kitab   The Qur'anic identification of the "People of the Book" which can refer to Jews, Jews and Christians, or Christians alone, depending on the context and usage.

Ahmadi or **Ahmadiyya**   Ahmadi is the title of new sect of Islam founded by Mirza Ghulan Ahmad in 1889. He claimed he was the long awaited Messiah or Mahdi. It is essentially an attempt to revise and revive Islam. The movement has spread to over 200 countries with from 10 to 20 millions as adherents.

Aisha   614–678, the daughter of Abu Bakr, the third and favorite wife of Muhammad. Married to Muhammad at age 9, given in marriage to Muhammad by her father. She was literate, wrote poetry and spoke well. A childless widow at the age of 18. She exercised much influence in early Islam.

Akhira   This is Arabic for "hereafter" one of the three primary subjects of the Qur'an, which have to do with the Day of Judgment, Paradise, hell, and all other things to do with "last things."

Al-A'raf This designates a location between paradise and hell, and is close to the same ideas of the Roman Catholic purgatory. This is where the faithful abide until they enter paradise.

Al-Awar The name for one of the evil jinn who encourages wild and wicked behavior.

Al-'ayn The impact or influence of the evil eye.

Al-Batin One of the 99 names for Allah, meaning "the hidden"

Al-Bukhari 810-870, from Bukhara, the compiler of the most revered collection of hadith, which are stories about, and sayings of Muhammad not found in the Qur'an. It is said that Al-Bukhari spent 16 years compiling the hadith and that he started with 600,000 different entries and boiled them down to half of that.

Al-Huda This sometimes title for the Qur'an means guidance, in that the Qur'an is guidance and wisdom for Muslims.

Ali or **Ali ibn Ali Talib** Both the adopted son and son-in-law of Muhammad. Ali married Muhammad's youngest daughter, Fatima. Ali, the fourth caliph after Muhammad's death, but the succession was a cause of schism and Ali's followers, the Shi'a (the "a" standing for Ali), broke off from the branch to be called the Sunni.

Al-Janna This is Arabic for garden, and refers to one of the four stages or levels of Paradise according to the Qur'an.

Al-Jahannam The term that designates hell. Al-Nar and Dozakh are synonyms for hell.

Allah or **Al'lah** This is God's name, the essential name. Allah was used as the name of God prior to the Islamic period among Jews, Christians, and pagans in the Arabian Peninsula. It is not identified with Yahweh, the covenant name of God given to Moses as described in Exodus 3. In pre-Islamic times, Allah had intercessors, and three of these were daughters, Allat—the goddess, al-Uzza—the mighty, and Manat—the goddess of fate. Originally, Allah was derived from al-ilah meaning simply, "the god."

Allahu Akbar Allah is Great, or, Allah is Greater

Al-Muslim 816-873, a compiler of the second most trusted collection of hadith. It is said his collection was personally gathered from 300,000 hadith.

Al-Nar A word that means fire, the fire that all Muslims must pass through after death that cleanses or purges away bad deeds. Other terms that mean close to the same are: Laza-the blaze (Surah 97:5); Al-Hutamah-the crusher (Surah 104:4); Sair-the blaze (Surah 4:11); Saqar-fire (Surah 54:47). Also related terms are: Al-Jahim-the hot place and Hawiyah.

Alawites, Alawis, or **Nusayris** A branch of Shi'a Islam, centered in Syria and which is part of the Twelver school. Said to be founded in the 9th century by ibn Nusayr. Alawites compose about 11% of the Muslim Syrian population. Alawites also have a presence in Turkey and Lebanon. Their doctrines are little understood, but there appears to be the notion of a godly triad, made up of three aspects of the one God. Alawites have been persecuted for these beliefs.

Al-rafiq al-a'la The highest of the seven levels of heaven.

Al-Taqiyah (see **taqiyya**) To defend or promote Islam, Muslims are permitted to lie to and deceive an enemy of Islam. Whatever one says for the sake of Allah and for Islam is forgiven. ("The Greatest Deceiver" is one of the 99 names of Allah.)

Al-Zahir One of the 99 names for Allah, meaning "the revealed."

Amil The title used for exorcists in India and Pakistan.

Amir Or Emir, meaning one who rules, a commander or chief.

Ansar The term means "helpers" and refers to those in Medina who helped Muhammad in this early struggles upon emigrating from Mecca.

Ar-Rahim This refers to Allah's merciful nature.

Ar-Rahman A term that refers to Allah's merciful character.

Arkan-ud-din The pillars of religion -- the Five Pillars of Islam.

Ashura A central and core religious event that commemorates the martyrdom of Husyan that took place at Karbala, Iraq, during the Islamic month of Muharram. It is the most significant event in Shi'a Islam. During this time the Ta'ziheh, or passion play that acts out the martyrdom of Husyan, is presented. (also see Matam)

Asr The afternoon or third prayer of the day.

Ayah A verse from the Qur'an

Ayatollah This is the designation of the highest-ranking imam amongst Shi'ites. The word means "A sign of Allah" and an ayatollah is qualified to issue binding fatwas. There are few of such high rank, and their authority over Shi'a Islam is large. Mainly seen in Iran and Iraq.

'Aza In Shi'a Islam, it has to do with standardizing formal mourning for the remembering the death of Husayn, the son of Ali.

Azazil A name for the devil and means one created by fire.

Barzakh The word means obstacle or separation. It came to refer to an intermediate state where souls go to await judgment. It is also the waiting room or place for souls before they are blown into the bodies or embryos of humans.

Baraka This refers to a spiritual power that is present when the Qur'an is read in Arabic, the original language that the Qur'an was given by Gabriel to Muhammad. It is also associated with tombs of faithful Muslims especially prophets and refers to blessings from Allah to the faithful dead.

Basmalah or **Bism'Allah** The term means, "In the name of Allah" or "God the Merciful, the Compassionate" and is used in many circumstances. A full "incantation for protection is: "Bism'Allah Al-Rahman Al-Raheem".

Bassamat Alfarah Literally the "smile of death" and refers to the facial expression of one who dies as a martyr or Mujahad.

Batin Mostly in Shi'a Islam and Sufism, the term refers to the secret, hidden meanings of the Qur'an, which only the imam can understand and communicate. The two major branches of Islam are in conflict over this as knowing the "secrets" of the Qur'an is of major significance in the rivalry between the two groups.

Baya'a Allegiance, as in swearing allegiance to the Islamic State.

Bida   A prohibition of any innovation or adapting Islam for modern times. Every innovation may be considered bida and thus heresy.

Bila Kayfa   In regard to right practice and doctrine, this term means something akin to "don't ask why" and is used by traditionalist Islamic scholars who defend doctrines and laws whose foundation or authenticity is murky, even impossible to discover.

Breaking the Cross   Since the cross is a primary symbol of Christianity, breaking the cross means to destroy Christianity.

Burqa   From the Urdu language, the term for clothing that completely covers a woman when she is out in public.

Caliph   Successor, referring to those who succeeded Muhammad, as Abu Bakr, Umar, and Uthman. Muslims, according to pure Sharia Law, believe that Allah has invested in a caliph complete authority over religious and civil governance.

Caliphate   It is a form of Islamic government led by a caliph. The caliph is the ruler. For instance, Al Baghdadi of the Islamic State, is proclaimed (proclaimed himself) as the spiritual leader of all Islam but not all Islam follows or acknowledges him.

Collections of Hadith   The following listing is adhered to or appealed to mostly by Sunni Muslims. Sahih Bukhari, d. 870, made a collection of hadith, often considered by Sunnis as the trustworthiest accounts of Muhammad's life. Sahih Muslim, d. 874, made a collection of hadith considered as very reliable. Sunan Ibn Majah, d. 886; Sunnan Abu Dawud, d. 889; Mami' Tirmidhi, d. 892; Sunan Nasa'i d. 916; Muwatta' of Malik Ibn Anas, d. 795; Sunan of Ibn Mansur, d. 841; Musnad of Ibn Hanbal, d. 855; Sunan of al-Darimi, d. 868; Sunan of al-Khashshi, d. 895; Sunan of al-Daraqutnie, d. 995; Sunan of al-Bayhaqi, d. 1065. Al-Tirmidhi is a separate collection of hadith widely used and is a compilation of other collections of hadith. Shi'a Muslims have a separate collection of hadith and consider some of that which is attributed to Muhammad in the above collections to be forgeries.

Companions   The name for those who knew Muhammad in both Mecca and Medina during the seventh century, like Abu Bakr, Umar, and Uthman.

Dabiq   The field of battle where many Muslims believe Armageddon will begin. Also the name of ISIS's glossy magazine

Da'if   A hadith that fails to reach the status of completely reliable, or hasan. The isnad is the first part of the hadith that describes how it was handed down or transmitted.

Dajjal   The full title for the antichrist is Al-Masih ad-Dajjal, and means liar. 'Isa, or Jesus, upon his return at the end of the age destroys Dajjal, the Antichrist and all the demons.

Dar al-Harb   Arabic for "the House of War" and refers to those lands and peoples where Islam is not yet dominant.

Dar al-Islam   Arabic for "the House of Islam" and refers to all those who are Muslim and also Muslim controlled land

Dasim   One of the evil jinn who causes discord between a man and wife.

Daw   The calling of Muslims to defence of Islam. Islam combines into one what Christians normally call evangelism and apologetics.

Dawa   The name used for Islamic evangelization with the prospect of seeing non-Muslims embrace Islam.

Days of Ignorance   All of history prior to Muhammad and the revealing of the Qur'an are collectively known as the days of ignorance, that period when humans did not have the true and final revelation from Allah.

Dhikr   This refers to the remembrance of Allah and is to be the goal or all Muslim worship. Faithful remembrance of Allah yields Allah's favor and thus rewards.

Dhimmi   A dhimmi is a non-Muslim who is subject to the Islamic state and pays the jizya tax.

Dhimmitude   The state of being subject. See Surah 9:29.

Din   The practice of religion; doing the works of religion.

Du'a   Personal prayer, made in any language, in distinction from the salat, the formal prayers, that are only performed in Arabic. In contrast to prayer made five times a day known as salat, which is the ritualized prayer, du'a is individual, personal prayer to Allah.

Demon possession   Muslims believe that demon possession is a very real phenomenon and mostly happens at night and entry may be made through the nose.

Durud   Prayer for Muhammad that he may escape the torments of hell and go to Paradise.

Eid (Id) al-Adha   Eid means "day" or "day of the feast" and is held on the 10th day of the last month of the lunar calendar, and is highly important for Muslims. It has to do with what Christians refer to as the Akida, which is God providing Abraham a ram to be sacrificed rather than his son Isaac. Muslim scholars are divided as to whether Abraham was about to sacrifice Ishmael or Isaac. (see Qur'an 37:100-108 especially 107)

Eid (Id) al-Fitr   A major Muslim holiday, marking the end of Ramadan.

Evil Eye   'ayn in Arabic, a look from a person who has evil intent and such sends an evil jinn or curse upon the one receiving the evil look.

Fajr   Name of the first prayer of the day, the dawn prayer.

Fard   Refers to the individual duty or obligation of a Muslim such as the prayers, or a collective duty, such as jihad.

Fatiha   The name given to the first surah in the Qur'an, and is to be recited by Muslims each day.

Fatima   The favorite daughter of Muhammad and Khadija, she married Muhammad's nephew Ali and was the mother of the Shi'a martyrs Hasan and Husain. She died six months after Muhammad's death.

Fatwa   A formal legal opinion decreed by a mufti or other Muslim leader or jurist when other forms of interpreting the Qur'an by means of literalism, consensus, or analogy could not be applied.

Feday   Those men who sacrifice their lives for the cause of Islam

Fiqh   The term for Islamic jurisprudence that includes that of the four primary schools of interpretation of Sharia Law.

Firdaws   The highest level of the gardens of Paradise to which martyrs go.

Fitnah   Literally the term means corruption and disorder. It refers to strife or disagreement, and is thus viewed as dangerous and something that could lead to a division within the Muslim community. It is also used to refer to temptation and primarily the temptation experienced by men at seeing women, which excites men producing a fitnah, or a 'fit' of uncontrolled and compelling desire and lust. This is one of the reasons Muslim women are to wear clothing that hides the female form.

Fitr To break a fast, especially after Ramadan.

Five pillars of Islam The fundamental practices required of all Muslims. One: The testament of faith or Shahada, which is to believe and profess that there is no God but God (Allah) and that Muhammad is the messenger of God (Allah). Two: Prayer, the Salat, which are five formal ritual prayers a day. Sunni Muslims do these prayers separately during the day. Shi'a Muslims pray each one three times each day. On Fridays, each Muslim is required to pray with the congregation in the Mosque a prayer known as jum'ah or Jummah. Three: The fast of Ramadan that extends from sunrise to sundown each day for thirty days. Muslims then will abstain from eating or drinking, anything, if they are physically able to do so. This is a time of focusing on all forms of self-dis cipline, including refraining from anger, gossip, and all forms of bad habits. Four: Almsgiving, the zakat, at least 2.5% to 20%, depending upon the particular sect's practice, and given to the poor. Muslims are also encouraged to give to other charities. Five: Pilgrimage or Hajj, and this to Mecca once in a lifetime for those Muslims who can afford or are physically able to.

Fuqaha Name for those who practice fiqh; those trying to live out the Shari'ah Law.

Gaalo This term refers to infidels, non-Muslims. It is a derogatory term that means one who is unfaithful to Allah.

Ghazi Arabic for "warrior" and refers to one who has fought against infidels, has faced death, and lived. Also a highly regarded veteran, a living martyr.

Giblab The direction Muslims pray toward. First it was Jerusalem; later Muhammad declared the proper direction to face in prayer was toward Mecca.

Ghusl The term means "bath" in Arabic and involves preparation for salat or prayer. Ghusl, the washing of the whole body is necessary after sexual intercourse, discharge or effusion of semen, and completion of menses.

Hadd One of the three categories of criminal offenses and means "most serious." The other two are Quesas and means serious and Tazir that means least serious.

Hadith The actions, statements, and teachings of Muhammad and his companions that forms the core of the Islamic tradition. The hadith literature comprises the essence of the Sunnah and is the primary lens through which the Qur'an is interpreted. An individual narration is determined to be "sound" (sahih), acceptable or good (hasan), weak (daif), or fabricated (mawdu). An ahad hadith is one that is narrated by only one source. Hadith Qudsi is a special kind of hadith wherein Muhammad quotes the words of Allah. The two most authoritative collections of hadith for the Sunni are Sahih Al-Bukhari and Sahih Muslim. Other important collections include the very early Muwatta of Malik ibn Anas, Sunan Abu dawud, Sunan ibn Majey, Sunan al-Nisaa, and that of Jamie at-Tirmidhi. Shi'a Muslims consider many Sunni hadith collections as forged in regard to the succession 'Ali to the caliphate. The two most important hadith of Shi'a Islam are those of Mohammad Ibne Yaqoob Abu Ja'far Kulaini and Usual al Kafi and Forroh al Kafi.

Hafiz The designation of one who has memorized the entire Qur'an.

Hajar al-Aswad This is the name given the "Black Stone" that is said to have fallen from heaven and is placed in one corner of the Kaaba in Mecca. Pilgrims attempt to get close to the black Stone to kiss it during the hajj or Umrah.

Hajj One of the Five Pillars of Islam, hajj is the pilgrimage to Mecca undertaken at least once in a faithful Muslim's life (if health and finances permit) involving reenactment of elements of Muhammad's life and the circumambulation of the Kaaba. The pilgrim's left shoulder faces the Kaaba and circles it 7 times and touches or kisses the "black stone" once. It takes place in the twelfth lunar month of the Islamic calendar.

Halal/Haram Allowed=Halal, forbidden=Haram. Halal designation is used for food often. The Kaaba and the Grand Mosque around it is Halal.

Hamduallah Arabic for Praise be to God.

Hanafi A religious school founded by Imam abu Hanifa, died 767. It is dominate in Central Asia and India. It is seen as the most diverse and broadest (liberal) understanding of Sharia Law.

Hanbali A religious school founded by Imam Ahmad ibn Hanbal, died 855, who held to a traditionalist view of the Qur'an, meaning the Qur'an was co-eternal with Allah and thus was the very word of God. He lived during the Islamic form of inquisition and refused to side with the ruling caliph al-Mus'tasin who wanted to consolidate all rule over Muslims separate from the ruling Muslim scholars, the Ulama.

Hanifism A pagan religion that was prominent in western Arabia, known as the Hijaz, in the sixth century, and one which Muhammad would have been familiar with. It was monotheistic, not polytheistic. A Hanifi leader, Zayd, preached against polytheism prior to Muhammad's time. Muhammad's wife Khadija is said to have been well disposed toward Hanifism.

Haram That which is forbidden. Doing an act that is haram brings punishment yet there is no reward for avoiding acts that are haram. Haram is one of the designations of material in hadith that speak of that which is forbidden.

Hasan A category of hadith considered "good" and meaning the source of the hadith is known but its reporters are not the best.

Hawd al-Kawthar The prophet's cistern or body of water that lies at the end of the bridge that all must cross in order to arrive in Paradise. It is filled with wonderful liquid, which the faithful will drink of.

Hijab A head and neck scarf worn by Muslim women. It is said to function as a bane or protection from Satan and to prevent the lust of men from being aroused. It is thought that an uncovered woman is easy prey for Satan.

Hijaz (Hejaz) The strip of land on the western border of present-day Saudi Arabia, which includes the Islamic holy cities of Mecca and Medina.

Hijra(h) Literally means "migration," in particular the migration of Muhammad from Mecca to Medina in AD 622, marking the beginning of the Islamic calendar. A second meaning is jihad by emigration. It means moving to a new land in order to bring Islam there and is considered in Islam to be a holy and revered action. "And)whoever emigrates for the cause of Allah will find on the earth many locations and abundance, and whoever leaves his home as an emigrant to Allah and His Messenger and then death overtakes him, his reward has already become incumbent upon Allah." (Qur'an 4:100)

Hinn The weakest of the jinn and also those jinn who appear in the form of black dogs.

Hirah A mountain some three miles from Mecca where Muhammad retired to a cave on that mountain and where the angel Gabriel began to recite verses to him that would become the Qur'an.

Hooris The term means "voluptuous maidens" and refers to female spirits that serve men in a variety of ways including having sexual relations with them in Paradise.

Hubal One of the primary gods worshipped in the Arabian Peninsula during, and long before, the days of Muhammad. The main center of worship of Hubal was in Syria. The image of this god was the last one Muhammad destroyed after he returned to Mecca and "cleansed" the Kaaba.

Hudood Consists of six major prohibitions found in the Qur'an: 1. Drinking alcohol; 2. Fornication or adultery; 3. Apostasy; 4. Theft; 5. Robbery; 6. Falsely accusing someone of illegal sexual activity.

I Aqdir The word means the absolute decrees of both good and evil. It is the sixth article of basic Islam creed, which is that Allah directly causes all that happens in the world. It is the doctrine of complete and absolute fatalism.

Ibadah Arabic for acts of worship and devotion.

Ibadi Ibadi is the name of the school of Islam dominate in Oman, which is also found in Algeria, Tunisia, Libya, and East Africa. Founded about a generation after the death of Muhammad and so is believed to predate both Sunni and Shi'a Islam. The Ibadis are strict interpreters of Sharia Law, while at the same time they are considered moderate and tolerant.

Iblis This is the term most often used for Satan or the devil and it refers to a jinn who refused to worship Adam who was made of mud unlike the jinn who were made of fire. Evidence for this is in Surah 7:12 and 18:50. Some say that Iblis was an angel as implied in Surah 2:34. Islam has never reconciled this contradiction. Shaytan is another word used for Satan. The primary characteristic of the Devil is hubris. His primary activity is to incite humans and jinn to commit evil through deception, which is referred to as "whispering into the hearts." Satan appears in the Bible as a serpent, in Islam as a dog and thus dogs are considered unclean animals.

Ifrit A particularly powerful and crafty jinn.

Ihram The name of a white garment worn by a Muslim who desires purity. It especially applies to the donning of white garments at the beginning preparation for the Hajj, the fifth pillar of Islam. It may also be worn at Friday, Jummah, prayers. The white garments denote a state of purity and sacredness.

Ijma The term refers to consensus in the ummah or community primarily as expressed in Sharia Law. Anyone who does not conform to the consensus will be damned.

Ijtihad Deductive logic and personal evaluation of arguments, which is the final method of understanding the Qur'an.

Ilham A form of inspiration of an angelic nature which is intended for the ummah or community of Muslims.

'Illiyyin A high level of the seven heavens.

'Ilm al-Rijal The science of biography, examination of accounts of report of the words and deeds of Muhammad as to their reliability.

Imam The one who stands in front; a leader in the mosque.

Iman According to Gardet in the Encyclopedia of Islam, the orthodox consensus view of Iman is, "the internal conviction, the verbal expression, the performance of the prescribed works." Faith and works are both necessary to achieve paradise.

Inshallah or Insh'allah God Wills, or If God Wills

Iqama or Iqamah This is the second call to prayer, after the adhan, made just before the congregation begins the obligatory, or fard, prayer. This prayer is the same as the adhan except for the addition of the phrase, "Prayer has started." The prayer then is: "Allah Akbar, I bear witness that there is no God but Allah. I bear witness that Muhammad is the apostle of God. Come to prayer. Come to prayer Come to divine service. Come to divine service. Prayer has started. Allah Akbar. Allah Akbar. There is no God but Allah."

'Isa The Arabic name for Jesus. Also "Isa ibn Maryam" Jesus, son of Mary.

Isafil The angel who will blow the trumpet on the Last Day.

Isha The night prayer, the fifth prayer of the day.

Islah A term that means reform and is the goal of many Muslims who reject the "traditionalist" position and seek to reform or renew (tajdid) Islam and that principally by means of democratization. It is not a rejection of Islam, but the desire to see Islam function like it did in the beginning when Muhammad was in Mecca and prior to the immigration to Medina.

Islam Refers to the religion of those of are in submission to Allah. A Muslim is one who is totally submitted to Allah.

Ismailis Another name for the Seveners.

Isnad Having to do with the transmission of hadith, the transmissional chain that is usually found at the beginning of a hadith. An isnad may be strong, weak, or fabricated.

Istislah This refers to that which has to do with the welfare of the ummah or Islamic community, and has to do with how some Qur'anic verses are understood. (See ijma, qiyas, and ijtihad.)

Izzart The word means "honor" and is used when a family member or other person must be harmed or killed due to dishonoring the family. For instance, if a Muslim converts to another religion, he is considered to have dishonored the family and therefore may be harmed or killed. The issue is what others in the community think. Honor may be restored by punishing or killing the one causing the dishonor.

Jafar The sixth Imam of Shi'a Islam. (see below) He died in AD 757 and his son Ismail was designated by him to be head of the community. However Ismail died before his father and was then replaced by another son of Jafar, Musa al-Kazim. (see Seveners below)

Jafari School of Jurisprudence The Shi'ite school of jurisprudence, named after Jafar ibn Mohammed al-Sadiq (AD 702-AD 757), the sixth Imam.

Jahaliya Ignorance, or the time of ignorance, specifically the ignorance of Islam of the pagans prior to the coming of Muhammad. Muslims speak of the period of "juhaliya" to refer to the time prior to the ministry of Muhammad among the Arabs.

Jamaat or **Jummah** Arabic for a meeting of Muslims, an assembly, a group, or denomination. It is held on Friday, the Muslim holy day.

Janannum The name of a purging type of hell that all Muslims must go through and which is spoken of in Surah 19:68-72.

Jibreel Arabic for the angel Gabriel.

Jihadism A contemporary movement that seeks to establish an Islamic state and ignores fixed national boundaries. The goal is to see Islamic Law be the only law on the planet and all peoples would be under the authority of the Islamic entity. It is fundamentalistic in nature. All people in the mind of the Jihadist are either "people of heaven" (themselves) or "people of hell."

Jinn A name used for demons, some of which are good but many are evil. The Arabic word "jinn" comes from the verb janna that means to hide or conceal. Practically Muslim people will employ various occult arts to protect themselves from evil jinn. Even though such are officially considered unIslamic, like fortune telling, the use of amulets, and the "evil eye", still this is common in folk Islam. The jinn are created beings and also die as humans do.

Jizyah An obligatory tax placed upon the People of the Book who refuse to convert to Islam. (Surah 9:29) Failure to pay jizyah may result in going to hell.

Jummah Arabic for Friday and refers to the Friday gathering for prayer.

Kaaba, Ka'ba, Kaba Arabic for cube, it is the cube-shaped building in the Grand Mosque in Mecca. Muslims believe Abraham and his son Ishmael initially built it. Others say it was build by Adam. The Black Stone is embedded in a corner of the Kaaba, and it is toward it that the Muslims bow in prayer. According to some Muslims, the Kaaba was first built in heaven.

Kabira The great sins.

Kahin (Kaheen) Pre-Islamic pagan officials who acted as shamans and fell into trances and provided guidance and revelations.

Kalam The term refers to questions of Islamic theology, what one believes, as opposed to fiqh or what one does.

Kalim Allah This term means, Speaker with God, and refers to Moses.

Kawaa'ib A synonym for hooris, the beautiful maidens (perpetual virgins) who satisfy men sexually and otherwise in Paradise.

Khabaith A female evil jinn, which may be present when one enters the toilet and thus a protective phrase is to be uttered for protection from Allah when entering the toilet.

Khadija 556-619, the first wife of Muhammad, married twice before, she chose Muhammad, much younger than herself, as a husband due to his skill at managing her business affairs. Muhammad married no other women until after her death, which he grieved over greatly.

Khalil Allah This term means, Friend of God, and refers to Abraham.

Kharijites An early extremist group that sought to define what and who a Muslim is and must be and emphasized purity of heart and mind. This "political" group developed under Uthman, the successor to Umar. The Kharijites thought that Uthman was not qualified to be the head of Islam due to wrong practices. The Kharijites, the first sect of Islam, are known as the Puritans of Islam. Their successors into the modern era are those who settle for nothing less that extreme and pure seventh century Islam as it was in the days of Muhammad and the pious ones.

Khateeb   A speaker, the one who delivers the *khutbah*, or sermon

Khitan   The term for female circumcision.

Khutba   The sermon preached by the mosque leader, Imam, at the Friday mid-day prayers. It consists of two parts. First, the Imam praises Allah along with prayers for the Prophet Muhammad. Second, he prays for the welfare of all Muslims.

Killing the pigs   A term that refers to destroying Jews and Christians.

Kismat   It means, "it is my lot" and refers to Allah's predestined will.

Klubuth   A male evil jinn, which may be present when one enters the toilet and thus a protective phrase is to be uttered for protection from Allah before entering the toilet..

Kufir/Kafar/Kafir   Unbelief /unbeliever. The root in Arabic refers to "covering over," i.e., in unbelief. Popularly a derogatory term for someone who is not an orthodox Muslim.

Kufr   Ungratefulness. It refers to ungratefulness to Allah.

Kutub   Arabic for books and refers to an original 104 books written by prophets. Only four are known: The book of Moses, or the Taurah, the Torah; the book of David, the Psalms; the Injil of Jesus, or the Gospels; and the Qur'an. According to Islam the first three books were changed and distorted and is then the reason Allah gave Muhammad the pure book of the Qur'an.

La ilaha illa Allah   Arabic for "there is only one God worthy of worship," and these are the first words of the *Shahada*. All prophets sent by Allah have been united by this one message.

Madrasa   An Islamic school where the Qur'an and hadith are taught. Sometimes other subjects are taught as well.

Maghrib   The evening prayer, or fourth prayer of the day.

Mahdi   One "who guides divinely;" a title reserved for the last Imam, who ushers in the Day of Judgment and restores Islam to be what it should be. For those who followed Imam Ismail, the seventh Imam, who disappeared (the occultation) close to the middle of the 8th century. (Ismail is the son of Ja'far as-Sadiq) This faction of Shi'a Muslims is referred to as the "Seveners." Another faction in Shi'a Islam known as the "Twelvers" believe in a twelfth Imam, the hidden Imam, will return at the day of judgment and re-establish Islam. Sunnis and Shi'a have differing views on this, the Sunnis largely have moved away from the concept of a Mahdi. The Mahdi must be of the stock of Muhammad.

Majinun   A term used to describe a person who is insane. The term is derived from the word jinn.

Makara   Arabic for schemer or deceiver. Allah can lead astray and is the best of schemers per Surah 3:54.

Makruh or **Makrooh**   One of the divisions of material in the hadith and refers to that which is repugnant. The doing of such acts brings punishment and the avoidance of which brings reward.

Maktub   It means, "it is written" and refers to Allah's predestined will.

Malaikah or **Malak**   Arabic for angels, of which there are good and bad. This word is not used to describe the evil spirits like the jinn.

Malik   The name of the main guardian angel of hell. (see Qur'an 43:77)

Maliki   A religious school founded by Imam Malik ibn Anas, d. 795. Reportedly he said, "this religion is a science" meaning Islam concerns all of what a Muslim does in life, rituals conducted, and beliefs held. He tended to rely upon the traditions of understanding Sharia Law in Medina during the days of Muhammad and the Companions. This school is dominant in West Africa.

Mandub   One of the divisions of material in the hadith, here meaning the doing of acts, which brings rewards, but not doing them does not bring punishments.

Manam   Arabic for dream or vision.

Maqdur   It means, "it is decided" and refers to Allah's predestined will.

Marfu   In the Hanbali school of jurisprudence, refers to a hadith that is directly attributed to Muhammad.

Mashur   A category of hadith that is "famous" and is reported by more than two or three transmitters or reporters.

Masjid   A Muslim place of worship, often called a mosque.

Maskh   The doctrine of abrogation, the concept that what was spoken later by Muhammad or recited to him annuls that which was given earlier.

Masru   One who is possessed by a jinn.

Mass   One, who due to being possessed by jinn, goes mad or is touched by a jinn and therefore out of his or her mind.

Matam   The funeral procession of Husayn reenacted during the Ashura that commemorates the death of Husayn.

Matn   The matn follows the isnad, which is the chain of transmission, and is the actual content of the hadith.

Maudu   A category of hadith and means fabricated or forged, and is a saying that contradicts other sayings.

Maut   Arabic for death.

Minbar   In a mosque, this is a raised chair or seat, like a pulpit, where the sermon is given out. This spot is reserved for the leader of the congregation.

Mi'raj   Muhammad's ascent into heaven after his night journey.

Mizan   The cosmic scale of Allah where the deeds of humans are measured; the outcome determines one's destiny to paradise or hell.

Mubah   One of the designations of material found in hadith and refers to acts which are permissible, the doing of which brings neither reward or punishment and the Muslim then has free choice.

Mubinun   The word means clear, easily understood. The Qur'an is claimed to be mubinun, as well as pure.

Muezzin   The one who makes the call to prayer from a minaret. The first two words called out are "Allahu Akbar."

Mufti   An Islamic scholar amongst Sunni Muslims, a leader in the Muslim community, a jurist/scholar who is able to make binding decisions for the community as in declaring a fatwa.

Muhaymin   Means a guard or protector. The Qur'an is said to be a protector of the previous revelations, as in the Old and New Testaments in particular. (see Surah 5:48) Most Muslims believe this means it corrects, or in most ways, supersedes, previous revelations.

Muhkam   Designation of the verses in the Qur'an that are said to be incapable of being misunderstood. They are clear and explicit.

Muhrim   The designation of someone who enters the worshipful state of Ihram, especially during Hajj and the donning of the white garments. (see Ihram)

Mujahad   A soldier engaged in jihad or holy war and who is prepared to die as a martyr.

Mujtahidin or **Mujtahid**   Scholars of Islamic doctrine and jurisprudence amongst Shi'a Muslims, who alone should lead Muslim states or nations.

Mullah   An esteemed member of the Ulama.

Munafiqun   Refers to hypocrites especially those who lived during the days of Muhammad and who pretended to submit to Islam but actually did not.

Munkar and **Nakir**   The names of the two angels who are on the shoulders of all people and who record good and bad deeds, and are involved in bringing about the death of each person. They will question all people at their death as to whether they have been good Muslims or not.

Muslim   A Muslim is one who is totally submitted to Allah.

Muslim Brotherhood   The Society of Muslim Brothers formed, principally in Egypt, to combat the decline of Islam in Muslim dominated countries and also to spread Islam in the West. It is still a major force behind the jihadist movement around the globe.

Mustahad   Recommended or virtuous acts. As opposed to Makrooh or Makru, which which mean distasteful acts.

Muta   Name of a marriage contracted for a limited time, even an hour, when a Muslim man is away from home, on a pilgrimage, or jihad. The word means, "enjoyment".

Mutashabih   Qur'anic verses which are not clear but are implicit or allegorical, and are known only by Allah. Shi'a Muslims believe these verses are simply those with deep meanings and are thus more difficult to comprehend.

Nabi Allah   A term used for Noah and means "the prophet of God."

Nabi   The word for prophet in Arabic.

Nafl   Practices that are considered optional for the Muslim worshipper. (also see Sunnat)

Nafs   Arabic for the soul or human spirit. Over time, the term mainly referred to the human spirit.

Najas or **Najis**   Impure, defiled, or unclean, especially in regard to water.

Naskh   The traditional idea of abrogation: Muhammad shifted his statements to relate to changing sociologic conditions, not theological or policy changes. It allowed the Islamic community to make adjustments in policy. An interesting example has to do with the drinking of alcohol, which is evident when the following verses in the Qur'an are examined: 2:219, then 4:43, and 5:90.

Nass A text from the Qur'an or hadith.

Nikah Marriage, which is recommended for those who are able to afford it.

Niyyah or **Niyya** The essential concept is intentionality, that is, Muslims are to go about their religious duty with sincere and intentional obedience -- and all for the glory of Allah.

Nushrah The term for charming away sickness, diabolical possession, or insanity.

Original sin Islam does not embrace original sin passed from Adam to offspring. Each person is born neutral and may do either good or evil.

Pak Refers to that which is clean, especially in regard to water.

Pir A Pir is a mystically oriented Sufi who functions as a spiritual guide. A pir will employ various aspects of magic. They specialize in direct union or connection with spiritual power. They will attract followers who honor them as faultless and pure holy men.

Qadar or **Al-Qadar** Refers to power, but came to mean Allah's divine decree concerning all things in time. Qadar is central to the Islamic understanding of predestination, extending to the idea that all things, good or bad, are the will of Allah.

Qadarites Early in the formation of Islam, due to contact with Christian theology, some Muslims questioned the extreme fatalism currently embraced and advocated a form of free will. These became known as Qadarites as opposed to the jabr who held to "blind compulsion" or fatalism.

Qadis, Qadi, Kadi An Islamic scholar and leader in the Muslim community, a jurist, judge, who is able to make binding decisions for the community as in declaring a fatwa.

Qarin A type of jinn that "accompanies" each person from birth to death, but may not die with its host; thus it is the name of the jinn that contacts persons after death, much like the spirit of the dead are said to contact the living. Muhammad said this kind of jinn flowed in the bloodstream

Qawm Arabic for tribe.

Qaynuqa In the Medina region of Arabia, a Jewish tribe who would not submit to Islam and whom Muhammad subsequently attacked and dispersed.

Qibla This refers to the direction in which one bows in prayer, historically first to the Temple in Jerusalem then to the Kaaba in Mecca after Muhammad was not able to convert the Jews to Islam.

Qiyas This is the use of analogy by Islamic scholars when confronting differences between the days of Muhammad and modern times. Analogy, comparisons, and then aiding in determining complex issues.

Qudsi "Holy" and refers to those revelations that came to Muhammad directly from Allah and not through Gabriel.

Quesas One of the three categories of criminal offenses and means intermediate. The other two are Hadd, which means most serious, and Tazir, which means least serious.

Qur'an The name of Islam's sacred and holy book, which negates or supplants all other sacred literature. Literally, "The Recitation."

Qur'anist Those who reject interpreting the Qur'an based on centuries long understandings of the meaning of the text, but approach the Qur'an differently, which is more consistent with those who are interesting in the reforming of Islam.

Quraysh Muhammad's own tribe, which was dominate in Mecca during the early days of Islam. This Arab tribe strongly opposed Muhammad and were eventually defeated by the early Muslims.

Qurayzah Another Jewish tribe in the region of Mecca other than the Qaynuqa who opposed Muhammad's Islam. He organized the destruction of this tribe after they backed out of an alliance with the Muslims.

Qurra A class of early Muslims who received the words of the Qur'an directly from Muhammad. The term means, "Qur'an readers." These began to die off and Uthman, the third caliph, began then to consolidate the recitations into a consistent document. Also designates those people who had memorized the Qur'an in the seventh century. The killing of these during the Battle of Yamama in AD 633 stimulated the compilation of the Qur'an.

Qutb Sayyid Qutb, 1906 to 1966, an Egyptian, who was greatly responsible for the rise of radical Islam. He witnessed the decline of Islam and advocated for a complete overhaul of Muslim dominated countries via Islamic control over all aspects of a society including economic, social, and political arenas. It was to be theocratic rule by the Islamic Ulmma. He argued for a complete overthrow of all that is not Islamic and by any means necessary.

Qyis Analytical reasoning employed by Muslim jurists when an issue is not directly addressed in either the Qur'an or the Hadith.

Raka'ah A unit of prayer. In the five daily prayers, there will be at least two units, or *raka'ats*.

Ramadan The ninth month in the Islamic calendar, the fasting month, wherein Muslims fast from sunrise to sunset.

Raqa or Raqyah The term meaning to charm someone by invoking Allah and is used in exorcism sessions.

Rashidun Refers to the first four successors of Muhammad, the caliphs Abu Bakr, Omar ibn al-Khattab, , Othman ibn Affan, and Ali ibn Abi Talib.

Rasul Arabic for messenger and is used in reference to Muhammad as the messenger of Allah and the one to whom an inspired book is revealed.

Rationalists The view of the Qur'an is that it is a created document as opposed to the Traditionalists who hold it be as eternal as Allah. Those Islamic scholars look for hidden meanings in the Qur'anic verses and will view such in light of contemporary culture and circumstances as opposed to the Traditionalists who insist on a static and literal interpretation. Present era Muslim extremists favor the traditionalist method of seeing the Qur'an. Rationalists are open to reform.

Recording angels Two angels sit on the shoulders of each person, one on the left and one on the right. The angel on the right records good deeds, the one on the left bad deeds. These may be named Munkar and Nakir.

Riddah Wars   The wars during the first caliphate, that of Abu Bakr, as he attempted to unite factioning tribal groups.

Risala   One of the three main categories of subject matter in the Qur'an, and having to do with prophet-hood, those things related to Muhammad and his office.

Ruh Allah   Arabic for spirit of God and refers to the angel Gabriel.

Ruh al-Qudus   Arabic for spirit, and early on meant breath or wind by Arab people. The word is derived from the Hebrew.

Rul Allah   Arabic for the Spirit of God and is identified with Jesus.

Rul ul'Amin or **Rul al-Quddus**   Arabic for the Holy Spirit, who is identified with the angel Gabriel.

Rumi   The renowned Sufi poet/mystic, died 1273, who is widely read today by Sufis and other mystics.

Sadaqa   Voluntary offerings.

Sadiq   The sixth and very important Imam, who died in 765, who founded the Shi'a school of Islamic law. This school developed a separate set of hadith from the Sunni schools.

Safi Allah   The name in Arabic given to Adam and means "Chosen One of God."

Sahabah   Refers to the "pious" companions of Muhammad who reported what Muhammad said, did, or did not do.

Sahih   Arabic for "authentic" or right and pious. A category of hadith meaning sound or genuine, with a reliable chain of transmission with no weaknesses.

Sahih Bukhari   Sahih Bukhari, d. 870, a collection of hadith, often considered by Sunnis as the most trustworthy accounts of Muhammad's life.

Sahih Muslim   Sahih Muslim, d. 874, gathered a collection of hadith considered as very reliable.

Salafi   Refers to the first few generations of Muslims after Muhammad, the great and pious forefathers who are considered the "best" people. Salafi refers to one who follows after the early companions of Muhammad, and who hold to a literal, conservative, or traditional interpretation of the Qur'an and Sunnah. Salafi is often used as a synonym, in American usage, for the term fundamentalist. The Salafi are a major force in Egypt and Saudi Arabia.

Salah   The collective name for the Muslim ritual prayers.

Salam   Means "peace" and is used as a greeting much like "hello".

Sar   The most common Arabic term for spirit possession. This term is also used for "fits" epileptics experience.

Salawat   "Peace be upon him" refers to Muhammad and is an invoking of blessings upon Muhammad. This is highly important as it may mean the difference between going to paradise or hell. It is related to the intercessory work of Muhammad. Those who practice the salawat will receive help from Muhammad. One blessing of Muhammad will be rewarded as ten blessings from Allah. The concept of Wasilah (below) is connected with salawat.

Sawm The act of fasting.

Seveners The Seveners are a sect of Shi'a Islam. The sixth Imam of Shi'a Islam, Jafar, died in AD 757 and his son Ismail was designated by Jafar to be head of the community. However Ismail died before his father and was then replaced by another son of Jafar, Musa al-Kazim. A faction of Shi'a Muslims refused to accept Musa, objecting that Jafar as Imam could not have made an error in choosing a successor and insisted that Ismail had not died but had gone into "occultation" or hiding and would return as the seventh Mahdi at the end of history.

Shafii A religious school founded by Imam Muhammad bin Idris ash Shafii, died 820. This school dominates in Southeast Asia.

Shahada or **Kalima** This is the term used for the Islamic confession of faith, the means by which one becomes a Muslim. In English, the Shahada for Sunni Islam is: "There is only one God worthy of worship, and Muhammad is His prophet." In English the Shahada for Shi'a Islam "There is no god but God, Muhammad is God's Messenger, and Ali is God's Executor."

Shaheed The term used by Allah in the Qur'an that refers to Muslims who achieved martyrdom in violent jihad. Such a designation elevates one's status in paradise.

Shayton Iblis or Satan.

Sharia or **Shariah** This is the name for Islamic law, which is derived from the Qur'an and the Sunnah. Sharia Law mostly concerns behavior, which fall into five classes: (1) that which is obligatory and may be rewarded or punished; (2) right action, not absolutely required and may be rewarded but not probably punished; (3) Neutral behavior, no reward or punishment attached; (4) disapproved behavior, which may be punished; (5) disapproved behavior, which are both forbidden (haram) and punished. There are five schools of Islamic law. There is one Shi'a school of law and it was founded by Ja'far as-Sadiq, died AD 765. The four schools of Sunni law are: the Hanbali School, founded by Ahmad ibn Hanbal, died 855; the Shafi School, founded by Muhammad ash-Shafi, died 820; the Maliki School, founded by Malik ibn Anas, died 795; the Hanafi School, founded by Abu Hanifah, died 767.

Sheikh A Muslim leader, a tribal leader, or an expert in Islamic theology.

Shiite or **Shi'ite** or **Shi'a** A follower of Shi'ism, the second largest sect in Islam, comprising about 10 to 20% of all Muslims. The conflict between Shi'ism and the Sunni sect goes back to the earliest decades of the Islamic movement and is centered, historically, in the succession of power in the Caliphate after Muhammad's death. Shiites believe the proper successor to Muhammed was Ali ibn Abi Talib (601 or 607 to 661), Muhammad's cousin and son-in-law, who married Muhammand's youngest daughter, Fatima. Instead, Abu Bakr the first convert to Islam was the first caliph, followed by Umar (Omar), then by Uthman. All three of the first three caliphs were assassinated. Ali was to be the fourth caliph but rejected that title and became the first Imam. The succession struggle resulted in the Battle of Karbala in AD 680 in which Hussein, Ali's grandson, and more than seventy of his family, were slain by the Sunnis. The martyrdom of Hussein is central in Shiite lore and even theology, and has led to many of the developments in theology that separate the Shiites from the Sunnis in belief, practice, and outlook.

Shi'a School of Law This school interprets Sharia Law for Shia. Founded by ja'far as-Sadiq, died 765.

Shirk/Mushrik This is the name of the sole unforgivable sin. It is the association of another deity with the one true God, Allah. Shirk is unforgivable because it is an essential negation of the central truth of Islam, that of Tawhid, the oneness of Allah. A Mushrik is one who practices shirk. For instance, according to Islam, Christians practice shirk as they associate Jesus and the Holy Spirit with God, thus they are seen as polytheists.

Sifa One of the four different types of information found in hadith and are reports of the character of Muhammad.

Sihr Arabic for the idea of magic, i.e., control of nature and other forces by means of rites, rituals, incantations, formulas, etc.

Sirah or **Sira** A biography of Muhammad's life.

Sirat A very narrow bridge crossing the fires of hell which all people must cross over. Many will fall into hellfire. The bridge is very thin and sharp.

Siyam Fasting, one of the five pillars of Islam.

Subhan il' aha Arabic for God is pure.

Sufi A subset of Islam where a direct, mystical experience with God is sought. Exercises are conducted in order to induce a trance-like state. Sunni Muslims, in particular, consider Sufism to be unorthodox. Sufis are considered apostate by some Muslim groups. It tends to be monistic in theology whereby there exists only one God who is without an external reality, much like what is found in some forms of Hinduism. s

Sultan A head of local governments that Islam absorbed through conquest.

Sunnah The Sunnah is the habits, customs, practices, actions, paths, of Muhammad, primarily communicated through the means of the collections of hadith, and are the primary traditions of Islam. The Sunnah is the norm as it interprets the Qur'an through the life and teachings of Muhammad.

Sunnat The term refers to those practices of worship, particularly prayer, that are not obligatory but are optional.

Sunni One who is on the path; a Muslim who correctly following the habits and customs of Muhammad. This is the name of the largest sect of Islam, comprising from 80 to 90% of all Muslims. Sunnis believe the first four Caliphs are "rightly guided;" which is in opposition to Shiites.

Sur This refers to the blowing of a trumpet on the Last Day, which stuns, but does not kill, unbelievers.

Surah/Surat Surah is singular, surat is plural, and refer to the chapter(s) in the Qur'an. In its present form the Qur'an has 114 surat.

Sut The name for one of the evil jinn, and the jinn who inspires lies.

Tabiun The Arabic word for the second generation of Muslims, that generation that followed the "companions."

Tafseer This is the term for a Muslim scholar who seeks to explain, expound, or disclose the meanings of the Qur'an especially as the attempt to understand or uncover the will of Allah as conveyed in the Qur'an. These complex process includes the following: determining the style of the text and its eloquence, defining unknown or otherwise less used words, the clarification of the meanings of verses, extraction of laws and rulings, explaining the underlying thoughts in metaphors and figurative speech, reconciling verses that seem contradictory, and finding out the underlying reasons for parables.

Tafsir bi'l-ishara Refers to commentary and explanation of the meaning of the Qur'an and is the classical science of interpretation and explanation of the Qur'an, which was consolidated in the 10th century. It has to do with the literal meaning of the Qur'anic verses, and is the preferred means of understanding the Qur'an by the Traditionalists. (see Ta'wil)

Taghut This term means "tyrant" in Arabic and is one of the names for the devil. Allah is the "avenger" and the "just," who exacts punishment upon tyrants, especially in Shi'a Islam. For instance, the Shah of Iran, deposed in 1`979, was considered a tyrant and thus must be opposed by faithful Muslims.

Tahahhud A Sunnah prayer made after the midnight and before the morning prayer.

Taharat In Sharia Law the word refers to "purity" and is associated often with the purity of water.

Tajdid The term means "renewal" and is closely linked with the concept of reform. (See "islah")

Tajwid This word has to do with the proper recitation or reading of the Qur'an. It involves complicated rules about word and letter pronunciations, when to breathe or not to breathe, and when to stop reading or pause, in the reading of the Qur'an. It also has to do with methods of prostration and bowing.

Takbir This is the formal name for the greeting, Allahu Akbar, "God is the most great," and which opens Muslim prayer. Also, it is speaking words of praise of Allah, in addition to being the call that units all Muslims, despite differences, to fight infidels.

Takfir This refers to one Muslim accusing another Muslim of apostasy. It can also refer to excommunication from the House of Islam, which may result in execution. It is reserved for Muslims who are considered weak or apostate.

Takwah This refers to Muslim piety and has to do with observing the Five Pillars of Islam, especially the haj, or pilgrimage to the Kaaba in Mecca.

Talaq The word used by a husband in divorcing a wife. Uttered three times by the husband, the marriage contract is voided.

Tanzil The term used to describe the Qur'an as being sent down from heaven – a direct revelation from Allah and therefore cannot be questioned.

Taqdir The Arabic word for the concept of predestination. Maktub–it is written; Maqdur–it is decided; Kismat–it is my lot; Inshallah–by God's will–these are expressions used to describe predestination or fatalism.

Taqiyya The term refers to being given permission by Allah to deceive in order to defend or promote Islam. It originated among Shi'a Muslims during the period of time while waiting for the appearance of the final Imam. Taqiyya, or "cautionary dissimulation" developed then during a low period in Islam, and served as a covering or defense against the outside world. It however has come to be appropriated by Muslims today. It is noted that one of the 99 names of Allah is "The Greatest deceiver."

Taqlid To follow or to be in conformity with the Ulama, the religious scholars, and to do so without question. That which is to be followed, primarily, is Sharia Law. It is often used in a derisive manner.

Tariqah In Sufi Islam, the term refers to the mystical journey that brings one away from a focus on the external to that which is internal, and much the same is found among many mystics such as in Shamanism.

Tarteel Chanting of the Qur'an. In a hadith, the Prophet said, "Whoever does not chant the Qur'an is not among us."

Tasawwuf The state of being a sufi.

Taslim The greeting known as the salamu alaykum, or peace be upon you, which is said at the end of the salat or ritual prayer.

Tawaf The seven fold circumambulation of the Kaaba.

Tawhid This is the central affirmation of Islamic theology, found in the first words of the Shahada – "There is only one God worthy of worship." Tawhid refers to the oneness of Allah. Different forms of Tawhid can be identified in Islamic thought, such as Tawhid ar-rububiyah, Tawhid of lordship; Tawhid al-uluhiya, the Tawhid of worship; and Tawhid al-Asma was-Sifaat, the Tawhid of Allah's names and attribute. The negation of Tawhid is to commit the unforgivable sin known as shirk.

Ta'wil Refers to the hidden meanings of the Qur'anic verses as opposed to the literal meanings (see Tafsir). A method of interpretation of the Qur'an favored by the rationalists.

Tayammum This term refers to mindfulness or intentionality, that is to be aware of what one is doing especially during making the prayers and performing other religious duties.

Tazir One of the three categories of criminal offenses and means the least serious. The other two are Hadd and means most serious and Quesas that means intermediate serious.

Ta'zayeh The Shi'a passion play that dramatizes the death of Husayn.

Tir The name for one of the evil jinn who brings about calamities and accidents

Traditionalists In the 8th century, during the Islamic "Inquisition," this is a word used to describe a group of Islamists who held that the Qur'an is not a created document but is co-eternal with Allah. This is the thought of the Maliki School of Sharia Law. Most of the violent jihadists are of the traditionalist mindset.

Twelvers The "Twelvers" refer to the rest of Shi'a Islam who are not Seveners and who look forward to the twelfth and final Imam who will usher in the Day of Judgment.

Ulama The community of Islamic scholars, clerics who are responsible for defining and interpreting Islamic law, or Sharia Law. There are four such schools in Sunni Islam, and one in Shi'a Islam.

Umar or **Omar** The second caliph, died in 640, at first a fierce opponent of Muhammad, then after his conversion to Islam, he became Islam's fiercest warrior. He established the foundations of the Islamic State. He ruled with a puritanical ruthlessness. He was assassinated.

Umm al-Kitab Arabic for "Mother of Books." Located in heaven and from which all other sacred revelations, the Bible, Old and New Testament, as well as the Qur'an, came. (see Qur'an 13:39)

Ummah Refers to the community of Islam, the entire body of Muslims. It may refer to just the Sunni branch, the Shi'a branch, or both of these.

Umrah The lesser pilgrimage other than the Hajj during the month of Ramadan. It is a pilgrimage to the Kaaba in Mecca at another time of the year.

Uthman or **Othman** The third caliph and one of the first converts to Islam. He died 656 in a bloody assassination. He was a rich merchant and married to Ruqayya, a daughter of Muhammad. Opinions are varied as to his effectiveness.

Wahhabi This refers to a particular Sunni sect, but it is often used interchangeably with Salafi. This is a very conservative Muslim group, traditionalists, founded by Muhammad ibn abd al-Wahhab, in the late eighteenth century. He was a Muslim reformer who popularized the views of Ibn Taymiyya (1263-1328), and who emphasized Tawhid and a literal interpretation of the Qur'an and the Sunnah along the lines of the early, pious Muslims.

Wahy Refers to personal inspiration.

Wajib One of the designations of material found in hadith and refers to acts that are obligatory, the doing of which is rewarded and the omission of which is punishable, such as prayer.

Wali From the Arabic word meaning "executor" and is the term used for Ali, the founder of the Shi'a branch of Islam. The "executor", or Imam, is to be without sin or error. Ali, the first imam in Shi'a or 4th caliph in early Sunni Islam, was infallible as are all those executors who have followed.

Wasilah The office or position of Muhammad as an intercessor in order that he may release persons from hell. Muslims must pray that Muhammad may receive the status of intercessor.

Watan al-Arab Means "the Arab Nation" and is a term used to refer to all who live in lands that have sizable Arab populations.

Witr It means "one" and is used of Allah. Allah is Witr.

Wudu The word means ablution, and is the washing of parts of the body, especially before performing salat or prayer. This preparation is complex and detailed.

Zabir This term has to do with the reality oriented aspects of Islamic life, mainly the Shari'ah Law, as opposed to batin or the inward life. For instance, the Sunni, and Shi'a, are more concerned with zabir while the Sufi's focus is on the batin.

Zahir The Zahir are Muslim spiritual leaders, imams, who can convey the explicit or ordinary message of the Qur'an, which all Muslims can understand. (see Ta'wil)

Zaidi or **Zaidiyyah** The term refers to Arab descendants of Zaid bin Ali, the great grandson of the Prophet Muhammad. A descendant of Muhammad may be referred ton as Sayyid, which is a title of honor given to those of the line of Muhammad. Those of this line who left present day Saudi Arabia and settled in Iraq, Iran, Pakistan, and Afghanistan have used the surname Zaidi.

Zainab bint Jahsh A cousin of Muhammad's, considered a rare beauty then, 590-630. She was married to Muhammad's adopted son, Zaid. Pressure was put on Zaid to divorce Zainab so that Muhammad could marry her and he did so when she was 35 years of age. She was Muhammad's second favorite wife and became close friends with the favorite, Aisha.

Zakat One of the Five Pillars; it is an obligatory alms giving. The word means "purification" and has to do with community responsibilities to care for the poor.

Zakir(s)   Those who act out the events associated with the commemoration of the death of Husayn at Karbala, Iraq.

Zalambur   The name for one of the evil jinn who presides over places of traffic, as in caravans of camels.

Zaydis   Name for those who follow a descendant of Ali, Zayd ash-Shahid, and have broken away from the main body of Shi'a Islam.

Zamzam   A well from which the Prophet drank.

Zina   The Arabic term for adultery or fornication.

Zindaq   A person who holds to a dualist philosophy, an equality between good and evil. Ancient Iranian or Persian religions such as Manichaeism Zoroastrianism were dualist, thus adherents of these were considered heretics.

Ziwaaj   Marriage.

Ziyara   Refers to a visit to the tomb of Muhammad at Medina.

Zuhr   This is the prayer made soon after mid-day.

Annotated Bibliography

A bibliography on Islam and related themes could include hundreds of titles, as many authors are focusing on Islam at this point in history. The objective here is to present books I have found helpful in my research, and to some small degree, acquaint the reader with what each book contains. Most of the titles have been acquired via the internet; some are eBooks; most are hard copies.

***

Abram, Simon, compiler, editor, publisher. *Islamic Hadith* (in English), 2011.

    Amazing document, the whole of the hadith by subject. Available only on Kindle from Amazon. 1681 pages, $2.00 total cost to download. A must have for anyone engaging in debate with Muslims.

_____. Editor. *Islamic Sharia Law: Qur'anic Law*. 2011.

    As amazing as the book above, this one costs $3.00. Very helpful and a must for those who want to go deep into Islamic thought.

Anonymous. *Hadith of Bukhari*. Forgotten Books, 2008.

    Volumes I, II, III, IV only of a longer set of stories about Muhammad, both what he did and what he said. Al-Bukhari receives the highest respect of those who made collections of the pattern, or sunnah, of the Prophet Muhammad. Next to Qur'an, the Hadith are the most important sources of authority for Muslims. This volume is easily read with generous white space and a readable font. Over 700 pages.

Aslan, Reza. *No god but God*. New York: Random House Trade Paperbacks, 2011.

    The author declares himself a Sufi and was converted to Christianity from Islam at age 13 but then returned to Islam's sub-sect, Sufism. Dr. Aslan, who teaches at the University of California at Riverside, quotes the Bismallah – "In the name of God, the Compassionate, the Merciful" and thus reveals his dedication to Islam. The book is well written and one of the most important pieces I have read on Islam. Dr. Aslan basically covers the history of Islam and the central core doctrines of the faith in a most detailed and yet entertaining manner. This book is a must for serious students of Islam, since it is absent atheist prejudices, Christian polemics, and political banner-waving. It was written prior to the Islamic State's and Al Qaeda's extremism. Like Ayaan Hirsi Ali (see below) he is hoping for a reformation within Islam that would restore one of the world's great religions. 338 pages with index and glossary.

Awde, Nicholas, translator and editor. *Women in Islam: An Anthology from the Qur'an and Hadiths*. New York: Hippocrene Books, Inc., 2005.

    Comprehensive coverage of what the Qur'an says about women plus what the Hadith says on the subject. It imparts a solid understanding of how Islam has viewed women. Some of it is shocking, and it would not surprise if most Muslims are unaware of what their religion actually teaches about women. Great index and bibliography. 256 pages, small font but generous white space.

Ali, Ayaan Hirsi. *Infidel*. New York: Atria Paperback, 2007.

This first of four books about Ayaan's fascinating story has a foreword by Christopher Hitchens and was a New York Times bestseller. Her life growing up in Somalia in a highly faithful Muslim family helped me to understand the hold any religion can have on a person where that religion becomes one's identity. Becoming an immigrant to The Netherlands, Ayaan negotiated that society and rose to become a member of its parliament.

_____. *The Caged Virgin: An Emancipation Proclamation for Women and Islam*. New York: Atria Paperback, 2008.

This second book has a preface titled "Breaking Through the Islamic Curtain," which sets the tone for the entire book. Ayaan writes from her own and from the life experiences of other women and intimately describes what it is like to be female in a Muslim-dominated country.

_____. *Nomad: From Islam to America*. New York: Atria Paperback, 2010.

In this third book Ayaan repeats some of what she reported in the first book, *Infidel*, and this time from a more seasoned response and reflective manner. She then goes on to tell the story of how she arrived in America and what happened next. To get a true sense of Ayaan and her concerns, it is best to read each of the three books just presented.

_____. *Heretic: Why Islam Needs a Reformation Now*, New York: Harper, 2015

In the fourth book, *Heretic*, also a New York Times bestseller, Ayaan seeks to appeal to Muslims to reflect upon and think critically about their religion. She does not attack but presents the reality of life as a Muslim person and the prospects for Muslims in the world now evolving.

Ayaan has moved to being an atheist, which makes her interesting and more reliable, as much religious bias is absent. She also moved from Dutch liberal to conservative politics, and in the fourth book her reasons for doing so become clear. This book should be a must-read for anyone concerned about the impact of Islam in the world today.

David, Joe. *The Infidels*. London: Thames River Press, 2014.

This is a novel that brings to life customs of Muslim people living through upheaval brought by Muslim extremists and how this impacted a young Christian girl. 189 pages and several hours pleasantly spent.

Deedat, Ahmed Hoosen. *Was Jesus Crucified?* 15th Edition. Chicago: Library of Islam, 2015.

See chapter 19 of this book for details.

_____. Combat Kit Against Bible Thumpers. Original 1992. Reproduced by Faisal Fahim via Amzon's CreateSpace Independent Publishing Platform, 2015.

See chapter 20 of this book for details.

Dunleavy, Patrick T. *The fertile Soil of Jihad: Terrorism's Prison Connection*. Washington D.C.: Potomac Books, 2011.

> Mr. Dunleavy, former deputy inspector general of the Criminal Intelligence Unit of the New Your State Department of Correctional Services, describes the radicalization of African Americans in our prison systems. His evaluation matches my own experience as a thirty-year volunteer at San Quentin State Prison in California. In any number of instances I watched as Muslim evangelism efforts brought black convicts into the Islamic fold.

Fahd al-Semmari, ed. *A History of the Arabian Peninsula*. Translated by Salma K. Jayyusi. New York: I.B Tauris & Co. Ltd, 2010.

> Sixteen Muslim authorities on Islam and the land of the birth of the religion provide essays on the nature and character of the Arabian Peninsula. The editor, Fahd al-Semmari, earned a PhD from the University of California, and the translator (from Arabic), Salma K Jayyusi, has a PhD from the University of London. The hand of Saudi Arabia and then Sunni Islam is firmly upon this book. 312 handsome pages, good font.

Garrison, David. *A Wind in the House of Islam: How God is Drawing Muslims around the World to Faith in Jesus Christ*. Monument, Colorado: WigTake Resources, 2014.

> Whatever David Garrison, Ph.D. writes on Islam, read it. A long time missionary with direct contact with Muslims, he has a heart for Muslim people. He is also a careful student of Islam and speaks in this book of what is taking place among Muslims of the world. He speaks of the "Nine Rooms" of Islam, which are the countries where Islam is dominant, and describes the moving of the Holy Spirit among these peoples. Great glossary, bibliography, and index. 300 pages, an easy and good read.

Guillaume, A. *The Life of Muhammad: A Translation of Ishaq's Sirat Rasul Allah*. Oxford: Oxford University Press, 1967.

> The Sira, or Sirat, is the life of or biography of Muhammad pieced together by Muhammad son of Ishaq who was born in Medina about A.H. 85 and died in Baghdad in A.H. 151. He is among those known as traditionalists of the second generation. He collected thousands of stories about Muhammad, and his work is considered the third most important document as to the doctrine and practices of Islam. The stories collected are astonishing at minimum, and as time goes on, due to the character of the material, Ishaq's work has less esteem among Muslims. Almost 800 pages, small font, somewhat difficult to read, but important in an overall evaluation of Islam.

Hazelton, Lesley. *After the Prophet: The Epic Story of the Shia-Sunni Split in Islam*. New York: Anchor Books, 2009.

> This stunning romantic historical novel about core Islam, its beginnings and early developments, was riveting and a pleasure to read. While not altogether factual, the author captures the culture of the day. I probably learned as much from this book as from any other. Lesley Hazelton has written other novels about peoples and places of that geographical location along the same vein as this book. 230 pages, well written, good font.

_____. *The First Muslim: The Story of Muhammad*. New York: Riverhead Books, 2013.

> Another fascinating and stunning historical novel, this one about Muhammad. Lesley Hazelton brings Muhammad to life and allows the reader to imagine what the place and times were like for the prophet of Islam. Life in the Arabian Peninsula in the late sixth and early seventh centuries is vividly portrayed and allows the reader to see that Muhammad was a man of his times. I could not wait for those hours when I could pick up Hazelton's books.

Ibrahim, I.A. *A Brief Illustrated Guide To Understanding Islam*. Houston: Darussalam, 1997.

> This colorful small book is written by the Imam of the Mill Valley (Sunni) Mosque who gave me the volume personally. He looks at what he considers to be scientific miracles in the Qur'an and then briefly explains major Muslim beliefs. 74 pages.

Jujjat-ul-Islam, Maulana Fasan Zafar Naqvi. *History of Kaba*. Translated by Huma Hasan. Karachi, Pakistan: Mahfooz Book Agency, 2005.

> A series of nine lectures by Hujjat-ul-Islam that provides a history of the Kaba in Mecca. Difficult reading but essential, as the Kaba (spelled in many ways) plays a key role in the early life of Muhammad and is a major monument in the lives of Muslims today. Here is a quote from the back panel of the dust cover: "The history of Ka'bah is as old as the time when Allah created the earth. When HE laid out the earth; Allah must have earmarked a place for the Ka'bah. He then waited for the builders who would be from pure ancestry because the construction of HIS house needed pure hands." 268 pages, easy to read font.

Khaled Abou El Fadl. *The Great Theft: Wrestling Islam from the Extremists*. New York: HarperCollins, 2007.

> The author is Muslim and a professor of Law at the University of California, Los Angeles. He makes a strong case that Islamic extremists are misrepresenting true and historical Islam. There appear to be clear instances of taqiyya (putting the best light on Islam despite what we see and hear) present, and the reader must be on guard. The book does make clear what are the differences between moderate and far right—or is that far left—proponents of Islam. One should have some understanding of Islam before reading this important book. 322 pages.

Khalifa, Rashad, Ph.D. *Quran, Hadith, and Islam*. Tucson, Arizona: Islamic Productions, 1982.

> Dr. Khalifa, at the time of the writing, was Imam at Mosque of Tucson, Arizona. The intent of the author is to show that the Qur'an is "indeed the infallible word of God." In a clear fashion he explains the chief doctrines of Islam. The Qur'an passages are presented in Arabic and English. Here is a most helpful and quick way to get to the core of what Muslims believe. 90 pages.

Love, Fran and Jelata Eckheart, editors. *Ministry to Muslim Women: Longing to Call Them Sisters*. Pasadena, California: William Carey Library, 2000.

> The contributors to this volume—all Christians active in Muslim minis-

tries—share their concerns, challenges, and rebukes. If you wish to minister the kingdom of God to Muslim women, this compendium will encourage, educate, and challenge you to think strategically and prayerfully about the task to which God has called you (quoted from the back cover).

Lutzer, Erwin W. *The Cross in the Shadow of the Crescent: An Informed response to Islam's War with Christianity*. Eugene, Oregon: Harvest House Publishers, 2013.

> Dr. Lutzer, senior pastor of The Moody Church in Chicago since 1980, has given us a very special and helpful book. Dr. Paige Patterson says, "The most provocative and salient monograph I have read on the subject of Christianity's response to Islam." Dr. Samuel Ezra Naaman adds, "I consider this one of the best books on Islam produced in the last 50 years." I am in complete agreement with these statements. 253 pages.

Malick, Faisal. *10 Amazing Muslims Touched by God*. Shippenburg, PA: Ambient Press, 2012.

> The author dedicates the book "to my Muslim brothers and sisters around the world seeking to know the way, the truth, and the life of God." There are 10 really amazing stories of how nine men and one woman, all devout Muslims, came to believe in Jesus. I have not read another book like it, and some of these accounts I have told over and over in various venues. Here is a book to learn from but also give away as an evangelistic tool to Muslim people. 170 pages nicely laid out and easy on the eyes.

Masri, Fouad. *Connecting with Muslims: A Guide to Communicating Effectively*. Downers Grove, Illinois: IVP Books, 2014.

> Fouad Masri is founder and director of the Crescent Project, one of my favorite outreaches to Muslims. I had the opportunity to meet him recently at an Oasis Conference in Brentwood, California. His is a ministry well worth supporting, and it provides a wide range of assistance to those seeking to share Jesus with Muslims. Highly recommended. The foreword is by Josh McDowell: "This present volume is about how to build bridges with Muslims in order to share the Gospel of Christ with them. Here is first hand, spot on, core information. A must read for anyone engaged in outreach with Muslim people."

_____. *Ambassadors to Muslims: Building Bridges to the Gospel*. Colorado Springs, Colorado: Book Villages, 2011.

> As above, Fouad Masri writes about reaching out to Muslims, and this volume is similar to his *Connecting with Muslims*.

_____. *ADHA in the INJEEL*. Colorado Springs, Colorado: Book Villages, 2004.

> This little booklet may serve as something to give away to Muslims, and is in English and Arabic. "Adha" refers to the sacrifice of a sheep or a ram when God redeemed the son of Abraham. The event is found in Qur'an 37:99-111. "Injeel" is Arabic for New Testament. Fouad Masri tells the story of the sacrifice of Jesus on the cross and relates in a way that a Muslim would understand. It is a wonderful gift to give a Muslim.

In addition to the three books noted above, Fouad Masri offers the following titles, short booklets that may be used to give to Muslim people but also useful in informing Christians about key concepts of Islam that connect with Biblical doctrine. Among these booklets, all published by Book Villages, are:

- *Is the Injeel Corrupted? My Search for the Truth about the New Testament.*
- *Do Christians Worship Three Gods? Al-Tawheed in the Injeel.*
- *Is Muhammad in the Bible? What Does the Injeel Say About the Prophet of Islam.*
- *Who is Isa Bin Maryam? My Search for the Truth about the Messiah.*
- *Who Died on The Cross? The Final Days of the Victorious Messenger.*

Maulana Muhammad Ali. *A Manual of Hadith*. Rutledge Curzon: London and Dublin, 1944.

> Here is the Hadith by subject prepared by a Muslim. It has been reprinted many times and is available on Kindle for $1.00 and in other forms as well. An important, authoritative document.

McCord, Kate (a protective pseudonym). *In the Land of Blue Burqas*. Chicago: Moody Publishers, 2012.

> The author left a significant career and headed for Afghanistan for five years where she immersed herself in the life of the people. A sincere and brave Christian woman, she experienced up close and personal life as a woman in a Muslim-dominated country. After knowing the details of Islamic doctrine, this book brings everything into sharp, real time, perspective. 312 pages; a page turner, nice layout and good font.

Meijer, Roel, editor. *Global Salafism: Islam's New Religious Movement*. Oxford: Oxford University Press, 2013.

> The editor of this important book presents eighteen essays written by scholars, many of them Muslims, to describe a revivalistic movement in Islam. There are five sections to the document: Salafist Doctrine; Salafism and Politics; Jihadi-Salafism; The Local and the Global Salafism; and Salafism and Identity. It is virtually impossible to understand contemporary Islam without knowing about Salafism. 462 pages, scholarly in character, and balanced in its evaluation of Islam.

Murray, Abdu H. *Grand Central Question*. Downers Grove, Il. InterVarsity Press, 2014.

> An essential description of a main concept of Islam: God is Great and there is no greater. "Allahu Akbar" means God is Greater. The author explores this concept in Islam, contrasts it with the God of the Bible, and concludes it is greater than all other conceptions of God. This is an insider's presentation in a clear, scholarly, and Biblically solid book.

Parshall, Phil. *Bridges to Islam: A Christian Perspective on Folk Islam*. Downers Grove, Illinois: IVP Books, 1983, 2006.

> Phil Parshall is a noted expert on Islam and from first hand experience. His work is especially valuable in regard to Sufism, which is a mystical approach to Islam. He outlines in a most respectful manner the actual practices of Sufis

and gives suggestions on reaching Muslim people. Very readable with good font style. 160 pages. Dr. Phil Parshall has also written *Muslim Evangelism* and *Lifting the Veil*.

Qureshi, Nabeel. *Seeking Allah, Finding Jesus: A Devout Muslim Encounters Christianity*. Bonita Springs, Florida: Zondervan, 2014.

If there was one book I would like to give to everyone who has any interest in Islam or who is a Muslim, it would be this book. It is the story of a young man studying to be a medical doctor, in a friendship with a Christian whom he debates energetically, but finally brought to faith despite his protestations. It is a terrific story and Nabeel now fully engages in outreach to Muslims. I had the opportunity to meet him in 2014 in Atlanta, Georgia at the Christian booksellers convention. He is part of the Ravi Zacharias ministry. If anyone is looking for a place to start, *Seeking Allah, Finding Jesus* is it.

_____. *No God but One: Allah or Jesus?* Grand Rapids, MI: Zondervan, 2016

A tremendous and most useful book for Christians who desire to understand contemporary Islamic thought with the purpose of meaningfully engaging Muslims with the message of Jesus. It is thorough, sensitively presented, and I recommend it to the highest degree.

_____. *Answering Jihad: A Better Way Forward*. Grand Rapids, MI: Zondervan, 2016.

Nabeel concludes, "Even though Muslims are often raised with the teaching that 'Islam is the religion of peace,' when they study the texts for themselves, they are faced with the reality that Muhammad and the Quran call for jihad. They will stand at the crossroads for only so long before they choose what path they will take—apostasy, apathy, or radicalization." He calls for Muslims to "re-imagine" Islam, since a true allegiance to its foundational teachings always and necessarily results in violence.

Riley-Smith, Jonathan. *The Crusades: A History (3rd edition)*. New York: Bloomsbury, 2013.

Absolutely everything anyone would need to know about the crusades. A very scholarly work but accessible for the serious reader. Lots of maps and other illustrations. It would be a prize in anyone's library.

Sanger, Richard H. *The Arabian Peninsula*. Ithaca, New York: Cornell University Press, 1954.

Here is a delightful account of the land where Muhammad and Islam grew up. The people, the places, and the sights and sounds bring one back to Mecca and Medina long centuries ago, where things have changed very little over time. Out of print but I found it on Amazon.com. 295 pages, good font and wonderful old black and white photos.

Schneier, Marc and Shamsi Ali. *Sons of Abraham: A Candid Conversation about the Issues That Divide and Unite Jews and Muslims*. Boston: Beacon Press, 2013.

Rabbi Schneier is founder and president of the Foundation for Ethnic Understanding and founding rabbi of the Hampton Synagogue in Westhampton Beach, New York. Imam Ali is the spiritual leader of Jamaica Muslim Center,

New York City's largest Islamic center. The two are friends and work together in projects concerning Jews and Muslims. Former President Bill Clinton wrote a foreword, and Samuel G. Freedman wrote an introduction. There are three parts of the book: one, Who We Are; two, What We Believe; and three, Our Shared Future. The two men wrote one or more chapters on these subjects. I found it helpful to see their faith positions, but found their desire to be conciliatory overdone and thus somewhat fanciful. I think I detected a little taqiyya on the part of both. 220 pages, a well done book.

Siddiqui, Moulana Mohammed Abdul-Aleem. *Elementary Teachings of Islam*. New Delhi, India: Islamic Book Service, 2012

A small booklet freely given out at the Mill Valley Islamic Center in Mill Valley, California on a Ramadan related event called Itfar wherein the public was invited to the mosque for a presentation and a real feast. The purpose of the book is to educate non-Muslims on the actual observance Muslims are required to make, especially having to do with prayers, Ramadan, and the Hajj. It details the ritual washings or ablutions necessary before times of salat or prayers. It is unlike anything I have ever encountered, but it produced a sadness, for me at least, to see the extreme ritualization the average Muslim must go through on a daily basis.

Sookhdeo, Patrick. *Understanding Islamic Theology*. McLean, Virginia: Isaac Publishing, 2013.

Sookhdeo's book is the reason for this present book. For years I have been trying to understand Islam so that I might be equipped to debate Islamic scholars. I am not there yet, but this book has gotten me closer to my goal. It is theology at its best, supported by passages from the Qur'an, Hadith, and Islamic jurisprudence. It is not a book that can be rushed through; it is not tedious, but requires careful attention. The format works well, and the manner in which Dr, Sookhdeo presents his material is remarkable. My sense is that it is truly a must read for anyone who wants to understand Islam and Muslim people. 466 pages with extensive indexes, bibliography, and glossary.

Spencer, Robert. *The Truth about Muhammad: Founder of the World's Most Intolerant Religion*. Washington. D.C.: Regnery Publishing, Inc., 2006.

Robert Spencer is the director of Jihad Watch, a program of the David Horowitz freedom Center, and is one of the most well known Islamic scholars. His work is hard hitting without apology. The focus of this book is Muhammad and is as clear a description of the prophet in print today. The author breaks it down slowly and carefully based on the records known today. His tone is harsh but honest. 224 pages, good design and font.

_____. *Religion of PEACE?: Why Christianity Is and Islam Isn't*. Washington D.C.: Regnery Publishing, Inc., 2007.

Robert Spencer is one of the most prolific writers on the subject of Islam and must be considered an expert in his field. In this volume he compares and contrasts Islam and Christianity. He hits hard. His arguments are well documented and clearly explained. He has also authored: *The Truth About Muhammad, The Politically Incorrect Guide to Islam (and the Crusades), Islam Unveiled*, and *Onward Muslim Soldiers*. 264 pages. Good font size.

_____. *Did Muhammad Exist?* Wilmington, Delaware: ISI Books. 2012.

> A third book by Robert Spencer that proved very helpful. In this volume he takes a close and critical look at the origins of Islam with a focus on Muhammad and the Qur'an. It is solid and authoritative. Probably must be described as a must read. 240 pages, good format, design, and font.

Wagner, William. *How Islam Plans to Change the World*. Grand Rapids, Michigan: Kregel Publications, 2012.

> Dr. Bill Wagner, a friend and fellow Southern Baptist, served long years as a missionary in Germany and Northern Africa, and in the latter field of ministry, directly with Muslims. He is indeed a first hand expert on Islam. Past professor of missions and evangelism at Golden Gate Baptist Theological Seminary in Mill Valley, California, he never retires and is actively engaged in outreach to Iranian-born Muslims. Dr. Wagner balances hard-hitting facts on Islam with a tender heart toward presenting the Gospel to Muslims. 345 pages, good font and nice book design.

Warraq, Ibn. *Why I Am Not a Muslim*. Amherst, New York: Prometheus Books, 2003.

> A most helpful book, written by a former Muslim who thoroughly understands the world of Islam both past and present. He moved to atheism from Islam, being persuaded by any number of factors that there is no god at all or of any kind. His critique of Islam is sharp and penetrating. "The Rushdie Affair" is chapter one and is an excellent presentation of how Islam is defended by Western apologists; I consider it a must-read. Ibn Warraq goes into the history of Islam more completely than anything I have come across, and his treatment of the person and message of Muhammad is straight forward and without much bias.

White, James R. *What Every Christian Needs to Know About the Qur'an*. Minneapolis, Minnesota: Bethany House Publishers, 2013.

> Solid piece of work on the Qur'an and much more. I found it very useful. Great glossary, bibliography, index, and more. He is the director of Alpha and Omega Ministries, focused on Christian apologetics. He writes on a wide range of subjects. 310 pages, good font and style.

Zwemer, Rev. S. M. *Arabia: The Cradle of Islam: Studies in the Geography, People and Politics of the Peninsula with an Account of Islam and Mission-work*. New York: Fleming H. Revell Company, 1900.

> I cannot say enough about how valuable this book was to me. It is absolutely incredible. It takes the reader back to a time when the world knew nothing of the Islamic State and the effort of the radicalized Muslim to spread Islam by whatever means necessary. The author loves Muslim people and labored to teach them of Jesus and the Gospel. His is firsthand experience—being present, knowing Muslim people at deep levels, and interacting with them and their religion closely and personally. It is all in this detailed and thorough presentation. I will go so far as to say it is a must read for anyone who desires to understand Muslim people and their religion.

INDEX

Note: No entries will be listed for the most common terms such as Allah, Muhammad, Qur'an, Hadith, Muslim, etc., nor what is found in the Bibliography. Also consult the Glossary for terms not listed here.

Abd al-Wahbab 151
ablution(s) (also washing) 8, 38, 50, 60, 99, 100, 170, 187, 289, 289, 297, 320, 340
Abraham(ic) 3, 9, 11, 12, 39, 42, 46, 47, 50, 51, 62, 145, 148, 199, 208, 212, 213, 214, 231, 237, 243, 260, 261, 268, 277, 278, 281, 284, 303, 318, 325, 326
abrogat(e, ed, es, ion) 24, 29, 40, 41, 44, 45, 73, 88, 93, 206–11, 237–38, 248, 313, 324, 325
Abu Bakr 5, 17, 18, 32, 43, 69, 78, 84, 143, 145, 166, 231, 308, 313, 316, 327, 328, 329
ad-Dajjal 46, 54, 317
Adam 11, 12, 38, 39, 46, 47, 50, , 51, 53, 66, 118, 119, 148, 150, 232, 243, 282, 323, 325, 333
adhan 8, 121, 122, 123, 287, 297, 313, 321
adulter(er)(y) 27, 34, 61, 79, 85, 85, 86, 87, 90, 98, 137, 139, 238, 239, 264, 271, 322, 340
Afghan(istan) 20, 134, 139, 147, 152, 196, 299, 304, 340
Aisha 5, 30, 41, 98, 144, 162, 170, 227, 270, 313, 333
akhira 30, 94, 313
al-Amin vi, 50, 236
al-Bukhari (see Sahih al-Bukhari)
al-Ghazali 138, 308
al-janna 60, 61, 296–98, 314, 322
al-Muslim (see Sahih al-Muslim)
al-Tirmidhi 31, 36, 50, 52, 56, 57, 59, 60, 62, 63, 66, 75, 87, 296, 298, 316, 318
Ali Talib 17, 314
Allahu Akbar 314, 324, 331

'amil 121
Aminah 161
angel(s) 4, 6, 8, 9, 14–15, 29, 36, 37, 38, 39, 40, 41, 48, 51–52, 56, 59, 69, 74, 84, 117, 118, 119, 127, 130, 136, 143, 161, 200, 206, 208, 213, 221, 222, 224, 225–28, 229, 230, 231, 232, 233, 234, 238, 242, 258, 273, 278, 279, 297, 320, 321, 322, 324, 325, 327, 328, 333
apostasy 11, 17, 25, 88, 119, 137, 139, 156, 186, 229, 237, 262, 320, 331
apostate(s) 20, 26, 34, 61, 63, 77, 88, 97, 128, 130, 135, 136, 138, 139, 140, 141, 191, 202, 249, 262, 330, 331
Arabia(n) 6, 17, 18, 19, 20, 23, 25, 26, 34, 36, 38, 39, 40, 48, 54, 57, 61, 90, 108, 113, 122, 131, 133, 134, 140, 143, 145, 147, 151, 152, 153, 155, 162, 163, 169, 190, 192, 198, 199, 200, 202, 231, 232, 234, 241, 243, 260, 301, 302, 307, 314, 319, 320, 326, 328, 333
archangel 4, 6, 11, 37, 87, 200
Ash'arians 66
Ashura 148, 315, 328
Aslan, Reza 2, 20, 142, 154, 155
ayah 41, 116, 121, 317
Ayatollah Khomeini 144, 178
Bab 303, 304
Babis 304
Baha'u'llah 303, 304
Bahai 2, 51, 300, 301, 303
Bahrain 34, 122, 163
Banu Nadir 7
Bapak 305, 306
barzakh 52, 53, 117
Basilides 242, 251
Basmalah 49

bassamat alfarah 60, 315
batin 315, 333
Batini 118
Battle of Al-Qadeseyyah 164
Battle of Arsuf 180
Battle of Badr 22, 55, 162, 168
Battle of Karbala 329
Battle of the Trench 7, 162
Battle of Tours-Poitiers 20
Battle of Uhud 162
Battle of Yamama 43, 331
Beatific Vision 47, 59, 60, 63
Bridge over Hell 57, 58
Byzantine(s) 20, 55, 163, 181
Cabu Musab al-Suri 141
Charles Martel 20
Christophobia 140
Classification of Hadith 32
Colonialism 140, 151, 219
companions (of Muhammad) 30, 41, 43, 45, 57, 60, 61, 68, 69, 73, 74, 76, 87, 108, 109, 123, 132, 143, 152, 164, 166, 170, 218, 288, 316, 318, 324, 328, 330
Crescent and Star 2, 163, 164
Crusades 10, 11, 20, 21, 85, 179, 181, 182, 184, 195, 196, 219, 240
Dagestan 19, 163, 309
dawa 114, 115, 135, 316
days of ignorance 62, 317
Day of Judgment 13, 50, 51, 53, 58, 69, 71, 149, 250, 271, 294, 314, 318, 327, 339
Day of Resurrection 7, 47, 53, 109, 117, 170, 242, 318
dews 14
dhikr 151, 307, 309, 317
divorce 16, 25, 34, 71, 82–83, 112–13, 148, 159, 225, 340
Egypt(ian) 3, 19, 21, 122, 128, 134, 143, 148, 151, 153, 163, 164, 165, 179, 180, 181, 231, 239, 251, 260, 261, 268, 277, 282, 292, 300, 304, 309, 325, 327, 328
emigrant(s) 143, 319
eschatological abodes 58

Evil Eye 15, 38, 117, 120, 121, 314, 325
exorcis(t, m) 1, 15, 39, 116–125, 146, 315, 327
Exordium, The 43
fard 8, 75, 93, 317, 321
fast(ing) 6, 9, 34, 84, 88, 93, 100, 103–04, 108, 122, 137, 146, 199, 226, 296, 306, 318, 327, 329, 330
fatalism 8, 64, 65, 127, 139, 155, 244, 320, 326, 331
Father Bodar 135
Fatima 17, 55, 135, 148, 314, 317, 329
fatwa 76, 147, 193, 194, 316, 321, 328, 330
fiqh 33, 47, 57, 58, 78, 82, 87, 98, 146, 147, 315, 317, 325, 326
firdaws 60, 61, 147
Five Pillars of Islam 4, 8, 10, 14, 35, 60, 62, 91, 146, 147, 315, 318, 319, 330, 331, 333
folk Islam 38, 39, 116, 147
fundamentalist(s) 23, 127, 128, 129, 131, 134, 136, 145, 146, 152, 156, 193, 322, 328
fuqaha' 33, 152
Gabriel 4, 6, 11, 14, 29, 36, 37, 39, 40, 41, 45, 48, 56, 74, 96, 109, 118, 134, 136, 145, 161, 162, 169, 206, 210, 224–34, 235, 238, 239, 241, 242, 245, 248, 219, 315, 320, 322, 326, 328, 333
garina 14
Gnosticism 3, 39, 149, 152, 188
Gospel of Barnabas 251, 252
Gospel of Thomas 49, 242, 271
Great Satan 34, 135
Greatest Deceiver 22, 42, 315, 331
Guillaume, A. 12, 69, 165, 166, 228
hafiz 31, 318
Hagar 3, 9, 260, 277
hajj 4, 9, 10, 60, 64, 84, 88, 93, 105, 106, 146, 212, 297, 318, 319, 320, 325, 336
halal 5, 33, 61, 70, 84, 139, 140, 319
Hamas 138, 139, 178

Hanafi (School) 18, 33, 47, 78, 89, 147, 319, 329
Hanbali (School) 18, 34, 147, 319, 324, 329
haram 5, 33, 61, 70, 75, 79, 84, 86, 88, 91, 94, 95, 139, 151, 218, 291, 319, 329
hasan (category of hadith) 316, 318, 319
Hasan (son of Ali) 17, 55, 108, 148, 317
Hasan al-Banna 151
hell(fire) 5, 6, 7, 17, 33, 36, 38, 52, 53, 56, 57, 58, 59–60, 61, 63, 64, 69, 77, 86, 96, 97, 118, 129, 143, 150, 152, 175, 191, 201, 214, 219, 222, 229, 238, 241, 247, 253, 317, 322, 324, 328, 330, 333
heretic(al)(s) 1, 11, 19, 51, 134, 136, 138, 155, 184, 309
hidden Imam 18, 149, 323
Hijaz (Hejaz) 143, 319
hijra 6, 93, 143, 162, 167, 319
Hirah, Mt. 161, 320
Hirsi Ali, Ayaan 1, 126–141, 142, 146, 155
Holy Spirit 3, , 27, 37, 39, 40, 48, 184, 191, 197, 200, 203, 210, 211, 219, 220, 223, 225, 226, 230, 231, 234, 236, 241, 245, 253, 263, 264, 219, 224, 274, 275, 276, 279, 293, 328, 330
homosexual(ity) 61, 86, 100, 111, 112, 126, 139, 203, 218, 284, 285
honor brigade 6, 11, 137, 219
hooris 61, 62, 63, 320, 322
Hubal 143, 320
hudood 137, 320
Husayn (son of Ali) 68, 96, 108, 148, 315, 324, 332, 334
Iblis 38
Ibn Ishaq 2, 5, 10, 12, 28, 165, 166, 186, 228
Ignaz Goldziher 144
ihram 320, 325
ijma 33, 34, 71, 76, 77, 78, 246, 320, 321
Imam(s) vi, vii, 8, 18, 22, 24, 30, 31, 34, 45, 55, 68, 69, 70, 73, 78, 79, 80, 81, 97, 100, 103, 107, 108, 110, 116, 141, 148, 149, 153, 176, 187, 216, 217, 235, 236, 246, 287, 303, 321, 323, 324, 328, 329, 331, 332, 333
iman 9, 35, 73, 88, 89, 91, 93, 94, 296, 303, 321
India(n) 20, 33, 34, 121, 122, 123, 147, 151, 163, 182, 299, 315, 319
Indonesia 34, 128, 300, 304, 305
infidel(s) 1, 37, 52, 54, 55, 64, 126, 130, 131, 138, 177, 179, 185, 190, 191, 194, 197, 318, 331
Inquisition (Christian) 182, 183, 184
Inquisition (Islamic) 244, 245, 319, 332
insh'allah 66, 142, 321, 331
intercessor(y) 57, 64, 294, 314, 328, 333
intermediate state 51, 52, 58, 315
iqamah 8, 121, 313, 321
Iran(ian) 19, 23, 26, 34, 54, 113, 134, 142, 144, 147, 148, 151, 152, 163, 300, 303, 304, 309, 315, 331, 333, 334
Iraq 33, 34, 73, 78, 131, 134, 136, 153, 163, 179, 300, 304, 315, 333, 334
'Isa 13, 48, 316, 321
islah 154, 321, 331
Ishmael, son of Abraham 3, 9, 25, 42, 47, 51, 212, 214, 237, 261, 278, 317, 325
Ismail Radwan 138, 139
Ismail, son of Jafar 12, 149, 321, 323, 329
Ismailis (also see Seveners) 302, 321, 329
isnad 32, 73, 76, 147, 165, 316, 321, 324
Israel(i)(ite) 32, 49, 85, 113, 141, 163, 173, 174, 201, 208, 209, 224, 230, 237, 238, 239, 241, 245, 262, 263, 265, 267, 268, 269, 270, 273, 276, 277, 278, 281, 285, 286, 292, 300
Jabrians 66
Jafar 149, 321, 329
Jamaat (also see Jummah) 322
Jesus (also see 'Isa) vi, vii, 2, 3, 4, 5, 10, 11, 12–13, 15, 21, 22, 27, 29, 32, 35, 36, 39, 40, 41, 42, 45, 46, 48–50, 51, 54, 55, 57, 67, 69, 103, 116, 124, 125, 132, 135, 142, 143, 145, 147, 148, 168, 169,

170–74, 175, 176, 177, 178, 182, 183, 184, 185, 188, 189, 190, 191, 192, 193, 194, 195, 197, 198, 199, 200, 201, 203, 204, 205, 208, 209, 210, 211, 214, 215, 218, 219, 220, 221, 222, 223, 225, 226, 229, 230, 231, 232, 233, 234, 236, 237, 240, 241, 242, 243, 244, 245, 246, 247, 249, 250–59, 262, 264, 267, 268, 269, 271–277, 278, 279, 280, 281, 283, 284, 286, 289, 292, 293, 303

Jew(s)(ish) 6, 7, 11, 22, 37, 41, 42, 44, 47, 48, 49, 50, 52, 53, 54, 55, 59, 60, 64, 74, 81, 87, 88, 93, 109, 111, 112, 118, 128, 129, 134, 136, 140, 141, 144, 145, 162, 163, 164, 167, 171, 172, 173, 179, 183, 184, 186, 190, 195, 198, 200, 206, 207, 210, 214, 216, 226, 230, 231, 243, 248, 251, 252, 254, 256, 258, 259, 260, 262, 269, 273, 275, 276, 277, 280, 282, 283, 284, 288, 292, 313, 314, 323, 326, 327

Jibril 87, 118

jihad(ist)(ism) 6, 9, 10, 14, 23, 24, 26, 34, 57, 62, 85, 86, 93–95, 104, 105, 106–07, 114, 115, 129, 133, 135, 137, 138, 140, 141, 144, 145, 152, 153, 155, 181, 184, 186, 187, 194, 210, 216, 218, 220, 221, 222, 248, 249, 297, 317, 319, 322, 325, 329, 332

jinn 5, 8, 14, 15, 29, 37–9, 41, 46, 75, 99, 117, 118–25, 132, 133, 146, 159, 162, 189, 227, 229, 231–34, 238, 247, 287, 313, 314, 316, 317, 320, 322, 323, 324, 326, 330, 332, 334

jizyah 93, 95, 322

Jordan 105, 151, 163, 209, 226, 275, 300

Judaism 3, 143, 146, 194, 199, 200, 208, 213, 214, 246, 269, 278, 283

Jummah 115, 318, 320, 322

Kaaba (Ka'ba, Kaba) 9, 10, 101, 105, 143, 148, 162, 167, 199, 214, 319, 320, 322, 326, 331, 332, 333

kalam 146, 322

Kalim Allah 47, 322

Kashmir 19, 309

Keeper of the Keys 143

Kenya 131, 133, 300

Khadija (wife of Muhammed) 6, 41, 62, 63, 143, 161, 162, 167, 227, 228, 232, 233, 317, 319, 322

Kharijites 145, 151, 322

kismat 66, 323, 331

kufr 59, 77, 323

Kuwait 33, 163, 300

Last Day(s) 16, 24, 50, 53–58, 61, 73, 91, 94, 110, 154, 183, 189, 207, 234, 238, 248, 273, 321, 330

Latihan (also Latihan Kejiwaan) 305, 306

Lebanon 34, 163, 301, 314

Libya 19, 134, 301, 302, 309, 320

literal interpretation 327, 333

Luqman 143, 158

magic(al)(ian) 15, 29, 39, 44, 59, 63, 84, 117, 120, 121, 123–24, 125, 132, 146, 173, 183, 233, 239, 241, 326, 330

Mahdi 18–19, 55, 97, 149, 313, 323, 329

makara 65, 323

maktub 66, 323, 331

Malala Yousafzai 140

Malaysia 34, 35, 301

Mali 19, 309

Malik (angel) 59, 118, 324

Malik (Imam Malik Ibn Anas) 31, 33, 72, 78, 165, 318, 324, 329

Maliki (school) 18, 33, 64, 65, 79, 147, 165, 324, 329, 332

maqdur 66, 324, 331

martyr(s)(dom) 14, 42, 52, 57, 60, 61, 62, 63, 65, 117, 138, 148, 197, 198, 210, 218, 315, 317, 318, 325, 329

Mary (mother of Jesus)(also Maryam) 3, 36, 40, 48, 49, 143, 145, 157, 173, 188, 208, 225–26, 231, 238, 241, 242, 245, 246, 271, 274, 284, 321

Mary (Magdalene) 257, 258

mass 119, 324

matn 31, 76, 324

Mecca 4, 6, 9, 10, 11, 12, 18, 19, 24, 29, 36, 41, 43, 54, 64, 73, 101, 105, 122, 129, 136, 137, 140, 143, 144, 146, 148, 157ff, 161, 162, 166, 167, 169, 192, 199, 207, 221, 260, 288, 302, 313, 315, 316, 318, 319, 320, 321, 322, 326, 327, 331, 333

Medina 4, 6, 7, 11, 12, 24, 29, 33, 36, 41, 43, 54, 73, 93, 136, 138, 140, 143–44, 152, 157ff, 162, 165, 166, 167, 169, 192, 207, 302, 313, 315, 316, 319, 321, 324, 326, 334

messenger (Muhammad as) 4, 8, 9, 13, 14, 35, 46, 49, 51, 54, 55, 60, 63, 64, 67, 73, 76, 77, 79, 80, 83, 87, 89, 90, 93, 94, 96, 101, 104, 107, 109, 112, 129, 144, 149, 188, 207, 228, 229, 234, 242, 246, 248, 249, 294, 295, 296, 303, 304, 318, 319, 327, 329

Messiah 13, 48–50, 67, 188, 195, 198, 200, 208–10, 238, 241–46, 251, 254, 255, 278, 279, 292, 303, 313

Miriam (sister of Moses) 48

Moderate Muslims 24, 127, 136, 140, 196

Monotheis(m)(tic) 3, 142, 142, 234, 247, 303, 319

Morocco 301, 302

Moses 11, 12, 36, 39, 40, 42, 45–49, 51, 146, 148, 171, 226, 230, 232, 237, 239, 240, 243, 265, 266, 279, 292, 303, 314, 322, 323

muezzin 8, 324

mufti(s) 33, 68, 76, 141, 153, 317, 325

muhkam 43, 325

mujah(ad, ideen) 61, 64, 315, 325

Munkar 14, 52, 118, 325, 327

Muslim Brotherhood 137, 151, 201, 217, 325

muta 32, 43, 44, 111, 112, 161, 246, 325

Nakir 14, 52, 118, 325, 327

Nabi Allah 46, 325

nafs 117, 325

Neo-Sufism 309, 310

Nigeria 34, 128, 301

Night Journey (of Muhammad) 40, 157, 162, 166, 167, 170, 324

Noah 11, 12, 46, 47, 51, 148, 159, 243, 282, 325

Oman 34, 163, 301, 320

original sin 38, 326

orthodox(y) 18, 33, 34, 146, 180, 292, 301, 321, 323, 328

orthopraxy 146

Ottoman(s) 33, 164

Pakistan 19, 20, 34, 121, 122, 123, 136, 139, 148, 196, 301, 309, 315, 333

paradise 2, 7, 13, 14, 16, 29, 33, 36, 40, 42, 45, 50, 52, 53, 57–59, 60–65, 69, 75, 80, 86, 96–98, 101, 102, 107, 115, 117, 127, 128, 130, 138, 146, 155, 162, 164, 170, 175, 177, 178, 185, 187, 189, 197, 210, 220, 232, 233, 234, 238, 245, 296, 297, 298, 300, 307, 314, 317, 319, 320, 321, 322, 324, 328, 329

pari 14

Paul (Apostle) vi, 66, 135, 190, 191, 210, 211, 221, 229, 241, 243, 244, 246, 251, 254, 262, 265, 273, 276, 277, 281, 286

People of Heaven 152, 325

People of Hell 152, 322

People of the Book 16, 23, 24, 81, 91, 93, 136, 145, 206, 207, 313, 322

Perfect Man 30, 234, 294, 307

Pious Ones 23, 127, 145, 155, 323

pir 150, 326

polytheis(m)(t)(tic) 3, 36, 44, 63, 64, 96, 97, 111, 143, 145, 162, 246, 248, 319, 330

predestin(ed)(es)(ation) 4, 7–9, 53, 58, 60, 65–66, 69, 205, 244, 267, 270, 323, 324, 326, 331

pre-Islamic 46, 81, 143, 163, 167, 199,

260, 314, 322
progressive Muslims 127
progressive revelation 41, 206, 208, 210, 237
prophet(s) (other than Muhammad) 4, 9, 11–13, 42, 46, 48, 50, 51, 69, 84, 97, 117, 145, 158, 162, 170, 190, 195, 200, 232, 237, 241, 243, 244, 250, 251, 264, 270, 271, 273, 274, 277, 279, 282, 292, 293, 315, 319, 323, 325, 328
Prophet's Cistern 57, 319
Qadari(ans)(tes) 66, 326
qadis 33, 326
Qatar 34, 163, 301
Qaynuqa Jews 22, 326, 327
qibla 101, 102, 167, 291, 326
qiyas 33, 34, 71, 77, 78, 246, 321, 326
qudsi 32, 318, 326
Quraysh(i) Tribe 10, 54, 74, 78, 160, 162, 166, 199, 327
qurra 43, 145, 327
Qutb, Sayyid 151, 307, 327
Ramadan 4, 9, 38, 73, 88, 103, 104, 146, 296, 306, 317, 318, 327, 333
Rasul 69, 103, 165, 327
rationalist(s) 38, 146, 152, 244, 245, 327, 332
recitation(s) 4, 8, 11, 12, 24, 28, 29, 41, 45, 120–23, 136, 142, 145, 194, 206, 226, 239, 309, 313, 327, 331
Recording Angels 37, 118, 327
reformation (of Islam) 136, 140, 141, 153–55, 335
Reformation, Protestant 154
resurrect(ed)(ion) 4, 7, 9, 47, 50, 53, 56, 97, 109, 117, 125, 159, 168, 170–72, 175, 182, 191, 192, 194, 200, 203, 226, 238, 242, 243, 247, 259, 266, 272, 294
Rightly Guided Ones 145
risala 30, 328
Risale-I Nur 309
Roman Catholic(ism)(s) (Church) 58, 64, 82, 179, 180, 193, 314
Roman Empire 54, 181
Ruh Allah 48, 328
Rumi, Jalal ad-Din 150, 309, 328
Russia(n) 19, 152, 180, 309
Sadiq, Jafar ibn Mohammed al- 97, 109, 104, 108, 110, 112, 321, 323, 328, 329
Sahih al-Bukhari (about) 73, 75, 76, 137, 169, 314, 316, 318, 328
Sahih al-Muslim 5, 314
Saladin 21, 179, 180
Salafi(sm)(st) 23, 186, 218, 300, 301, 302, 328, 333
sala(h)(t) 4, 8, 74, 88, 93, 317, 318, 328, 332, 333
sar 119, 328
Sarah (wife of Abraham) 3, 9, 260, 261, 277, 284
Sassanid Empire 163, 164
Satan, satans (see also *shaytan*) 5, 14, 15, 34, 37–39, 46, 54, 80, 102, 118–21, 124, 125, 150, 193, 207, 221, 223, 228, 229, 232–34, 238, 249, 263, 265, 275, 282, 288, 319, 320, 329
Satanic Verses 193, 208
Saudi Arabia 6, 19, 23, 26, 34, 113, 122, 131, 140, 145, 147, 151, 152, 169, 190, 192, 198, 202, 301, 302, 319, 328, 333
sawm 4, 9, 329
Sevener(s) 19, 149, 321, 323, 329, 332
Shafi'i school 33
shahada(h) 4, 8, 35, 146, 318, 323, 329, 332
Shari(a)(a')(ah) Law 1, 2, 7, 17–19, 26, 68–79, 81–95, 96–113, 114, 115, 120, 128, 136–41, 147, 148, 167, 180, 193, 196, 204, 219, 221, 245, 246, 287, 289, 293, 299, 316, 317, 319, 320, 324, 329, 331, 332
shaytan, or *shaitan* 15, 37, 80, 88, 118, 320
Shi'a Statement of Faith 148
Shi(a)('a)(ite)('ism) 2, 9, 10, 17–21, 22,

23, 32, 34, 41, 43, 45, 50, 55, 64, 99, 105–07, 110, 112, 129, 134, 142, 144, 147–49, 151, 163–65, 178, 179, 299, 300, 301, 302, 307, 314, 315, 316, 317, 318, 320, 321, 323, 325, 328, 329, 331, 332, 333, 334

shirk 36, 48, 60, 123, 124, 145, 330, 332

Signifier 308

sihr 120, 330

Sira (biography of Muhammad) 2, 4, 5, 10, 12, 28, 29, 33, 57, 58, 69, 87, 165–68, 182, 186, 227, 228, 279, 330

sirat 56, 58, 69, 165, 330

Somalia 1, 19, 128, 131, 302, 309

Son of Mary 36, 40, 49, 188, 238, 241, 242, 245, 246, 321

spirit possession 117, 119–21, 328

Striking (Casting) Terror into the Heart 7, 11, 15, 26, 197, 248

Subud 2, 303–07

Sudan 34, 122, 128, 147, 151, 302

Sufi(s)(sm) 2, 19, 20, 45, 64, 142, 147, 149–52, 300, 302, 303, 306–10, 315, 326, 328, 330, 332, 333

Sultan 179–81, 330

sunna(h) 11, 17, 18, 32, 34, 71, 72, 74, 77, 78, 80, 81, 83, 84, 93, 95, 96–98, 107, 109, 120, 123, 245, 316, 318, 325, 328, 329, 330, 331, 333

Sunni vi, 1, 4, 9, 10, 17, 18–20, 22, 23, 26, 31–33, 41, 43, 45, 50, 55, 60, 64, 66, 68, 70, 72, 74, 76, 78, 80, 82, 84, 86, 88, 90, 92, 94, 97, 108, 114, 117, 119, 129, 134, 145, 147, 148, 150, 152, 163, 165, 168, 187, 188, 244, 246, 269, 287, 299, 300, 301, 302, 314, 316, 318, 320, 323, 325, 328, 329, 330, 332, 333

sura(h)(t) 4, 11, 24, 29, 36, 43, 44, 47, 50, 102, 138, 157–60, 239, 317, 330

Suwayd 143

Syria(n) 33, 131, 134, 143, 151, 153, 163, 302, 314, 320

takwah 63, 331

taqiyya(h) 22, 78, 235, 315, 331

tariqah 150, 332

tawhid 4, 9, 30, 96, 145, 244, 245, 330, 332, 333

ta'wil 45, 146, 149, 331, 332, 333

traditionalists 18, 134, 146, 147, 148, 152, 153, 155, 156, 234, 240, 245, 316, 319, 321, 327, 331, 332, 333

Trinidad 122

Trinity 3, 4, 36, 42, 48, 134, 145, 226, 231, 233, 238, 246, 251, 253

Tunisia 19, 151, 302, 309, 320

Turkey 20, 33, 35, 113, 134, 153, 163, 164, 179, 180, 302, 314

Twelver(s) 19, 34, 103, 149, 299, 300, 302, 314, 323, 332

Twelfth (Imam, Mahdi, or Caliph) 19, 45, 55, 149, 303, 323, 332

ulama ('*ulama*) 33, 71, 76, 77, 81, 147, 153, 154, 319, 325, 331, 332

Umar (also Omar) 17, 32, 69, 78, 145, 167, 231, 316, 322, 329, 332

ummah 5, 34, 42, 60, 63, 71, 76, 77, 89, 91, 115, 128, 144, 145, 152, 318, 320, 321, 332

United Arab Emirates 302

Uthman (or Othman) 5, 17, 29, 32, 41, 43, 69, 78, 145, 231, 232, 239, 316, 322, 327, 329, 333

visions (and/or dreams) 6, 39, 120, 132, 143, 151, 212, 224, 226, 227, 233, 255, 258, 266, 285, 304, 324

Wahhabi(sm)(st) 18, 34, 301, 333

wali.. 149, 333

warner (term for Muhammad) 13, 50, 53, 57, 294

Weighing of the Deeds 56, 97

West(ern)(erners) 1, 5, 10, 16, 21, 23, 26, 33, 34, 38, 39, 50, 54, 71, 80, 92, 107, 113, 115, 127, 128, 129, 130, 131, 132, 133, 134, 135, 139, 140, 141, 151, 153,

154, 180, 181, 182, 183, 187, 193, 195, 196, 218, 219, 221, 251, 287, 290, 307, 308, 309–10, 325
witr 64, 333
Yemen 33, 43, 78, 134, 151, 302
za'am(a)(ii) 166
Zachariah (also Zechariah) 48, 213, 224, 225, 262, 264
Zayd(is) 143, 319, 334
zakat 4, 9, 52, 56, 101, 105, 318, 333
Zoroaster 303

If Allah Wills is dedicated to my Muslim friends, neighbors, and all seekers after the Creator who has made us all in His image and loves us with an everlasting love.

ALSO

*False Prophets Among Us:
What is the New Apostolic Reformation and Why Is It Dangerous?*

Memoirs of a Jesus Freak

Christian Basics: Lessons, Debates, and Conversations

Deliver Us from Evil: How Jesus Casts out Demons Today

*A Matter of Life and Death:
Understanding True and False Conversion*

*The Soul Journey: How Shamanism, Santeria, Wicca,
and Charisma Are Connected*

Why I Am a Christian

If the Devil Wrote a Bible

Spiritual Health

Biblical Christianity Is Evangelical

The Preposterous God

FOUND AT WWW.EVPBOOKS.COM OR WHEREVER FINE BOOKS ARE SOLD

www.ingramcontent.com/pod-product-compliance
Lightning Source LLC
Chambersburg PA
CBHW081208230426

43666CB00015B/2682